Aberfan –
Our Hiraeth

An anthology in

Poetry
Prose and
Pictures

ABERFAN - OUR HIRAETH

Compiled by Maureen Hughes
Aberfan & Merthyr Vale Writers and
History Group

Published by the
Aberfan & Merthyr Vale Community Co-operative

MARCH 1999

ISBN   0 9534868 0X

Printed and bound in the U.K. by
RAINBOW PRINT (WALES) LTD.
Merthyr Industrial Park, Pentrebach, Merthyr Tydfil CF48 4DR
Telephone: (01443) 691114   Fax: (01443) 690276

Contents

Hiraeth
Chapter One

1.   Hiraeth *

When the waters of life are muddy and clouded,
Return to the clear crystal cool of a healing source
When the hills are puffed with effort and grind
Return to the green of the valley and the parallel road.
When talk is punctuated with anger and hatred
Return to your native tongue, soothing and understanding
When arms flay with pugilistic might,
Return to the shawled bosom of your childhood.

When the noise of the oppressor drowns all sound,
Return to the singing heart and the cadences of the mind
When existence itself is as a pointless star,
Return to the inner soul where heaven abides.

Where is this place? Where will peace be found?
Return to be renewed
Where love, warmth and caring abound
In the hills, in the streets, in the homes, in the schools,
In the Chapels,
In the hearts.

Return once more to my beloved Aberfan.

WENDY HOWARD
October 1990

* Hiraeth - Longing

View of new road facing Brecon

2. Foreword

After long exile from South Wales it would be presumptuous of me to claim an intimate knowledge of life in Aberfan and Merthyr Vale over the last half century and as profitless as Li-Po's fishing for the moon in the Yellow River. I feel some political 'Prominente' should have been selected to supply the introduction to this ambitious venture. Nevertheless, I am deeply touched and honoured by the invitation, consoling myself with the thought that - just possibly - the transformations that have taken place in the intervening years between my callow youth and more-or-less philosophic old age make such changes stand out in sharper focus. At least this Merthyr Tydfil Odysseus returning to his Ithaka-on-Taff hopes he is better informed, if not wiser.

I find my memories do not build up in any logical sequence. They are disconnected mental images that still contrive to emphasise the metamorphoses between the late Twenties and the early Nineties.

Visiting two local schools last autumn, I was struck by the heartening contrast between the pinched, deprived children of my schooldays in Pantglas School and the present healthy, well-shod, friendly and confident generation. Somebody, I mused, must have worked with dedicated devotion, imagination, courage and sheer, hard graft to effect such progress.

One must doubt if any manuscript adequately could convey the 'atmosphere' of Aberfan in the 'Good old Days', unless, of course, the pages were left on the banks of the Taff on a nice warm night when the coal grit came whispering down and chemical effluents were drifting down from Merthyr to eddy round the marges of the Coffee Tavern Field. Yet, should such papers be put on the fire, after the initial spurt of flame, tiny sparks would wander over the ash surface like miners' lamps moving to the early shift on some winter morning long ago. Ultimately such hopeful glimmerings, like the coal miners' occupation, disappear into prophetic darkness. "When Truth is driven underground," thundered Emile Zola at the Dreyfus trial, "it grows and grows in the dark until it acquires prodigious strength, and when it bursts forth, it shatters everything." Alas, Truth driven underground in the local coalpits by the King Coal Captains of Industry shattered only the occupation and prospects of a fine breed of men.

Yet one can discern a Phoenix rising from the flames even though the furnace is not coal-fired. If the wings of this legendary bird are somewhat bedraggled and the tail feathers scorched and smouldering, this avian symbol of re-birth gamely struggles upward from Aberfan, perhaps first having cooled itself in a cleaner, sweeter Taff than the polluted river I remember. If this bird shared a parrot's ability to talk, it would not squawk vain repetitions but tell a tale of pathos, pride, triumph and disaster - and, in spite of all adversity a kind of sober quiet triumph.

Disaster? I have not the words to write about the catastrophe that attracted the black limelight of the world in 1966, but with John Donne, the metaphysical poet, I feel, "No man is an island … I am involved in Mankind." Aberfan has managed perfectly well without me but, nevertheless, I am involved with this small village. I was born here in 1909. I attended Pantglas School when old Jones Cannonballs was the Headmaster. My father, mother and only brother have long been asleep in the quiet cemetery above the now dry-eyed canal.

Earlier this year Selwyn Pritchard, a hard-bitten, sardonic writer of angry, vitriolic verse, wrote to me. He is an Australian poet with Celtic roots but no connection with Glamorgan. "Selwyn, my Doppelgänger," he wrote, "when I heard about Aberfan, I cried."

Across the ages one hears the voices of Pericles of Athens in his funeral oration. "The story is told, not only over the native hearth but lives on far away, without visible symbol, woven into the stuff of other men's lives."

"Sub speciae aeternitatis" all tragedy fuses into a timeless whole, part of the multi-coloured pageant of humanity. Such easy generalisations may be of small comfort to my little mining village of Aberfan that found the cliché 'the rich tapestry of life' turned out to be threadbare and shoddy. Yet, from whatever fabric available, the people of Aberfan have fashioned something worthwhile and permanent.

I would like to make it clear that I have had no part whatsoever in the preparation of this book. All credit lies elsewhere but I feel the presence of old friends - Sarnicol, once a near neighbour and now a scholarly, gentlemanly ghost, Lionel Richards, my early, unofficial Guru, still with us, and new friends like Maureen Hughes, whose warmth and welcome greatly has been appreciated.

To these and everyone involved in this undertaking, I send my sincere good wishes, with all encouragement and confidence in those concerned in this most laudable literary exercise.

SELWYN RUSSEL JONES

3.   An Introduction

Our villages are found in the middle of the Merthyr Valley. Here the valley of the Taff has been subject to a number of processes which shaped it. For instance, the general cross section of the valley with its flat bottom and steep sides indicates that a glacier formed the valley. A valley formed by a river on its own would have the outline of a letter 'V' but the flat glacial floor gave room for the villages to be built without a struggle to climb steep mountain sides.

On the Aberfan side the Troedyrhiw road makes a wide bend between Pantglas Fawr and Park Place in Troedyrhiw. The road is dodging around a spur between the large hollow of Pantglas and the stream of Cwmdu that came down past St John's Church. Normally spurs would gradually slope down to the main river but this spur forms a high bank at the edge of the road because the glacier rubbed away the nose of the spur. The consequence is that steep slopes at the edge of the spur have prevented the building of houses so that Aberfan and Troedyrhiw are quite separate. On the other side of the valley the very steep mountainside with bare rocks peeping out of the valley wall above King's Hill prevent the building of houses there too. That particular scenery is also typical of the glaciated mountainside.

Where the villages occur the river makes a wide bend. On the Merthyr Vale side, that gave some lower land for the farms of the area, namely Danyderi and Ynysowen. Usually the land on the inside of the bend is low lying and in this case it gave the stretch of flat land on which the colliery was built. On the other side of the river, a large hollow, Pantglas, "the green hollow" was formed by the many small streams that ran down the mountainside. Within this hollow part of Aberfan was eventually built.

Landslides helped to isolate the position of the villages. The landslide in Troedyrhiw, where the 'Lido' was built, occurred before the end of glacial times because the mound of rocks on the valley floor was swept away. The Darren, beyond Aberfan Fawr and opposite Darren Las, happened after the last glacier and the mound of broken rock existed as a wonderful playground for children. The area presented problems for the builders of the Glamorgan Canal, the Rhymney Railway Line and the new road. When they built that, the evidence of the landslide was buried.

This is a brief account of what happened on the surface of the earth as far as our villages are concerned. But we must also consider what lies beneath the surface. First there is the fact that the rocks held coal seams. When they decided to build the colliery the aim was to extract all the coal between Troedyrhiw and Cefn Glas Farm and it was estimated that they would produce ninety million tons. Some coal was already being produced at Danyderi level, still to be seen, and very small workings at the edge of the Canal. The spoil heaps of these are evident just past the cemetery wall, the lower end of Bryntaf and near Pontygwaith. The coal from the levels was intended for Merthyr's iron industry. In addition there was also solid rock to be obtained, hence the quarries we see around the villages. Most of the older houses are built of this rock and the Pennant Sandstone, as it is called, gave interesting buildings because the stone could be grey, blue, rusty or brown, often in the same wall. The variety of colours creates an interest in the buildings. Besides, the rock was solid and hard wearing, a great help for building our industry and two villages.

BILL GRIFFITHS, 1991

To Merthyr Tydfil and Brecon
A4054
A470
Troedyrhiw
N
Aberfan
Merthyr Vale
Mount Pleasant
Merthyr to Cardiff railway
Route of Glamorganshire Canal (now part of the Taff Trail)
KILOMETRES
0   1   2
MILES
0   1
A4054
A470
River Taff
To Pontypridd and Cardiff
BRYAN DAVIES

4. Our Book

We are gathering all our treasures
Our precious children
Into the arc of our love.
We are gathering all our words
Into the continuity of the ages.
We are gathering all our syllables
Like the Sonata
Raising the roof of a Church hall
In Merthyr Vale so long ago.

We are part of Thee
And of the love of this village
Of the ages of man
We will tell thee,
Of the civilisation
Of brotherhood and sisterhood
And of the simplicity
Of the soul
Made whole
By shared love
And endeavour.
Will we ever tell thee
Anything so important again?

MAUREEN HUGHES, 1991

Aberfan and Merthyr Vale Writers and History Group

Back Row
Reg Chandler, Bryn Carpenter, Bill Griffiths, Cyril Vaughan, Norman Jones, Mair Williams, Emily Griffiths, Maureen Hughes, Stephanie Davies, Julie Jefferson.

Front Row
Albert Lloyd, Sheila Lewis, Marlene Jones, June Vaughan, Mair Price, Beryl Roberts.

A Lloyd '90

Hafod Tanglwys Isaf Farm, Aberfan

5. Hafod Tanglwys

At the edge of the cemetery in Aberfan and between the new road and the canal bank there is an old farmhouse. Its name Hafod Tanglwys, is witness to important features of Welsh history. Tanglwys is described in the 'History of Merthyr Tydfil' as the sister of Tydfil. 'Hafod' denotes that the area was a summer time grazing ground. The event that took place is dated to 450AD or 480AD in that history book. So our story links together the results of the Romans leaving Britain and the coming of Christianity in the person of Tydfil, her family and other settlers to the Merthyr Valley. The third thread in our story is the development of a pattern of life.

First, the period following the withdrawal of the Romans is often called the "Dark Ages", implying a collapse of civilisation. Since the Romans had invaded South Wales in 50AD and because our region had forts at both Penydarren and Gelligaer and there existed a Roman road to join them, it can be assumed that soldiers and inhabitants were at least aware of each other. South East England did become Romanised and maps of the region often show "Celtic fields" existing alongside Roman villas which featured fine buildings and central heating. This showed a good degree of inter mixture between Roman and Briton. Villas were even built in the Vale of Glamorgan, but our hill country with its steep slopes, colder and wetter weather, poorer soils prevented profitable agriculture. Roman settlers would not therefore be attracted to our region. The conclusion drawn by one historian was that

> * "the average Welshman of AD400, like his ancestor at the time of the Roman conquest, was still in the pastoral stage, clad in skins and subsisting on flesh and milk of his flocks and herds and still using, it may be added, implements made chiefly of flint and stone."

What the Romans did leave was a large number of Latin words which helped to convert the Celtic Brythonic language into Welsh. A table shows some of the topics and some of the words relating to them that transformed the language.

Topic	Latin Word	Welsh Word	English Meaning
Literature	Liber	Llyfr	Book
	Littera	Llythr	Letter
	Scribenda	Ysgrifen	Writing
	Auctor	Awdur	Author
Building and Fortifying	Murus	Mur	Wall
	Castellum	Castell	Fortress - Castle
	Fossa	Ffos	Ditch - Trench
	Pons	Pont	Bridge
	Lorica	Llurig	Cuirass - coat of mail
The Human Body, Clothing and Home	Corpus	Corff	Body
	Bracchium	Braich	Arm
	Coxa	Coes	Leg
	Bucca	Boch	Cheek
	Palma	Palf	Palm of the hand
	Manica	Maneg	Glove
	Pexa	Pais	Petticoat - Undergown
	Parietum	Pared	Partition
	Postis	Post	Pillar - Post
	Porta	Porth	Door - Entrance
	Fenestra	Ffenestr	Window
	Coquina	Cegin	Kitchen
	Candela	Cannwyll	Candle
	Flamma	Fflam	Flame
	Cultellus	Cyllell	Knife

* A. H. Williams - An Introduction to the History of Wales. Page 59.

This is by no means a complete list of Latin borrowings, but they provide evidence of the antiquity of our language. In the isolation of Wales that followed the departure of the Romans and the Anglo Saxon conquest our literature started to evolve. In the pre-Roman times we had no writing but poetry, legends and history were handed down by word of mouth from one generation to another. By the seventh century, written Welsh poetry was not only recording history but also keeping alive the strong rhythm, rhyming and alliteration which had belonged to the ancient, oral, pre-Roman tradition. This development of language and literature, becoming Welsh, is one change to which Hafod Tanglwys silently testifies.

In the History of Merthyr Tydfil we are told that Tydfil was descended from Brychan Brycheiniog whose Welsh mother had been married in Ireland. Brychan is described as Christian and a long list of sons, grandsons, daughters and grand-daughters includes many people who either founded churches or were Celtic saints. Two important developments had happened in South Wales with the collapse of Roman power.

First there had been an invasion of Irish settlers into the south western regions like Pembrokeshire. This movement is shown by a trail of standing stones spreading from the far south west of Ireland across to Wales with one famous stone being found in Southern England. On these "were carved a special form of writing called OGHAM by which letters were notched to form a stroke alphabet on the edges of memorial stones."* A famous stone found near Narberth in 1895 shows the name of a dead man in Ogham. Sir Cyril Fox, in his book on the "Personality of Britain", gives a drawing of the writing, on page 94. The man's name was also carved in Latin capitals and the symbol of the Celtic cross stood at the head of the stone. The dedication *Memoria*, Latin for *to the memory* was used instead of the usual *HIC IACET, 'here lies'* found on British tombstones. *Memoria* was habitually used in North Africa. What had converged on South Wales, an invasion of seaborne traffic from the Atlantic coasts of France and Spain such as had happened in prehistoric times. Then the route from Carmarthen, Llandovery and Brecon and beyond had brought gold ornaments into South Wales but with the coming of Brychan that road carried a form of Christianity that made Wales into a land of saints and monasteries. The faith that had arrived in Merthyr was quite different to that which had been brought by the Romans.

This new faith had started life in the eastern half of the Roman empire. From the earliest days of Christianity some converts had shown extraordinary enthusiasm for a holy life. Gradually this enthusiasm for a life of prayer and good works was channelled into forming communities mostly of simple people working to maintain themselves and joining in worship and public service. Both ideas and disciplined practice were carried across the Mediterranean to southern France and from there across to the Atlantic and so to Ireland and South Wales by sea. Gwladys, sister to Tydfil, established her community on Gelligaer mountain at the edge of the road that leads from Cross Inn to Bargoed. There you can see the remains of a small building and pick out a surrounding enclosure or 'llan' that formed the church and the consecrated ground. While the church accommodated only the priest and the altar, the congregation occupied the 'llan'. The headwaters of the stream lie near-by and the probability was that the huts of the members of the community were scattered on the surrounding slope. Such an explanation is possible because similar features built of stone remain in Ireland. Missionary work had always been a feature of Christian history and this was maintained by these Christians too. Gwladys' son, Cattwg Cadoc, established churches at two places called Llangattock, one near Abergavenny and one near Llandovery. In addition we find another Cadoxton near Neath, where there is at present a dispute about the stone altar in the Church, and another Cadoxton near Barry. This is the way that Celtic Churches and monasteries were established by Celtic Saints. There is no doubt that Tydfil belonged to one of these communities and that Tanglwys and Rhun were fellow members.

Finally, we have to ask how did these people live. Working for a living was a feature of their discipline but in our hill country farming had its' difficulties. Of course, some hunting, fishing and collecting wild products could provide some food. Growing crops would need patches of ground to be cleared of trees. Then that field would need to be fenced to protect it from animals. The ground would have to be ploughed and that required everyone to help. Grain was grown for bread. This is shown to us by archaeologists. At a famous 'dig' near Dinas Powis a great deal of information about this period was obtained. Here were found broken querns, the hand operated grindstones which ground the ears of the corn into flour. Circular slabs of sandstone were probably griddles on which thin sheets of bread were baked, bread not Welsh Cakes. In the rubbish heaps of the settlement "were

* E. G. Bowen. *The Settlements of Celtic Saints in Wales. Page 19.*

found great quantities of animal bones" writes the archaeologist, "cattle, swine, sheep and a few fowl" he adds. There were also remains of fish and limpets. Obviously most of the food supply came from the animals but, in addition to the meat, cheese and butter and useful raw materials like skins and hides, wool, bones, sinews and gut for stitchings were obtained. Polished stones showed that they had helped to make leather. Wool was spun into yarn by using bone spindle whorls which gave loose strands a twist to make it into a single thread. The yarn was woven into cloth and that was shown by a fragment of a loom weight. Bone was carved into pins, plaques and combs. These last were shaped like those fine toothed combs that mothers had occasion to use on us as children.

This kind of farming is called pastoral farming. Grazing and herding of the live-stock was a very important part of the people's activities. In the summertime, the live-stock would be driven into some lonely spot to make the job easier. Such a place was called the "Hafod" after the Welsh word "Haf" for summer. Hafod Tanglwys was an ideal grazing ground. It was not too far away from the community at Merthyr. A large green hollow in the mountainside provided the Welsh name Pantglas and gave a pocket of land which could easily be watched over. The hollow stretches from Ynysygored to Perthygleision Farm. There are about six streams providing plenty of water, even in summer time drought, as well as patches of tall grass for grazing and patches of bog and ponds for keeping cool. Well wooded slopes provided fire wood and timber for the huts that would be used year after year. There would be plenty of opportunity for carving wooden utensils required for domestic purposes. Between patrolling the area, shearing the sheep, milking, making cheese besides cooking, tending fires, keeping the camp clean; it would not be idyllic but of course much of the work would be carried out by the older children of the settlement.

Then one year there was a cattle raid in which Rhun, brother of Tydfil, was killed. Retribution followed when, Nefydd, son of Rhud, put the 'pagans' to the sword. This stresses the fact that the raiders were non-Christian tribesmen probably from not very far away. That was the incident that put Hafod Tanglwys into the history books. It may have happened fifteen hundred years ago but amazingly the memory has been preserved. I have tried to show that this adventure was not an important fact. The story goes on. Part of the Hafod Tanglwys Farm was taken to build the Glamorgan Canal about 200 years ago. Another slice was taken to build the Rhymney Railway line just over 100 years ago. The new coal mining village of Aberfan was built on some of the farm's lower fields. Would it not be ironic that at some time in the future, Hafod Tanglwys would be associated with a coal industry in South Wales on the strength of a small coal tip sheltering against the cemetery wall when the signs of a coal mining industry will have vanished?

BILL GRIFFITHS, 1992

References:

Sir Cyril Fox	The Personality of Britain.
E. G. Bowen	Saint David. The Settlements of Celtic Saints in Wales.
Local Histories	Merthyr Tydfil. The Gelligaer Story.
Leslie Alcock	Arthur's Britain - Wales in the fifth to seventh centuries AD.
	Prehistoric and Early Wales. Foster and Daniel.
A. H. Williams	An introduction to the History of Wales. Vol. 1.
	Prehistoric times to 1063AD.

6. Hafod Tanglwys - The Summer Palace

These are the jewel colours of my Summer Palace,
Silver blue, flashing green,
Myriad hues of light.
These are the stars and moon
Of my lord and lover
Who brings me home
To our Summer bower
Of leafy trees
And overhanging branch.
A bed of twisted sinews
Twigs and leaves.

This is my Summer Palace
The birds are flying overhead
And the blue skies
Mingle with the green trees.
The men are coming home,
Singing and laughing with my Lord.
The mosses make grassy cushions
Of dark green velvet
With white fronds of spume.

This is my Summer Palace
The sky is a canopy of silver and blue,
The clouds are fluffy fronds of swansdown
And my love is bringing me
An armful of flowers
To decorate my Summer Palace.
"Welcome," my Lord.
"This is my special bower
Where life and love become one
In my arms,
And where love and peace dwell
Side by side with the healing spring
And where I found you
In the voluminous waters of my love."

R.CHANDLER

This is my Summer Palace.
The stars shine green, blue and gold
Upon our Love.
All our nights are spent in Peace and Harmony,
And Love reigns supreme.
The mists of time
Roll around my head,
The green haze of the woods
Blends into the mountainside,
And the crystal stream
Lilts down to the plain.
The craggy rocks lie overhead
And the ferns are crackling
Beneath my feet.
The trees are bending to whisper
To my love and I
"This is your Summer Palace
You have come home to your leafy bower
Of overhanging branch
And bed of twisted twigs and leaves."

This is the Summer - Autumn afternoon
of my Love.
Gathered here is the totality of my life
With my love buried deep within my heart
And the shimmering haze of Summer fading
Silently into Autumn.
This is the Summer Autumn evening
Of my Love
A precious seed will be buried within
My heart,
Until you return to the Summer Palace.

R·CHANDLER

My Summer Palace is shrouded in
Despair
The bower droops with tears
As a million raindrops
Gather in the branches
Of my leafy trees,
The sky is tinged with pink and purple
The calm before the storm
Of our catastrophe.

My Summer Palace is at rest
Snow has covered the hills
The sky is pink and blue
The trees are bare,
And the birds sing through
All the short days of winter
Winds moan through the branches
Of the trees,
And we wander, you and I
Through the Summer Palace
Of our Youth
Turned to wintry sleep.

But now we walk hand in hand
My dearest Lord
Wrapped together in the warm Summer air,
Only the sound of faint singing
And laughter
From the Summer Palace
Disturbs the warm balmy air
As I turn for the warmth of your embrace
Sweet Lord and lover of the Summer Palace.

Maureen Hughes 1989

R.CHANDLER.

15

7. Some of the Story of the Aberfan Farm - Tir Aberfan

The Aberfan Farm and the Ynysowen Farm were opposite each other on the banks of the Taff. They were neighbours across the river and this is the beginning of the close association between the twin villages of Aberfan and Merthyr Vale. When the colliery came in the 1870s this became more apparent as houses were built on the two estates to accommodate the quickly growing workforce.

The Aberfan Farm was an historic one. Within its confines, 1154 feet above sea level, near to the source of the Fan stream, was to be found Capel Y Fan. The old name of the Chapel was Capel Y Cyndynfan. This was a wayside chapel, a house of prayer and dated to the middle of the eighth century. Travellers would have passed this way along the open treeless upper slopes of the mountainside and stopped at the chapel to offer up prayers. During this early medieval period (400-800AD) the lower slopes of the mountainside would have been forested and the native population living on the upper slopes.

A castle or 'castell' is indicated on the mountain. 'Hen Castell Llwyd' is shown lying to the south of Capel Cyndynfan and is located in a field north west of Cefn Glas Farm. This 'castell' may not have been man made but a natural feature.

On the mountain top, the Aberfan Farm had a summer 'grazing homestead', Ty Cefn y Fan. The homestead was permanently occupied by a member of the same household and belonged to the family for centuries. The Aberfan Farm remained with the family of William Lewis ap Rees from March 1536 until the twentieth century. At one point, a descendent of William Lewis ap Rees, Lewis William Lewis, was the owner occupier of Tir Aberfan. His mother was the daughter of William Meiric Thomas and another of her sons occupied Ty Meirich Coch. The Pantglas Schools were built on some of this farm land. The family were heavily involved in the Dissent Movement in Merthyr Tydfil and the surrounding area. They were amongst those who were meeting at Cwmglo and struggled peaceably for the right to worship according to their own conscience.

During the Interregnum, Richard Thomas Lewis of Tir Aberfan acted a Parish Clerk for Oliver Cromwell. He was one of the six leaders of the Merthyr Dissenters. He was the Parish Clerk from 1639-1653 and possibly until 1660. His cousin from Hafod Tanglwys Uchaf, William Howell Lewis was indicted on a treason charge, probably relating to the implementing of Parliamentary laws before the Royalists were defeated; once this happened, the trial never took place. Another cousin lived in Ynysygored Farm. He was an unpaid Puritan preacher, was labelled a fanatic by the Royalists and his congregation referred to as 'Highland Tribesmen'. He was one of the sons of Lewis William Lewis of Tir Aberfan.

Lewis William Lewis' daughter married Griffith Lewis and there were three sons. One of these sons, Jenkin Griffith, was living in Tir Aberfan by 1715. He died in 1727. He had kept the family traditions and was a Deacon at Cwmglo. The fortunes of the family steadily improved and Jenkin Griffith converted the leasehold into freehold. By 1737 Richard Jenkin Griffith of the Aberfan Farm was one of the wealthiest farmers of the period.

Their descendents were still in the farm in the early 1800s and the family name had become Jenkins. The third son, Richard, built up the estates with the help of his uncles. He was a linear descendent of the old Dissenting Conventicle of Cwmglo on the Aberdare mountain and he was a member of the Unitarian cause at Cefn Coed. He was linked by marriage to many of the other prominent Dissenting families. He was a member of the Vestry that oversaw local government in these times (1830s) and was in office at the time of the 'Merthyr Rising'. Richard was one of the people who shaped the town. Richard Jenkins of Aberfan was one of the philosophers of Merthyr who formed the Philosophical Society in December 1807. Like Richard Jenkins, most of them were associated with the Unitarian cause in Cefn and had strong family connections with Cwmglo. The Philosophical Society purchased scientific instruments. Amongst them were a good reflecting telescope, a pair of globes and a microscope. Every member subscribed a guinea and books were also purchased. Among their discussions they dwelt on religion, politics and philosophy for they were deep thinkers and people of intelligence. Richard Jenkins was an auctioneer and was celebrated as such throughout Glamorgan and Monmouthshire. He was still living in Tir Aberfan in 1841 and was seventy years of age.

By 1851 the head of the household in the Aberfan Farm was William Thomas although the owner was one Thomas Thomas. William's wife was called Cathrin and they had three sons and a daughter living there with them.

In 1856 Rowland Thomas Griffiths married Sarah Miles, a farmer's daughter of Llancaiach, Gelligaer and by 1861 they were living in Tir Aberfan.

MAUREEN HUGHES, 1991

References:

The Farms and Farmers of Senghenydd Supra prior to the Industrial Revolution.
The Parish of Merthyr   Prof. T. V. Davies.
The History of Merthyr Tydfil   Charles Wilkins.

Aberfan House showing the extension added by Mrs R. T. Griffiths

8. "Nothing was saved."

Someone who knew the Aberfan House well was Mary Jones. She went there to work as a very young girl. The only baby born there, in the new extension added by Mrs Rowland Thomas Griffiths, was Mary Jones' namesake, her daughter Mary. She was put to sleep in a beautiful mahogany four poster bed.

Mary Jones remembers the house being surrounded by fields. "We used to go picking blackberries in the hedgerows. The house was substantial and the earliest parts of it dated from the 16th century. There were eighteen rooms and three staircases in the house. There was a bathroom there bigger than most peoples' living rooms and two large basements, one of which was a wine cellar filled with rack upon rack. The other cellar was filled with marble slabs for salting the pigs.

There was a large hallway in the new extension and from here a mahogany staircase wound its way upstairs to the two master bedrooms and the master's dressing room. A colourful mosaic of tiles covered the entire hall floor and the door to the main house was so large and the patterning so intricate that when it needed painting, the labourer who had come with the painter, asked him if he had seen the door, remarking how much paint would be needed for the job. The decorations in the front rooms were such that people would come to view them. There were as many as seven doors leading from one of these rooms and if a new door was needed, great pains were taken to match it up to all of the other doors, which were three inches thick, with beautifully patterned glass in all colours. An unusual feature in the best room was the marble fireplace where the ashes were gathered into a sort of tunnel and were emptied through the kitchen grate backing onto the main room.

When the farmer retired to a villa nearby, the farmhouse was sold to be used as the Vicarage. Sadly, the first incumbent, painted over all the beautiful decorations."

Mary Jones was helping her son move into a new house nearby when she saw the Aberfan Farm House being pulled down. She went over to find out what was going on and one of the workmen told her that there had been problems with subsidence there. "Look at that big hole, for example", he said . He was very surprised when she told him that he was referring to one of the two large cellars. Mrs Jones felt very sad when she saw the beautiful wood and glass doors being burned. Nothing was saved.

"Will the Milk" (1st left) Llewellyn Roberts (middle) and Jacky at the dairy on Aberfan Farm

9. The Aberfan Estate at the time of the Civil War

The Civil War, which began in 1642, was fought between King Charles Stuart and his followers, known as 'Royalists' and 'Cavaliers', and the followers of Oliver Cromwell, the 'Parliamentarians', who were also known as 'Roundheads'. We know that this Civil War divided families; some sons took opposite sides to fathers and brothers in some of the battles, and bitterness existed for generations to follow. We also know that King Charles Stuart was beheaded at Whitehall in January 1649, and the Monarchy was replaced by a Puritan republic which was to be dominated by Oliver Cromwell.

Our area was divided during this time, but the Welsh people in the main tended to remain loyal to the King. Wales was known as the 'nursery of the King's Infantry' because of the support it gave to the Royalist cause. Following the King's defeats at the battles of Marston Moor and Naseby, the King himself visited South Wales to gather men and money to defend his throne. One of the men he met was Colonel Edward Pritchard of Llancaiach Mansion near Nelson, who had gathered at one time a force of 4,000 men for the King. We know that upon leaving our valley the King stayed at Brecon following his visit to Llancaiach Mansion on 4th August 1645, and he wrote a warning letter to his son - "Charles, it is very fit for you to prepare for the worst."

The King knew that the Welsh had become tired of the Englishmen who commanded Royalist troops and of the high handed way in which they plundered their way across South Wales and he detected the resentment of the people who had formerly come to his aid. Within a few days Brecon was taken for Parliament and the County of Glamorgan also went over to Cromwell. Colonel Pritchard of Llancaiach Mansion changed sides and by September 1645 he shared command at Cardiff Castle as a Parliamentarian on the side of Oliver Cromwell.

One who did not leave the King was John Thomas Williams of Merthyr Tydfil who was by then the High Constable of Caerphilly. Another family who remained loyal was that of Lewis of the Van who owned an ironworks at Pontygwaith.

In 1648 Roundhead troops were sent from Brecon under the command of Colonel Marten to put down a Royalist rising in Glamorgan. At Cardiff 8,000 men had gathered to support the King - the Battle of St Fagans on May 5th 1648 resulted. There is a local story that while travelling towards Merthyr the Roundheads saw and destroyed Morlais Castle, which seems a costly and time consuming waste of energy, and there is another story that the Cromwellian soldiers stabled their horses in the Parish Church at Merthyr Tydfil.

A third legend which concerns Aberfan, must have its roots in the fact that the destruction of Lewis of the Van's ironworks at Pontygwaith took place on Colonel Marten's journey from Brecon to Cardiff, or else upon the return journey after the Battle of St Fagans, which seems more genuine to the writer now.

The story is that the Cromwellian soldiers stayed at the farm near Bryngoleu owned now by Mr Bonsall Price, and that several of them died and were buried in the field opposite the farm, which is now the playing green in front of some of the Aberfan Fawr houses. Trees were planted, seven of them, one for each dead Roundhead. Many people will remember the tall trees which were removed after the Second World War, because of their great height.

Perhaps some soldiers were attempting to make their exit from the Battle of St Fagans with severe wounds, and perhaps they did die in Aberfan, or could it be that while they were destroying the ironworks at Pontygwaith there was opposition and they were killed there and later buried in a 'safe house'?

Another story does have it that the farm had Puritan connections and that a secret exit was built under the ground as an escape route, that would have been a 'safe house' for Roundheads if the owner shared their Puritan faith.

HILARY CLARKE, 1994

Reference
"Merthyr Tydfil, a Valley Community" -   17 & 18 Centuries in Merthyr Tydfil.
                                           MANSEL RICHARDS

When we were children growing up on the Aberfan estate, we were told these stories by older children about the Civil War. They would be centred around the Aberfan Fawr Farm. They were stories of secret tunnels and people hiding in the huge oak tree outside the farm. They were stories peculiar to this part of the village, and had been handed down to each generation. All the more intriguing to find out that the Parish Clerk to Oliver Cromwell at the time of the Inter-regnum was Richard Thomas Lewis of Tir Aberfan.

Similarly in the Grove area of the village. The children here have always been referred to as Picts and Scots. The houses were built on land belonging to the Ynysygored Farm.

MAUREEN HUGHES, 1994

Aberfan Fawr Farm at the beginning of the century

10. A Gentleman and Farmer

Delightful weather at the end of August 1875 saw the children of the Baptist Sunday Schools in Troedyrhiw making their way to Aberfan for a monster picnic. With their pastor, teachers and members of the Church they walked through the streets of Troedyrhiw to Aberfan. The church choir led the procession and various music selections were sung in a spirited way. The children carried several new banners and flags.

They were making their way to a field belonging to Rowland Thomas Griffiths of Aberfan House. His estate encompassed the original Aberfan and took its name from the Fan stream which ran down the mountainside. Nearby, the cottages that housed the workers on the estate were called Aberfan Row, and when a new hotel was built on the edge of the estate in the 1870s, this hotel was called "The Aberfan".

The Glamorganshire Canal ran through the estate and Sunday School Scholars had been known to come down to the farm field from Troedyrhiw in canal boats, courtesy of W. C. Crawshay. They would have walked through country lanes past the Aberfan Fawr Farm to reach the fields of Aberfan House. But on this beautiful August day a large muster made their way by foot. But not only the field was placed at the disposal of the Sunday School; Mrs Rowland Griffiths 'threw open' her house for the preparation of tea and cakes and assisted with the preparations herself. Indeed she was praised for her great kindness.

Mr and Mrs Rowland Griffiths were not blessed with children of their own. They had an extension built on to the original Aberfan Fach Farm House in the hope of having children. But there was only ever one child born there and she many years after the time of the Rowland Griffiths.

Not only was Rowland Griffiths a farmer, he owned the Perthygleision Colliery or the Aberfan Colliery as it was sometimes known. The colliery was about a quarter of a mile from Aberfan House. In 1879, the level produced nearly two thousand tons of coal. The company tendered to the Board of Health and supplied coal to the newly built Merthyr Vale School. In the census returns Rowland Thomas Griffiths was described as "a gentleman and farmer", and a few weeks after the 'monster picnic' a grand 'field day' was held, when he released a young fox, belonging to himself, in the neighbourhood. The fox had a few hours start before the hounds assembled and, although the cry went up 'fast and furious', the fox 'Reynard' 'ran to earth' on the adjacent mountain, after an exciting chase.

On the Thursday previous to the fox hunt, Mrs Rowland Griffiths was laying the foundation stone of Capel Aberfan. The weather on this occasion was so bad that the children's choir from Troedyrhiw was prevented from singing. Mrs Griffiths gave £20 to the chapel funds and was presented with a silver trowel and mahogany mallet. Several of the visitors were entertained by her and Mr Rowland Griffiths at Aberfan House, and by Mr Edwards and family of Aberfan Fawr Farm. Others were entertained by Rhys Rhys at the nearby Aberfan Hotel.

The Aberfan Hotel

Mr Edwards had a very narrow escape a few years later whilst at Mr Griffiths' "Aberfan Colliery". A boiler explosion at the colliery shook all the houses, even in Merthyr Vale, and the people ran out onto the streets. Mr Edwards was at the colliery with his horse and cart. The horse, when he heard 'the loud bang', bolted with his master and they avoided the falling iron and stones. But the force of the explosion hurled the upper portion of the boiler two hundred feet high and sent it up into the woods, a long distance away. The whole of the engine house and stack was sent flying in all directions and the engine was damaged. The boiler had been there for many years and Mr Rowland Griffiths lost no time in replacing it and in setting men to work upon repairing the engine house and premises.

At the time of the Abercarn explosion Rowland Thomas Griffiths headed the list of subscribers to the Relief Fund with a donation of 5 guineas. He became the President of the Cricket Club and had his health drunk with musical honours at their first annual meeting at the Aberfan Hotel in 1879.

In 1875 he had begun building houses on his land, realizing, by then, that the future of the Merthyr Vale Colliery was assured. He entered into partnership with John Nixon to put up the first bridge crossing the river from the Aberfan estate into the new colliery at Ynysowen. When the bridge in Troedyrhiw was damaged by storms in 1878-79, and had to be closed the Board of Health rented the use of the colliery bridge to get into Aberfan.

The delay in the bridge in Troedyrhiw being reopened caused someone to sing at a concert in the Rechabite Hall

"Just above you know full well
The boundless River Taff
Has burst the bridge
And Troedyrhiw is cut right slick in half
There's no bridge yet
Though months have gone
So I must prophesy
That bridge will be completed when the pigs begin to fly."

Rowland Thomas Griffiths and his wife were a young couple in their thirties when the colliery was coming into being. He was descended from an ancient South Wales family in these parts. Eventually he became elected to the Board of Health and the Board of Guardians who administered the Poor Law. He was instrumental in securing some of the farm land at Hafodtanglwys for the Cemetery in Aberfan.

When Rowland Thomas Griffiths died in 1887, his widow continued to live at Aberfan House, until she died in 1913. She had become known as "Lady Aberfan". She was very fond of Pleasant View which she could see from Aberfan House whilst looking up towards the mountain but dreaded houses coming in between, on her farm fields. She said that she hoped she would be dead before any more houses came.

Today there are housing estates over the fields that she loved so much. But I like to think that she would have been her usual kind, generous self towards the children. She seems to have had a special affection for young people.

MAUREEN HUGHES

Capel Aberfan

11. "A Beloved Minister"

Rowland Thomas Griffiths of the Aberfan Farm was descended from an ancient South Wales family on his father's side as well as his mother's. His father's roots went back to the Neath Valley, in the County of Illtyd, long before there were any accounts written. His grandmother Eleanor, was the daughter of a farmer of repute and she married a carpenter who was called William. Daniel who was the father of Rowland Thomas Griffiths, was the youngest of their six children.

Eleanor was deeply religious and influenced many people including her own children. When he was very young, Daniel would take a lantern and go across the fields to meet his mother from prayer meetings. Sometimes he would catch sight of his face and the lantern, reflected in the stream that ran through the fields and he would be very frightened, but this did not stop him from going to meet her.

His mother and father died when he was still young and his eldest brother, William, assumed responsibility for him. Daniel went to live with his sister Mary and her family. They would tease him and call him an 'old man' because he liked reading the Bible. He was allowed into the adult meetings of the chapel when he was only nine years old. He was so knowledgeable that he was able to discuss things with the ministers. Daniel remembered these meetings all his life and the wonderful deep feelings that he had. When he became old enough he went to work on the "camlas", canal, and became a wonderful carpenter, working very hard to learn his trade at this time.

Daniel became a worthy Sunday School teacher in Melin Cwrt in the Neath Valley and he learned the Epistle to the Romans by heart. He used to recite this in chapel meetings and eventually he learned the whole of the Epistles from memory which brought him to the attention of the whole of Wales. The Sunday School children followed his wonderful teachings.

Soon he was preaching throughout the Neath Valley and many joined him which made him very happy. In 1822 Daniel had the opportunity to move to another part of Wales to preach. Glamorgan was afraid of losing him and they worked very hard to keep him. He was preaching at this time in many chapels, but they were all too small for his congregations.

The Secretary of the Neath Independent Chapels was Rowland Thomas. He was very rich and was anxious to help Daniel Griffiths. He had a daughter, Jennett, and she was helping Daniel with his work. Daniel and Jennett talked about a new chapel, but they themselves had no money and no land. Daniel prayed about all these things and eventually Mr Rowland Thomas told him that he had bought a large piece of land to build a chapel at Melin Cwrt. A beautiful chapel was built by wonderful workers and they named it Soar.

Miss Thomas and Daniel Griffiths married and had children. The eldest was called Daniel after his father. He was born in his grandfather Thomas' house near Caerphilly but he died at sixteen years of age. Rowland Thomas Griffiths was the second born in 1831 and was called after his grandfather. He inherited the Aberfan Farm through his mother's family. His brother William and he inherited the Aberfan estate. William was given the name of Daniel's father and elder brother. He became a wholesale ironmonger in Merthyr Tydfil and lived in Courtland Terrace. They were both worthy sons of their father. William was a faithful and loving Sunday School teacher to the very end of his life at Market Square Chapel where he was also a deacon and treasurer.

Daniel's health began to fail after the death of his brother William. He had a narrow escape when a big tree fell by his side on the way back from the funeral. Shortly afterwards his horse fell underneath him and Daniel was as dead, on the road. His arm was 'out of place' for five weeks but he still kept preaching. He was having bouts of illness and his beloved daughter Mary Ann would be struggling to breathe in one room and he could hear her as he was struggling to breathe in another. His health did not improve and he preached his last 'Gymanfa Ganu' in Llwyni in May 1845. He preached with great 'hywl', fervour, but he didn't preach in a Gymanfa after that.

On April 1st 1846 he was talking and singing hymns at three o'clock in the afternoon. He died peacefully that day at six o'clock.

Thousands attended his funeral. Twenty seven ministers attended. Hymns were sung from his home to his beloved chapel. There were so many people thronging around that some of the ministers had to climb in through the windows. The Mayor was in the Chapel and he asked the people outside to stop pushing from outside because he feared for the lives of the people inside. The crowds had become out of hand. But at long last, he was laid to rest.

Neath had never seen such a funeral. Many of the great men of the time were present.

As a tribute to a beloved minister and leader, the Church went without a minister for twelve months, and gave the year's wages to Daniel Griffiths' widow and children.

It was said that he was one of the most brilliant scholars and Preachers that Wales ever raised.

References
Remembrances of Rev Daniel Griffiths
P. Griffiths, Altwen 1847, translated from the Welsh by Ethel Lloyd 1994.

History of Zoar Church - Neath 1823 -1983
Nantlais Jones - Deacon Zoar Chapel.

Rev Daniel Griffiths

Many thanks to those people who helped me with documents and information on the Aberfan Estate - Diolch yn fawr

MAUREEN HUGHES

Chapter Two
Merthyr Vale Colliery

1. Introduction

The Merthyr Vale Colliery opened on 23rd August 1869 and closed on 23rd August 1989. Thousands of families relied upon the colliery for their livelihood over those 120 years. Generations of fathers and sons followed each other into its workings. All of us grew up with its vibrancy, knew its every mood and the light from its lamps lit up the dark places in our community.

Standing above the village after the site was cleared, everyone could see and be amazed by the amount of land that the colliery had covered. A third of the village had been taken up by its mass. Now it has become a brooding wasteland in the middle of our community. There is an air of sorrow about the deserted site abandoned by man after so many years of productivity.

Merthyr Vale Colliery

2.   John Nixon - 'No Clutcher at Straws'

With its inevitable final claim on life, the public cemetery sits so quietly within our communities, and none less so than the 'Aberffwrwrd' Mountain Ash in the Cynon Valley.

Guarded at its rear by the strong, steep, eastern hillside; flanked on the one side with high grassy mounds of colliery waste and on the other the swift, tumbling clear 'Ffwrwrd', it has gathered within its walls those who have passed through the community outside, which they have served according to their inherited and acquired talents.

Yet one of the graves found here hides a story which is so closely linked to many of the others which surround it. For here in the front of the burial ground lies the remains of John Nixon, a man who shaped the destinies of two Welsh valleys, the Cynon and the Taf, though born on 10th May 1815 in the small village of Barlow, seven miles from Newcastle-upon Tyne, County Durham.

Until he was fourteen years of age, it was at that village school he received his formal education before progressing, as expected, to the farm where his forebears had from many years carried out a tenancy-ownership. This Nixon however, was to break this centuries' old tradition after only two years 'on the soil.' Instead, he became an apprentice with a Mr John Gray, a noted local mining engineer of Garesfield, who also carried the office of chief mining agent to the renowned Marquess of Bute - two names which were to play an important role in Nixon's long and distinguished mining career.

To augment his young zeal for the emerging steam and coal trade in County Durham, the former farming lad entered a famous academy at his native Newcastle, namely the Dr Bruce, rubbing shoulders with other young visionaries, Robert Stevenson and George Elliot, soon to make such an impressionable impact upon Britain's industrial revolution. Elliot, of course, later, to find his future too, in the South Wales valleys.

Little time was wasted before the young John was to climb the greasy ladder to success, when after the termination of his apprenticeship, he became overman at the Garesfield Colliery, at the then handsome wage of 3s.6d. per day (17p). The two years he spent right in the heart of coal mining must have provided him with a valuable insight into the skills required by the collier, and no less, the expertise of successful liaison with those upon whom later in the Welsh valleys, he would have to depend for his success.

To such a keen student of coal mining the call would inevitably come to put his knowledge and experience to the test. It was no surprise therefore to those who closely followed this prodigy, when he replied to an advertisement placed in the northern newspapers by no less a personage than Mr Crawshay Bailey, who required a manager for his Nantyglo collieries. Nixon must have had no small prescience of the impending growth of the South Wales coalfield because, in the true entrepreneurial spirit, he relinquished his post as overman at Garesfield and headed south west; his link with the Welsh valleys was made.

Here, however, we find no clutcher at straws, for at this vital interview he was to decline a more than generous offer from Crawshay Bailey of becoming eventually to chief managership of a colliery group at Nantyglo. At just 24 years of age he did not relish the thought that acceptance meant another losing his position, a rare quality which many would have to acknowledge in Nixon years ahead.

There appeared though, an offer which was to bring him a step nearer to his ultimate goal at Taf and Cynon. Following a successful interview with Lord Bute's agent at Llandaf, he was commissioned to survey the Dowlais property, prior to a new lease being granted to Sir John Guest. True to the fastidious quality he possessed, he was able to conclude an acceptable and accurate report for the agent. During this exhaustive survey he enhanced his knowledge of mining as his keen insight observed wasteful and dangerous methods of coal production, something he would later turn to his own advantage when he would sink his own collieries.

It was here also that he made his first and impressionable contact with the superior Welsh steam coal - at Penydarren Pit. He quickly saw the potential in this coal which generated such an intense heat yet required so little stoking and gave off little smoke; he knew that his own native Newcastle coal took second place to this new find. True to his growing skills, he moved quickly and effectively to exploit the growing markets which would snap up this type of coal.

It was not in Britain alone that he canvassed orders. Indeed, he dared to load a boat with it at his own expense and crossed the channel to France. Success favoured this brave venture as the French manufacturers agreed with Nixon's findings. His successful salesmanship did not, however, end with the manufacturers. He even approached the French Naval Authority and frigates bearing the Tricolor were to be propelled by Welsh steam coal before our own Navy were to become impressed.

Armed with his new victory there was nothing going to stop the young genius sinking his own collieries; the former farming lad was not to win his bread from off the land, but by delving many hundreds of yards below it and it was ironic that in this process, acres of good farming land would be swallowed at a stroke. Progress, however, is only achieved with casualty.

And casualties there were, as this Newcastle genius earned in later years the accolade, "Amongst all the personalities of the Welsh coalfield, there is not one which stands out with greater prominence than that of John Nixon. For, not content with one sinking, this man masterminded at least four in the Cynon valley - Deep Duffryn, Nixon's Navigation, Abergorki and Cwm Cynon. It was no wonder a twelve foot cross rises above his grave to look out over the wall to his former colliery sites."

Falling into financial difficulties because of the rising momentous costs in drilling through rock of almost impenetrable thickness, he accepted partnership with a Bristol financier, Evans, and later with another famed name in Welsh coal - William Cory. The partnership prospered and the objects achieved.

Here, I suppose, most men would have been happy to sit back and bask in the acclaim won, but not so John Nixon as he gathered himself for a final venture which was to overshadow anything hitherto - the sinking of Merthyr Vale Colliery, just over the mountain from the Cynon Valley. Speculation had abounded for some time amongst those whose business it was to know, that deep down in this Taf valley lay a rich tract of coal, hitherto thought completely inaccessible. But whereas many coalowners jibbed at the mammoth project, Nixon gambled on one last throw of the dice as he set to the unthinkable. Encouraging no others to his invitation for partners, the steel in the man coupled to his vast store of mining experience, decided him to go it alone. Many times over the next five years his skill was called upon to overcome one obstacle after another, and the day eventually came in 1875 when the first 'dram' of coal saw the light of day. Another rung, indeed, the final rung to the top of that ladder to fame!

What a career for the young Barlow lad, five firsts in sixty glorious years, and it is only in retrospect we enjoy the luxury of time to assess this man who stood astride others in his profession. We may well ask and ponder as to the 'whys' and 'wherefores' of his illustrious career amongst us here. From where came the irresistible drive, the unquenchable desires for success? I doubt if we shall ever know; there is the strong possibility he himself never knew the answers. Other than a 'reredos' (an ornamental screen) together with a wall plaque at St Margaret's Church, Mountain Ash, he does not seem widely recognised in our communities, yet he lived to see villages spring up around, and because of, his collieries. He retired from general managership of his coal mines in 1894, and spent the latter years of his life in London and Brighton where he died on the 3rd June 1899. Fathering no son by his wife Elisa, Nixon was succeeded in his business by a nephew, Mr H. E. Gray.

The simple inscription on his tomb, 'I am the resurrection and the life' prompts my hope that the prodigious coal giant had found throughout all his meteoric career "a vein that runs not out!"

CYRIL JOHNSON, 1991

Merthyr Vale Colliery: showing the three stacks

3.   Globychau newyddion Ynysowen - Merthyr Vale Colliery

Dacw'n llesg y mae en esgyn
Fwg ac ager uwch y dyffryn
O lobyllau Ynysowen
Tua'r entrych glan.
Lle nad oedd na thwrf na chyffro,
Drwy'r holl oesau aethant heibio
Ond hen Daff yn araf llithro
Dros y cerrig man.

Y mae'r fuan ysgyfarnog,
Gyda'r ffwlbert swrth a'r draenog,
Wedi redeg yn anfoddeg
I rye gilfach draw;
Ac yn lle gwaedd oer y fulfran
Athw hw y nos ddallhuan
Y mae'r ager gwillt yn clecian
Yn y graig uwchlaw.

> Gwilym Glan Taf
> William Edmunds
> Merthyr Express 26 December 1874

News from Ynysowen Colliery - Merthyr Vale Colliery

There is the languid smoke and steam
Ascending above the valley
From the Ynysowen Colliery unto
the firmament above, where there was no
thunder or excitement,
though the ages they went by,
But the Old Taff slowly gliding over the small stones.

The early hare, with the sluggish polecat and hedgehog,
They have run discontented, over to a safe refuge.
Instead of the cold cry of the vulture, and
the too-hoot of the night owl,
the wild steam is cracking in the rock above.

Translated from the Welsh by Ethel Lloyd 1991

4.   A Red Letter Day

"To the Parish of Merthyr the event is of the highest importance, for it is like the opening of a purse which has long been closed, and the best of the matter is this, that as the purse gets more and more opened so it will yield an ever increasing benefit to the Parish with no fear of early exhaustion." From the "Merthyr Express" on the successful sinking of the Merthyr Vale Colliery, January 1875.

When John Nixon leased the land for the sinking of the Colliery, from Lord Windsor in 1867, there were nine farms in the vicinity of Aberfan and Ynysowen and eventually the Ynysowen Colliery, subsequently the Merthyr Vale Colliery, was sunk on the cornfield of the Ynysowen Farm.

Sarah Edwards was about nine years of age when she climbed the mountain to the Danyderi Farm fields with her father Will. The hill was steep and he carried her on his shoulders part of the way. The year was 1869 and the month, August. As they looked down into the valley they saw a knot of men gathering in the cornfield below. "You are seeing history being made here!", Will Edwards told his young daughter as they watched the first clods of earth being turned over for the sinking of the Ynysowen Colliery. Will Edwards had come originally from Pembrokeshire, as had his wife Lucy. He was a plate-layer on the Taff Vale Railway and lived in Danyderi Cottages. There was a small settlement of railway workers in Danyderi, other plate-layers and some railway police. The Taff Vale Railway ran very close to their homes.

Before the sinking of the Colliery began on the 23rd August, the picture of Aberfan and Merthyr Vale was one of almost rural domesticity. But there were a few other features. As well as the nine farms, there was a substantial colliery level known as Danyderi. Some of the workers employed there lived, like Will Edwards, in Danyderi Cottages, others in Troedyrhiw. There was also the Windsor Hotel nearby, and a Welsh Baptist Sunday School met in Danyderi.

In Aberfan there was the Perthygleision level or the Aberfan Colliery, as it was known sometimes. The owner of the Colliery, Rowland Thomas Griffths lived in the Aberfan Farm. Nearby was Aberfan Row where the people employed in the farm house and on the farm, lived. On the canal bank were two cottages called Perthygleision Bridge, the "Red Cow" public house and the Lock House. The Lock House attached itself firmly to the hearts and minds of succeeding generations of villagers but was demolished in the 1980s when the trunk road was being extended. Why the house was removed isn't clear, but the site is still there.

Aberfan began to grow in importance with the sinking of the Colliery and the building of the village. Rowland Griffiths went into partnership with John Nixon for the construction of the first substantial bridge from Aberfan to Merthyr Vale Colliery and houses for the workers and their families began to be built on his land.

The safety standards of the Colliery, when in production, were a source of pride to John Nixon but the sinking of the Colliery brought some very bad incidents. Part of the problem was the deep water which flooded into the workings and at some points in the sinking, was ever present. The coal was not easily won. The shafts were sunk near to the River Taff and the sinkers had immense problems with water from the first. Quick sands eventually flooded the pit to the very top with slush and at one point, from eighty to a hundred gallons of water per minute was rushing into the shaft. This problem and the that of quicksands were overcome by lining the shaft with a vast iron tube. But before this was accomplished, there were several fatal accidents and in 1873 a sinker named William Morris lost his life when water rushed into the pit forcing out a piece of sheeting which knocked him into thirty feet of water. Eventually his body was recovered from water 150' deep. Ironically, he had been knocking in wedges to prevent water flooding into the pit. Poignantly too, is reported the death of a twelve year old boy, Thomas Gillard, who was working on the branch line to connect the Colliery with the Taff Vale Railway. Mrs Gillard had recently been widowed and had lost her eldest son and her mother since coming to live in Ynysowen.

'For a long time past many disappointments and anxieties have been experienced through various causes, such as inundation and giving way of the shaft, but thanks to untiring energy, success has crowned their efforts and "Old King Coal" now reigns supreme'.

This success had come at the very end of 1874 and the vein of Merthyr smokeless steam coal had been struck at a depth of 430 yards. The seam was a thickness of 6'8" and of the very finest quality.

There was a great outburst of rejoicing at the discovery and the next day was given up to widespread celebrating which was recorded by huge cannons which could be heard clearly four miles away in Merthyr and over the mountain in Mountain Ash "while the sundry pieces of bunting hung out at the most conspicuous points of the new settlement told the railway passengers that there was a red letter day in the history of Merthyr Vale." The coal was put on display in various shop windows in Troedyrhiw.

The Merthyr Express eulogised over the breakthrough to the famous four foot seam at Ynysowen and commented that the place would be better known in the future by its English name of Merthyr Vale, and that serious obstacles had been triumphed over by an "inexhaustible resource of energy, resolution and fertility of invention". Singled out for mention were George Brown, the Manager, Walter Bell and Mr Douthwaite the resident engineers, and John Thubron, the master sinker.

Mr Nixon had leased four thousand acres, from summit to summit of the mountain and from the edge of Mr Fothergill's Castle Pit in Troedyrhiw to Cefn Glas in Pontygwaith. Merthyr Vale was intended to be the largest or one of the largest collieries in South Wales. Everything had been built on a scale to meet the demands of an enormous out-put of coal. The railway connections and sidings had similarly been planned for a substantial accommodation of traffic. The Colliery was connected directly with the Taff Vale Railway and through that with the Rhymney Railway at Quakers Yard and was thus well placed for the ports of Cardiff, Newport and Swansea.

The workmen who were already employed by the Nixon Company were accommodated in a large village but this was added to for the new workmen and their families, who flocked to Merthyr Vale for employment. The Merthyr Vale Colliery was sunk against a background of slump in the iron trade and a consequent slump in the established coal trade in the Merthyr Valley. There were nearly two hundred empty houses in nearby Troedyrhiw. In Merthyr, there were children, termed "street arabs", by some, wandering aimlessly and between eight and ten thousand children of the 'poorer classes' were being fed in soup kitchens. This was why the successful completion of the sinking of the Colliery was an event of the "highest importance" to the Parish of Merthyr.

MAUREEN HUGHES, 1991

The Bell of St Benedict's Roman Catholic Church

5.   The Second Master Sinker

A court case at the end of 1875 throws an interesting side-light on the fortunes of one of the men who had sunk the colliery.

The case concerned a Nathanial Walker who brought an action against Nixon, Taylor and Co. to recover the sum of £10/16/8 which he alleged was due to him.

The story is as follows:

In April 1871 Mr Thubron had come to his house and offered him 33/- per week, with house, coal, and flannel, to come to work in Merthyr Vale Colliery. Mr Thubron was the head sinker at the colliery. The terms had been agreed and he had come to work at the colliery. He rose to become second master sinker and was paid £10/6/8d per month.

Obviously the completion of the sinking of the colliery meant that his job as sinker was coming to an end. He was told to cut coal and his wages from now on would be "what you can make, the same as another man". When he refused he was given notice to quit his house.

Walker maintained that all the other sinkers did not go on cutting coal. A bone of contention with the company seems to have been that the sinker had gone to Durham to work the year before, when wages had dropped, without giving any notice. The judge reserved his judgement.

Compiled from the Merthyr Express.   MAUREEN HUGHES

6.   The Double Shift Dispute

The first recorded strike in the Merthyr Vale Colliery took place in March 1876. A meeting of the colliers was held at the Aberfan Hotel and almost every collier was present. The miners' agent for Merthyr and Dowlais was present because the men had been given a month's notice which had run out a few days before. The miners' agent, Mr Isaac Connick, spoke in both English and Welsh. The dispute was over the working of a double shift system which apparently was not the system being worked in the rest of the South Wales coalfield, but was used when a new pit was being opened.

Mr Connick said that the colliery at Ynysowen was still in this stage, that is, still being opened out and he advised the men to resume work.

Two resolutions were proposed and seconded and after all the various points had been considered, passed.

They were as follows:

1.   "That this meeting of the workmen of the Ynysowen Colliery, seeing that the work cannot be said to be opened out, taking into consideration the depressed state of the trade and the large amount of capital expended on this enterprise, together with the manager's trouble in contending with difficulties already met within the pit, we deem it our duty to resume work until such time as we are able to consider the question under more favourable circumstances.

2.   It having been intimated that some of the men who have taken part in the strike would be 'marked out' this meeting considers it their duty to request the manager that all men returning to work have their own working places back again."

Four men left the meeting and the manager Mr Brown received the deputation most cordially and gave them a satisfactory answer to the resolutions.

The reply was brought back to the meeting which at once agreed to resume work the following morning.

A hearty vote of thanks was given to Mr Connick for his presence and advice.

Compiled from the Merthyr Express.   MAUREEN HUGHES

7.   A Serious Gas Explosion

The first serious accident from an explosion of gas occurred in the Merthyr Vale Colliery at the beginning of December 1877. This happened in the four foot seam, a seam that was 440 yards deep. Four men, all residents of Merthyr Vale, were engaged in timbering. A piece of timber was knocked out of place and a fall followed. This was succeeded by a 'blower' indicating the presence of gas. The men, being alarmed, fetched a comet lamp, a rather indiscreet thing to do as the flame of the lamp protrudes through an aperture. The lamp was held to the roof to test the gas which immediately exploded. The flames burnt the men about the back, face and hands very severely. One man, working nearby, was blown ten yards by the force of the explosion and was very much cut about the face and hands. The explosion was heard by the men who were working at the top of the pit and they descended to the rescue of the sufferers, as well as to the other men working below. The injured men were taken home immediately and given medical attention. Two of them, William Herbert, who was the foreman and Evan Watkin, one of the workers, were still in a critical state a week after the accident.

Compiled from the Merthyr Express: 8/12/1877.

8.   The Building of the Village -1

The Colliery continued to grow in influence

The new cemetery had been established at Aberfan on part of the Hafodtanglwys Estate following many public meetings. The land had been purchased and the Chapels built at a cost of £3,200. The first burial was of a young man from Troedyrhiw in April 1876. The official opening of the cemetery was in August 1876. By March 1878, seventy five burials had taken place in the cemetery. One hundred and six feet of wall was being rebuilt there and a scheme for widening the road was being carried out. Later in the year there were trees planted and four benches purchased. When repairs to the road were needed, workmen from the Merthyr Vale Colliery carried them out. Now the Board of Health would take over the road.

Trade was causing concern to the Merthyr Vale Colliery. Trade was not good and only three or four turns were being worked. The average price per ton of Merthyr Steam Coal was nine shillings and threepence and a skilled, adult, collier's wage was sixteen shillings and sixpence. The colliery had continued to grow in influence, the well being of the whole community being tied to its varying fortunes. In 1879 it could be reported that trade was again somewhat depressed but that great relief had been felt that the workmen's contracts, that were coming to an end, were being renewed.

With such growth in the community, came the call for the division of Ynysowen and Aberfan, from Troedyrhiw. The principal rate payers from Ynysowen, Aberfan and Treharris signed the petition for the division. This seems to have been well received by the powers that be, unlike the acrimony that greeted the similar petition that had been inspired by John Nixon in 1868.

By 1880 the community was on the way to being established. The colliery, chapels, schools, some shops and many social activities, were in evidence.

Two of the principal ratepayers who had signed the petition for the division of the parish were Walter Bell of Ynysowen House, and Rowland Thomas Griffiths of Aberfan Farm. Walter Bell was the agent for Nixon and Rowland Thomas Griffiths described himself as a gentleman and farmer. These two men between them oversaw the building of the community of Merthyr Vale and Aberfan.

MAUREEN HUGHES, 1992

9. A True Friend

A young man rode out from the Stables of Ynysowen House, Merthyr Vale. The night was dark as he crossed the small bridge over the River Taff and galloped onto the Aberfan estate of Rowland Thomas Griffths.

The night rider was Walter Bell. He was a Scotsman from Dumfries and the General Manager of the Merthyr Vale Colliery. He had come to South Wales as a very young man, probably around twenty years of age. For four years he was an engineer with the Rhymney Railway and then he worked with Nixon's Navigation for thirty six years.

At first he was employed at Mountain Ash and then, in 1869, he came to Ynysowen when the company began sinking a new pit. He was in charge of the surface operations at Merthyr Vale at the age of thirty two.

With his responsibility for the new colliery came a commitment from Walter Bell to the new community. He threw himself into the campaign to secure a Board School for Merthyr Vale. As an earnest and businesslike member of the Board he was able to overcome the opposition of some of the other members to the provision of the new school. Nearly two hundred empty houses in nearby Troedyrhiw, caused by the slump in the iron trade, meant that there were empty places in the local school and there were those on the Board who were of the opinion that the children from Merthyr Vale should fill those vacancies. The Vicar of Troedyrhiw was amongst those who thought this way. He was the agent for the land-owner of the site chosen for the new school in Merthyr Vale. But with great determination, all difficulties were overcome.

The new school was opened in March 1878, some of the new pupils being present at the ceremony. Mr Bell entertained the visitors at Ynysowen House. There was no railway station for Merthyr Vale at this time and a special halt was provided at Danyderi, near the new school, for the distinguished visitors. Some months later it was reported to a School Board meeting that Walter Bell had sent urgently for the school accounts because some parents were in arrears with their children's school fees. He had secured the books within half an hour from the headmaster, Mr Jenkins. The Merthyr Vale parents would have had a firm but sympathetic hearing, for Walter Bell had a real interest in education. A Roman Catholic, he had attended a meeting of fellow Roman Catholics in July 1878 and urged the

Mr Walter Bell, JP

parents who were present to send their children to school. If they could not afford to pay, he advised them to approach the Board of Guardians or the School Board. He assured them that there was no shame in "appearing before the Board." He called upon those who were poor and could not pay and therefore had good cases to come before the Board "without delay." Walter Bell had been elected to the very first School Board. He was extremely public spirited. He was a member of the Board of Guardians, the Board of Health and in 1880 he served on the Committee organising the prestigious Art and Science Exhibition in Merthyr Tydfil. He was raised to the Magistracy in 1894. He was a diligent supporter of the Temperance Movement and was opposed to the Sunday opening of public houses.

Within the community of Merthyr Vale and Aberfan his influence was crucial. A branch of the Volunteers was formed and Walter Bell became the Commanding Officer. He was a marksman of outstanding merit. Major Bell was the Commanding Officer at the time of the "awful calamity" at Lavernock and when Sgt Ball won the Prince of Wales Cup at Bisley, the praise given to Major Bell by James Ball at that time was well deserved. He worked tirelessly to keep the newly emerging community gathered around the Merthyr Vale Colliery, to the fore.

Walter Bell was a Roman Catholic when this could have meant narrow sectarianism but he was described as the 'most broad minded of men' and was a true friend to the other denominations in Ynysowen. There are references to be found to his deeds towards the Zion English Baptist Chapel when they were establishing their new church and to the lending of his fields to the Anglicans and the Primitive Methodists for their Sunday School Annual treats. He presided over numerous concerts held in the chapels for a variety of good causes. A contemporary source declares that he was "quite incapable of refusing kindly assistance to every Protestant denomination that sought his help."

Major Bell has been described as a fine dignified man who "in private life found his greatest happiness among his family." He and his wife Mary, also a devout Roman Catholic, had three children and enjoyed a loving relationship. Their home in Merthyr Vale was Ynysowen House which was the original dwelling house of the Ynysowen Farm. From its windows in 1878 they would have had a clear view of the work going on to erect the massive iron framing for the new No. 2 pit of the Merthyr Vale Colliery. This pit was to give work to a further three hundred colliers.

A novel feature of Ynysowen House was to be found in its stables. Chaff was cut there and sent to the mouth of the pit in small trolleys on narrow gauge rails laid out for the purpose. When the colliery was being demolished in 1990, following its closure, these rails were clearly revealed adjacent to the pit shaft, after being buried for many years under coal and other debris. The chaff had been fed to the pit ponies who worked underground.

Mr Bell could be found at this time presiding over a meeting, in the Presbyterian Chapel, which had been called to raise a fund for those left destitute by the explosion at Abercarn Colliery. Walter Bell became the Treasurer of the fund. Soon donations were coming in from workers and employers alike. Twenty pounds were contributed immediately from the men's own Sickness and Accident Fund. This had been established by the men themselves at the Merthyr Vale Colliery some three or four months earlier.

Eventually, Walter Bell became General Manager of the company with responsibility for overseeing Mountain Ash and Merthyr Vale, both vast concerns. From contemporary sources we learn that Walter Bell was a man of good family and high integrity. Independent in politics, he kept his promises and was straight in his dealings with the workmen. He was a courteous and faithful friend, kind and true hearted. After more than a quarter of a century of devoted service to the community that he had seen develop around the Merthyr Vale Colliery, he died very suddenly on Thursday morning 6th February 1886, after complaining of feeling weak. His wife, Mary, was devastated. Within months she moved to Canonbie House on the Aberfan estate, to live, and died there a few years later. A small room was found in the house, too small for two people to stand up in - it was the prayer room of the Bell family.

When his funeral cortege arrived at the Aberfan Cemetery, 'God's Acre', as it was known, a throng of over two thousand people were gathered there to pay their last respects to Walter Bell. "Truly", it was said in his funeral address, "there was something deep and estimable in the character of a man who could command the respect and affection of such a diverse gathering". He had kept the balance of justice between master and man. Workmen and professional men of business were all there, as well as his doctor, the local MP, the local councillor and representatives of the various bodies with which he was associated.

The Priest who conducted the service spoke of Walter Bell's character, the main strengths of which had been his thoroughness, his justice and his gentleness. He added that Walter Bell had always put the safety of his workmen above monetary interests. When he had been elevated to the Magistracy he had received congratulatory addresses and handsome pieces of plate from the workmen under his direction. Under his management there had never been a single strike and the colliery had been free from the serious accidents that were happening in other collieries in the South Wales coalfield at this time. The workmen from the nearby Plymouth Collieries, who were on strike at the time of his death, were most reverent in their attitude towards him. At the meeting called to discuss the strike they removed their hats and stood in silence remarking afterwards that "it would be well for working men if there were more employers' representatives like Mr Bell. He could be approached by even the humblest of workmen." He was held in respect and affection. The Temperance Movement lamented that they had lost a good, strong, supporter.

When Walter Bell was a very young man starting out at Ynysowen, he had represented John Nixon in his dispute with the Board of Health over the discharge of effluent into the River Taff just above the colliery. The dispute was acrimonious and the Board had gone so far as to invite Walter Bell to drink the waters of the Taff at Troedyrhiw; these had been described by an Inspector of Mines as "a blackish turgid stream little different from the effluent sewage which was pouring downstream". Since that time Walter Bell had become an influential and respected man in the town and now the Board lamented that they would miss a very faithful member and a dear friend.

The three things most associated with Walter Bell in the community have disappeared. The Merthyr Vale School so carefully and lovingly built, was replaced in 1968 by the Ynysowen School which was provided for Aberfan and Merthyr Vale school children following the Aberfan Disaster. The Merthyr Vale Colliery closed in 1989. His name, however, is still in common usage with the hill climbing from the old level crossing gates to Station Square, Merthyr Vale known as "Bells Hill". Ynysowen House was situated on this hill but now houses cover the site.

MAUREEN HUGHES, 1994

District Intelligence.
Merthyr Express
July 3rd, 1880. Merthyr Vale.

10. The Friend of the Family

On Thursday night, Mr David Hopkins, of Hafod Tanglwys, was carting stones from Aberfan quarry for Mr Bell's new villa, and, when backing "Darby" with a load on the canal bank, the weight of the cart overbalanced the horse and turned him in a somersault into the canal, where poor Darby's life was in peril for some time. Mr Hopkins, with "Dafydd ei fab", managed to keep his head above water until assistance came, and the unfortunate animal was rescued. The horse has been "the friend of the family" at least a dozen years, and is very feeble.

11. "Lead Kindly Light"

On a more sombre note, there was always a great camaraderie among the community of Aberfan, especially with the miners. When a miner passed away, there was always a collection made from door to door to give to his mother or widow, so that she would have enough money to cover the expense of the funeral, and every miner of his shift would follow him in his glass hearse to the cemetery and they would all be singing 'Lead Kindly Light' on the way.

MARY MAGLONA, MELBOURNE, AUSTRALIA, 1990

Merthyr Vale Night Stokers, 1912

12. Merthyr Vale Colliery 1920s and 1930s

'When a man was given a place of his own, I am referring to a collier, he had to buy all his tools for himself and for the boy working with him. This is a list of the tools he had to buy:

1.   Two shovels (round-mouth)
2.   Two picks
3.   Two steel curling boxes for carrying coal
4.   One steel bar
5.   One sledge hammer
6.   Clamp and wedge
7.   Stone wedges
8.   Axe
9.   Measuring stick
10.   Lock and bar for tools
11.   Chalk
12.   Caborundum stone to sharpen axe'.

TED DUGGAN, KNIGHTON, 1991

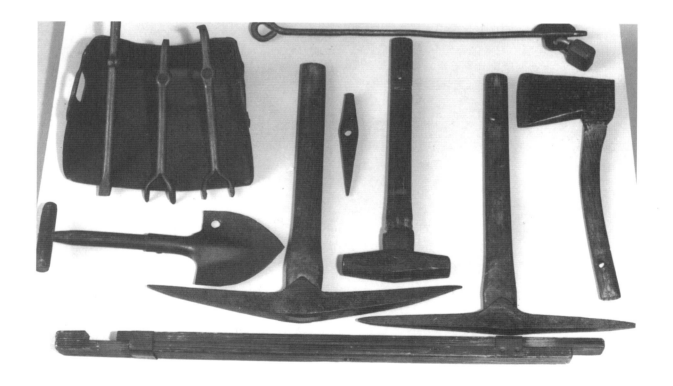

Set of Collier's Tools

13.   A Bowl of Soup

Ted Duggan now lives in Knighton, Powys, but began his working life as a miner in Merthyr Vale Colliery. He was fourteen in 1928 when he started work. He was up at 5 a.m. and walked to the colliery from the Grove where he lived. Each man had his own lamp and number which he checked when he collected it from the lamp room. He blew into the glass and if the light flickered the lamp was given back because it was damaged; either the washer or glass needed replacing.

During the night coal would be wound up the pit and then the men would be wound down at 6 a.m. The shift would last until 3.45 p.m. Merthyr Vale was a half a mile deep and the men had to walk a mile to the coalface. Merthyr Vale was a bad pit for gas. If there was a mist on the mountain they would probably have to go back home because the mist affected the air in the pit. There would be a bad circulation of air. "We would be rushed home and we weren't paid because we hadn't produced anything. We were paid by the ton. We weren't allowed to use a shovel. All coal had to be filled by hand. If you were caught with a shovel then you would be sacked; there was a man coming around to make sure that we didn't have any shovels. There was no muck and no small coal allowed: no pay for muck and small coal.

The coal was put into a curling box and carried to the dram seven or eight yards away. We were working in the nine foot seam. There were several hundred men mainly working day or night shifts; they were all working in stalls about about fourteen yards between them and you'd have to walk right around to reach the coal face. There would be hundreds of men working, all in conjunction. The bottom of the pit was like a honeycomb.

I was fourteen years old and working with my father. I went to the lamp room to collect my lamp. There would be other boys there collecting their lamps. Some of the boys would be smaller than me; the lamp would be a foot long, then the handle would add another foot so their lamps would be nearly touching the ground. They were just children really. People wouldn't accept it today. There would be twenty four of us in the cage going down to the bottom of the pit. We would be stacked up and hanging on. Between six and seven o'clock it would be all winding men up and down the pit.

At sixteen a boy could start night shift and would earn more money. He would work one day and a fifth and have an extra day's pay a week, The pay was as follows:

Aged 14	2/6 per week
Aged 14$^1/_2$	2/10 per week
Aged 15	3/4 per week
Aged 16	4/3 per week
Aged 18	6/8 per week

No-one was wanted after 18, too much of a raise to 8/3. This was a man's wage. The boy was got rid of and a new boy taken on, because the man you were working with would be paying your wages. Some of the boys would have a place but about 50% would be out of work.

I was working on the night shift and every night we went down the pit and we would wait for our pals about 100 yards from the pit bottom, then in one single file we would all walk on to the coal face which was approximately one mile. We would be singing in full voice and anyone listening must have thought we did not have a care in the world. There were a couple of songs that stick in my mind.

"I am wasting my time
Down Merthyr Vale mine
Filling three drams every day.
Boring top hole,
Clearing shots holes,
During the cut all the way.
Put two pairs of timbers
Three pairs of flats
And a monster big gog
In the Face.
When it comes to the end
There's nothing to spend
For I'm wasting my time anyhow."

The other song went like this:

"Morning always comes too soon,
When you're working afternoons.
And through this lousy shift
The coal boils out around me.
The drams are hard to get,
The boss is always grumbling.
The money we can't get
So to the office we strolled one day
To get our few bob pay
And then we signed the dole".

A. LLoyd

There were big, brown cockroaches underground. They were an inch long. They lived in the damp timber. There was a post there that was 9' high. We couldn't put a finger where there wasn't a cockroach. One night there were all cockroaches flying around. They were bustling about and the place was alive with cockroaches on the move. Then the place fell in. They knew by instinct somehow and left the post before the place fell in.

When I was $16^1/_2$ I was working with a chap called Jerry Williams. The man next door was filling water into the tank. Mr Williams said to me, "He's a long time coming back. Go and have a look where he is". We were filling coal at three o'clock in the morning. I went to have a look and the place was choc-a-block. We couldn't get out. Blocked in and couldn't do anything about it. We could hear sounds but we were not out until eleven o'clock when we were cut out over a corner. Nothing was said. But my mother said to me "What happened the other night?" "Nothing" I said. "One of the neighbours told me that you were blocked in." But we never mentioned what went on in the colliery. Never mentioned what went on in work.

Half of the pit closed. Seven hundred men from the colliery were out of work. I was working in the 9' seam when it finished. We worked in appalling conditions in the 9' seam. Gas, cockroaches and in some parts, water. There was a man from Aberfan Road, Mr Alec Lewis, he was working in the main place and the water was falling on him, off some galvanised sheet, like rain and he was soaked to the skin all day. This was a high seam and very dangerous; there was a long fall and the men had to work close to the seam. I remember one Sunday a gang of us boys went for a walk. With us was a fellow called Ritchie Morgan. "I've got a good place now in the 9' high seam. Coal is boiling out", he said. "Oh aye", I said. Friday there was an ambulance. Face had had him. A high piece had fallen out and killed him.

When I was eighteen, three districts finished.. The vestry of the chapel near the station in Merthyr Vale was being used as a labour exchange. The chap there said to me, "There's no prospects here but there's a retraining scheme you can go on." I was sent to Sholden, Hereford, where there was a training camp and I was there for three months. On the way to the station we picked up people in Dowlais, Troedyrhiw, Merthyr and they were all men from the employment exchange. We had a warrant to travel by train to Hereford and then we were met by open lorry. Sholden was miles from anywhere. We had to pick up the following clothes and equipment. Corduroy trousers and boots. Three planks and tressles six inches high plus a plate, knife and fork and an enamel mug. Also an army blanket. I had to report to number seven hut. There were thirty two of us in the hut. The three planks made a bed when placed on the 6' tressles. There was a straw mattress plus an army blanket.

In the morning there was an inspection of bedclothes and towel. There were about two hundred of us in the camp. We were gathered together like you see in the POW films. Captain Leadbetter was in charge and we were put to work in gangs of twenty. We travelled about half a mile and we were breaking stone all day, from 4" down to $2^1/_4$". Then we would work in Sholden quarry, also breaking stone. I remember working in the cookhouse, cleaning utensils, Saturday and Sunday as well. The pay was 4/- a week, 8p a day.

There was a song that we used to sing:

Men at work, Merthyr Vale Colliery

"Working in Sholden
Working all day
Working in Sholden
For eight pence a day.
If you would grumble
The boss would say
"Get in the office
And go on your way."

Less than in the pits. I was eighteen. I had been having 6/8. For recreation we'd go to the YMCA and there'd be billiards, table tennis and boxing matches. There was rivalry between North and South Wales. They'd fight for a couple of packets of Woodbines. Hammered themselves to pieces but there were no hard feelings. In three months, I went home. They were sending men away to work the sea-wall at Brighton but they didn't send me. When I asked why, I was told that I wouldn't be paid enough to live on. I would get a boy's wage because I was only nineteen. So I went back home to the pit, started the same week; my father found me the job. I worked there from 1932 to 1937. That's how it went. I left the mines and came to Radnorshire because an uncle of mine came down on holiday and said "That boy's looking bad isn't he? If he stays in the mines he won't be with us much longer. If I find him a job, can he come to Radnorshire?" "Up to him", my mother said. Within a few weeks he had found me a job as a building labourer on houses. I was getting $8^1/_2$d an hour. I knew others were getting 9d.

I went to the boss. "What?" "If it's not good enough, finish," he said. I finished for a week and then I was sent back again. This time I had 9d the same as the others.

Whole families had gone to Aberfan and Merthyr Vale from Radnorshire. There had been plenty of work as the pits were being opened out and plenty of houses. Those who started coming told those back home. There were several people from Radnor in our street.

At one time there were thirty two seams in the Merthyr Vale Colliery and now only seven are being worked. The seam that I worked is still there.

In the 1930s there was a lot of coal stocked because of the depression. The coal was waiting to go to Cardiff. Sometimes the pit was three days on stop. No surplus allowed now. Don't care about people, now close the pit. Now it's like a child with a bowl of soup. Picking the best and leaving the rest."

TED DUGGAN, 1988

*Ted Duggan after
he had left the colliery*

14. "Go to L"

Around 1930 Merthyr Vale pit was working short time, three days on and three days off. The days that you had off you had to sign on the dole at the labour exchange, which was the vestry of the chapel about 50 yards from Merthyr Vale station.

The clerks at the labour exchange had a bright idea so they put cards above each clerk with the letters of the alphabet such as A to E and F to M and so on. Everybody queued in order with their name. I, being Duggan, would go to A to E. So one day a man by the name of Charlie Louch from Cottrell Street went into the wrong queue and when he got to the clerk, the clerk asked him his name and Charlie said "Charlie Louch". The clerk said to him "Go to L" so Charlie caught him by the coat and said "Who are you telling to go to Hell?".

TED DUGGAN, 1991.

Trinity Chapel, Merthyr Vale

15. A heaving, seething mass

We were a group of ten girls going on a visit to a local coal mine. They did say that we were to be suitably dressed and when we were given helmet and lamp we felt that we could have passed as Bevin boys. We had been told stories of how, for the fun of it, the winder would drop the cage in such a way that a ride on the Big Dipper would be as a ride on a go-cart compared with it; this was only a story, because we journeyed smoothly down to the pit bottom.

They told us that we would find it dark and damp, and at times frightening, also the changes in temperature would be disturbing, it was all of those things. They told us that the smell of horses would make us want to vomit; horses who only saw daylight for two weeks of the year; horses who had to be led with great care through the streets to a nearby field where they went wild with delight with their freedom; horses who had lost their sense of sight because of the fifty weeks of darkness; horses who were cheered on their way by children and adults when they passed through the village streets. They were speaking the truth when they tried to describe the smell of the underground stables, we did not linger long.

Then they told us that when we saw the places and conditions under which some of the miners worked at the face, we would be shaken. They were not exaggerating. We said that no money could compensate for having to work in such conditions.

What they didn't say was that we would see the stable door covered with a heaving mass of black beetles, which at the tap of the overman's stick dropped like a broken icicle in one piece, to shatter in various directions.

That to me was the horror of my first visit to a coal mine.

JUNE VAUGHAN, 1981

16. Man under Journey

Ted Duggan was born in 1913 at 8, Ynysygored Road, Aberfan. His parents both came from Radnorshire and met and married in South Wales. Ted has been away from Aberfan for over fifty years but still regards Aberfan as home.

He relates a sad story about a friend of his father's, also from Radnorshire, a bachelor who lived with his sister at 14 Ynysygored Road. His name was Pryce Jandrell.

In 1928 the Merthyr Vale Colliery went into liquidation. Eventually, it was taken over by the Powell Duffryn Company. Ted remembers that when it closed down, "Mr Jandrell, my father and I, went to dig coal on the tips about two hundred yards from where we lived. Mr Jandrell and my father were big friends. He said to my father, "Ned. Have a pipe of tobacco, my sister in the Post Office in Felindre has sent tobacco to me." They sat down for a chat. After this they shared the coal and arranged to go digging again the next day, the weather permitting. The next day was a nasty, miserable day so they decided not to dig for coal but to go up to the top tip for sticks, that is, timber." We could see a journey in the distance. A journey was a succession of twelve trams or trucks, each carrying a ton of waste to the top of the mountain. We lined up to jump on one of the shafts in between the trucks so that we could ride to the top tip. Mr Jandrell went up in front; he was a rider underground. The trucks were made of iron. What we were doing was strictly illegal of course. The journey started up the incline. When it had gone thirty or forty yards someone shouted, 'man under journey'. The power was knocked off but nothing could be done. I was sent down to the stationary engine house to tell the man there that there was someone under the journey. That was the last I knew of Mr Jandrell. He must have slipped.

I knew that he was buried in Radnorshire but I knew nothing of Radnorshire in those days. Eventually I came up here to work when my uncle found me a job away from the pit. I was working on the road improvement to Knighton, by Beguildy Church and in the lunch hour I went to have a walk around the Churchyard and there I saw Pryce Jandrell's gravestone, 'Pryce Jandrell died Merthyr Vale, aged 46, 1929'.

I was fourteen and a half at the time of the accident. I was about twenty-five when I saw the gravestone. Mr Jandrell was always smiling, jolly and roundfaced. There was no compensation. We weren't supposed to be there. Those tips have been taken away, flattened. A playing field was made of the waste."

TED DUGGAN, 1988.

A. Lloyd

Drawing of the Black Bridge

17. Merthyr Vale Colliery 1984-85

"Many a man lay in the cemetery broken hearted, working all week for poor wages, Saturdays included. Many men in the family wouldn't see daylight."

WILL JOHN O'BRIEN, 1984-85.

Most mornings I rose in the dark to go down to the picket line. I saw Aberfan in a way that I had not seen it before, very quiet with the houses and people asleep. I crossed over the bridge by the Church and into Merthyr Vale. I joined the rank and file and Union officials who had gathered outside the colliery. We were waiting for the police vans who escorted the two men into work. Some mornings the weather was bitterly cold with a thick frost covering the pavements of Nixonville and we stamped our feet and blew on our hands to keep warm. Often I was the only woman down there but I never felt out of place. The police would line up in rows opposite the waiting miners. This was to prevent them from surging forward when the vans approached. I was there when a mass picket was held; there were ugly scenes.

Every morning after the two men had gone into the colliery and most of the police had left, we would go through the gates to the Ambulance Hall, which was being used as the Union Headquarters. There we would have a cup of steaming hot, strong, sweet tea, very welcome after the bitter cold outside, and a convivial chat with the Lodge Secretary, 'Comrade King', and Chairman, Ivor John. There were many other Union stalwarts there, most of them never missing a morning.

Every day at lunchtime I would take a tin of cakes, usually Welsh cakes, Teisan Lap or Pikelets down to the Lodge hut. One night the hut went on fire. Bryn Carpenter ran to the police on the yard and asked if he could use the telephone in the Fan Room to call the fire brigade; they refused. "Duw", he said to me the next day, "I had to run to a house in Nixonville to use their phone", he added as an afterthought. "Your tin is alright, Maureen, but the butter all melted". Needless to say the damage to the hut was extensive.

The miners in our colliery received a lot of local support. A massive public meeting held at the Social Club, gave them unequivocal support. At this meeting the Vicar, Rev Neil Davies, who had witnessed the events outside the colliery and who knew South Africa, likened them to the scenes he had witnessed in the black township of Crossroads.

He was one of three local ministers who came to see what was happening on the picket line. A Methodist Minister, Rev Judy Davies and Rev Kenneth Hayes, the Baptist Minister, were the other two. Mr Hayes was a frequent attender coming nearly every day until the vans started coming at just after four o'clock instead of just after five. "A little too early for me, I'm afraid", he said. Sometimes I too slept late, then I would hear the vans screeching through the village, disturbing the quiet morning air.

The villagers gave other tangible support. House to house collections by the Ward Labour Party raised hundreds of pounds at a time, for food parcels. The refusals to give hardly entered double figures. Members of the Ward Party gave regularly every week and together with members of the Whitchurch Labour Party gave hundreds of pounds towards food parcels. The Chapter Video Workshop also gave regularly to the NUM and raised hundreds of pounds towards the food parcels. Fund raising for the single miners by Eunice Tovey and other women in the Support Group enabled every single miner to receive a Christmas gift of money; very few of the single miners were receiving Social Security payments. Things came to my house from I know not where. With Christmas approaching I made up parcels of extras where I knew there were a few children. My family and I tramped around the village, the all too familiar thick, cold frost covering the pavements, to deliver the parcels.

A Baptist Chapel in Llanishen gave a roomful of gifts. A small donation to the food parcels fund secured Christmas presents for any miner's family because of the Chapel's generosity. One young mother called with her daughter; she told her little girl that the scene reminded her of when she herself had been a child and so many things had been sent at the time of the Disaster, "So many things, freely given" she said quietly.

A man in Australia sent £80 by registered post, in one pound notes "to help the miners along", he wrote. The Women's Support Group distributed money to families with children, their share of the money being raised nationwide. Wantage Labour Party and Ruskin College supported the Merthyr Vale Lodge throughout the strike and many close links were made. The BBC in Bristol gave money that was used to buy coal. Money was raised from churches and chapels all over the country for the same purpose. All denominations seem to have contributed. Police cars regularly patrolled the back lanes, or 'gullies' as we call them, of the streets near the colliery, to protect the vast stock piles of coal which for years had prevented one side of the village from seeing the other.

I myself visited the homes where there would be as many as four children under twelve and no coal in the house. I wrote to Ted Rowlands, our Member of Parliament who contacted the Chairman of the Coal Board in South Wales. Back came the reply that a letter from the family doctor or from the Social Services Department, would secure coal for those in need. I know of at least one family doctor who did not charge the customary fee for these letters.

There were many individual acts of kindness, neighbours and friends helping each other, sharing meals, visitors to the Memorial Gardens giving donations to the fund for food parcels. The Support Group from Oxford arrived on two separate Saturdays in December with enough food to give every family involved in the strike a wonderful Christmas Party. And they came as if it was a pleasure, cheerful and hardworking and they must already have worked very hard to raise all the money to buy so many things and to come so far.

A Theatre Group of youngsters, some had hitch hiked from afar afield as Leeds, arrived to provide hilarious entertainment. Long suffering friends of mine, some I realise now, with policemen in their families, were prevailed upon to make cakes for my fund raising. Not one of them refused, all the money going to the food parcel fund. On a lovely, sunny afternoon in June 1992, I remember all this help and kindness towards this beloved spot and I thank them once again.

"Then suddenly, despite South Wales remaining firm, it was all over."

MAUREEN HUGHES, 1992

18. No Surrender in the Valleys

Hywel Francis and Gareth Rees

What the NUM leaders in South Wales feared most at this time was not a collapse of the strike, but a violent backlash from communities which had hitherto been so disciplined but which were increasingly penned in by police and poverty. Harrassment by some police of men, women and children taking coal from anywhere they could find it, became a dominant feature of daily life. Finding fuel, often by means of organised 'picket' teams cutting large areas of neighbouring forests, was now as important as food distribution, to the maintenance of family and community morale. It was in this tense atmosphere that an ominous exchange had taken place between Weekes and his cousin, the Labour MP for Merthyr and Rhymney, Ted Rowlands:

> "Ted had rung me up, saying that his wife Janice had been down the picket line and it had been extremely unpleasant. And for one of the first times during the strike, I lost my temper and I said, "I've not heard a word from the Labour Party for the last six months, and now you're telling me I've got to stop two men who demand to go to work. I'm not going to do it!" He said, "there's going to be trouble then". I said that it was up to the NUM and that was it. I put the phone down on him. Within two days, Ted was right, and David Wilkie was killed. That was a hard one for me to swallow, that was the worst, the lowest point of the strike."

The taxi-driver, David Wilkie, was killed by a concrete block dropped from a bridge, as he drove a scab to work at Merthyr Vale Colliery on the morning of 30 November. His death was described by one church leader as 'the blackest day of the strike. The real culprits were those who were prepared to see the dispute go on and accept unnecessary casualties.' What made Merthyr Vale such a flashpoint was its' location on the doorstep of historic Aberfan, scene of the 1966 disaster, in the midst of the most solid district in the British coalfield, the central valleys of South Wales. Compounding the problem were the police roadblocks, which prevented Merthyr Vale miners from travelling to their own colliery to picket. Nevertheless the death of the young taxi-driver, the immediate appearance of Margaret Thatcher on television to condemn the 'murder', and the subsequent arrest of three young miners, two of whom were to stand trial for murder, did little to weaken the strike in South Wales, simply because it was such an aberration. It did however, have a calming effect on the coalfield, best symbolised the following morning by Bill King, the veteran Merthyr Vale lodge secretary. A young miner recalls the scene on the picket line:

> "we stood in the pouring rain, Bill King asked for two minutes silence for everyone that had died as a result of the strike that was forced upon us. And we stood there, police and pickets, rain dripping off our noses, stunned virtually. But still Williams, the scab, came back to work in the convoy."

THE 1984-85 MINERS STRIKE IN SOUTH WALES BY HYWEL FRANCIS AND GARETH REES, REPRINTED FROM "LLAFUR" - JOURNAL OF WELSH LABOUR HISTORY, VOLUME 5 NO. 2

19. Afraid - Angry - Upset *

I had heard, read it, all before
In the poems of Idris Davies.
A lanky talkative youth
Had quoted "Gwalia Deserta"
And "Tonypandy", and
"Do you remember 1926?"
Hung on our wall
Thirty years later.

But this was no poem
Of a past prophet
This was happening in our streets
Where
We had walked hand in hand,
And to those people
Who had shared
Our youth and childhood.
This was happening now,
In a time when we thought
That it could not happen
In 1984 and 1985
And without any real protest possible.

Mute we stared at the police
Lined up in front of us.
Afraid, afraid of what
we had read in the papers
About prisoners in cells in Chile,
South Africa and Northern Ireland.
Afraid of the power
Of the State
That the police represented.
Angry at what was happening
To the boys in our pit,
And angry at the interlopers in
Our community.
Upset at what was happening
In our villages,
The twin villages
of Aberfan and Merthyr Vale.
Sickened by the churning
of our stomachs,
The dread and despair in our hearts,
And at the degradation
Of those raised in the Sunday Schools
of Non-Conformity
And on the Politics of Need.

MAUREEN HUGHES, 1985

* QUOTATION BY ESME KITTO FROM MERTHYR VALE AND ABERFAN WOMEN'S SUPPORT GROUP
VIDEO - PRODUCED BY RICHARD DAVIES

20. Hope

I dream of a world full of equals
A world where all thinking is free.
I dream of a freedom for everyone
And there is never a you or a me.

I dream of a peace universal
With hatred and killing no more
I dream of an end to all weapons
No barriers. Just open doors.

I wish that all civilised countries
Would join in this wonderful scheme.
I wonder will this ever happen
Or will it remain just a dream.

TOM ABBOT, 1989

March back to work, 1985

21. Miners' Fund

The pre-Christmas Fundraising activities of the Single Miners' Support Group brought in over £800. This was distributed as money gifts to the single miners resident in Merthyr Vale, Aberfan and Mount Pleasant. The Group wishes to thank those individuals and organisations who gave so generously. We were staggered by the extent of the response we had. It overwhelmed us, and we are even more aware now of how fortunate we are to be part of a community which shows its support and concern so willingly and open-handedly.

INDEED, THANK YOU ALL.

Women's Support Group 1984-85, Merthyr Vale Colliery

HEADWAY, FEBRUARY 1985
GERALD CAMM, EDITOR

22. 12 Months On

On March 6, 1984, the miners strike began. There can be few who considered it would last twelve months. Without attempting to unravel, or judge the causes it is none the less impossible to ignore this most central, dominating fact of our community life this past year. Either through direct experience or as witnesses, we are all aware of its effects locally and nationally. The hardship of many families and the attempted support of varied groups are two of its features.

Whilst it would be imprudent to list names now, there are many in both categories. Headway was recently urged by a mother with a young baby to give thanks to those who give coal, a special blessing at the coldest time of winter.

Other positive effects would seem to be the links forged between the village and people from other parts of the country. The picketing of Didcot Power Station by men from Merthyr Vale Lodge has resulted in a bond between our village and the Wantage area of Oxford. And too, with the students of Ruskin College. Happily, and very personally, is the union of Gerald and Sylvia Williams. Gerald, from Glyndwr Street, met his bride while picketing in Didcot - CONGRATULATIONS!

HEADWAY, MARCH 1985
GERALD CAMM, EDITOR

The march back to work, Bridge Street, Aberfan, March 1985

23. The March Back to Work

I remember the morning in March when we all walked back to the pit. We gathered at the Community Centre whilst it was still dark, children and adults, miners and villagers, and supporters from outside the village. There were hundreds of us there. I saw the Rev Hayes hovering across the road, I shouted to him to come across and join us. He came across and joined in the march.

The Lodge banner was raised. The Women's Support Group banner was held high and we all set off for the colliery yard. Lights were going on in the houses along the route as we went through Aberfan Road and Bridge Street. Everywhere was dark and the pounding of feet echoed around the streets. As we crossed the bridge, the main bridge between our twin villages, I remember looking up into the hills above Merthyr Vale, the morning was beginning in earnest and the sky was lightening as we entered the colliery yard.

Bill King made a short speech and called upon everyone to sing the "Red Flag". Some people knew the words better than others, but everyone did their best. A quick look around to see that everything was there and things began getting back to normal.

At the end of the day, as Bill King, NUM secretary of Merthyr Vale Lodge for twenty four years asks "was it all worth it?" Not just the struggle in 1984-85 but all of it. He doesn't think so.

Standing amongst the rubble today, as the Merthyr Vale Colliery is being dismantled, he compares the broken rubble to the broken health of the men who worked there. The seams being worked were extremely dry and dusty and the consequent suffering was too big a price to pay. He knows that more care should have been taken of the men's lives and health. He remembers the numerous widows that he had to deal with, their husbands' health broken by their work in the pit.

The colliery closed on 23 August, 1989, one hundred and twenty years to the day that the first moves were made to sink the colliery.

Although the original reason for most of us being here is no longer in our midst, we have built up a network of strong cultural and social links and we will survive.

MAUREEN HUGHES, 1990

Crossing the bridge from Aberfan to Merthyr Vale, March 1985

24. All Change

The post-strike period finds Merthyr Vale Colliery with a changing face - in physical structure and personnel. Plain for all to see are the tall lines of the new bunkering facilities. Soon it is expected a railway spur will join directly to the main line at the screens area. If this development means a reduction in the level of lorry traffic, a collective 'Hooray' will issue from local residents. Despite representations, resulting in some dust-laying measures, the dirt and noise factors persist to an intolerance degree. All who live along the lorry convoys route vouch for the wake of filth that is inflicted. Anyone who has been engulfed in a storm of coal dust on Bell's Hill or in the Station Square will have a nasty taste of what the people who live there put up with daily. This is a problem of which we feel sure the Colliery Manager is aware. The man-in-charge, Mr Caddy, took up his post during the strike. Previously he had been Under-Manager at Cwm Colliery. As Mr Caddy starts his association with Aberfan and Merthyr Vale, another has come to a close. After twenty four years as Lodge Secretary of the NUM, Bill King has retired. While the last twelve months were the most dramatic of his tenure - the level and style of policing in Nixonville last winter remains vivid for him as does the steadfast support of the women which bolstered the resolve of the union, and the enduring bonds forged with outside groups - Mr King has many other changes to reflect on during his stay. Changed levels of workforce with many now coming from outside our village. Increased mechanisation, in particular the disc-cutting method of coal winning - better safety standards due to the modern use of cogs gives him special satisfaction.

Bill leaves at a time when, nationally, the future of the industry is unsettled. However, while not wanting to appear too sanguine, he is optimistic for a healthy local future if the required investment and development occur. May his judgement be right.

HEADWAY, AUGUST-SEPTEMBER 1985
GERALD CAMM, EDITOR

25. The Price of Coal

In the first few days of February, there was a sharp reminder of the inherent dangers that can exist in coal mining. Thankfully the underground explosion at Merthyr Vale Colliery did not extend to serious human injury, though it did put a temporary stop to coal production.

To those of us whose knowledge of mining is had by repute rather than first hand experience, it was evidence that it is only the most stringent of safety standards that prevent a repeat of past industrial disasters.

Above-ground concern has been expressed at the growing stocks of coal at the colliery. Looming tips are very obvious, especially at the northern end of the yard. Besides their unsightly appearance, there is apprehension that they are a potential trouble spot if they are long term features.

However, information reaching us indicates that recent difficulties at the washery was a factor in the build up and that a start has been made to reduce the stock. We trust this is so and that none of us has to endure prolonged and avoidable nuisance.

HEADWAY, MARCH 1986
GERLAD CAMM, EDITOR

26. The Good News

1987 ends on a more optimistic note for the village. Judging by reports of a joint British Coal - unions' review, held in the first week of November, Merthyr Vale Colliery's productive life will continue in 1988. With confident expectations for the future. This is a big relief for the industry after alarming rumours earlier in the autumn.

At the same time news was filtering through of Merthyr Borough Council's decision to assume control of the Aberfan and Merthyr Vale Community Centre.

Protracted discussions between the Fund Trustees and the local authority have resulted in a satisfactory solution to the financial crisis that has beset the Centre.

It is expected that the Council's take-over will be complete by 1st April. Then it should be plain what changes have come about. Between now and April, HEADWAY will try to keep you informed of how the set-up affects us.

For the present it is pleasing that the next community activity, the Senior Citizens' Supper will take place in a celebratory mood.

You are reminded that the supper is in the Centre on the evening of Thursday, 10th December. A ticket charge, refundable on supper night, will be made.

HEADWAY wishes all *bon appetit* for what we are sure will be a splendid occasion of feasting and fun.

And to readers in general - *Happy Christmas and a Peaceful Prosperous New Year. Nadolig Llawen A Blwyddyn Newydd Dda i' Chi Gyd.*

HEADWAY, DECEMBER - JANUARY **1988**
GERALD CAMM, EDITOR

27. The End

The life of Merthyr Vale Colliery was snuffed out on 23rd August, 1989. Hopes of saving the pit, even with plans for a reduced workforce, were finally dashed.

To some the intent of British Coal was inexorably fulfilled. No argument for continued production, no matter how valid, was likely to be heeded. And so it proved. Now part of the workforce will have been placed in one of the few remaining South Wales collieries. Other men will have taken redundancy.

The shock felt throughout the village concerns not just the closing, which had a certain inevitability, but the manner of the end. No run-down or phasing-out. Instead a brutal cut off. Wednesday production, Thursday no more!

But much as the community at large will be distressed, it is the individual miners and their families who shoulder the real burdens. Trying to decide either to place their future at another colliery, whose fate might soon repeat Merthyr Vale's, or accept redundancy payment, but possibly be on the dole for ever after. And with the job losses at Hoover swelling the number of those whose lives are now shaken by unemployment, optimism is not high. It is a cruel dilemma faced by many of our fellow villagers and others in neighbouring communities. Although only a minority of its workers were local, the pit still belonged to the village. Now, what becomes of a mining village without a colliery?

For almost a hundred and twenty years this village's reason for being was Merthyr Vale Colliery. The pit, for us, was always here. It is sobering to realise mining was underway a score of years before our oldest citizen was born in 1892. None of us knows what will be without a colliery. While we acclimatise to the new situation, HEADWAY is sure many, in and out of the industry, have opinions to share. We will be glad to publish such views.

In the meantime, our sympathy goes to all directly and immediately affected by the death of Merthyr Vale colliery.

HEADWAY, SEPTEMBER **1989**
GERALD CAMM, EDITOR

28.   The End of an Era

Merthyr Vale colliery has come to a halt
The wheels no longer turn round.
No more the double decker cage
Will take the men below the ground.
The jobs have all been sacrificed
No matter that we yearn
Not a butty left to do the work
And the coal no more to burn.
The washery's idle, the drams are still
and there's rust along the ropes.
They have taken away the winding house
And with it go our hopes.
Some will say good riddance
While others will feel sad
Especially those that have worked there
Ever since they were young lads.
The Tories call it progress
And I guess they always will
But the miners have found it hard
To swallow the bitter pill.
Aberfan has taken knocks before
And come out of it with pride
The world will always remember
The day the village nearly died.
Thank God for the valley people
They are a race that's set apart
And though I left you years ago
Aberfan is always in my heart.
It's the village where I met my wife
And my ways of life did learn
And Aberfan I promise you
One day I will return.

Tom Abbot, 1989

Merthyr Vale without the colliery

29. My Valley

My valley once was wild and green
The mountainsides so full with life.
Then came the days of coal
And soon my valley knew of strife.

For coal brought life to many men,
No thought by owners of the cost,
The men who worked beneath the earth,
How many maimed? How many lost?

My valley then was black with dust
But free from school we ran and played,
No cares but those of youthful days,
Secrets shared and friendships made.

Up to Maggie's scrumping apples,
Then to the park and on the swings,
But time soon steals your youth away
It flies too soon on silent wings.

The coal has gone, no pit there now,
I watched them blow it all away,
And so my valley should be green again
But still I will regret that day.

Another blackness is o'er us now
What of the men who stand and wait
For work they know will never come,
What is our destiny - What is their fate?

MARGARET HARRIES, 1991
NEÉ ABRAHAM

30. Lament

God I saw thy world,
Green and brown mountains,
Between two pit wheels,
Grown silent now
After so many years.

MAUREEN HUGHES, 1990

31. The Question Why

With another untimely death, tragedy strikes the community once again. We have lost three young men this year in harrowing circumstances. We are not alone. The mining valleys have in recent times all suffered similar deaths. It is time we asked the question WHY? Is it deprivation, the loss of jobs, the hopelessness of many young people who can't find work? In this, the age of plenty for some and nothing for others, are we so indifferent to the suffering of others? The official answers appear to be to build more prisons, create a hard regime, for our young; it goes on and on. These are not answers, they are not even solutions. Often young men have been corrupted by their experiences in these places and have come out changed for the worse. Meanwhile, the young, surrounded by the trappings of the material world, naturally want to reach out and enjoy the multitude of goods they see all around them. They cannot enter the glass world of their T.V. screens. They can only dream and grow older.

And so they take their frustrations and, indeed, hopelessness and seek their own solutions, sometimes through the only too easily available drugs. Make no mistake, it's another way of dreaming, even though it ends up a nightmare. In the 1940s and 1950s most people learnt to smoke, lots learned to drink; can we therefore assume that if drugs had been available then many of that generation would have become addicts? We must wonder why some of our young people have become such easy prey.

EDITORIAL,
HEADWAY, 1995.

Nixonville

Chapter Three
Disaster and Aftermath

1. Introduction

Coal mining was the main occupation of the people of Aberfan and Merthyr Vale for over a hundred years. Then in the 1970s, because coal mines closed in other parts of the South Wales coalfield, miners started coming from these areas to work in the Merthyr Vale Colliery. When the colliery closed in 1989 about one fifth of the men who were employed there were from Aberfan and Merthyr Vale. In common with other South Wales mining villages our history and the neglect of the environment by those in authority, caused the accumulation of huge spoil tips of colliery waste.

In 1966 this neglect brought about a great tragedy in Aberfan when our village school and part of Moy Road were engulfed by a moving mass of waste material. One hundred and sixteen of our children were killed along with twenty eight adults. There has been great sorrow and suffering in our community because of what happened.

The Valley, Aberfan

2.   "The school is down"

A baker's round in Merthyr Vale and Aberfan for over forty years brought with it an intimate knowledge of the residents living there, and there has been a happy sharing in the important events in their lives. And because a roundsman is often the first person to detect the "unusual" about people's domestic circumstances, it has been my sad lot to enter homes and discover the unfortunate stroke victim, the person who has died suddenly and even the home where fire has taken its inevitable fatal toll. It has all been part of the job. None of these unfortunate incidents however, prepared me for the events of Friday, 21 October, 1966.

When I left the Perthygleision Bakery at 8.30 that morning with a loaded van, it was just another Friday morning and as I travelled down to Aberfan Road it was a case of passing the same folk as always nodding and acknowledging them as is our custom in Welsh villages.

Stopping near Danybryn, Aberfan Road, I got out to start my deliveries and was greeted, as usual, by my customers as their daily bread became a reality on their doorsteps. The weather was seasonal, I recall, with layers of thick Autumnal mists lining the valley sides. Villagers were going about their normal routine, shopping, or wending a way to various jobs; children were meandering towards the school in groups, some on public transport of course. It was an ordinary Friday morning, like so many that had gone before.

From Aberfan Road it was around the Mackintosh Hotel and into Angus Street for more deliveries and it was there, I later realised, that the first indication came of the impending major catastrophe. There was, as it were, a loud banging noise which I wrongly assumed was the delivery of a load of coal to one of the miners' homes. A glance at my watch showed it to be 9.10 a.m. I continued into Cottrell Street without thinking any more about the noise, after all coal delivery was such a common place happening in our villages.

Seconds later though, I noticed a girl about eight years of age coming around the corner out of Angus Street. She was very distressed, crying and sobbing. It was a natural instinct to enquire of her why she was crying and through her tears she replied, "The school has fallen down" and ran off down Cottrell Street. I didn't know her at the time and I have never discovered her identity since.

The school down! The school down! This just could not be true, the words sounded almost unbelievable. This was my school, our school. I had spent almost five years of my young life at Pantglas School, from 1938 until 1942. It took me only seconds to turn around the van and speed back along Angus Street and from there up to the first houses of Moy Road. Leaving the van, I ran in the direction of the Junior School; the roads at that moment were clear and there were very few people around. Then came the water from the 'mains' which ran on the canal bank at the rear of the schools; the pipes had been catastrophically ripped open by the avalanche of slurry hurtling off the mountainside towards the school and houses. And, when in moments I had mounted a window ledge at the front of the school and looked inside the classroom, I was to discover the horrendous import of that 'bang' heard down in Angus Street. On the left hand side, as if flung there by a giant hand, was a mound of the evil, black morass whilst on the other side the desks and chairs had been swept up into a shambling heap and below them, THE INNOCENTS, some of whom I had seen laughing and joking, on their way to school just half an hour ago; indeed an image on the mind for a life-time! But I also saw about six men there, who were feverishly, in such a nightmare situation, attempting to reach the children, and this they did and were successful in passing to me three of them. Their eyes were wide open but they uttered not a word. I passed them down singly to three men below me outside the classroom, from where I believe, they were carried over to the houses nearby. I had no recollection of the names of the children, neither the identity of the handful of us who worked there together, it didn't seem relevant anyway, there was only one thought and object, in us, saving precious lives.

Soon in Moy Road, outside the devastated school, help began to pour in as we saw the miners racing from the colliery carrying their picks and shovels. Here were men trained over many years to deal with such a gigantic problem. I drew aside as they prepared to continue and expand the rescue that we had commenced. Sirens, horns, gongs, etc. then heralded the arrival of ambulance, fire tender, rescue service and police. Slowly the full implications of a major disaster was breaking on our numbed minds, we braced ourselves for the endless anxious period which was to follow these early moments.

The ensuing days and weeks proved heart breaking as we tried to pull together the broken threads of our village life. Homes, to which it had always been so much pleasure to go with my bread, were now sad and quiet, and words seemed almost meaningless as the losses were carried in heavy hearts. We mourned in families; we mourned in streets; we mourned as a community for those we loved.

Today, the grief still remains, but masked now in the necessity of carrying on for the sake of others; thus the bowed heads look up again and smiles have formed on once sad faces.

TOM ARSCOTT, 1992, ABERFAN

3.   Bernard Thomas

My name is Bernard Thomas, and this is the account of my personal involvement in the Aberfan Disaster.

I was nine years of age at the time of the Disaster. I will always remember that in 1966 we went on the school trip to Bristol Zoo on my birthday at the end of June, and that, on the return journey, the engine became detached from the rest of the train, and we were left stranded for about an hour before a replacement unit came to pull the remaining carriages the rest of the way home.

Very often, it is little things like this that can stick in one's memory for a lifetime, and can often be recalled when also remembering major events in one's life, such as the Disaster was to all of us who had any involvement, however small it may have been.

My story is fairly typical, I should imagine, to the stories of us who went through the tragedy and survived, as is, I also believe, the fact that it is the mental injuries that remain within us that are worse than any of the physical injuries that any of us suffered. A physical injury normally heals fairly quickly, and, more often that not, leaves little or no outward sign of its having occurred to the person. This is not so with regard to the damage done to someone's mind as the result of such a traumatic experience. It can be very difficult to put into words one's exact feelings and emotions regarding involvement in a catastrophe such as that which occurred here in Aberfan. Many of us received little or no counselling or help to come to terms with what had happened to us. I had a small number of sessions with Dr Cuthill, a psychiatrist at the Park Hospital in Bridgend. Many people misguidedly regard having treatment in such an institution as a sign of what they deem to be "madness" or some kind of mental disorder. These people obviously have no conception of what someone like myself was going through, or had previously suffered. As I have already said, there are a great number of emotions and feelings involved in such a complicated situation. There is the feeling of guilt that you have been left alive, while your friends and classmates died. One wonders, "why me?" The confusion and these feelings is really indescribable . My late father decided, perhaps mistakenly, that there was no benefit to be had from these visits, so he stopped us, i.e. myself and my brother, Andrew from going for any more.

I will always remember walking to school on that fateful morning. One of the main reasons is because of the fog. It was so thick that the group of us who were walking together could barely see each other. I didn't know it then, but this was the last time that I would see many of those children, many of them friends, alive again. I was always a little slow at making friends, and just as I was starting to get over this, the Disaster came and snatched away the few close friends that I did have, two of them my cousins. It is chiefly for this reason that I have no time or respect for people such as the National Coal Board as it then was, or those who were in charge of it, such as Lord Robens. He categorically seemed to deny any responsibility for the incident. There is also the matter of the cover-up carried out by the Labour Government of the day. A certain amount of the blame could also be laid at the feet of our local council and MP at the time, for not forcing the issue with the Coal Board. It is also shameful that the men working on tip no 7 were afraid to speak out, for fear of losing their jobs. As far as I am concerned, no justice was done because those in charge got away scot free with corporate manslaughter. Heads should have rolled, metaphorically speaking, and the ones who were responsible should have, at least, been jailed. They probably would have been, had the Disaster happened in a country where there were stricter laws controlling the dumping of mining waste. The community of Aberfan and an entire generation of children were very badly let down by those whom we had elected to look after our interests.

As I have said, I remember the walk to school on the day of the tragedy. I remember that we had the assembly as normal. We were looking forward to that afternoon, because school was breaking up for the half term holidays, which meant a week off. A whole week of freedom.

I was a pupil in Mr Howell Williams' class at the time when it actually happened. I was sitting at my desk reading a book, which would have been one of my first tasks of the day. I remember hearing a loud rumbling sound as the tidal wave of slurry approached the school. Mr Williams shouted for us to run, and pandemonium broke out. Everyone seemed to be trying to escape in a blind panic, which was hardly surprising. I remember the thought crossed my mind "Oh, that will stop outside". The next second, for some of us at least, could have meant the difference between life and death, depending on where one was at the time. I remember the deafening crash as the avalanche of mud hit the wall of the school, demolishing it like a wall of cards. I was lifted by the sludge, and seemed to be carried by it across the room, still sitting at my desk. I must have been knocked unconscious, for a time at least, because my next recollection is that of coming to, and of hearing all the others screaming and crying for help. It is a sound that haunts me now, after over 30 years. Somehow, I don't know how, I wasn't completely buried by the engulfing slurry. Something had stopped it from coming over the top of me and covering me altogether. I was lying up against the interior wall of the classroom, practically on top of the sludge, which, by now, filled the room to a depth of almost half its height. My first thought was to get out of the building as quickly as I possibly could. I found that I was still able to move, so I managed to sit up. When I looked around, I saw my teacher, Mr Williams, who seemed to be freeing his foot from a desk or some other such object. I instinctively made my way over to him, and he helped me out through the top of the classroom door, which had consisted of small panes of glass with wooden strips in between. These had been smashed by the flying debris. I also remember looking over, and seeing a gaping hole where the outside wall of the school building and the windows through which I had initially seen the approach of the slurry had once been.

We managed to climb out of the remains of the building through one of the open windows of the main hall. I am not sure of the time, because I don't know how long I was unconscious, and the fact that I was, naturally, in a state of shock. As with most events of this nature, the full magnitude tends not always to hit one immediately, even those directly involved.

I seemed to wander around for a while in somewhat of a daze. I eventually found my brother Andrew, and Stephen Gerlach and his sister Clare. They were concerned for their brother Christopher, who they had not yet accounted for. He was, thankfully, rescued alive some time later.

By this time, a number of rescuers had reached the scene, and were starting to get organised. We were taken to a house across the road from the school, and from there by ambulance to hospital in St Tydfil's. It seemed like utter chaos. No-one was prepared for such an event, especially when it involved an entire school, the pupils and staff, although no-one can say that there hadn't been prior warnings. There had been a previous slip of the same tip about two or three years earlier, besides the fact that a former headmaster's wife had raised the issue in council meetings on several occasions, warning of the possible consequences of continued tipping on the mountainside above the Pantglas School. There were also a small number of villagers who did support her, and tried to assist by the getting up of petitions and the like, all to no avail of course. Some of this could be put down to the apathy of the people, and the fears that the colliery would close if the tipping had to stop. It could be said here that the people of Aberfan were ever so slightly responsible themselves for not supporting these campaigns.

I do not make the above remarks with the intention of offending or upsetting anyone in the community, but we are all able, generally, to see things a little differently or perhaps, more clearly, with the benefit of hindsight. Anyone can say "If only I'd listened to her", or, 'If only I'd signed the petition/ gone to the meeting", etc. Life, for many of us, is only too full of those "if only's".

I hope that you will see that my stance from the above remarks is, that if anyone is really guilty, and to be held accountable by the people of Aberfan in any way, it is the aforementioned National Coal Board and, to a greater or lesser degree, the Government of the day, for allowing the disaster to happen in the first place and, prior to that, fobbing off the people and the council, our local representatives with all the cock-and-bull stories that they gave them. Although the danger began to exist when the first shovel-full of earth was dug by the people employed by the Nixon Navigation Company when they started to sink the shafts of Merthyr Vale Colliery, it was the National Coal Board who "owned" the mine, on the Government's behalf -albeit "for the benefit of the people" - when the Disaster actually happened and, as such, it is they who were ultimately responsible. It is chiefly for this reason that I now find the arrogance of Lord Robens in, more or less, categorically denying any culpability whatsoever, particularly hurtful and disgusting. The likes of him and his cronies seemed to be nothing more than contempt for the people of Aberfan and their suffering and grief in the wake of the Disaster. To me, the Tribunal was little more than a sham, an attempt to pacify the villagers of Aberfan, even though it laid the blame for what happened here directly at the feet of the NCB.

There is also the matter of the Disaster Fund. This was set up with the intention of trying to alleviate the suffering of the bereaved parents and families of those who lost their lives, and to help those of us who survived the tragedy to be able to have some sort of ease from our suffering, not to help the government and Coal Board cover up their incompetence and ineptitude. It more than added insult to injury when the Fund was made to pay £150,000 towards the cost of removing the tips from the mountainside. The villagers also had to fight for this to happen as the government and Coal Board, in their doubtless infinite wisdom, saw "no need" for the tips to be removed, there is little doubt in my mind that, if they had had their way, they would have waited for things to, hopefully, calm down, and then carried on dumping on the same site as if nothing had happened. To me this would be typical of the type of authority and people that they were. It is only recently, after 31 years, that the money has been returned to the Fund's Management Committee, and that after an almost continuous battle with the various governments. They also only paid back the bare amount. I know that this is all that the Committee were asking for, but they should have paid interest on the money on principle, if only to try and bring it up to an equivalent value and buying power at today's rates. Also involved here is the matter of so-called compensation. Initially, the NCB were only going to pay a small amount, something in the region of a paltry £50 per child lost. To me, the amount is irrelevant. No amount of money could ever compensate a parent for the loss of their child. For my part, it could never really make good the damage that was done to me all those years ago. In a way we were all bereaved, immaterial of whether we lost a brother, sister, a son or a daughter. All of us children who survived lost friends and playmates, as well as relatives. There was hardly a household in Aberfan that wasn't affected. Each one was touched by the disaster in this way, even if only indirectly, by having known personally one or more of the tragedy's victims.

I also remember that this was the very day my father resumed smoking, a habit from which he had refrained some three years earlier. At the time he was working in Teddingtons Aircraft Controls in Cefn Coed, Merthyr as a capstan lathe setter/operator. The first message received at most workplaces was for anyone from Aberfan to go home immediately, as a wall had collapsed at the school. This was because the immediate scale of the disaster was not apparent at first. Volunteers flooded to the village when the full magnitude of the accident became obvious. Naturally, my father was worried sick as to the fate of my brother and myself. He didn't know whether we were alive or dead. It was while he was here, at the school, that someone offered him a cigarette, which he was probably only too grateful for at the time, thinking that it would help to calm his nerves during the crisis. He and my mother didn't find out for several hours that Andrew and I were safe and in hospital.

It was also during the stay in hospital that I remember seeing the first television reports on the various news programmes about the Disaster. There were, of course, the usual interruptions to the scheduled T.V. programmes, such as there were during the sixties, and the radio reports. But, I expect like everyone else, I was too dazed to really take in the full magnitude of what had actually happened. At nine years of age one can barely understand the concept of people dying in old age, let alone having one's friends and classmates killed around one, and nearly losing one's own life into the bargain. It is almost impossible to put into words how I felt when I eventually came home from hospital and asked my mother and father what had happened to my friends. Friends like Dyfrig Hayes, whose father sadly also passed away (over the Christmas period 1997). Just as unimaginable is how they must have felt at the thought of trying to explain to a child of nine that one of his few close friends was dead. I have never really been able to come to terms with this, a thing which I believe to be true of every one us involved. It is also true that the parents never got over the loss of their children in such a manner. It is almost impossible to accept the death of a child from a fatal illness, but for nearly a whole generation of children from one village to be wiped out in school, one of the very places their parents expect them to be totally safe, beggars belief.

As I got older, mainly, perhaps when I was in my teens and for some years after, I would often go and sit in the cemetery, especially close to where the children were buried. It was as if this was the only way that I could actually believe that the Disaster had happened. It all seemed too unreal for words, like some bad dream from which I would eventually awaken. Sadly this is not so. The Disaster did happen, I have to accept that - in so far as I can. But that does not mean to say that I am able to forgive or forget what happened. I cannot find it within myself to forgive those responsible. And I will certainly never forget what happened.

Involvement in the Disaster has also had an effect on me in later life. For one thing I have suffered with what could be regarded as a drink problem, much of which, I believe anyway, from trying to blot out the memories of the Disaster. It also resulted in many other things in my behaviour which might otherwise have been different. Naturally, this caused a great deal of friction at home, much of which I now regard as my own fault, but which stemmed from, I believe at least, being directly involved in the Disaster. I suppose that, in the light of today's knowledge in this field, my problems would probably be given some convenient label or other by those who purport to be experts in such matters. I know that many people who are not experts have tried to do so (note my earlier references to "madness" etc.). This, I believe, also stems from these people's own personal inadequacies . They see something or someone they don't regard as what they deem to be the "norm" and immediately commence to ridicule them out of hand, or to rubbish the object or that person's ideas etc., just because it doesn't quite shape up to what they think or believe, though this does not automatically make the majority of the people right in what they think, or make their idea of the so-called "norm" correct.

It is in the light of my own experiences that I am able to sympathise with people who have survived recent disasters, such as Hillsborough or Zebrugge and the like, or those who survived the horrors of the concentration camps during the dark days of the war. My memories will haunt me until I die, as will theirs. It is all too easy for people, especially outsiders who had no involvement whatsoever to tell someone such as myself to "snap out of it", and that "life goes on" and to "let go of the past". Talk is cheap, and people who don't know what they are talking about always seem only too ready to hand out "good advice" to those of us who are suffering the aftermath of events such as that which happened here in Aberfan. It is really easy for such people to use all of the trite and hackneyed cliches and phrases that I have just mentioned, and probably a few more to boot. They are not the ones who have to live with the memories that those of us involved in the Disaster have to. When they visit our community, it is, or it has been only for a short time. They can pack their bags and leave it all behind them when they return to where they came from. Those of us who were involved and who still live in the village cannot. Neither can those who moved away from here after the event, really speaking. As they say, "you can run, but you can't hide". The memories will always be with you, wherever you may go.

I recently attended the Town Hall in Merthyr with a group from Aberfan, for the unveiling of the web site on the computer Internet which has been created to provide information about Aberfan, and the events surrounding what happened here. This was brought about, in part at least, by the efforts of Professor Iain McLean of Oxford University, and Martin Johnes who assisted by working on various papers which have been released under the 30 years ruling on official secrets. This was somewhat of an eye-opener, even for someone who was involved. It makes me realise that, perhaps, I was a little harsh on the local council in some of my earlier remarks. It is the Coal Board who should bare the brunt of the blame for, as I stated, fobbing the Council off.

I believe that it is a good thing that these documents have been preserved for posterity. If anyone wishes to have an in-depth look at this information, it would open their eyes to at least some of the underhand dealings that went on between the Government and Coal Board. It may also be possible to see most of the letters that went to and fro between the various Government Departments involved, including the one from the then Secretary of State for Wales, the Rt. Hon George Thomas, later to become Lord Tonypandy, which mentions the people of Aberfan as "acting irrationally". For one thing, what would he know? He never married or had children. Anyway, no-one related to him was directly involved, which may back up to some degree at least, my remarks about most outsiders not knowing what they are talking about. Someone in his position perhaps, could not be expected to understand the behaviour of people in a village which had just lost almost a whole generations of its children. Is it any wonder, then, that I have no respect for such people?

That, basically, covers most of my experiences of being involved in the Aberfan Disaster, in pretty general terms anyway. Who knows? I may decide to enlarge upon this at some future date.

1998

The Tragic Scene at Our Beloved Schools

4.   A View from a Hospital Bed

Crisp as lettuces, they bobtail down
The tiled warrens, sisters of mercy
Nipped in the bud of their uniforms,
Scurrying each to its own burrow.

Like magicians they can suddenly
Appear down the corridors
And with stealthy hands they can
Conjure up a quickening mixture of magic phials
To dampen the boiling cauldron of the mind.

They offer hope where there is none
They give peace where there is turmoil
They place cool hands where the head is burning
And they smile when they could shed tears.

At the evening of the day, do they
Shut the door of memory, fast against the night?
I wonder.

WENDY HOWARD

First Printed in 'Countryside Quest'

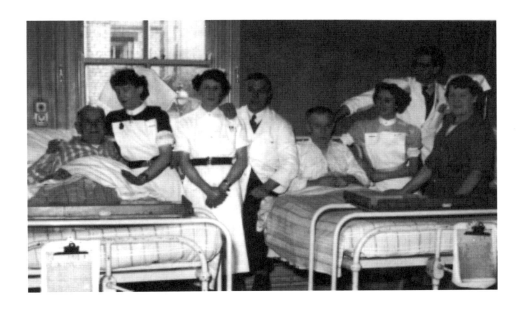

5.   Something that no-one could ever forget

On the morning of 21 October 1966, at about 11 a.m., there was a broadcast by a special radio newsflash, of a disaster at Aberfan, South Wales, where a school for young children had lain directly in the path of a massive landslide from a mountain of coal waste towering above the village. This slurry, which had parted from above was, at the time of its downhill sweep, in the form of a very wet cement, many feet in depth, demolished a small farm-house and continued down to engulf the school-yard, toilets, and taking the end walls of the school children, teachers, and people in adjacent houses in Moy Road. The roof of the school, without its supporting walls, was left hanging down over the debris. There was a heavy loss of young lives but the actual figure was unknown at that time.

Throughout that dark Friday, news was being given out at intervals with requests for helpers, or working volunteers, as further slides or falls were expected at any time, which would eliminate any hopes of continued rescue attempts. Hearing these sad reports and thinking of so many little Welsh children trapped, possibly, in the school building, I couldn't settle without wondering what might happen in the stricken village and decided to drive to Aberfan on the morning of Saturday 22 October.

I put a protective helmet, spade, torch, gumboots and oilskins into the back of my V.W. Beetle, went back into the house, told Olwen that I was off to South Wales, at which she was at first taken aback although, perhaps, had anticipated the departure. I drove down fairly quickly without mishap until going over the Brecon Beacons, when, to my annoyance, the nearside rear wheel went flat. A quick change to the spare and off again; great, until driving through Merthyr, more snags; I was stopped by a police inspector in the main street. He said to me "I am sorry, no traffic is allowed to proceed towards Aberfan". Whilst notifying me of this order, he was at the same time looking over my shoulder into the rear compartment of the car. The inspector then, to my surprise, remarked, "Oh I am sorry sir. I see that you are already working there. What is the position there now?" I replied truthfully, "Well its really hard to describe." And, "Have just had a break for something to eat." "Right, well carry on up to the top of the road but when you reach the junction at the top, you'll have to leave your car as no traffic is allowed down to the right into Aberfan, to allow a clear way for trucks bringing slurry out of the village. You'll have a lift from a returning empty vehicle, without any problem". Thanking him, I carried on and duly reached the 'stop' area, a concrete structure and about five roads, the one on the right going down-hill towards the village. Here I locked up and left the car, carrying my equipment across and, without delay, a disaster-bound lorry stopped and picked me up, to stand in the back - thereby I lost my best cap, in the wind. He dropped me in Aberfan Road which was the road below Moy Road.

As I remember, going down into the village, one could see a moving mass of men and machines on the opposite hill across the roofs of the houses, around the school remains. The slurry had passed through the school and houses of Moy Road and was up to the roof gutterings of the houses of Aberfan Road, and had slid between the buildings so filling the lower ground and gardens. This was in the form of wet cement with large pieces of shale instead of chippings. My first job was, with a few others, in the gutter farthermost from the slide, to shovel the slurry along until it reached the street at ninety degrees where it would be washed down hill by the water flowing through as the slurry drained from Moy Road.

At that time, being a stranger to this type of work, I had not visualised their intentions, or what they had in mind, so joined the uppermost team above the school. As the trench had already progressed some good few yards with rows of toiling men shovelling stuff from one to another, along corrugated iron sheets, back along the trench to waiting lorries in the road. Two worked on the face with shovels, whilst I tried to help by cutting into it from above, as my spade was more effective with its stouter edge. The material had, by now, turned into a nearly dry cement.

During this non-stop period through Saturday night and Sunday morning wonderful work, much appreciated by the 'lads', was done by the Salvation Army People, some young ladies, who all through the night were coming around the workers carrying loads of milk bottles and bananas on cinema type ice-cream trays slung from their shoulders. From their efforts on this one night one must hold these people in high regard. After midnight, sometime, one of the lads, perhaps a miner, blond haired and stripped to the waist, as were a lot of them in the trench, called up asking me to swap my spade for his shovel. This spade was new and although never used again in the twenty five years that have passed since that time, the handle is worked smooth. The spade, when hurriedly thrown back into the back of the car to come down, its natural white wood handle was brand new, was blackened and smoothed by hard work. At last, in the early hours of Sunday morning, the two trenches met, without deviation, and must have been guided from above, making a clearway around the school. Wondering what was going to happen next, again the novice, I stood near the big 16" calor gas floodlight on its high tripod of five foot. Two of these had been in use, one at the head of each trench. At that moment, a man who seemed to be in charge of the digging of our trench, shouted up asking if I could manage the lamp and cylinders of gas, about four feet high. I found out what was required of me and I slid down the side with the tripod and cylinder, into what was now the farther-most end of the school yard. He told me that our small group, about six of us and a small track vehicle were going to start clearing the toilets, about four, if I remember rightly, at the far end, and then clear the yard through into the classroom, which, devoid of its wall, was now as part of the yard and the roof hanging down at an angle attached seemingly by one side. At this time, I think back to the trench diggers, who as mentioned, had stripped and placed their shirts and pullovers on the top side of the trench above where they worked. There were quite a few people wandering around, no doubt with their own very personal reasons for doing so and when the man in charge asked me to operate the flood lamp and cylinder along with the team because there were these people around, he told me that should anything be uncovered to swing the light away immediately. He also instructed us to pick up and keep any items, perhaps clothing, to check for any identification in case there were names attached. I found a small garberdine collar, very small and grey. There was no identification.

When daylight came, it came not alone, but with a different people, wandering around in and scuffling through the debris that we had moved during the night. Again I wondered why, perhaps through tiredness, until the terrible reality dawned on me when they asked various questions, indicating that here were people who had lost someone near to them but still had hope. One gentleman I spoke with was looking for his daughter and another for his nephew or niece. I think that just before midnight on the Saturday, a lady was found across the road from the school. A covering of sheets was put around her and two rescuers in white singlets were inside for some considerable time bringing her out. Their work must have been made more difficult because by now the slurry was setting into a dry cement-like substance. Just nearby to this sad find was a car held vertically against the wall of a house.

Unfortunately, apart from those already mentioned and some that I met near a chapel where I went for a drink, I met none of the people of Aberfan. On the Sunday afternoon I lay on the grass for a short time and then cut across to the road where I was given a lift to the top road and my car. I arrived home in Llandudno at about 7.30 p.m. on Sunday, having no idea of the state that I was in, and had even stopped in Ross on Wye and slept for an hour in a street whilst passing through.

BILL OLIVER, LLANDUDNO, 1991

6. Sunbeams on Disaster Morning

"Where can I park? O.K." - then returning with shovel in hand, "I've come from North Wales, where can I help?"

"You can have these" and thirty pairs of brand new gum boots were tossed from a van before it drove away as fast as it came.

"Oxygen will probably be needed!", as a number of cylinders were carefully laid on the floor. "Who can I say delivered?" was drowned in the vehicles' quick getaway.

"Here is a list containing the names of a few who have escaped from the school." From a parent who knew his son was not to be on it.

"You can use our house!", from a resident of Moy Road to Authority as it sought location for incident post.

"Oh! Love him!" as she tenderly washed the first victim to Bethania Chapel and fought back the rolling tears.

'An Aberfan Policeman'

7. "I remember they stood in the rain so patiently, love them, waiting for news of the children. They stood on Bethania Hill, so patiently."

An Aberfan Nurse

Bethania Hill

I can picture them
Because I know them
So well.
The men would be
In their caps.
The women in their
Headscarves.
The men would be
Smoking rolled cigarettes
Shuffling about
On the kerb.
They would all be
Bending their heads
On times,
Looking at their shoes,
The rain falling
Onto their faces
When they raised
Their eyes.
Pity, capture their tears
In your hands
For they are bound to fall.
Love help bear their burdens.
They are bound to come.

Maureen Hughes, 1991

Dedicated to Gwyneth "Jennie" Probert (neé) Hodkinson and Joe Probert.

The Newly Built Pantglas Secondary School Circa 1906

8. Merthyr Vale Primary School Log Book 1966-67

October 1966.
Colliery waste tip engulfed Pantglas Junior School and several houses, causing many casualties.

21 October
Soon after the start of the morning session we heard of the tragic disaster at Pantglas. We endeavoured to maintain the school as normally as possible in the circumstances. Children were escorted home at dinner time, and in the afternoon, by the staff.

Before leaving the school, a meeting was arranged for the evening when an attempt was made by various means to gather information relevant to the compiling of a nominal roll of Pantglas School. This meeting broke up at 1.30 p.m. to be recalled on the following day.

22 October
Meeting was called and food had been prepared by School Meals Staff. This meeting was of short duration and the food was packed and delivered by hand to the scene of the disaster for distribution to the workmen. A message was brought back informing us of a shortage of drinks at the site. Mineral waters were obtained from nearby shops etc. and despatched as quickly as possible. At approximately 5.30 p.m. the Medical Officer of Health informed us that the school was to be held in readiness for use as a Rest Centre. Classrooms were cleared and arrangements made for cooks and staff to be available. Food supplies were obtained from various sources. Several orders for meals were made and the food prepared, only to find that the expected men did not arrive. Food was several times sent to the site of the rescue operation.

During the small hours of Sunday morning large quantities of bedding were delivered to the school and rest rooms set up. Help was provided by volunteers from the teaching staff of the Borough and some friends. This service was soon organised on a shift basis.

The school had now been completely taken over and by Sunday evening there had been established a Feeding Centre for meals consumed on the premises, food was prepared for distribution to various key points, a bulk Food Store had been established under Civil Defence control, a clothing depot established and five classrooms plus other smaller rooms were used as rest rooms.

23 October
During the remainder of the week the pressure on the services available at school increased steadily and a valuable contribution was made to the overall operation. It is impossible to report the effort in accurate statistics as no time could be spared during the week to keep records. It is fair to estimate that thousands of meals were served and eaten on the premises. Greater quantities of food and drink were sent out to other venues than those actually eaten at the school. Hundreds of personnel connected with the operation were fed, including miners, voluntary rescue workers, Civil Defence, W.V.S., Red Cross, Ambulance, Police and Military.

The temporary sleeping quarters were used extensively and great efforts were made by all concerned to maintain a high standard of feeding, efficiency and, perhaps above all, cleanliness.

No praise is too high for the unselfish service given by the scores of people involved in organising and running this centre. To list names would be invidious as it is sufficient to give heartfelt thanks to those who helped to make the contribution to the general effort a truly valuable one.

29 October
The centre closed down officially at 8 p.m. today and immediately the work of restoring the school to its proper function was put in hand. Fumigation was done during the night and the school was cleaned and re-adjusted on the Sunday.

31 October
Donation of £2 received from Rose Easton, Liverpool. Money placed in school account. School re-assembled this morning after a half term closure which has been described in the fore-going pages.

We were pleased, and indeed proud, that we were able to function with some measure of normality after such a disturbing time. Overall attendance was 88%. Several mothers visited the school to express their apprehension regarding the tip above Brynteg. After a long discussion, I was able to re-assure them to some extent but promised to do my utmost to obtain an official statement as soon as possible. I have attempted to do this through the Town Clerk.

No Aberfan children have reported.

Footnote to October 23-29
During the week three mobile classroom units were being erected in the school yard to cater for the children of Aberfan. This work has gone on through all the turmoil and disorder.

November 1966

1 November
A few parents again visited the school to discuss the safety of the tip.
Attendance today is 93%.
The task of clearing the school of surplus equipment gathered during the last week is still continuing.

2 November
The Chairman, and some members of the Education Committee, with Mr Beale and Mr Roberts, visited the school to inspect the progress of the new classrooms. Mrs Jenkins, kitchen staff, who was rendered homeless by the disaster has returned to duties today.

3 November
Attendance is still quite normal.

4 November
Parents visited the school this morning to seek assistance in obtaining transport home for the children. Arrangements have now been made for transport to be available at 3.30 and 4.00 p.m. as from Monday 7 November.

7 November
School was visited by a deputation of mothers from Aberfan who were brought by Mr Beale, Mr Roberts and Mr Williams. They inspected the school premises which, unfortunately, were not in top condition due to the bad weather and the large number of workmen using the school. In addition the electricity had been cut off during the afternoon.

8 November
The three extra classrooms are nearing completion but the school is still inundated with workmen.

11 November
The school is still very much disturbed by the inconvenience of workmen and large quantities of furniture which are at the moment stored in the hall.

18 November
During the last weeks several donations have been made to the school by various schools and individuals. Money and a large consignment of library books have been delivered and these items are being held pending developments regarding the future of the Aberfan children.

23 November
A meeting of Merthyr Vale residents was held in the school this evening to discuss and receive reports on matters concerning the residents. The safety of the tip above Brynteg, the question of retaining walls, etc. The headmaster attended this meeting and at the close of the meeting it was pointed out to me that one or two people were trying to persuade parents to withdraw their children from school because of the danger of the tip. The majority of parents pointed out to the people canvassing them that they felt the report given to them in the meeting, of the inspection of the tip had been a re-assuring one and they could see no useful purpose in the proposed action.

24 November

Three families of children, nine in all, are absent from school. It is not known whether it is a result of various individuals after the meeting last night. It should be pointed out that the persons convening the meeting had nothing to do with this action. The matter has been reported to Mr Beale.

26 November

Money received from E. P. Collier School, Reading. Money placed in school account and the gift acknowledged.

Families have returned to school.

14 December

Furniture from temporary rooms sent to Perthygleision and Mount Pleasant. (Schools catering for Pantglas children.)

21 December

School party held today. I must express thanks to the teachers and ancillary staff for their wonderful co-operation.

23 December

School closed for Christmas holiday.

10 January

School re-opened with all teachers present. The classrooms in the yard are not in use because of the refusal of Aberfan parents to send their children to the school. Stock is still held. (Ordered by Miss Pitcher.)

9 February

The top class of the school was taken today to the language laboratory at Quakers Yard School for the first of a regular weekly lesson in Welsh. We are excited at this new venture and have high hopes that the development will prove profitable to the learning of the language.

TUDOR J. EVANS

9.   A Cry from "The Heart" of Aberfan (As we forgive them)

There was a black tip, above Aberfan,
Put on our green hills by the hand of man
One day it fell upon House and School,
Pushed there by a damned-up pool.

Now, I must forgive the N.C.B.
For taking my child away from me,
With eyes so bright, and cheeks so red,
All that is gone - She's white; She's dead.

In their coffins side by side,
Below ground someone's joy and pride;
All people in this vale of sorrow,
Mourn those for there's no tomorrow.

The Mothers here who suffer loss
Are like to Mary, at the Cross,
What grief for her so meek and mild,
When she saw killed her first-born child.

Grief it seems must be our lot,
Grief at times is all we've got,
I cannot die and join her yet,
My husband needs me, my children would fret.

Maybe I'll live in peace once more
When death and heaven open door
I trust I'll feel a great Amen,
When with my babe I am again.

May God's wisdom shine on me
So I'll forgive the N.C.B.
Then I can live in peace -
Then I will live in peace.

SHARON LEWIS' MOTHER.
CHRISTMAS EVE, 1966

Funeral Service

10. From 'Chaos to Calm'

The Diary of the Gordon-Lennox Education Centre
Thursday November 3 1966 to Thursday December 1 1966

The Director of Education for Merthyr Tydfil, Mr John Beale, M.A., set up on Monday October 31st, 1966, an educational centre in Aberfan Park namely, two caravans, manned by the Acting Head of Pantglas Secondary Modern School, Mr Ken J. Davies. It was to act as a supply base where a wide range of school material was stored and which children could call for and take away to their homes. A communication base where parents could keep in touch with all the recent developments. An interviewing base where there would be space and time for private and confidential interviews. A friendship base where it was hoped the education committee could build up a close relationship with parents in order to restore them to their happy normal routine. During that Monday 60 - 70 senior pupils and 20 junior pupils reported to the trailer. With just two caravans at our disposal, Mr Ken Davies thought that these arrangements were unsatisfactory. With very inclement weather, one caravan was proving to be unsuitable, so children had to amuse themselves the best they could. Toys, books, equipment, like pencils, crayons, coloured pencils, colouring books etc., were distributed to parents and children.

I negotiated with the Secretary, Mr R. Colston, with regard to rental or hire of the Gordon-Lennox Club. Mr Colston arranged for me to meet the President and the Committee on Tuesday, November 1st, 1966. The Committee unanimously agreed to let us have the Hall. They would not consider the question of monies.

Meanwhile more pupils were reporting to the trailer, 75 seniors and 34 juniors. With extreme kindness, the Ebbw Vale Council placed their magnificent modern swimming baths at the children's disposal. The visits were frequent and as time went on clearly therapeutic.

The Club was inspected by the Director of Education, Assistant Director Mr Eddie Roberts, Ald., Tal Lloyd Chairman of the Education Committee and Committee members. Mr Roberts, H.M.I., visited the Centre to see for himself what arrangements had been made.

On Thursday November 3rd, 1966, the Centre opened and as the rehabilitation of children into an educational environment was one that had not yet been experienced in the Merthyr District, in the hope that it might one day be of interest to future educationalists, I kept a diary of the day to day activities undertaken by the Staff involved in the Gordon-Lennox Club and it reads as follows.

First day at the Centre opened at 9.30 a.m. until 12 noon. Afternoon 2 p.m. until 4 p.m. During the morning 40 - 50 children assembled. As the day progressed we had up to 120 school-children of all ages. One could see the grief and shock written on many faces. No-one smiled. The movement of a table made a rumbling sound, which resulted in an unhealthy silence in the hall, as this was immediately associated with the rumble of the descending slurry. All children were given painting books, drawing books, crayons, pencils, etc.

The job of Mr Ken Davies and his Staff, using the utmost humility, was trying to restore the children to a normal way of life. Also to let parents gain confidence in letting their children out of sight once again after such a traumatic experience. The Staff organised and set up activities, according to their professional ability and interests. Mr Eric Jenkins set up a Reading Section and Library; Mr Reg Chandler set up an Art Section with painting and drawing facilities; Mrs Joan Williams and Miss Mair Morgan ably assisted with the juniors and infants. Miss Jane Morgan assisted with the films and projector. I had a History and Geography Section, where pupils could read about the past, draw and illustrate, read Geography books about different parts of the world, anything to get their minds off what they could see every day, the desolation of their schools, the black mass of slurry, their village in turmoil. Mrs Ann Hickey set up a Needlework Section. The children heartily accepted the place, finding it both spacious and friendly.

Miss Gwyneth Evans, Music Teacher at Pantglas Secondary School, together with Mr Cyril Vaughan, had been requested by the Merthyr Tydfil Education Authority to visit every parent to enable them to talk about their lost children, arrange school photographs, and to try to comfort them it proved to be a very heart-rending task. Following the disaster, many children wanted to hide at home, school had become a place of terror. But the apperance of Teacher Mr Cyril Vaughan, well known in the village, at the door, had become a matter of joy. A bond had grown between teachers and parents that had never existed before, 'Aw Miss', said a little girl to Miss Evans, 'My mother said you've been working hard.'

On Friday November 4th, 1966, the weather was not on our side. In very wet conditions, the Centre opened as promised on time at 9.30 a.m. We were glad to welcome 120 children, 100 seniors and 20 juniors. They dispersed to the activities according to individual interests.

Miss Gwyneth Evans, Deputy Head, accompanied by Mr Melville Thomas, County Drama Adviser for Monmouthshire (Gwent), arrived to make arrangements for a visiting touring Drama Group. Various notices were displayed. Firework display Aberfan Park, Saturday 5th November 1966 at 6 p.m. Swimming Ebbw Vale Baths, Monday 11 a.m.

On Tuesday 8th November 1966 the Centre opened at 9.30 a.m. Numbers of pupils arriving each morning increased. Visit of newspaper reporters for the Evening Standard. During the morning Mr Ivor Duncerton of BBC "Twenty Four Hours" Programme arrived to negotiate arrangements for filming at the Centre. On the 4th November I received a letter from Mr W. A. C. Hall, Capitol Theatre, Cardiff extending the hospitality of the Capitol Theatre for the children to see the film "The Sound of Music" starring Julie Andrews. Made arrangements with Mr W. A. C. Hall to accommodate 190 pupils and staff to see the film 'The Sound of Music' for the 2.30 matinee, on Thursday 10th November 1966.

Visit of a London Drama Group in charge of Mr Melville Thomas, Drama Organiser for Monmouthshire. Mr Ronald Chenery and his team of players: Jenny Moody, Claire James, David Gilpin and John Griffiths (formerly of Troedyrhiw) performed an excellent play which was thoroughly enjoyed by all present, and held the children enthralled by its audience participation. It was a pleasure to see the young audience appreciate live entertainment, for some their first experience of the theatre. Today 240 children were present both the morning and afternoon sessions.

On Wednesday November 9th, 1966, usual morning activities. Mr Roberts H.M.I. paid a visit to the Centre. He was surprised to see that numbers were increasing, both juniors and seniors.

Mr Fyfe Robinson of the BBC visited the Centre to make arrangements for filming.

88 pupils taken by Merthyr Transport with Staff to Ebbw Vale Baths. Members of staff proceeded to Cardiff to collect a new batch of films, from Sound Film Services, 27 Charles Street, Cardiff.

BBC team of six began filming in the Centre , over 200 pupils were present. Senior pupils present 160, juniors and infants 90, total 250.

On Thursday November 10th 1966 at 12.35 p.m. 190 children and staff proceeded to Cardiff in two double decker buses, provided by Merthyr Tydfil Borough Corporation to see the film 'The Sound of Music'. We arrived in Cardiff at 1.45 p.m. Cardiff Constabulary assisted in traffic control allowing the buses to pull up in front of the Capitol Theatre. We were met by Mr W. A. C. Hall, the Manager of the Capitol Theatre, Cardiff. Children were televised by both BBC and TWW cameras. The Management excelled themselves in giving the children a great welcome. Each child received a bag of sweets, and during the interval free ice-cream, drinks, etc., were distributed. At the end of the performance, the children were televised by 20th Century Fox, for distribution in America.

Mr Stan Rees, Manager of the Concrete Block Factory, Aberfan, arranged free transportation for the Saturday Football Match, Merthyr Town playing Kettering.

On Friday November 11th 1966 the Centre opened at 9.30 a.m. with roll call, and the usual activities.

On Monday November 14th 1966 a party of 80 pupils proceeded to Aberavon to the Avan Lido, where they were officially received by the Mayor and Mayoress of Port Talbot. They were entertained at the Sports Centre where the senior boys chatted with Jeff Jones (4 for 93 for England against the Aussies) and Alan Rees, former Welsh rugby international and still a Glamorgan cricketer, and then with ex-Empire welterweight champion Eddie Thomas, a great hero still revered in Merthyr by every boy of five upwards. An excellent free lunch was provided and the afternoon was spent in the Lido.

The remaining pupils carried on with recreational activities at the Centre. During the morning we had a visit from a team from Italian State Television. The production was to be called "Aberfan - One Month After" under the Director F. Bianacci. The team took many photographs and interviewed the three infant and junior teachers.

On Thursday November 24th 1996 the centre opened at 9:30 am. Preperations were now being formulated for the closure of the Gordon-Lennox Club, for senior pupils. Mr Michael Moynihan of the Sunday Times visited the Centre to report on its activities for his newspaper.

On Friday November 25th 1966, the Centre was to carry on for another week for seniors and for another fortnight for infants and juniors until they moved to Merthyr Vale Junior School. The senior pupils and staff were to move to Troedyrhiw Secondary Modern School on Thursday December 1st 1966. Three days were given to move equipment and stock.

The Aberfan Social Club organised a Christmas Party for all children on Thursday 22nd December 1966.

Mr and Mrs Jones kindly arranged at the Gordon-Lennox Club a farewell party for the seniors on Tuesday December 6th 1966. Mr and Mrs Jones spared no costs and excelled themselves with the arrangements. Mrs M. Hayes kindly arranged a small present for each child delivered from the Baptist Church. O.P. Chocolates, Merthyr kindly donated 300 novelties. The party was a momentous occasion thoroughly enjoyed by all.

The juniors and infants had their party on Thursday December 15th 1966. Mr Wilding, Manager of Morlais Bus Services, kindly placed at our disposal a number of coaches to transport the children free of charge to see the pantomime 'Mother Goose' at the New Theatre, Cardiff.

To climax all the proceedings and to bring our eventful month at the Gordon-Lennox to a close, the Bath Trades and Labour Institute, Social and Democratic Club arranged a memorable day's entertainment.

On Saturday, the 3rd of December 1966, 210 children left Aberfan at 8.30 a.m. accompanied by Mr H. Watkins, Mrs T. Watkins, Mr Cyril Vaughan, Miss G. Evans, Miss M. Morgan and Mrs N. Morgan with eight club members, for Bath.

At 11 a.m. we crossed the Severn Bridge where we were met by members and proceeded to Bristol, where we assembled at Oldlan Common where tea and biscuits were kindly provided. Each coach was then escorted by two people of the Bath Welsh Speaking Society. The party was honoured in having a police escort into Bath, where we assembled outside the old Police Station. A party of 100 pupils and staff went directly to the Roman Baths for a conducted tour. 50 went to see the Roman Abbey and 50 to the Pump Room. After the tour it was back to the coaches for a short ride to the Bath Trades and Labour Institute, Green Park, where we were kindly met by Mr Felton, President and Chairman and his Committee members. The children were entertained to a hot lunch of fish and chips, a sweet, etc. At 1.30 p.m. we were given a tour of the beautiful City of Bath, before arriving at Hillside Hall for a cinema show, entertainment from a comedian and a Beat group. At 4 p.m., the children were given a delightful tea. After a most delightful day and having thanked Mr Felton, Mr A. Downing, Vice-Chairman and Mr W. Wedlock, Secretary for their kind hospitality, we departed for the return journey to Aberfan.

The momentous day arrived, Thursday December 1st 1966, when we moved as a school to Troedyrhiw Secondary Modern School to be accommodated in the mobile classrooms. Here we were to remain until our final move to become part of Merthyr's first Comprehensive School.

People all over the world still expressed their kindness in many ways. Invitations for holidays abroad to Greece, Italy, France, Brittany, Germany and many holidays in many parts of the British Isles.

The boys and girls who went through that dramatic period in their lives are now parents themselves, whose sons and daughters attend Afon Taf High School.

Over the years the pain has diminished with time but can never wholly be wiped away.

The name 'Pantglas' will always be remembered.

TAKEN FROM THE DIARY OF HUGH WATKINS,
DEPUTY HEAD LOWER SCHOOL,
AFON TÂF HIGH SCHOOL, 1993

If I keep a green bough in my heart, the singing bird will come.

OLD CHINESE SAYING

10B525
MARIAN HEATH
SUDBURY, MASS.

To the people of Aberan,
We wish we could help. We can't do much, but we are praying for you. We are thinking of you right now.

Sincerely Yours,

Ack

Jeff Davis
Kathy Meyers
Joan Hicks
Vickey Dyer
Susan Nason
Linda Nohe
Arti Truesdell
Larry Smith
Steve Smith
Father Eugene Botello

Two years ago, the Merthyr Tydfil Borough Council moved from the Town Hall in the High Street to a new Civic Centre in Castle Street. Housed in the basement of the Town Hall were the thousands of letters that had poured into the Borough at the time of the Disaster in Aberfan. The letters were given into the safe keeping of the Librarian. I read a few thousand of these letters for the purpose of this book. I chose some two hundred of the letters as being representative. I have quoted from thirty five of them which convey the tone and spirit of so many others that were sent here.

MAUREEN HUGHES, 1992

11. "The Singing Bird will Come."

Thousands of letters poured into Aberfan and Merthyr Tydfil following the Disaster.

Slate quarrymen of Llechwedd Quarry, Blaenau Ffestiniog, wrote "there were no dry eyes amongst us when we heard the horrible news on Friday." An exiled North Walian in Quebec, Canada, wrote that he had never felt closer to the people of South Wales. His family too, had toiled in the slate quarries of North Wales. His was "a letter of sorrow." "Cofion gwlad benllywydd tirion." he wrote. A lady sent a sympathy card from Los Angeles, "with a Welsh heart full of love and prayers for all of you. My people are from the Rhondda Valley." Welsh people everywhere felt the loss. Another exile wrote from Nuneaton, "my heart goes out to all them back home." An elderly lady wrote from Harrogate to say that her parents had been from Cardigan and that her "dear father bought horses and ponies for the various South Wales Collieries. I saw Aberfan on the lists." She continued, "Our Rev Carter knows the Rev Hayes very well, in fact, I think that they were at college together. All my love to the people of Aberfan." The St David's Welsh Society of Kansas city, Missouri wrote, "we sing the Welsh hymns and speak about that grand country of Wales. May God bless them, as we in Kansas City will pray for them in their times of troubles and sorrows." The Women's World Day of Prayer, Wales, wrote from Cardiff, "we pray that our Heavenly Father will comfort them in their dark hour."

The Darby and Joan Club of Corris, Machynlleth, sent their deepest sympathy and prayers to the "brave people of Aberfan in the great sorrow and adversity that has befallen you. We feel that Corris is a part of Aberfan as there are so many family connections here." The Whitland branch of the Federation of Old Age Pensioners Associations wrote "we are proud of the men, women and children who without thought for their own safety went immediately to their assistance. A lot could be written about the heroism of the teachers and the various acts of bravery performed even by little children." The secretary of the organisation who wrote the letter, came originally from Merthyr Vale and had worked in the Merthyr Vale Colliery. He regretted that, because of illness, he had not been able to help in the rescue operations.

There were numerous contributions from the Trade Unions. Cardiff dockers of the National Docks Labour Board sent £132 to the Disaster Fund. London busmen from Hendon Garage sent their sympathy and a cheque. They too appreciated the "tremendous effort of all engaged in the rescue operation." Building trade workers of Merthyr wrote that they felt "most deeply" and "shared the sorrow of all concerned in the worst period of our sad and unhappy valley." Whilst the Treharris branch of the Amalgamated Engineering Union wrote, "We of the Welsh mining valleys have witnessed tragedies in the past, tragedies with which the mining communities have been plagued in the quest for coal but this catastrophe is a burden that we will bear for generations." Agricultural workers wrote from Yorkshire. The Ryhope, Durham Area, branch of the N.U.M. wrote "We are a mining village of about the same size as Aberfan and therefore we know the terrible hazards of mining and its terrible disasters. On the day of your disaster we were told that our own pit of 850 men and boys was to be closed down in one month's time, this was a big blow to all of us but I am quite sure, nothing to compare with what's happened to our mining friends in Aberfan." Gestetner Duplicators Limited wrote to offer their services to the Appeal Fund itself. "Please tell us of your needs", they said.

From Israel came flowers stuck to a sheet of paper. They were from students in a teacher training college of the Labour movement. "How sad and dark can life be without the sound of laughing children. We all know how dangerous work in the mines can be. We are pupils in a school that belongs to the Labour movement, and can identify ourselves with your sorrow." Echoing the theme of the flowers, they wrote, "the children, the fresh little flowers, have gone away. Who will keep the devastated ground well-watered with tears to grow up new plants again. Who will bring the light again in Wales?" From St Paul's School, Kansas City, came a card from the pupils and the Roman Catholic Father, which quoted an old Chinese saying, "If I keep a green bough in my heart, the singing bird will come."

A headmaster from Yorkshire wrote of his own children's primary school education in Wales. "This disaster has produced inexpressible sadness in my family and myself." Whilst the headmaster of a school in Czechoslovakia wrote to say that he had lost his wife and child in a similar way in the Second World War. "I can appreciate the grief of the children's parents." A man wrote from Philadelphia, Pennsylvania, "I am a refugee from Hitler's holocaust in Europe. My mother, father, a sister and a brother, died in German gas ovens. My surviving sister was saved by the help and goodness of the English people. Time does heal wounds. If not altogether, but to the largest degree, by the Grace of God." The British Embassy in Tel Aviv sent on a letter from Mr Pesah, who remembered "the good boys from Wales" with whom he had served in the British Army, in the Second World War. He ends "in peace and preventing wars, will be the consolation." Pupils from a school in France, extolled their "little Welsh friends" to "believe in our kindness." And schoolgirls, also from France, wrote, "we share in your trouble and we are near you in your pain."

"A tiny little school", the children's own description, in Skegness, sent over £52 which was raised by a Beetle Drive. "Mums and Dads came and helped us to raise this money." Mount Stewart Infants School, Harrow, Middlesex, sent £10:10:0. "We would very much like you to use this money towards a Christmas Party for the children. We shall be having one and we thought that they might like one too." A boy of eight, a pupil in the British School, Hanover, Germany, sent £1:4:6 which he had collected from the children in his street. "We would like to give this money to the children of Aberfan," he wrote.

An elderly widow, "one time schoolteacher", wrote from Rhymney, Monmouthshire, that she had been "chilled to the marrow." Hackney Teachers' Association, spoke of their "deep sense of shock and sorrow." As teachers "whose job it is to work with children every day, we can feel very close to all those who have suffered such overwhelming loss." The Welsh Executive member of the National Union of Teachers, wrote from North Wales concerning the teachers of Pantglas and Merthyr Vale Schools, "the devotion of our colleagues to their pupils and their personal sacrifice on their behalf, will always be remembered by the profession and the people at large as the outstanding example of selfless heroism. I visited Merthyr Vale County Primary School last Thursday and I was tremendously impressed by the quiet efficiency, warmth of feeling and genuine kindness, which I witnessed on the part of the teachers there." A lady from Croydon, in Surrey, sent a poem to be passed on to the Rev Hayes. In the poem she likened the cross on the hill above Aberfan, to a "school of flowers."

A Welsh Presbyterian Sunday School in the Vale of Clwyd, sent a parcel of toys and books "for the surviving children of Aberfan." A minister wrote from his Sunday School in Manchester, with the £10 that they had helped collect. As a "little lad", he lived in Moy Road and attended Pantglas School. Sunday schools had also donated to money sent by two Anglican Churches in Wiltshire. "In loving sympathy for those children of Aberfan's Sunday Schools, that died." The Sikh community of Manchester referred to the children as "the most precious treasure" and as if to give weight to their words, a very small child wrote from Hawarden near Chester, "I hope that everyone is keeping well now." And a six year old from New Barnet, Herts, wrote, "I had this 10/- for my sixth birthday. Now I want you to have it. God bless you all."

12. Letter from Irene Downing

The Mayor of Merthyr Tydfil

96 Shorncliffe Road
Folkstone
23 October 1966

Dear Sir,

During the last war my husband A. B. Downing was welcomed to your town with about 350 boys from the Harvey Grammar School, Folkstone. You welcomed them warmly and with sympathy for they were "evacuees" and they shared your homes, your schools and your affections. This kindly act will never be forgotten, you were kind to our children. Now your children have suffered and I feel that a prayer will be said by many a young man in Folkestone who was given hospitality by you as a boy, a prayer for your suffering and that you may all be comforted.

My husband had affection and regard for Merthyr, he died some years ago. Had he lived it would have been his wish, as indeed it is mine too, to send sympathy and a little cheque that perhaps may be used to bring comfort to those who suffer, to Welsh folk who were good to our children so long ago.

Yours sincerely
Irene Downing

13. The Lovely Garden

Irene Downing is now over ninety years old. Blind these days, she still lives in Folkestone. Her association with Merthyr spans half a century. She was one of the first people to send a donation to the Disaster Fund in 1966.

At the beginning of 1992 she sent a poem to the village of Aberfan.

Here the scent of roses perfumes the air.
Pause a moment and say a prayer
For those who died too soon.
Stand still and listen,
You will hear the sound
Of children's voices
Laughing, talking, singing.
These sounds will never die.
They are alive in the perfume
Of the roses.
Do not weep.
Know that they are now in heaven,
A place of beauty and happiness
Beyond our comprehension.
So be happy in the lovely garden.

IRENE DOWNING, 1992

14. The Rememberance Garden, Aberfan

This lovely garden is situated at the end of the Cemetery Memorial. Even after twenty six years people come to visit in large numbers, to pay their respects and they can all remember what they were doing at the time of the Aberfan Disaster.

Visitors are now part of the lives of the people who live here. They arrive frequently to visit the graves of those who died in October 1966. The new garden is lovingly cared for by the Cemetery Memorial Committee whose Chairman is Bryn Carpenter.

In October 1991 the Welsh Office expressed a desire to fund a project that would mark the twenty fifth anniversary of the Disaster in a special way. A remembrance garden for visitors, only a dream, due to lack of funds, could now become a reality. Born of an idea of Sheila Lewis, designed by architect Michael Davies and planted by garden designer Sue Gill, the garden is a beautiful and fitting way of expressing the thanks of the community of Aberfan to people everywhere for their continued support.

Sheila Lewis, 1992

Rememberance Garden

15. "Those who suffered"

News of the terrible tragedy that struck our village on 21st October 1966 was quickly disseminated world wide. The expertise of the media and the unprecedented coverage immediately produced an overwhelming response of sympathy, support, help and guidance. The Mayor of Merthyr Tydfil, Ald. Stanley Davies, after taking counsel, decided to appeal for financial relief for those who suffered. The response of the appeal was of such magnitude that it overwhelmed those who had instigated it. In under six weeks from the announcement of the appeal over £1,000,000 had been received. Donations were received not only from the United Kingdom but from sympathisers throughout the world. Substantial donations were received from America, Australia, New Zealand, South Africa, Italy, France and Germany. In addition, personal possessions were sent and holidays offered throughout Great Britain, Channel Islands and the continent of Europe. The final amount of donations to the Aberfan Disaster Fund rose to over £1,750,000, which in today's terms would be valued at ?

The avalanche of money poured into the Mayor's Parlour at Merthyr Tydfil. We are greatly indebted to the staff at the Town Hall, augmented by many volunteers, whose work was of inestimable value during this crucial period. Mr Selwyn Jones, the Town Clerk, and Mr Joseph Crossland, the Borough Treasurer, became respectively the Secretary and the Treasurer. All these people gave freely of their time, energy and enthusiasm.

It was apparent that a body of responsible people needed to be appointed to manage the Fund. Consequently a Provisional Management Committee was established. The Committee met on five occasions during which time arrangements proceeded for the establishment of a Trust Deed. Mr Elvet Francis Q.C. was invited to advise the Committee. It was agreed, after much deliberation, that there should be six life members consisting of people who had experience, knowledge and long association with the Merthyr Borough. In addition, there were to be four ex-officio members and it was agreed after consultation, there would be five elected Aberfan members.

With the establishment of the first Management Committee, Ald. Stanley Davies, C.B.E., J.P. became Chairman and Sir Alun Talfan Davies Q.C. Vice Chairman. The Management Committee were:

Life Members
Councillor Stanley Davies, C.B.E., J.P. Chairman.
Charles W. Bridges Esq., J.P. Chairman of the Magistrates for the County Borough of Merthyr Tydfil.
S. O. Davies Esq., M.P.
Alderman David J. Williams.
Colonel Reginald Freeman, D.L.
Mr Claude Neville D. Cole

Ex-Officio Members
Alun Talfan Davies Esq., Q.C. Recorder of Merthyr Tydfil; Vice-Chairman.
Alderman S. G. Edwards, J.P. Mayor of Merthyr Tydfil, 1968/69.
The Most Reverend Glyn Simon, D.D., Lord Archbishop of Wales / as Lord Bishop of Llandaff.
Colonel Sir Cennydd Traherne, K.G., T.D., Ll.D., J.P. Her Majesty's Lieutenant for the County of Glamorgan

Aberfan Members
William D. Tudor Esq.
Trefor Jones Esq.
Cyril C. L. Vaughan Esq.
Arthur Goldsworthy Esq.
J. Chris Sullivan Esq.

On the demise of Alderman Stanley Davies in 1968, Sir Alun Talfan Davies Q.C., became Chairman and myself Vice-Chairman. We continued in office until the Aberfan Disaster Fund Management Committee was dissolved in 1988. Over our period of office there were changes in the representatives on the Management Committee; names of committee members are included in the appendage, as indeed are the names of members of the Finance and Community Promotions Executives who played an important part in the running of the Community Centre and community activities until May 1988.

It was necessary to appoint a Secretary/Treasurer and Mr Gerald Davies, a barrister and administrator was appointed in May 1967. In April 1968 a new Secretary was appointed, a Chartered Accountant, Mr Geoffrey Morgan. He retired in March 1974. From then Secretarial duties were performed by Mr D. Davies of Deloittes and Company, Rev Derek Nuttall, Mr Ray Cottrell and Mr Geraint Davies of Grant Thornton, Chartered Accountants. The latter played a vital role in the management and distribution of funds until the Disaster Fund Committee had its last meeting on 14 May, 1988. His expert advice and the efficient way that he carried out his duties for the ultimate benefit of the community, was of inestimable value. He has been joined by Mr Elwyn Roberts of Coopers Lybrand Deloitte in advising and administering the last two charity committees of the Fund, namely Aberfan Memorial Charity and the Education Charity.

The administration of the Fund from the period 21 October 1966 to August 1968 was published in the 'First Report of the Management Committee of the Aberfan Disaster Fund.' Copies of this, and subsequent reports were given to residents in the 'Area of Benefit' and libraries. The Report gave an account of initial problems facing the Trustees and how they dealt with them. It describes how over £800,000 had been expended. The activities of the Management Committee under the Trust Deed were as follows.

Consideration of Major Cash Grants to Bereaved Families and Final Conclusions.
Eligibility of Bereaved Families and Persons for Major Cash Grants.
Injured Children.
Parents of Seriously Injured Children.
Injured Adults.
Payment of Rents and Removal Expenses.
Grants for Loss of Homes.
Repairs to Damaged Houses.
Grants to Grandparents of Schoolchildren lost in the Disaster.
Holiday Schemes.
Miscellaneous Grants to Organisations and Individuals.
Projects.
        Public Memorial at Aberfan Cemetery.
        Aberfan Development Study.
        The Community Centre.
        Memorial Garden.
        Industrial Project.

Within months of the publication of the 1st Report, Mr Stanley Davies C.B.E., J.P., died. The Mayor had worked unstintingly on behalf of the people of Aberfan. The concern, effort and time he spent ungrudgingly in the administration of the Fund for the benefit of the community will always be remembered.

Sir Alun Talfan Davies Q.C. , became Chairman and remained the Chairman until the Disaster Fund ended. It is fair to say that he never missed a meeting. His knowledge, expertise, management skills and guidance through the twenty two years was a tremendous asset to the Committee. He worked diligently to enable the views of Aberfan to be realised and tackled the various problems associated with the administration of the Fund with vigour and determination. His contribution was inestimable.

Mr W. Siberry will always be remembered for the invaluable support that he gave as a link with the Welsh Office and on his retirement he became a member of the Disaster Fund, in 1973.

During the period covered by the Second Report of the Disaster Fund, a sum of £150,000 was paid towards the Government's scheme for the complete removal of the tips. The tips were a constant reminder of the great tragedy. Initially it was contended by the Welsh Office that a partial removal of the tips would provide complete safety and therefore the additional cost of the complete removal could be avoided. Representatives of the Aberfan Committee met the Secretary of State at the Welsh Office and made plain their demands regarding the tips. It was in these circumstances that the Welsh Office asked for a contribution towards the cost from the Disaster Fund. Prolonged negotiations took place. The Welsh Office put forward a figure of £250,000. Eventually the figure of £150,000 was agreed upon. The Management Committee agreed to pay this figure, with the exception of Mr S. O. Davies

M.P., who resigned from the Committee in protest against the decision. However, at that time there was a sense of urgency and the avoidance of delay in the removal of the tips was essential. The removal of the tips at Aberfan led to a large scale removal of tips throughout South Wales. It should be noted that in the early Summer of 1976, as a result of representations made by Sir Alun Talfan Davies, (Chairman), Mr Ted Rowlands M.P. and Mr Alec Jones M.P., the National Coal Board, through the good office of Mr Phillip Weekes, the Board's Chief Executive, made a gift of £30,000 to the Fund, a gift which greatly assisted the Trustees in pursuing their objectives.

Throughout all the years that he has represented Merthyr Tydfil in Parliament, Mr Ted Rowlands has also been a Trustee of the Aberfan Disaster Fund. His contribution has been tremendous. Many doors have been opened as a result of his enquiries and knowledge. He has always worked diligently in his unassuming way, giving advice and working hard for the people of Aberfan.

A major problem that confronted the Trustees was the assessment of the payments that should be made to those families and individuals who had suffered as a result of the Disaster. The Law at that time was to the effect that appropriate compensation for the loss of a child was £500 and this was the figure adopted by the authorities. However, the Trustees took a different view. The bulk of the money had been donated by sympathisers from all over the world for the benefit of the bereaved parents and those who suffered. It was agreed that the sum of £5,000 should be paid to the parents who had lost their loved ones. The Chairman, the Secretary and Aberfan Representatives visited the Charity Commissioners' representatives in London. Subsequently, the Charity Commissioners visited Aberfan and agreed the figure put forward by the Trustees. All benefits to those who suffered and all those who were injured in the Disaster were completed. In determining the size of every injury grant, the Management Committee relied entirely on the recommendation of Mr Tasker Watkins V.C., Q.C., who later became the Rt. Hon. Deputy Lord Chief Justice for England and Wales. His work was detailed, difficult and considerable when considering reports that emanated from medical consultants in psychiatry and orthopedics.

Another major work of the Committee was the planning of the Community Centre. Our architects, Messrs Burgess and Partners of Cardiff and Messrs Sawyer and Horsburgh were responsible for this as well as the Memorial Garden on the site of Pantglas School. Mr A. F. Colwell, Director of Parks and Cemeteries, Merthyr Tydfil Borough Council, designed the Cemetery Memorial. Messrs E. Turner and Sons Ltd., Cardiff carried out general constructional work and Messrs E. W. Bull and Son of Rayleigh, Essex were responsible for the monumental work. Colonel Sir Cennydd Traherne K.G., was Chairman of the Projects Committee. His lively interest, gentlemanly support, knowledge, concern and guidance and his contribution to the administration of the fund was considerable. In all this work we were always ably assisted by the Liaison Committee of the Aberfan and Merthyr Vale Community Association with its Chairman, Mr Cledwyn Davies. It was necessary that month by month reports were made available to all households in the area of benefit and we are indebted to the stirling work of the village newspaper "Headway", pioneered by Rev Erastus Jones and his wife, Lun.

Tribute must be paid to all local Trustees of the Fund. They faced much of the public relations work in Aberfan and willingly shouldered these onerous duties and devoted a substantial amount of time, effort and concern on a voluntary basis to the varied and intricate problems the Fund had to face. Their loyalty and efficiency carried out the decisions of the Management Committee for the benefit of the community.

The Community Centre, with its swimming pool was popular and widely used. Its success rested with the voluntary work provided by members of the Community Association. The complex was opened by Her Majesty, The Queen in March 1973. The Queen and her family have shown continuing concern over the years. In August, 1986, twenty years after the Disaster and thirteen years after the Official opening, the Centre found itself in need of further financial support. Consequently the Fund Management Committee invited Messrs James Ritchie and Partners to appraise the Centre's problems. The conclusion reached stated, "Regrettably, the fundamental conclusion of this report must be to state that the financial losses of the Centre will eventually eat into the endowment fund to the extent which will collapse the Fund and render the Centre untenable."

Out of the £1.75 million, outgoings included £350,000 to build the Community Centre complex, £250,000 was invested in gilt edged securities to provide an income that was aimed at maintaining the complex. The fund being on a fixed income suffered the ravages of inflation. Unemployment and a National Coal Strike had an adverse affect on finance. Rates, lighting, water rates and bills were continually escalating the cost. We unequivocally claimed that the Centre was understaffed and indeed the staff were underpaid. To run the Community Centre complex under a strict economic budget presented difficulties, particularly to the Aberfan Trustees.

There were two realistic options. One was for the Merthyr Tydfil Borough Council, possibly with extra Welsh Office help, to take over the Centre. The other option would be for an injection of cash into the Disaster Fund but we were advised that there was little prospect of this taking place. A transfer to the Borough Council had always been considered to be the best solution but attempts made in the past had failed.

In 1987/1988 meetings were arranged between representatives of Merthyr Tydfil Borough Council, the Welsh Office, Mid Glamorgan County Council and the Disaster Fund. We are indebted to the guidance of Mr Roger Morris, Chief Executive of Merthyr Tydfil Borough Council, his officers, the Borough Councillors, Welsh Office observers, Charity Commissioners and members and representatives of Mid Glamorgan County Council for the successful transfer of the Community Centre, a very valuable asset worth far in excess of £1,000,000 into the hands of the Local Authority. The Welsh Office assisted in arrangements for the Urban Aid Grants. The Disaster Fund donated its investments valued at over a quarter of a million pounds, to the Local Authority. In addition there was to be financial help from Mid Glamorgan County Council. This ensured that a corporate body of representatives of the Merthyr Tydfil Borough Council, will, through its elected members, be responsible for a building that in itself reflects the prestige and importance of Aberfan in contemporary history.

The District Council took over the Community Centre on June 1st, 1988. Only two funds of the Aberfan Disaster Fund remain. The Aberfan Memorial Charity and the Aberfan Education Charity. The former is under the hardworking and dedicated Chairmanship of Mr Bryn Carpenter. The committee comprises the remaining Aberfan Trustees and local members of the Aberfan and Merthyr Vale Community Association with its initial accumulated fund of £106,000. They are responsible for the maintenance of the Cemetery Memorial and the Memorial Garden on the site of the Pantglas Junior School. The Education Charity with an initial accumulated fund of £31,347 is also made up of the remaining Trustees. I am its Chairman. The financial aspects are supervised by our accountants Mr Geraint Davies of Grant Thornton and Mr Elwyn Roberts of Coopers Lybrand.

The Disaster Fund Committee over the years has been helped by many people in its work, some by offering their expert advice and in certain areas, acting as co-opted members. We are grateful to our financial advisors Messrs Cazenove and Co., and the Bank of Wales for the day to day investment and administration of our funds; Barclays Bank at Merthyr Tydfil for their help and advice; our solicitors Messrs Slaughter and May and Martin Evans and Son, Merthyr Tydfil; the Merthyr Tydfil Borough Council; Mid Glamorgan County Council; the Welsh Office and the Charity Commissioners; the Executive Committees of the Aberfan and Merthyr Vale Community Association; "Headway", our local newspaper and the builders involved in our projects.

To all those who, over the years, have continued to show their sympathy and concern, we send our greetings and thanks. Your caring will always be remembered in our villages.

CYRIL VAUGHAN, 1992.
VICE-CHAIRMAN, ABERFAN DISASTER FUND.

Back Row - From Left
*Rev Ken Hayes, Geraint Davies,
Malcolm Jones, Glyn Jenkins,
Doug Pearson, Bryn Carpenter,
Bill Tudor.*

Front Row - From Left
*Cyril Vaughan (Vice - Chairman),
Douglas Badham,
Sir Alun Talfan Davies (Chairman),
Mary Cotter
Sir Cennydd Traherne,*

***Members of The Aberfan
Disaster Fund***

16. Those who Served

Aberfan Disaster Fund

Members of the Provisional Committee

Alderman Stanley Davies C.B.E., J.P. (Chairman)
Sir Alun Talfan Davies Q.C.
Charles William Bridges Esq., J.P.
Claude Neville Cole Esq.
Stephen Owen Davies Esq., M.P.
Col. Reginald Freedman D.L.
Alderman Albert John
Right Reverend Glyn Simons D.D.
Col., Sir Cennydd Traherne K.G., T.D., Ll.D., J.P.
Alderman David John Williams
Selwyn Jones Esq.
Joseph Crossland Esq.
Councillor James Williams Esq.
John Beale Esq, M.A.

The Aberfan Disaster Fund Management Committee
Life Members

Alderman Stanley Davies C.B.E., J.P., Chairman February 1967 - February 1969 deceased.
Sir Alun Talfan Davies, Vice Chairman Feb 1967 - Feb 1969, Chairman Feb 1969 - 1988 Life Member 1969.
Cyril C. L. Vaughan Esq., Vice Chairman Feb 1969 - 1988, Chairman of Local Trustees 1969-1988 Life Member 1971.
Charles W. Bridges Esq., J.P., Feb 1967 - 1968 deceased.
Stephen O. Davies Esq., M.P., Feb 1967 - August 1968 resigned.
Alderman David J. Williams, Feb 1967 - 1988.
Claude N. Cole Esq., Feb 1967 - Jan 1968.
Ben Hamilton Esq., June 1968 - 1988.
W. Arthur Goldsworthy Esq, 1969 - 1973 deceased.
Douglas Pearson Esq., J.P. - 1973 - 1988.
Bryn Carpenter Esq, 1973 - 1988.
William Tudor Esq., 1973 - 1988.
William M. Siberry Esq.

Ex Officio Members

Alderman Mrs A. M. Evans, Mayor of Merthyr 1967-68.
Alderman Mr S. G. Edwards, J.P., Mayor of Merthyr 1968-69.
Alderman Mr Albert John, Mayor of Merthyr 1969-70.
Alderman Mr David J. Williams, Mayor of Merthyr 1970-71.
The Most Reverend Glyn Simons, D.D.
Arch Bishop of Wales (as Bishop of LLandaff).
Right Rev. Roy Davies, Bishop of Llandaff.
Right Rev. Stephen Thomas, Bishop of Llandaff.
Col. Sir Cennydd Traherne, K.G., T.D., Ll.D., J.P. Her Majesty's Lieutenant, County of Glamorgan
Douglas Badham Esq., C.B.E., J.P. Her Majesty's Lieutenant Mid Glamorgan.
Sir Alun Talfan Davies Q.C., Recorder of Merthyr Tydfil.

Rt. Hon. Lord Justice Tasker Watkins V.C., Recorder of Merthyr Tydfil retired when he became Recorder of Swansea Judiciary.

Mr Phillip Owen Q.C.   (served briefly as Trustees during their appointments as Recorder

Mr Emlyn Hooson Q.C., J.P.   of Merthyr Tydfil)

Mr Ted Rowlands M.P. for Merthyr Tydfil.

Sec/Treasurers

Gerald Davies Esq., Geoffrey Morgan Esq., Raymond Cottrell Esq.

Financial Advisors

Sir Melvyn Rosser FCA, David Davies FCA, Stephen Rogers FCA, Geraint Davies FCA, Elwyn Roberts Esq., M.A., FCA.

Aberfan Elected Representatives

	Elected	Retired	Re-elected	Term of Office	
William Tudor Esq.	Feb 67	Sept 67	Oct 71	1988	
Trevor Jones Esq.	Feb 67	Sept 67	Oct 73	Jan 75	deceased
Cyril C. L. Vaughan Esq.	Feb 67			1988	
William H. Goldsworthy Esq.	Feb 67	Sept 67	Oct 67	1978	deceased
J. Chris Sullivan Esq.	Feb 67	Sept 67			
Harold Davey Esq.	Oct 67			1971	
Trevor Emanual Esq.	Oct 67			1971	
Douglas Pearson Esq., J.P.	Oct 67			1988	
John Prosser Esq.	Oct 69			1982	deceased
Bryn Carpenter Esq.	Oct 71			1988	
Mrs Mary Cotter J.P.	1977			1988	
Rev. Kenneth Hayes	1975				
Sidney Chilcott Esq.	1975			1988	
Malcolm Jones Esq.	1975			1988	
Glyn Jenkins Esq.	1977			1988	
Ray Cottrell Esq.				1988	

Co-opted Members

Sir Julian Hodge.
Sir Alfred Nicholas C.B.E.
Mr John Wright, Newport College of Art.
Mr Peter Jones, Welsh Arts Council.
Mr F. A. Colwell, Merthyr Corporation, Director of Parks and Cemeteries.
H. K. Tramnell Esq.
Wyn Thomas Esq., Burgess and Partners.
Mervyn Jones Esq., C.B.E.
Sir Thomas Parry Williams.
J. A. Thomas Esq.
J. Beale Esq., M.A., Director of Education Merthyr.
David W. Howells Esq., B.A., Headmaster Afon Taf High School.
Tudor Evans Esq., Headmaster Ynysowen Primary School.
John Isaac Esq., B.Sc., M.E., Headmaster Afon Taf School.
Martin Gay Esq., B.Sc., M.Sc., Headmaster Bishop Hedley High School.
Eddie Roberts Esq., M.Sc., Director Education Mid Glamorgan.

P. W. James Esq., James Ritchie Associates.

Liaison Committee of Aberfan and Merthyr Vale Community Association

Cledwyn Davies Esq.
David Evans Esq.
Rev. Kenneth Hayes
P. Emanuelli Esq.
Mrs Beryl Williams

Rev. Erastus Jones
Mrs Lun Jones
Rev. Derek Nuttall
Ray Cottrell Esq.
William Donoghue Esq.

Cemetery and Memorial Garden Committee

Bryn Carpenter Esq., Chairman.
Douglas Pearson Esq., J.P.
William Tudor Esq.
Trevor Emanuel Esq.
David Pryce Esq.
Wyndham Thomas Esq.
Maureen Hughes.
Cliff Minnett Esq.

Glyn Jenkins Esq.
Rev. Kenneth Hayes.
Cyril C. L. Vaughan Esq.
Mrs Sheila Lewis.
Mrs Elaine Richards.
Brian Hodkinson Esq.
Richard Davies Esq.
Mrs Emily Griffiths.

From Disaster Fund Two New Charities Established in December 1988
Education Charity

Cyril C. L. Vaughan Esq., Chairman.
William Tudor Esq.
Bryn Carpenter Esq.
Elwyn Roberts Esq., of
Cooper Lybrand Accountants

Douglas Pearson Esq., J.P.
Rev. Kenneth Hayes.
Geraint Davies Esq. of
Thornton Baker Accountants

Aberfan Memorial Charity

Bryn Carpenter Esq., Chairman
Glyn Jenkins Esq.
Malcolm Jones Esq.
Cyril C. L. Vaughan Esq.
Elwyn Roberts Esq.,
of Cooper Lybrand Accountants.

Rev. Kenneth Hayes
William Tudor Esq.
Douglas Pearson Esq., J.P.
Geraint Davies Esq. of
Thornton Baker Accountants.

Community Promotions Executive

Mr Cled Davies (Chairman)
Mrs Joan Bennett
Mrs Eileen Bunford
Rev. Judy Davies
Rev. Neil Davies
Mrs Enid Edwards
Mrs Beryl (Evans) Williams
Mrs Sally Fletcher
Mr William Griffiths
Ms Maureen Hughes

Mr C. Vaughan (Vice-Chairman)
Mrs Peggy Brunt
Mr Ray Cottrell
Mrs Mary V. Davies
Mr William Dinnage
Mrs P. Emanuelli
Mr Tudor Evans
Mrs Nesta Flynn
Mrs T. Iverson

Community Promotions Executive (continued)

Mr Jack James
Mr Cyril Johnson
Mrs Cath Jones
Mr Charles Jones
Mr Malcolm Jones
Mrs Sheila Lewis
Mr William J. O'Brien
Mrs Val O'Brien
Mr William Penn
Mr Robert Pye
Mrs Doris Richards
Mrs Beryl Rowe
Mrs Olwen Small
Mr Haulfryn Thomas
Mr Wyndham Thomas
Rev. June Vaughan, B.A.
Mrs Beryl Williams

Mrs Freda Johnson
Mrs Ellen Jones
Rev. Erastus Jones
Mr Derek Lavington
Rev. Derek Nuttal
Coun. Mr Thomas O'Brien
Mr Douglas Pearson, J.P.
Mr Stuart Phillips
Mr Glyn Rees
Dr Ken Roberts
Rev. Michael Short
Mrs Nanwen Smith
Mrs Alwen Thomas
M. C. C. L. Vaughan
Mrs Mary Veck
Mrs Delphi Williams

Administration & Finance Executive

Mr Cyril C. L. Vaughan (Chairman)
Mr Viv Bennett
Mr Sid Chilcott
Mrs Mary Cotter, J.P.
Mr William Donoghue
Mr John Emanuelli
Mr Colin England
Mr David Evans
Mr William Griffiths
Mr Jack Hamer
Miss Mair E. Jones
Mr Trevor Jones
Mr Michael Lynch
Mrs Sheila Mulcahy
Mr Terrence O'Connor
Mr Douglas Pearson, J.P.
Miss Phoebe Phillips
Mr Jack Prosser
Mrs Elaine Richards
Mr William Tudor

Rev. Kenneth Hayes (Vice-Chairman)
Mr Bryn Carpenter
Mr Ray Cottrell
Mr D. Cled Davies
Mr Jeffrey Edwards
Mr Pinno Emanuelli
Mrs Bernadette Estebanez
Mr Tony Evans
Mr Peter Gwyther
Mrs Lun Jones
Mr Malcolm Jones
Mr Glyn Jenkins
Mr Maldwyn Morgan
Rev. Derek Nuttal
Mr Terrence O'Brien
Mr John H. Phillips
Mr Tom Price
Mr David Pryce
Mr Emlyn Richards
Mrs Beryl Williams

17.   A Visit to Bristol Zoo - 1967

Michael came home from school breathless and excited, "Can I go on a school trip to Bristol Zoo?". My immediate reaction was, "No! You're too young", the coach may crash, you may lose yourself, or fall into the Lion's pit - all unspoken words. All irrational fears.

The real reason was the refusal to trust a child with anyone else since October 21st 1966. We tried to protect our children like the proverbial Mother hen, we attached them to our apron strings by a piece of elastic, we only allowed them to go so far before being zinged back to the safety of our arms.

'No' we want to say, but we cannot, we must not, we must let them go for their own sake.

Tuesday arrives equipped with sandwiches, cake, squash, apples, sweets, chocolate, money, new trousers, new anorak and Michael was ready. We met at the school and the children cheered as they saw the five coaches coming down the hill.

Mrs Bailey's voice boomed, "When the coaches come in do <u>not</u> move, stay where you are, do not move until your teacher tells you." Quietly and obediently they responded. "I wish they'd listen to me like that" says one mother. Quietly and obediently they get on the coach, class by class. We each seek our own child for that last contact, that last smile and wave from the window. They are ready to leave on time, no one was late.

One jovial driver looks towards us and shouts, "You don't want this lot back do you? I'll dump them on the way".

I'll never forget that moment, no one moved, no one spoke, it was meant as a joke but we couldn't appreciate it. If only that driver knew the wealth of his cargo, how much it has cost us to entrust our little ones into his hands. 'God let them come home safely' was our silent prayer. They leave, we strain to catch the final glimpse. We did not say 'be good', our constant prayer is 'Life be good to them'.

We return home to a silent emptiness that we had not noticed before when they were at school. It's 10.00 a.m. only six hours and they'll be home.

At 3.30 p.m. we arrive at the school. Mothers and fathers were saying, "I hope they won't be late'. The first coach arrives, we ask, everyone alright? trying to keep a normal pitch to our voice. "Yes, of course, what did you expect?"

We find our child and hold his hand, the hand we've longed to hold all day. At home he opens his duffle bag and pulls out the treasure; a pen for Judith, a knife for Peter (Mrs Bailey didn't see that), a lion's head for Mammy and Daddy, sticks of rock for Gran, Grandma and Grampa.

No more questions so off to bed; say your prayers, "Lord keep us safe this night'.

Thank you Lord.

JUNE VAUGHAN

Pantglas Junior School trip to Bristol Zoo

18. Gift from Aberfan

Just a fortnight after the Aberfan Disaster, the attention of the world was turned towards the floods in Florence. Some of our bereaved sent their children's clothes to help the children of that city.

Ties of kindness

This almost-forgotten act struck a chord in the hearts of some prominent Italians. They sought a permanent means of expressing their feelings. They wrote: "It is our wish that the memory of those children may live and be perpetuated - beyond death and suffering - in a token of gratitude and homage to the rush of solidarity of the mothers. A homage from a people who revere the cult and poetry of those feelings which bind together mankind with the simple and humble ties of kindness."

Marble Plaque

So they produced a bas-relief plaque on marble, measuring 36 inches by 28. It is the work of one of the donators, Angelo della Lorre, director of the Fine Arts Academy of Rome. They are presenting it "to the people of Aberfan" as an expression of "thankfulness of the Italian people."

HEADWAY, SEPTEMBER 1970

19. Community Conference

Merthyr Vale School, on Saturday, 11 May 1968, bore witness to the determined commitment of the community in wresting itself from the dismal depths of October 1966, in an effort to forge a way forward into the future. Individuals had, for some time, been successfully treading that difficult path, but now, it was together we met in hope and faith to envisage recovery on a broader front, no mean task for a community so ravaged.

Of course the conference called that day was not one of a spontaneous nature, much delicate and dedicated groundwork had been in motion for some time. Not least to thank for this spadework were the Canadian people, who so generously gave their money, culminating in the setting up of "Ty Toronto", a caravan which came to mean so much in subsequent days.

Staffing that caravan was the Rev. Erastus Jones and his wife Lun, two Welsh speaking folk. Soon they enlisted the experience of the Tavistock Institute of Human Relations and the Department of Sociology of University College, Swansea. Together, with local assistance, the group called the local community together. And the response was made in a positive manner when representatives of local 'groups' plus the Parents and Residents, formed after the Disaster, came to Merthyr Vale School that day and discussed 'Communication, Purpose and Programme' with earnest vigour.

Folk present enthusiastically voted the venture a measured success but appreciating full well that 'talking' although so necessary, had eventually to lead to 'doing', a transition to 'coats off' and 'rolled up sleeves' and not a few heartaches in the process.

It is a matter of history now that the transition was effectively accomplished and a hard working Community Association formed with a rising mountain of problems to face. Included in those was the management of the new Community Centre, something on which the young Association had to sharpen its teeth. The 'Way Ahead' for Merthyr Vale and Aberfan was not made without its tears, for tragedy had left behind mists of doubt and fears which sorely affected our deliberations and adjudications.

But thank God, we've arrived on the side of the many obstacles met on that road and there are many more positives than negatives to remember from those days. Of course, there is still the 'Way Ahead', it will always be so, and we can be confident that that challenge will continue to encourage leaders to rise from within our midst and meet and deal with it. What sort of community will be fashioned depends on many things, but one in particular that overrides the remainder, is you and if you do not find the standard of community that you hoped for … well!

Our own measured success in the local experience encouraged a further vision for Ras and Lun Jones as they lifted their eyes beyond our own community to those who lay on the other sides of our mountains, so close but not yet near.

So it was that in 1973 the call went out from our midst:

"We call upon the people during 1974 to examine themselves, to go back over their own story, to rediscover what has made them what they are, to choose together in a new age, what they are going to be."

Yes. That call too, was heard, conferences were held and for a while, the Valleys were stirred, to what extent only the future will reveal. Sufficient interest was generated to bring about a publication "The Valleys call for self-examination" by the people of the South Wales Valleys during the "Year of the Valleys 1974."

CYRIL JOHNSON, 1992

<u>Note:</u> "The Community Conference" written by Rev. Erastus Jones, from Ty Toronto, Aberfan 1976, contains a more detailed account of the two successful exercises mentioned above.

Community Exhibition for all organisation represented on the Community Association, 1980

20. Headway: The Early Years

Community newspapers have never caught on in the Valleys. After all, news can spread through a valley quicker than a journalist can plug in a word processor. Yet the people of Aberfan and Merthyr Vale have had a free community magazine delivered to them each month for over twenty years.

It all began in the immediate post-Disaster period. Many of the normal channels had become blocked while others were carrying rumour and supposition rather than hard fact. At the 'Way Ahead' village conferences there was general agreement that a regular and efficient means of communication was needed if the rifts and divisions in the community were to be repaired. The slogan that emerged was 'everyone must get the same story at the same time'. If that objective was to be met any proposed publication would have to be distributed free to every home.

While the financial and practical implications of that first principle were being discussed thought was also being given to the kind of publication needed. It was obvious at the time that the sensitive nature of the post-Disaster situation had to be taken into account. Many of the invaders from Fleet Street had shown how easy it was to touch the community on the raw. This danger was underlined when the cover of the first issue of our own magazine brought an angry reaction. One of the photographs reproduced was supposed to be of Merthyr Vale but at first glance, seemed to be just of the colliery.

So some carefully thought-out guidelines were laid down. The magazine should be positive not negative; objective rather than subjective; good humoured but not hearty; local without being parochial; confident but never arrogant; educative without being stuffy; entertaining without being silly. And when an eight-year-old suggested that it should be called 'Headway' we also realised that it had to be forward looking.

In the first issue of July 1969, the editor attempted a summary of the Headway philosophy. He underlined the difference between this magazine and most of the professional and commercial publications. Headway's aim was to build or repair the bridges by providing a reliable and consistent version of what was happening in the community. This rather novel approach was illustrated in the first edition by the fact that Prime Minister Harold Wilson's visit was reported on page 9 while the lead story was a transcript of an address on the topic of togetherness.

Yet even though many of Fleet Street's news values were being turned on their head, there was an attempt to copy the newsgathering and presentation techniques of the full-time journalists. So rather than have a committee we had an editor, an art editor, a photographer and a circulation and business manager. A team of regular reporters and feature writers was picked, and everything they wrote was given a byline. This meant everyone knew who was responsible for everything that was being published and the onus was on each individual to develop their skills and knowledge. While everyone accepted the challenge, those involved with the printing and production process experienced the greatest difficulties. For the first two years Headway was printed on an office duplicator operated by standing in an empty bath in the Ty Toronto caravan.

The July 1971 anniversary issue underlined the scale of the Headway operation. At that time there were around forty people involved in producing and distributing the magazine to every home. Some of those listed were occasional contributors, but the bulk of the editorial, production and distribution teams found themselves on a relentless treadmill. Their workload was increased when printing was transferred to a second hand offset press which required new layout and photography techniques as well as a crash course in the art of the master printer. Given the weight of that burden, it is not surprising that production ground to a halt in 1975.

But less than a twelve month later, the 'Merthyr Express' was heralding the re-appearance of its 'rival'. A few of the original team had returned together with a new band of volunteers. These included a network of district correspondents; a response to frequent complaints that outlaying areas, like Mount Pleasant and Aberfan Fawr were being neglected.

The first break in production illustrates the nature of the Headway enterprise and why it has survived over twenty years. It also gives an insight into the strength of community that still exists. For despite the immense sacrifice of time and energy involved, and the often unrewarding response, or lack of it, there has always been a sizeable number of people willing to become involved. This level of commitment is even more significant when we remember that all of them were amateurs faced with 'learning on the job' and under the scrutiny of the whole community. As the first editor remarked, whatever its' failings and lack of expertise, we could justifiably claim that Headway was 'all our own work.'

Many of the learners proved to have considerable talents. 'Old Timer', the first sports reporter combined a wide range of sporting knowledge with an elegant writing style. And 'Jane's Page' was from the beginning a splendid mix of pithy comment and practical advice. The magazine format provided the space for these special talents and allowed Headway to go far beyond 'telling everyone the same story.'

An example of this can be found in almost any edition during the first five years. In January 1970 for example, there was an article about the proposed clean up of Aberfan and Merthyr Vale. Jane was concerned about a slippery path leading from Bryngoleu to Ynysowen School and Ynysowen Choir received a glowing review for their first annual concert. Old Timer was attacking the spread of bad sportsmanship and the "Prize Puzzles" feature was offering a first prize of 10/-. A preview of the year looked forward to hearing more of 'the Ynysowen Sound', that was, Ynysowen Male Voice Choir, Ynysowen Junior School Choir, and the Darby and Joan Choir. New buildings to be completed during the year included Bethania Chapel, St. Mary's Church, the Nursery School, a new house for the catholic priest and public toilets at the foot of Station Hill. Also promised for 1970 was the plaque for the Memorial Garden, a new bridge to Perthygleision and the first stage of the new community centre. There was a 'stage whisper' about the proposed new drama group, an early reminder about the second community concert and of what was then, the Youth Centre Carnival.

That sample issue shows how appropriate the magazine's name. It did seem that the community was making Headway on a large number of fronts. In her book published in 1974, Joan Miller attempted to assess Headway's contribution to the process of rebuilding and redevelopment. While recognising how difficult it was to provide an accurate evaluation and admitting that some people thought that the money spent on the magazine was not justified, she did reach a generally favourable conclusion. In her opinion Headway had gone far beyond its original remit of 'simple rumour scorching and handing-out of official information … it has standards of journalism and design to be commended … it does much to make people know they belong together: it passes on local items of news: collects memories of the old days; includes comment on current affairs; and tries to include all matters that are, or should be, of interest to everyone in the village.' She concludes with a very flattering assessment that may contain an element of truth: 'It is hard to think of anything else that in so short a time could have produced a feeling of cohesion and solidarity in the community.'

KEN ROBERTS, 1991

21. A Fo Pen Bid Bont

I have learned, with a feeling of sadness, of the imminent move of the Rev. Erastus and Mrs Lun Jones from our community to Porthmadoc.

My first unforgettable meeting with Ras and Lun was in their caravan, Ty Toronto. It was sited opposite the old library near the bridge which joins Aberfan to Merthyr Vale. Lun, the ever-industrious and efficient typist and secretary, busy at the keyboard. Ras gazed out at the mist-shrouded hills. The bridge, Aberfan and Merthyr Vale, the mist and the two newcomers, viewed retrospectively, was a significant tableau. The symbol of the Community Association was to be a bridge and a torch. Ras and Lun became the bridge's keystone. They provided the vision that widened our enlightenment and helped disperse the mist of doubt and despair that pressed down on us following the devastating experience of October, 1966.

The arrival of Ras and Lun, when our village was riven by stress, conflict and despondency, with their practical Christianity did much to point our future way. Whenever they realised an objective was right, their determination to carry out that policy was unshakeable. They taught a lesson of the significance of the events and a real involvement being a balm to sensitive wounds.

I continue to admire the time and effort they devoted to helping restore our community. The careful planning of conferences which were the foundation of our Community Association.

Ty Toronto is a name which will always be linked with Valleys' history in the twentieth century. It was Ras who initiated the Call of the Valleys project. Their joint work with the Churches' Council and their inspiration and dedication to Headway continue to enhance village life. In the wider context, they have been zealous in fund-raising for the under privileged.

The motto of Pantglas Secondary School was 'A fo pen bid bont' - 'Whoever is head let him be a bridge'. Ras and Lun have been precisely that.

In their deserved retirement, I am sure our whole community will join me in wishing our friends health and continuing happiness.

CYRIL C. L. VAUGHAN.
CHAIRMAN, ABERFAN AND MERTHYR VALE COMMUNITY ASSOCIATION.
HEAD WAY, OCTOBER 1985

22. Presentation

Attending one of their last Headway Committee meetings the Rev. Erastus and Mrs Lun Jones were surprised guests of a presentation party.

To mark their many years of devoted service to Headway, other committee members had sneakily schemed a special evening in their honour.

Centrepiece was the presentation to them, by Editor, Lyn Evans, of a painting commissioned from artist, Mr Reg Chandler.

The picture, a striking representation of Merthyr Vale Colliery seen from a view point on the Canal Bank, was received with obvious pleasure by Mr and Mrs Jones.

HEADWAY, OCTOBER 1985

23. 20 Years

A message from Lord Cledwyn, formerly Cledwyn Hughes, a Government minister at the time:-

I am grateful to the Editor of HEADWAY for affording me this opportunity to send a message to all its readers and the community generally on this twentieth anniversary of the Aberfan Disaster. I do so in the knowledge that although time, mercifully, can heal, it can never entirely erase the memory and the pain of the appalling tragedy which befell Aberfan on 21st October 1966. On that fateful morning, I was opening the Alaw Reservoir in my constituency of Anglesey and during the proceedings a message came through that an accident had occurred at a school near Merthyr Tydfil. But as further information followed, it became clear that a grave and critical mishap had taken place and I arranged for a helicopter from RAF Valley to fly me down to Merthyr from Amlwch. It was not until I arrived that the magnitude of the disaster became apparent to Sir Goronwy Daniel, then Permanent Secretary at the Welsh Office, and myself. What followed was the saddest and most traumatic experience of my political life and it remains with me to this day. I was taken to the site and to the chapel which served as a mortuary. We were profoundly shocked and grieved and decided that we would seek to apply ourselves at once to the difficult tasks which had to be performed. I still recall with respect and gratitude the courage and devotion of so many local people and of members of the various services who worked long and unstintingly in a desperate situation.

The whole nation mourned the loss of Aberfan's children and its leaders came to Aberfan to show their deepfelt sympathy, and in the following days that sympathy flowed across national boundaries and became worldwide.

Our final thoughts, however, must be with those who lost their dear ones and I know that all of us send our messages of sympathy and understanding as we did twenty years ago.

HEADWAY, NOVEMBER 1986

24. My Memories of Aberfan over the last seventeen years

Sara Mclean, second from right front row.

I was only eight years old when the Aberfan Disaster happened. I honestly do not remember it at the time, I was into 'Blue Peter' and the like. So October 1966 meant nothing. It was at the age of eighteen that I learnt of the devastation and tragedy of the Aberfan Disaster. I learned how the world was drawn to the needs of that small community. Money and support came and went. In recent years I have learnt more about the tragedy as the many anniversaries occur.

I first came to Aberfan with an Ecumenical Youth Group at the age of eighteen. Even at that age I had no idea where Aberfan was. All I knew was that it was a mining village that had had this disaster many years before. The year was 1976, ten years after the disaster. My parents had visited Aberfan so they had filled me in on details that I had known little about. Our mission, if that is the word, was to build a garden near the Post Office and beautify the waste ground. Ron Scrivens, who had retired as a mason with the Borough Council, was in charge of the building work. There were about twenty of us young people. There were many Europeans. Germans and Swiss, Swedes and Italians. There was I, a very naive eighteen year old from Northern Ireland, having to share a large hall to sleep, eat and be merry in. I, who had never shared a room at home, let alone a room with several young men.

The leader of our group was a young Irish Jesuit priest called Charlie Davey and there was also a young curate who did his bit but was in charge of the Parish while his Vicar was on holiday.

There was a system when it came to cleaning the room and preparing the food. I remember the only thing I could cook at the time was tuna fish pie but tuna was too expensive for our budget, so it ended up mackerel pie which didn't quite have the taste to it.

The people of Aberfan made us most welcome. Maureen Hughes was the person I made most contact with. We had communicated by letter beforehand. I had written to her to find out what I needed to bring with me, a sleeping bag, etc. Maureen was most helpful and has been a friend to me to this day. She has a son the same age as I and we spent a few off hours walking the hills around the village. These hills are where the slag heaps were scattered. I visit Maureen as often as I can.

The Jenkins family were also very kind to me. They took me in when I was struck down with food poisoning, most likely my fish-pie! I was sorry to learn of Mrs Jenkins' death a few years ago. Dave Jenkins and I keep in touch though.

The garden that I helped build is still a centre point, to this day, of the village. The villagers are able to meet and sit and gossip in the fine weather.

Unfortunately, I have lost touch with the others from the group. Simone, the Italian guy, and I kept in touch for a couple of years. We met up again in Germany when I went there to live in 1977. There was another Northern Irish girl in the group. She is now married but that is all I know about her.

On my last visit to Aberfan in the Summer of 1988 I was able to see the change. My dog and I enjoyed our days walking along this part of the River Taff. The place looks totally different during the Summer months. In the Winter time, I could envisage a bleakness about the place.

Another point that I was very aware of during my initial stay in Aberfan, was the lack of young people my age around the village. This fact brought home to me the true devastation of the disaster.

The Community Centre, which was built from funds received during the Disaster Appeal, was an impressive building. The Youth Group used the swimming pool regularly during our time off. On our last day we were all given a reception at the Community Centre and presented with a plaque to remind us of our month in Aberfan. It is that reception that I will always remember.

Aberfan has taken twenty years to recover from the disaster and the Aberfan that I see now is full of optimism. I remember walking up in the mountains where the dreaded slag heaps used to stand and looking down on the valley below. The slag heaps are now scattered and a new road runs through the valley. These have been positive steps. I once saw a postcard of Aberfan showing these slag heaps. The photograph was taken in the early sixties. The whole village was in shadow. To look at the village today is to see a light and happy place which looks to the future but still remembers the sadness of the past.

SARA MCLEAN, OCTOBER 1990

Opening of Work Camp Garden

25. Remembering Aberfan

Places unknown, unheard of by the world at large, can suddenly hit the headlines. How many of us had heard of Bhopal or Chernobyl before the chemical and nuclear disasters put them on the map? Who, for that matter, has heard of Hiroshima or Nagasaki?

Or of Aberfan? Twenty years ago, on 21st October, 1966, tragedy struck the South Wales mining village of Aberfan. A towering coal-tip slithered on to a school, killing one hundred and sixteen children and several adults.

With a population of about three thousand, Aberfan was just another mining village with little to distinguish it from any others in South Wales. Following that terrible day, the whole world had heard of it. Few disasters have aroused so much emotion, probably because so many children were its victims.

Unable to do anything but send money, people across the world contributed with the intention of helping the bereaved families, providing resources for the children who survived, and rebuilding hope in the shattered village. One and three quarter million pounds was received.

I knew the village of Aberfan before 1966, and a while ago, I visited the cemetery in which the children were buried and stood alongside the orderly row of graves on its bleak hillside. It was hard not to weep. As I stood there reflectively, a woman I imagined to be a grandmother of one of the children, knelt by a tiny grave and placed flowers in a vase.

Life moves on, as it must. Last month I drove past Aberfan - in fact, right across where the lethal coal-tip lay, for recently a new section of motorway has opened there. That motorway, I feel, is symbolic; how easy it is to drive past without a thought. Motorists are not allowed to stop alongside motorways, but if they could, I can imagine an authorised lay-by, simply so that we could pause before this great sorrow and let it be a reminder of this and other human tragedies.

Yet that motorway symbolises a deeper truth. It takes us away from the tragedy. We cannot dwell on past sorrows - they have happened and nothing can undo them. Restitution, as far as humanly possible, has been made. We must try to commit victims and dear ones to God in faith and hope, knowing that the love we had for them does not end at death.

"Love is eternal" said Paul (1 Corinthians 13:8 GNB). Three times in the Book of Psalms we read: "The Lord is gracious and compassionate" (Psalm 111:4 NEB) and this is our greatest consolation.

We remember Aberfan, give thanks for all who helped, and pray that those who sorrow after twenty years may find the peace and strength of God, as well as hope in his gift of eternal life.

Remembering Aberfan.

In recalling a great tragedy, Rev. Dr. David Owen reminds us that love does not end at the grave.

REPRINTED FROM 'WOMAN'S WEEKLY' OCTOBER 1986

26. Yet Again

Cemetery Memorial Arches

Return again
The ceaseless pen
A path to climb, so steep
Parents stand
Hand in hand
Where little children sleep.

Pilgrims walk
And soft-voice talk
Beside the multitude
Others pray
Thoughts to stray
In soul-search solitude.

Life so still
Upon that hill
In silence, profound thought
How much coal
For each lost soul
The tragedy it brought.

TOM BELLION.

27. I Put Pen to Paper

Thank you for giving me the opportunity to make a contribution to this Commemorative Book. The tragic event which occurred on the 21st October, 1966 robbed you of so many of your younger generation. Your grief was shared throughout Britain and the world.

However, as was so clearly demonstrated in your commemorative television programme*, love and hope continued to shine through your sorrow and I was so stirred by this that I put pen to paper to share with you the ways in which your experience has also affected my own life and outlook and my future activities.

1966 was in many ways a year of sorrow for me too. In fact I began the year at the Midnight Watch Service at my church, praying to God for His help as I faced what lay before me. The year to begin was the one in which I knew I was to lose my beloved Mother "in the Spring" and I sobbed as the church bells rang out twelve times to herald the New Year.

Mum died on Sunday the 6th March 1966 and within a few months we faced new anxieties as my nine year old son fought against kidney disease under the care and treatment of Dr Kiedon, Consultant Paediatric Physician at Alder Hey Children's Hospital. Early in October, Dr Kiedon informed me that David's condition was proving resistent to conventional treatments so he intended to change to a new type of treatment which he was using on some of his leukaemia patients but it would be the first time he had tried it to treat kidney disease. Dr Kiedon emphasised that the treatment must be continued for a six week period if it was to succeed and David had to have frequent blood tests to monitor its effect.

On the morning of the 21st October 1966 my husband telephoned me from work to say he had just heard some awful news. My fearful response was "Dr Kiedon has died!!" - much to my husband's surprise! He corrected me by giving me the awful news about the disaster taking place in Aberfan, and we spent the remainder of that day in tears and prayers, and many times after that too, for your little ones. We knew so well what it was like to fear for the life of a loved one, the sense of helpless desperation.

I could not dispel my sudden apprehensions about the welfare of Dr Kiedon. My son was by then halfway through his new and vital treatment. We attended clinic on the 27th October. Dr Kiedon was late due to fog and my apprehensions niggled at me. After his examination of my son, Dr Kiedon gave us both a cheerful "Goodbye" and I looked back to see him sitting at his desk, waving to us. He died the next evening with cerebral haemorrage! My husband heard the news first and brought it home to me, and you can imagine our feelings, sorrow mixed with despair for our son's future health!!

At his next clinic check up a week later, David was seen by Dr Kiedon's Registrar who told me she had only been at Alder Hay for two weeks and by some miracle the only lecture she had been to had been by Dr Kiedon on the treatment he was giving my son and she would follow it through on the guidelines he had given. Six months later David was on the road to recovery and I hope that many other children benefitted too.

The association of events, the tragic loss of so many children in Aberfan, Dr Kiedon's death a week later, the continuation of his treatment beyond death, which saved my son's life and health, all served to awake in me the driving force to pay back our miracle, to share it by helping to save the lives of sick children.

In 1967 I first started fundraising through my son's school, Malvern County Primary School, Merseyside, for the provision of investigative urological equipment for Alder Hay. However, I wanted to extend this to something more enduring and in March 1968 I founded the 'Alder Hay Children's Kidney Fund'. I remained its Chairman for twenty one years, retiring in 1989, then becoming one of its Patrons. By then the Fund had raised one million pounds with much generous help from groups and the public, and established the first specialist children's kidney unit in the country, and two permanent Research Fellowships at the University of Liverpool under the direction of Consultants at Alder Hey, and many other facilities. This work goes on.

Our Annual General Meeting falls in October and I have never been able to approach this month without remembering the children and bereaved of Aberfan and Dr Kiedon. I believe he joined them in Heaven and will have helped to guard them too, as he did my son and countless other youngsters.

Because of those events of 1966, hundreds of sick children have benefitted from new cures found

* *"Aberfan - 25 years of Experience" Produced for Channel Four by The Video Workshop. Chapter Arts Centre, Cardiff*

through research programmes, helping them recover and avoid dialysis, and for those for whom dialysis was necessary, A.H.C.K.F. made it available when it was unavailable from other sources. Many of these patients have now had successful transplants, some are now parents themselves, several have come from Wales.

Please accept these successful endeavours, arising as they did out of shared grief, as a tribute to those you loved and lost, whose deaths influenced me to start them. May they rest in peace and may those who continue to mourn also find peace.

May I also offer my congratulations on the courage and manifold achievements of the people of Aberfan and Merthyr Vale since 1966 and thank them for their shining example in such grief.

May God bless you all!

AUDREY WILSON.

28. Children of the Valleys

Past and present meet on a nostalgic trip to South Wales.

We were strangers in the village, which is a few miles south of Merthyr Tydfil. But that day, my sister-in-law who was on a visit from New York, had expressed a curiosity about the mining valleys.

She wanted to see them, and the place where a terrible tragedy had occurred some years ago. So I offered to drive her there.

It was a very Welsh sort of day, low clouds, a westerly breeze, the rain just keeping off. The pylons were like monster guardians marching over the moors which stretched mistily on either side of the valley road.

'How can they do that to the landscape?' Jennie complained. 'Where are the Welsh poets? Why don't they rage, rage against this difigurement?'

It is hard to explain, but we are fond of our pylons. They are part of the landscape, making an honest Welsh statement. We are a bit ambivalent about tourism, and I recalled the so-called motto of the Welsh Tourist Board, taken from 'Men of Harlech': 'Ever they shall rue the day they ventured o'er the border.'

It took a while to find the village. Welsh sign-posting means that you really have to know where things are. The old familiar landmarks of winding gears have gone and sheep now graze where the slag-heaps were. But with sharp eyes the traveller can pick up clues: a letter box set into the front wall of a cottage and 'Penydarren Post Office' in small letters over the door.

Finally we reached our destination. A modest village it is, with rows of tidy new houses. On a street corner a group of youths started shouting at us. At first I ignored them; yobbos, I thought. Then I heard what they were shouting! 'You've got a puncture, lady!' They were right. 'Got a spare? Got a jack? We'll change it for you!' The boys crowded round, five of them, aged about 12 and 13. 'He's a mechanic. He can do it.' they insisted, looking at the eldest, who might have been 14.

'All right,' I said.

They found the spare and the jack. There was no spanner, but one of the boys happened to have one on him. They all got down to it, some of them hammering at the obstinate nuts, others offering advice. When it was done and everything put tidily away they said 'OK then' and moved away, back to their pitch on the street corner, not even expecting a tip.

"You won't find that in New York City,' said Jennie.

It had got quite late by now and we had a date in Merthyr. We looked up the hill to the cemetery through the trees and saw rows of identical graves. There wasn't time now to visit.

As we passed out of the village we passed a new school building. Of course we will never forget the children who died when the slag slid down the mountain. But now I shall also remember, with gratitude, the living children of Aberfan.

CYNTHIA LANGDON DAVIES, 1992.
REPRINTED FROM THE 'LADY

Bethania Chapel, Aberfan.
"Where the youngsters stand"

29. Bryn and Betty

Bryn Carpenter is the dedicated Chairman of the Committee looking after the Cemetery Memorial and the Memorial Garden. He is married to Betty. He has his own special way of saying her name, lingering over each syllable, which reveals how deep his affection is for her.

"Betty never complains. I am only able to carry out these duties thanks to her support" he admits. They met in the Merthyr Vale Colliery. Betty was working in the colliery canteen and Bryn was working in the lamp room. He would take a jug over to the canteen to collect tea for all the boys and Betty would fill the jug and that is how they met.

Everything that was served in the colliery canteen was home-made and it was not only the pit workers who came to the canteen for their meals, people who were working in the local shops, would also come there at lunch time. They would buy a check in the morning and surrender it when they came back for their meal. This way Betty and the other women working there would know how many were coming in for a meal and they would not have to be collecting money at their busiest time.

The canteen would be that busy that there would be nine women working on one shift. The first shift would start at five o'clock in the morning and the last one would finish at eleven o'clock at night. Out and about in the village, the women would be greeted by men working in the pit but they very rarely recognised them. Betty and the other women would be too busy to look up when they were working

Betty's father was known in the village as the "Welsh Caruso". He was well-known for his beautiful voice and a member of Ashton's Choir. Betty was well-known in the colliery for her "Teisan Lap". She recalls with amusement her days in Pantglas School and lessons with Miss Davies 'Cookery'. Miss Davies told Betty that she would never make a good cake because she didn't have light enough hands. Some years later, soon after she had married Bryn, Betty entered a fruit cake in the Bryntaf Carnival. There were a lot of entries, which had to use 'Nunbetta' flour. Miss Davies, 'Cookery' was the judge. "She didn't know who was who " laughed Betty, "and she gave me the second prize which was worth 7/6d."

Bryn was in the colliery all his working life. He was the longest serving member of the NUM Lodge. He says that Merthyr Vale was a 'family pit'. "You'd do your work but you would go to work feeling happy about going there."

Today Bryn works just as hard as the Chairman of the Cemetery Memorial and the Memorial Garden Committee. He does this work because he wants to serve the bereaved families, of which, his is just one. He has been the Chairman for over twenty six years. He pays tribute to all the individuals and organisations who, over the years, have donated to the upkeep of the Memorials and he strives to see that the standards are maintained. The Cemetery Committee bears the cost of all the shrubs and flowers and have made alterations for the better. Grass and lawns have proved beneficial to the appearance and maintenance of the Cemetery Memorial and the families appreciate the loving care that the memorials receive. Generous people, including many senior citizens and choirs who have given concerts, including our own Ynysowen Choir, have made this loving care possible. Visitors are pleased to see the area being so well looked after. Many of them may have given donations towards its upkeep or contributed to the Disaster Fund.

The Cemetery Memorial Committee is a source of strength and support to Bryn. He is full of praise for the Council employees working in the Aberfan Cemetery for their concern and understanding and commends the Cemetery Memorial's own gardener, Phillip Carpenter, for his care and dedication.

Dear Betty. Always the same, warm, welcoming and serene. Dear Bryn, dedicated and determined, honest and fair. A winning combination, formed when their eyes met over a jug of tea.

MAUREEN HUGHES, 1992

Bryn Carpenter retired as Chairman of the Cemetery Memorial Committee in 1994 after nearly twenty eight years of service.

Bryn Carpenter third from the left with Bryntaf Carnival Committee and Peter Hughes Perthygleision Farm and his tractor.

30. Aberfan At The Public Record Office

Now that thirty years have passed since the disaster, the public can see some of the papers about Aberfan in the Government and Coal Board records of 1966-1969. These were opened to the public at the Public Record Office in Kew, London, on 2nd January 1997. They include letters between Government Ministers and civil Servants in the Welsh Office and the Ministry of Power, and the files from the office of Lord Robens, the Chairman of the National Coal Board. They show that the behaviour of the Coal Board after the disaster was even worse than was generally realised at the time. I have written two articles about this - one of them appeared in The Observer on 5th January 1997 and the other in The Times Higher Education Supplement on 17th January 1997. I have found a number of other damaging documents, not mentioned in either article. For instance, Lord Robens simply scribbled 'Hard Luck - R' across a letter from Cyril Moseley, of Morgan Bruce & Nicholas (the solicitors for the Aberfan Parents' and Residents' Association) requesting a meeting of both sides' experts in April 1967.

The Public Record Office produced a guide to these records for journalists, and it is probably now available in the Search Room. Anybody may use the Public Record Office, and I would be glad to give advice on what records it might be helpful to look at.

I know that people's feelings in Aberfan about the disaster still run very deep. I have tried not to re-open any local hurt - apart from factual details of what happened, my articles are entirely about the behaviour of Senior Coal Board Officials, Government ministers, and civil servants. They deliberately do not name anybody from the Aberfan area who was involved in the disaster.

While I was writing the articles, I read the records of the disaster that are held in the Central Library in Merthyr. These are in bad condition, and I intend to apply for a grant so that they can be conserved and catalogued. If I succeed in raising the money, the work could be done in Summer and Autumn 1997. These records do not include the huge volume of letters of condolence received from all over the world and held until recently at Aberfan. I did not ask to see any of those.

My two recent visits to Merthyr to look at these records were my first visits to the area since the early 1970's (when I spent some time in Merthyr while writing my biography of Keir Hardie, which appeared in 1975). I am very grateful for the warm and helpful reception I got from everyone I spoke to. Please do not hesitate to let me know what you think about my articles - whether favourable or unfavourable!

Iain McLean Professor of Politics, Oxford University, Nuffield College, Oxford, OX1 1NF.

'Headway'
March 1997

31. Headway May 1997

Professor Iain Mclean, Nuffield College, Oxford writes to let 'Headway' know that he has applied to the British Academy for a grant to catalogue the papers in Merthyr Tydfil Central Library concerning Aberfan, and that he expects a decision in late May. In the autumn a further article by Professor Mclean on the issues surrounding the Aberfan Disaster and its aftermath will be published in 20th Century British History.

Copies of Professor Mclean's articles for the 'Observer' newspaper and the Times Higher Education Supplement are still available from the 'Headway' office or the Thrift Shop.

32. Oxford Don Gets Funds To Save Aberfan Papers

Iain McLean, Professor of Politics at Oxford University, has been awarded a grant of £4,000 by the British Academy to preserve and catalogue the records of the 1966 Aberfan Disaster that are held in Merthyr Library. The Library has one of the few extant sets of the evidence taken by the Tribunal of Inquiry into the disaster. The then government promised in 1966 that this evidence would be published, but it never was. Merthyr Library also has a poignant collection of newspapers from 22nd October 1966 - the day after the disaster - to early November 1966. These priceless old newspapers are crumbling away and urgently need to be saved.

When Merthyr Borough Council moved offices, the Library saved some other vital documents. These include a long memorandum from the National Union of Mineworkers (South Wales Area) on the causes of the disaster, and original letters dating from 1963 - 4, from Merthyr Council to the National Coal Board, complaining about the tips behind the Schools at Aberfan. Headed 'Danger from Coal Slurry being tipped at the rear of the Pantglas Schools', these letters played a key role in the Tribunal of Inquiry. The Coal Board fobbed off the Council with lies and evasions. If it had dealt with these letters properly, there would have been no disaster.

The money from the British Academy will pay for a Research Assistant who will work on the papers for three months at Dowlais Library. When the work is done and the room in which the papers will be permanently housed is ready, the papers will be available (by appointment) for readers from all over the world to learn about the causes and consequences of the disaster for themselves.

COUNCILLOR GLENYS EVANS, Chairman of the Borough Community Services Committee welcomed the news that money was forthcoming from the British Academy for the project. A former Mayor, and proud to be from Bryntaf, Aberfan, Councillor Evans said that 'the Disaster was a dreadful part of our coal mining history'. The preservation of the documents was essential for the future needs of our own youngsters who would want to know why this had happened and also to help prevent similar tragedies, although unfortunately they had occurred since. More importantly the Disaster should never be forgotten and this was another way of making sure that it never was.

SHEILA LEWIS writes 'I am very pleased that Professor McLean, through his interest in the history of the Aberfan Disaster, has acquired £4,000 for preserving and indexing the records and documents of that time. It is very satisfying for us, who were / are directly involved, to know that the truth will now be available for all to see'.

'HEADWAY'
JULY/AUGUST 1997

33. University Of Wales Graduate To Work On Aberfan Papers

Martin Johnes will be working, mostly in Dowlais Library, on Merthyr Library's collection of documents about the disaster. Iain McLean, Professor of Politics at Oxford University, recently got a grant of £4,000 from the British Academy to catalogue and conserve these papers, and he appointed Martin as the Research Officer. Martin will be working on this project from the start of October until the end of 1997. Martin holds a degree in History and Archeology from the University of Wales College of Cardiff, and is currently registered for a Ph.D. on association football in South Wales between the wars.

The papers to be catalogued include the Transcripts of Oral Evidence given to the Tribunal of Inquiry in 1967, and letters to and from Merthyr Borough Council both before and after the disaster. They include a series of letters from the Borough Council to the Coal Board, in 1963-4, headed "Danger from Coal Slurry being at the rear of the Pantglas Schools".

This collection does not include the letters of condolence received in Aberfan after the disaster. These letters are in a separate collection.

Iain McLean also expressed his pleasure at the decision by Secretary of State Ron Davies to return £150,000 to Aberfan in late July 1997.

"I was one of those who lobbied the Secretary of State about this", he said. " I sent him copies of my research on Aberfan, which I have been doing since the papers in the Public Record Office were opened to the public at the beginning of this year. I said that the case for giving the money back seemed stronger than ever, now that the full history of what went on in 1967-70 is coming to light. But I was astonished and delighted when I heard that they had agreed to give the money back".

HEADWAY SEPTEMBER/OCTOBER 1997

34. Aberfan On The World Wide Web Site

In February this year, Merthyr Libraries launched it's very first Internet Web Site. The web site is on the Aberfan Disaster. Unfortunately, the press mistakenly reported that it was a new exhibition on Aberfan. There is NO such display here in the Borough, but now academics and schoolchildren from all over Britain and across the world can log onto the web site and see historical information on Aberfan and a list of all material held on Aberfan in Merthyr Libraries.

All the vast amount of books, pamphlets, reports and so on held by the Library have been indexed and listed thanks to a British Academy Grant obtained by Professor Iain Mclean. The work was started in October by Martin Johnes, who successfully completed the project in January.

The web site only gives a glimpse into the 5,000 document archive. It is now possible just to give an Internet number and obtain the information required.

The web site will bring about awareness of Aberfan outside the area but local people don't need a computer to look at the material. By visiting Merthyr Central Library they can look at the actual books and records.

CAROLYN JACOB
REFERENCE LIBRARIAN
MERTHYR TYDFIL CENTRAL LIBRARY

35. The Pigeon Man

Return again to that sunlit hill
To reflect and quietly pause
Thinking of the tragedy
The total cost and cause.

Springtime bright the flowers
The golden and the pink
Sit awhile in sunlight
And of the darkness think.

There I met a stranger
Who was passing in his van
Selling corn for pigeons
A friendly, sincere man.

Asking of this tragedy
And of the lives defiled
So many carved inscriptions
Can ne'er replace a child.

Came the time of parting
And the shaking of the hands
Another grain of friendship
In life's mysterious hands.

TOM BELLION.

Chapter Four
God's World

1.   Introduction

Our mountains and green spaces have always meant a great deal to us. Roaming the hills we came to know each season thoroughly, with its own trees, flowers and animals. The colliery lay sprawling beneath us in the valley and there was the ever present starkness and bustle of the working pit community but the wind blew fresh and free on the mountainside where there was beauty, constancy and peace.

The year also had its social round and there were highlights in it common to us all. St David's Day brought celebration in the local schools with a very high standard of poetry, music, dance and drama. Palm Sunday came next and everyone would take flowers to the cemetery. The May Day Fair, the Sunday School Anniversaries and subsequent trips to Barry or Porthcawl were occasions of high excitement. Summer holidays from school brought visits to the Swimming Pool nearby, unless there was a polio scare when with much wailing and gnashing of teeth on our part, we knew that it would be closed for weeks on end. Back to school and soon, familiar faces would be missing as whole families went hop picking. Remembrance Day brought the sale of red poppies. My father always placed one above our mantelpiece in silence. Christmas came and with it plays in school and jam sandwiches eaten at our desks as our 'party'. There were more exciting things to eat in Sunday School parties with a visit from Santa Claus. But the beauty and joy of the Nativity Play still endures in school and chapel to this day.

"Looking Down" Local People Landscaping With The Groundwork Trust in Pleasant View

2.   The Seasons

The Seasons.

To a year there are four seasons
I love them all here are my reasons

First Spring arrayed in a dress of green.
Deckes the countryside untill its lovely
to be seen,
Then forests with children's laughter
shall ring.
And birds come back sweet songs to
sing

Then Summer with her gay flowers
Millions to fill lovers bowers
Golden corn rippling in the breeze
Yes I love all these

Next (or) Autumn dressed in gold
Bringing many joys untold
Nuts are brown, apples are red
Leaves came down that once hung
overhead.

Last Winter in her cloak of white
That covers the country in a night
Oh what joy to live, awake on
Xmas Day
Oh what joy to live, laugh and play

Patricia O' Brien

PANTGLAS SCHOOL, STANDARD 4
1949 - 50

3.   Mine Refused

There was much concern in the village when it was announced that a small mine operator had applied for planning permission to open a mine on the mountain near the approach road to Danyderi Farm, and very close to the copse of trees planted in memory for the victims of the 1966 Disaster, and entailing the felling of many of the trees.

Many local organisations, together with Merthyr Borough Council, objected. Mid Glamorgan County Council Planning Application Committee initially recommended giving permission, but the full Planning Committee ordered an investigation of the site. A good number of local people were present when this was done and on 27th November 1981, our views were clearly made known to the councillors.

On Friday, 11th December, the full Planning Committee met. A delegation from Aberfan and Merthyr Vale was present. Tom O'Brien, our County Councillor, made a strong and coherent plea for the rejection of planning permission and the Committee decided, almost unanimously, to instruct the Planning Applications Committee to refuse the application.

It is understood that the National Coal Board also objected to the granting of the licence for mining on that site.

HEADWAY, JAN - FEB 1982

4.   Marlene's Diary

February. As I walk around the garden, I see the crocus and snowdrops starting to pop out of the soil.

As the days go by I notice the buds starting to come on some bushes and shrubs. It is an exciting time because you can see the start of new life in the soil and Spring is on its way.

Primroses bloom, snowdrops and crocus in an assortment of colours. Also dwarf irises in purple and yellow seem to smile at you to brighten the day.

End of February and the daffodils are in bloom, also polyanthus and white and pink aralus trails over the walls. Tulips are coming along and we will have plenty of colour again as mother nature takes over her role.

Norman and I sit and watch the birds in our garden. They are all busy feeding from our bird table and nut holders. They give hours of entertainment, with the cheeky sparrows fighting over the tit bits and a robin that likes to show that it is his garden. He sometimes taps the window of the kitchen and he has come into the kitchen when I have left the door open.

The little blue tits and the great tits are very acrobatic; they hang from all sorts of places. We also have blackbirds, thrush and wrens in the garden. Last year we had nests of wrens, blackbirds and blue tits in our nest boxes. We had two sets of blue tits born in one of the boxes.

As the days warm, our fish start to rise on the ponds. Nature is a wonderful thing.

September. In the Spring we saved sunflower seeds from the wild bird food. My eldest grand-daughter, who is four years old, planted them with me. There was great excitement when, in the Summer, we measured both Athena and Sigourney, who is 2 years old, up against the flowers. Some of them had grown as high as eight foot. A few had flower heads on them. The birds enjoyed the flower heads very much so nothing gets wasted.

MARLENE JONES, 1992

5.   St. David

The Welsh Evening - Noson Gymraeg - held at the Community Centre on St. David's Day proved to be varied and entertaining. Over one hundred and forty people came together to celebrate our Patron Saint's Special Day. Following a traditional Welsh tea of Bara Brith, Welsh Cakes, Apple Tart and Cream, the compére introduced the evening's entertainment.

Local talent, helped by two friends from the Rhymney Valley on the guitar and flute, was brought together to provide an hour-long programme of recitations, songs and folk tunes. The evening ended with community singing vigorusly entered by all present. The Headway Committee would like to thank all those who contributed to this happy and successful evening, especially the ever-ready Education and Recreation Committee and all those whose gifts of food made the evening a cheap one for all to enjoy.

HEADWAY, APRIL 1982

St. David's Day, Mount Pleasant School

6. Unison, Conviction and Dignity

In the years before the beginning of the Second World War, I attended Pantglas Boys' School which later became Pantglas Junior School.

The journey from school was always by foot, regardless of the weather, over the bridge from the Perthy area of Aberfan, under which the last train passed in February 1951. Road alterations have removed all traces of that bridge. Then my eyes focused on the mountain side where stood the pyramids of black rubbish which the coal masters of Merthyr Vale Colliery had dumped on the beautiful mountain with no concern for anything but making massive profits. Below the monuments of toil and hardship were two schools, the boys' and the girls' schools.

On the other side of the valley was another tip scarring the mountainside and beneath it Merthyr Vale School. Between these black sentinels, that stood on either side of the valley, ran the River Taff, which was so inky black that fish had for many years forsaken its rushing, slithering path as it made its way to the coast, growing wider and blacker as it soaked in pollution from the tributaries that fed it. Often we peered into its murky depths where not a stone could be seen on its bed. Smoke belched from the three tall colliery chimneys and wisps of smoke rose from the chimney of every house in the village. Even the hillsides were denuded of trees; they had been felled for industrial purposes.

I hated the sight of these black dustbins of the coalmining industry on our hillsides. They became even more numerous until there were seven of them.

What a contrast our valley presented when viewed by George Borrow in 1854. Passing down the valley towards Aberfan he said, "The scenery to the South on the further side of the river became surprisingly beautiful. On that side, noble mountains met the view, green fields and majestic woods."

Today, the world knows Aberfan. The name is synonymous with terrible tragedy caused through industrialists' ignorance, ineptitude and lack of communication.

The village was transformed from a happy place to a place of silent grief.

We shall always be thankful to God for all those throughout the world who came to us with support, guidance, help, sympathy and gifts.

We could build for the future! We were heartbroken, devastated and every thing was chaotic. Our village looked an alien place. Even the dirt and mud around our streets mocked our intended efforts at restoring the former order.

We started the healing process by creating as much activity as we could. Our people came together for mutual support. We were determined that from now on, as we grew in strength, that vigilance was to be the key-word for the future wellbeing and security of the village.

We were able to ascertain that there were forty to fifty different groups with officers and committees. The Community Association, with its nucleus of the Parents' and Residents' Committee, welded the groups together so that from henceforth we would speak with one voice. People discovered they had hidden talents of leading and serving.

The hive of activity these committees engendered was therapeutic for all concerned. This was very necessary in our activities in which we shared our anger, our sadness, our problems and joy.

However, the tips were a constant reminder. They had to be removed. Our meetings in the village, the Welsh Office and in the N.C.B. offices at Llanishen eventually resulted in their removal but we had to pay an additional price, £150,000. This had to be paid by the Aberfan Disaster Fund. However, it was felt that as long as they remained, we could never look forward; their removal was necessary for our re-growth as a village and a community.

The Community Association continues to be a watchdog. Whenever difficulties or problems rear their ugly heads, we can quickly summon the villagers together to consider ways and means of tackling problems. Perhaps our motto should be, "Never take no for an answer". We are always ready to challenge experts, especially those whose ideas conflict with what we consider to be correct.

So it was when the Welsh Office announced its initial plans for the A470 road to pass through Aberfan.

Our village was just beginning to look lovely again. Most of the aftermath of the Disaster had been removed. People were painting their houses and making our village look attractive again, when it was announced, as a bombshell, that the road would bisect our village. It now appeared that another major disruption to our life was going to erupt. We were determined not to allow this to happen.

The calling of a public meeting resulted in a Road Action Committee being formed. It was successful in persuading the experts to re-route the road into its present path leaving our village to continue its regrowth. The new road now presents panoramic views of our valley and the Brecon Beacons and we hope encouraging new industries and increased employment.

We care for our environment. The scene has changed. The tips have all gone. The colliery has been erased. The river flows gently through the valley and the men and boys fish in its waters. The valley is growing more beautiful and wildlife once more is attracted to its beauty and security. Hardly a wisp of smoke is noticed during the daytime. Trees planted on the hillside present their beauty in varying shades of green.

The villagers have learned many things. Above all we would mention our gratitude to our friends, known and unknown, local and worldwide, who supported us in our dark times. Secondly, our pledge to ensure that whenever we see dangers rising in our community, that we will act immediately, in unison, with conviction and dignity, to right the wrong. It is the duty of all of us to keep God's world safe from the greed and exploitation of man in whatever way that greed seeks to express itself. We have, as citizens of the world, observed the effects of man's greed in Chernobyl, Bhopal and our own little village. We must ensure that dangers do not threaten our world and our existence. It is God's gift to us and we must cherish it.

CYRIL VAUGHAN, 1991

Stuart Phillips looking over Aberfan and Merthyr Vale from No. 7 tip, July 1966

7. The trees along the side of the River Taff

I walk along the pathway
The view is so beautiful
For the tips are now of the past,
The trees are budding their leaves
Ready for the Spring.
The river is clean
And the fish can be seen
At last. And
At night when it flows quietly by
My river sings a lullaby.

KITTY MAY JONES (NEÉ AYLWARD), 1991

The River Taff at night

8. The Spring

Hurrah! The Spring is here at last,
And now the Winter days are past.
The birds are singing in the air
Telling the world that Spring is here.

The flowers their gay colours show
When God on them his gifts bestow.
The trees spread out their branches long
Inviting the birds to sing their song.

**IRENE M. HOLDER,
PANTGLAS JUNIOR SCHOOL,
STANDARD 4, 1950**

9. Dawn in the Valley

In the early morning, before the sun rises, I stand in the dim light, looking over the bridge, gazing upwards towards the distant hills. The valley is hushed, the mist hides the river bank covering the activities of the night creatures, whose rustlings come faintly to my ears. The river splashes its way towards the bridge, rushing down the weir, running more gently under the bridge and downwards, hurrying to merge with other rivers, before reaching its final destination.

In the water beneath the bridge a quick 'plop' tells me that a water creature is close at hand. The valley seems to be holding its breath. Suddenly I hear the chirp of the first bird, followed by a short silence before a few others join in. Soon the soloists are followed by a full dawn chorus, such marvellous sounds coming from hundreds of little throats, echoing and filling the valley with their songs. The cuckoo makes his special contribution. The light gradually increases in strength.

The whirr of wings tells me that my friend, the heron and his mate, are taking their first flight of the day, flapping and stretching, winging their way along the river down towards their fishing grounds in Pontygwaith.

A breath of wind moves the misty blanket. Along the river bank, the mink makes his last forage, almost invisible. The ducks and moorhens, making sleepy sounds, slip quietly into the water, moving gently, wings flexing near the bank.

The valley is awake and waiting for the sunrise. The night sky pales more quickly now. I look towards the mountains rising steeply behind the houses in Merthyr Vale. As I gaze above the houses still shrouded in misty darkness, the first glow of the sun's rays bathes the mountain tops with a shimmering aura, higher and higher the sun rises, flooding the valley with warm and glorious light, the mist is banished, colour surrounds me.

A new day is born

I stand on the bridge and take a deep breath. The smell of growing things fills my senses. I have been witness to a happening that fills me with wonder and delight. For a short time, before everyday activities begin for me, I am at one with the valley and with the river bank.

With this infinite space, I glimpse past and future dawns stretching away into eternity.

My spirit soars. I turn away slowly. I am fulfilled and content and I breathe a silent prayer of thanks.

SHEILA LEWIS, SPRING 1991

'Toby Sam' on the river bank, 1988

10. Mount Pleasant
"God always feels nearer"

One of the early joys of life at 'The Mount' was to climb the mountain behind our houses and look down into the valley stretching up towards Merthyr Tydfil and down towards Treharris. This was our world in those days of infancy. Often on such walks with my father, we came across Vicar Evans of the Church that I attended at the Rechabite Hall. My father and I often exchanged conversation on those mountain walks and I recall on one occasion the comment that the Vicar made, "I like it up here Mr Keevill. God always feels nearer and I find inspiration for my sermons." What a gentleman he was, never failing to raise his clerical hat as passing.

Another extraordinary feature then to be found on the mountain was the sight of the wild cats which roamed the area quite freely. We were, as children, always relieved to pass them, never quite sure of their intentions.

PHYLLIS DAVIES, 1992

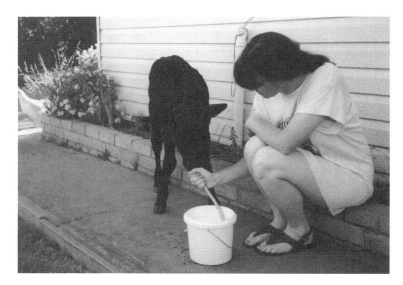

Caroline feeding the heifer, Yarambat, Melbourne, Australia

11.   The Beautiful Woodland

Just recently I lost a number of old dear friends, for that is what trees become when you grow up with mighty oaks, ash and beech surrounding your home. They become an integral part of your life - you live your childhood fantasies in and around them and then watch your children grow and do the same.

I have been lucky enough to live in Pleasant View for most of my life and you may imagine with what sadness I heard the final route for the A470 trunk road. I appreciate how badly a new road is needed and the relief that was felt by residents in Merthyr Vale and those of Aberfan whose property was affected by the route originally proposed but still the sadness remains in what we shall lose in terms of natural beauty.

I found it very distressing to witness the felling of magnificent, centuries old trees and finding that, within minutes, the view from my window, which had always been there, was completely altered forever. When construction begins in earnest, we wonder what will become of the great variety of birds and small animals whose homes are in and around the trees. There is large patch of rare violets in danger of being wiped out.

I would say to the people of Aberfan and Merthyr Vale, take a walk in the beautiful woodland on your mountainside very soon, one morning you could wake up and find it lost forever.

ELEANOR ABRAHAM, HEADWAY 1983

The above was written in 1983 and now, in 1990, we can see that the trees in question were felled quite needlessly. They were not in the direct line of the trunk road but interfered with a temporary power line needed for the construction work. Instead of lopping the high branches 'the powers that be' cut down many trees. Pleasant View is left with a row of tree stumps where there could have been a natural screen absorbing traffic, dust and noise.

We must learn by this experience. I urge everyone to ask questions and ascertain all the facts. Don't make it easy for mature trees to be felled, as in this case, quite needlessly.

ELEANOR ABRAHAM, HEADWAY 1990

12.   Great Trees Fall

Our woodland means so much to me,
Far more than concrete property.
I must confess it breaks my heart
To see it cruelly torn apart
By metal monsters' cruel teeth
Biting into earth beneath.
Huge drills boring through grass so green
Revealing earth and rocks long unseen
To me the unkindest cut of all,
As saw bites deep and great trees fall.

In spring no more will cuckoo call
In Autumn, no russet leaves to fall.
In winter, no branches glistening white
When soft, Pure snow falls overnight.
Where bluebells grow and children play,
Soon will run the motorway.
Where thrush sings by day
And owl hoots at night
Soon will shine the neon light.

ELEANOR ABRAHAM 1983

13.   An Easter Message from Father Barnabas

Christ's birth heralded the intrusion of God into this world. Throughout His life on earth there were glimpses of His hidden divinity as He went about preaching the good news of God's Kingdom, healing the sick, consoling the afflicted, and even calling back to this life some who had passed briefly into the next life. It was on the Mount of Transfiguration, Mount Tabor, that His hidden glory burst through most fully before Peter, James and John. He walked along the same road as we tread, suffering the agony of the Cross. But this was not the end of the story. The hidden glory burst forth in its fullness on Easter morning, when the disciples first beheld the empty tomb and later were greeted by the Risen Christ, radiant in His divine humanity, the same Jesus whom they had known and loved, who now reassured them, through his Resurrection, of the truth of his teaching. Until this tremendous event of Easter there was uncertainty about the next life; the Sadducees, a sect of the Jews, denied its existence. The Resurrection puts the seal of truth on life eternal and teaches us that death is not the end of our life, but simply an end to a phase of it and a preparation for when we join those who have gone before us.

ARCHIMANDRITE BARNABAS, 1991, HEADWAY

14.   The Pleasure Fair - Troedyrhiw

On Monday last this event, which is looked forward to with much interest, took place as usual, and being the only out door gathering of the year in this locality that is an established annual fair, it is usually well patronised by those from the neighbourhood and others who are interested in maintaining the attractions of the fair, which consisted of the usual amusements in the shape of standings of toys, nic nacs, eatables and drinkables of mysterious composition, also exhibitions of acrobats and wizards, astonishing and bewildering the optics by the performance of the hanky panky business. Amongst other things there were two novelties exhibited, one a clever model of a Cornish tin mine, also showing the mode of tin refining and the other, a roundabout, which was worked by a steam engine and was well patronised by the juveniles, as usual. In the evening a large number of people promenaded the streets, more particularly those in which the fair was held, and it is worthy of remark, that the usual unpleasant concomitants of fairs in general, were fortunately, for the most part, absent on this occasion and the streets were comparatively quiet and orderly.

MERTHYR EXPRESS, 7 MAY 1870.

15. Reflections

Lost on an island I'd love to be
Surrounded by palms and azure blue sea.
No dishes to wash or linen to press,
Relaxed and bronzed, enjoying the rest.
No homework to finish or room to keep clean
No errands or papers or quarrelling scene,
I'd stretch in the sun on that far distant shore
Contented, at peace, no knock at my door.
No worries or bills will blighten my day
And on every decision I'll have my own way.

But how lonely this world with no-one to share
The perfection of Nature, marine life so rare.
Alone to partake God's gifts to us all.
The beauty, the splendour, the wild sea birds call.
An island is great when you day dream alone
But so lonely at night when your thoughts turn to home
'cos life's meant to be shared with friends young and new
With loved ones, and old ones, and neighbours so true,
So forget all your yearnings for isles in the sun
Be happy, be grateful, God's made life such fun.

PAMELA N. LEWIS (NÉE SMALL)

16. Sunday School Anniversaries 1930-1939

Noah's Ark Chapel, Bridge Street, Aberfan.

I suppose I was privileged to be in at the 'beginning' of several anniversaries!

My father, Tom Small, was the Sunday School Superintendent of the Primitive Methodist Chapel (Tom Small's Chapel), call it what you like.

Anniversaries needed words and music so Dad would order the music and word sheets. These would arrive at home and would be opened there, hence my first paragraph.

The first conductor I recall was Watcyn Gittens, who apart for training us was also connected with the BBC Cardiff. It was Watcyn's task to turn the Sunday School into a choir, which he always did.

One aspect of Sunday School Anniversaries was an interesting one. Normally the Sunday School was well attended, but in later Spring our numbers would swell, children and adults would appear as the word got round - Anniversary Time. Things in those days had an ordered pattern. No one was turned away. All denominations merged on Sunday afternoons to practice, and towards the actual Sunday evening rehearsals as well.

We were joined by friends and relations, the Goughs and Lewis's would bring along their cousins from Troedyrhiw. Anyone who could find a soloist or reciter of poems was welcomed with open arms. There were very few instrumentalists. 'Auntie Blod' Edwards was the accompanist. Later she trained the Sunday School.

How was the Chapel changed into a concert hall? Today there is the Centre underneath with facilities for functions. Before the Centre was built there was a cellar beneath the Chapel, this was a veritable Aladdin's Cave. My Grandfather and Father stored equipment for their business of electricians and plumbers. However there was one side of the cellar which contained a pile of assorted shapes and sizes of pieces of wood. This was the stage on which the Sunday School would sit.

Before the Sunday preceding the Anniversary the pulpit was carefully removed by taking out several large iron bolts. The pulpit was reverently taken down to the cellar. Then the transformation began. Those odd shaped pieces of wood! Yes, they all had their place, each one fitted in to form first, the stage. This came out to the back of the first row of pews. The seating came next. Planks of wood supported by T shaped shorter planks carefully screwed to the stage. A rail at the front and steps to get on to the stage. There was no door to the left of the pulpit in those days. Then it was the women's turn, they covered the seats with material and also put the curtain on the front rail.

One or two practices on the stage and we were ready, for the great day. This was usually a day when new clothes would be worn, new hats from Watcyn's wife who kept a front parlour shop.

During the next week in time for the following Sunday, down would come the stage back into the cellar, up would come the pulpit, and a long wait until the next time the postman delivered the packet of Anniversary Songs.

There was a reward for all this effort, usually on the following Tuesday. Beedles and Stephens' Coaches would draw up outside the cinema, where the Sunday School (dressed for the Arctic!) would board, and take us to Barry Island and <u>once</u> to Porthcawl.

HARVEY SMALL.

SUNDAY SCHOOLS 1950s

When we were young we grew up in a very close community, we knew everyone in all the surrounding areas and helped each other whenever we could. I remember the street parties when the war was over and the annual Sunday School trip to Barry Island in a charabanc. Oh the excitement of that day! We went to Smalls Chapel, as it was known then.

IRENE HOLDER - 1991

SUNDAY SCHOOLS 1920s

In the winter nights we passed the time away by joining the Band of Hope at the Church of Christ, Bridge Street and the English Baptist in Nixonville. On a Sunday afternoon I went to the Church of Christ, that was the only way that we could get a trip to the seaside, which was Barry Island. We travelled by charabanc with Beedle and Stephens. They had a garage at the bottom of Pantglas Road.

TED DUGGAN, 1991

Disgwlfa Sunday School Outing

118

19. Marlene's Garden

Passing by 7 Belle Vue Villas, most people's heads turn to look at Marlene's and Norman's garden. Like many gardens, partly on a slope, and hard work to tame, this garden has overcome any limitations and is a picture.

"Marlene. Can we come and see your garden?" is a familiar request from friendly mothers passing by, taking their children to school. A side path and a flight of steps takes them to the main body of the garden where a myriad of plants meets the eye. Although brought up in this house, Marlene only moved back here to live twelve years ago. She has spent the intervening years, with her husband, Norman, restoring the garden to its present lovely condition.

"I often go into the garden to peg out the washing and end up spending hours out there." Marlene grows most of her own plants from seed. This allows her to splash out on the special plants that she comes across in the nursery or garden centre. Marlene loves her plants. She very tenderly showed me an Adstrantia Major that she had grown from seed. The plant looked very delicate. "I won't touch that" said Norman.

Sigourney and Athena helping in the garden

In the Summer, Marlene has some beautiful pink poppies over three feet high. The corollas are very striking, each one a shimmering, quivering, velvet brown sphere, surrounded by the pink gauze of the poppy petals. Stone creatures peep out from behind plants and line the fish pond. A stone kingfisher, hedgehog and dove were looking very much at home in their surroundings. A large egg shaped stone, rescued from the garden of an aunt, was covered in some very interesting lichen.

A particular favourite with Marlene's grand-daughter are the very tall foxgloves that grow in the front garden. Athena loves the garden already. "She won't pick a flower" said Marlene. "She will only smell them." Marlene is proud to be passing on her gardening skills to her grand-daughter. They spend hours together in the garden.

Marlene plants trees and climbing plants in clever combinations. She showed me clematis and conifers growing entwined together.

In fine weather, Marlene and Norman find time to sit in the garden and enjoy the fruits of their labour and their terrace looks out over the valley. The former Merthyr Vale Colliery was lying in their direct line of vision but like the many houses and shops of Aberfan Crescent, which lay opposite, has disappeared almost without trace. Now they have a clear view along the valley bottom and up to the hills of Troedyrhiw. MAUREEN HUGHES

20. Sheep Sheering Match, Ynysowen

July 1880 - The annual sheep sheering match in connection with the Gelligaer, Llanvabon, Merthyr and Eglwysilan Society took place on Monday in the rear of the Windsor Hotel, Ynysowen, situated between Quakers Yard and Troedyrhiw. This was the second year only that these matches had been held and they occasioned a very considerable amount of interest amongst the agricultural portion of the inhabitants. The entries amounted in all to thirty two. Last year when the shearing match was held at Deri, the entry had been twenty eight. The "Merthyr Express" for the following Saturday reported that the work was in general very well done and in some classes the judges had considerable difficulty in deciding upon their awards, so close was the competition.

There were some winners from Merthyr Vale. Rees Jones won second prize in an entry of eight for shearing five sheep within three hours. His prize was £1. A young man under thirty, Thomas Lloyd came first in a similar competition and won £2, and a young lad under twenty years of age, William Bowen from Forest Farm, came second after shearing four sheep within three hours. His prize was 13/-.

When the matches were over all the parties concerned sat down to a substantial meal at the Windsor Hotel. The prizes were subsequently distributed and the day finished very pleasantly.

"Looking Up": Landscaping with the Groundwork Trust at Pleasant View

21. The Lily of the Valley

Oh the lily of the valley
The crocus in the snow
The daffodils and tulips
Red roses lovers grow.

Purity of snowdrops
Cherry blossom on the tree
The beauty of life's bower
The small anemone.

The springtime of the primrose
That flowers in hedgerow shade
Crysanthemums, tall daisies
Nature's bouquet made.

The Grove, Aberfan

Carnations and cornflowers
The poppies in the corn
Stock that scents the midnight air
Which lingers in the morn.

No single graceful flower
Could ever you compare
You are my morning glory
The fairest flower there.

TOM BELLION

22.   Hop Picking

Over the centuries, September meant one thing in Herefordshire, hop-picking. The hop belongs to the same family as hemp and cannabis and is a relative of the nettle. A hardy, long lived climbing perennial, its shoots can reach 20' in length but die back to ground level every Winter. Not only is the hop used to flavour and preserve beer but has been used to make brown paper sacking, binders for sheaves of corn, brown dye for wool and as a substitute for oak bark in tanning.

Today the growing of hops is concentrated in the sheltered river valleys of the Frome and Lugg but hop-picking throughout Herefordshire has been recorded for over 400 years. The early pickers were the farm labourers' wives and children and by the middle of the 1800s a good picker could earn one shilling and sixpence a day. When the railways came they brought labour from South Wales and when the picking ended the pickers lined up to be paid. Many calculations had to be made before the South Wales pickers piled into the buses that had been sent to take them home. Sometimes they had 'subbed' so much of their wages during picking that they had little money to take home.

During the 1950s the South Wales valleys were still supplying hop-pickers and in September there would be as many as two hundred adults and one hundred children extra on one farm. "On a Sunday evening the singing from the covered cow-shed was beautiful." By the end of the sixties picking finally came to an end in the district.

Families from Aberfan Crescent went hop-picking to Herefordshire for thirty to forty years. Some unmarried boys and girls would go, eager to earn some extra money in hard times. Gwyneth Probert, neé Hodkinson was one of these youngsters. She remembers going to Little Frome in the 1930s.

REFERENCE -
POCKETFUL OF HOPS : HOP GROWING IN THE BROMYARD AREA
£6.75 - PUPLISHED BY BROMYARD AND DISTRICT LOCAL HISTORY SOCIETY
1988 - ISBN 0 9502068 49

23.   "We would make a bed of hay."

I lived in Aberfan Crescent and I started hop-picking around the farms of Hereford during the 1930's. I was about eighteen years old. I went every Autumn for three years. My brother and sister usually came with me. We would go in September and stay for about six weeks. A van would take our luggage and then we would catch the train from Aberfan Station into Hereford. There would be a lorry waiting for us to take us to the farm.

We would make a bed of hay and sleep in the barn. The next day we'd see the farmer and make a start. We were paid by the bushel and were paid 1/- for each bushel picked. We would usually pick thirty bushels a day. We worked from eight and finished at five. We only had one break at dinner time and then we'd have some sandwiches. The weather was usually fine but if it was raining, we had no work.

When the time came to finish work, we'd go to the farm and have potatoes and swede free but we'd have to pay for eggs. On the Saturday we'd go into Hereford and by butter, bread and meat to last the week. We cooked on a range outside the barns. We all got together. There were people there from all over Merthyr and we made friends with them. We had brought our own saucepans, tea-pots, kettles and other cooking things with us, along with blankets, clothes, towels and anything else that was essential. We always made a clothes line for the washing and washed by

Gwyneth (Jennie) Probert neé Hodkinson

121

hand in a big bowl. We had a stand pipe and we'd give ourselves a good wash down and there were wooden huts for toilets.For recreation we went to the 'locals'. We would have to drink out of jam jars - they wouldn't trust us with glasses! When the picking came to an end, the vans and lorries would take us back to Hereford station. Our belongings would be packed back into tea-chests. We'd all be searched to make sure that we hadn't pinched apples. As my sister didn't take to hop-picking, she had gone home early with my mother. My brother wasn't sorry, she had given him jam

sandwiches for his dinner break every day since we'd been there. We used to buy clothes out of the money. They would last us a while.

I wouldn't like to go now. I was young then and it was an adventure.

GWYNETH PROBERT, 1991
(NEÉ HODKINSON)

24. References to hop picking found in the Log Book of Aberfan Pantglas Boys' School

15 September 1933
Low attendance owing to exclusion for epidemics and absence of several boys in the hop fields.

13 September 1935
Some boys are still away hop picking.

11 September 1936
Attendance is low as several boys have been taken hop picking.

25. They even took their tin baths

I used to love to watch the people in our street, Aberfan Crescent, going hop-picking.

They would pack their belongings in boxes, suitcases and bags. Then all this would be loaded on the backs of lorries. They even took their tin baths. The families would all pile into the back of the lorries, pets as well, and they would be gone for weeks. Although it was very exciting to see everyone arranging and loading things it was very sad after they left because everywhere was so quiet. I suppose you could call it a working holiday, so many people did it then.

MARLENE JONES, 1991
(NEE WILLIAMS)

Aberfan Crescent and Martin's Paper Shop

26. Hop Picking Morning (early 1950s)

The whole of Aberfan Crescent looked like a railway platform, brown paper parcels, bags, boxes all tied with string, tin trunks and blankets tied up like giant swiss rolls. Children running here, there and everywhere; still more cord from Martin's to tie up yet another box. Mothers and fathers back and fro to their front doors looking for their transport. Everyone excited, looking forward to their hop picking, seeing old friends once again, memories of sing-songs and celebrations.

"Pop", George Martin, leaned against the wall puffing on his pipe, smiling to himself, his eyes twinkling. He loved to watch the children swarming about like "bees around the honey pot."

TINA MARTIN, 1991

27. Ministers' Corner

During the next few weeks the words 'All is safely gathered in' from a well-known harvest hymn will be sung in congregations up and down the land.

A friend of mine living in Zambia smiled when she joined in the harvest services and with a congregation of many hundreds sang in the Zambian heat, "He sends the snow in winter".

The failure of the harvest doesn't mean a great deal to us who expect the supply of the goods we need to be in the shops at a price. Unfortunately, in a world of want we are made only too aware of mountains of food-stuffs being thrown away.

For us Harvest is a time to remind ourselves of the goodness of God, of those who work to provide the harvest and distribute the results to our tables.

Everything we eat and drink has been produced by someone, somewhere in the world. Their hard work makes it possible for us to go on living.

Let us use harvest as an opportunity to thank God for all the blessings in our life, in our rich harvest may we learn to share.

Thanks be to God. The land has produced its harvest. God our God has blessed us.

HEADWAY, OCTOBER 1985

28. From Mount Pleasant

"Wayandah", Melbourne, Australia

Bathed in golden sunlight
The beloved village nestling
In the hollow, green hollow.
Pleasant View with hills behind,
Where we gathered catkins, bluebells,
Watched Autumn leaves fall,
Rode Sledges and picked velvet moss
For tin-lid gardens.
Rolled poly-roly down the hill,
The sky and the grass
Whirling into one.
Where my friend's sister
Ate desiccated coconut,
And we all tried to climb the trees.

MAUREEN HUGHES,
FEBRUARY 1988

29. A Walk by Moonlight

It was a bright moonlight night when I thought of going for a walk. So I wrapped myself up and started off. I passed through the sleeping village until I came to the dark forest. I walked through noticing everything as I passed and thought that it was very interesting. I walked on until I came to the very heart of the forest. The shimmering expanse of water and the silver-tipped petals shone like a star. The pale gleam of moonlight that shone in through the trees above me showed a little path. I wandered down and saw little animals moving about. It was very calm and quiet in the forest and the eerie silence made me shiver. I sat down on a log that lay beside me and watched a little rabbit playing among the leaves. When the rabbit had gone back to his burrow, I got up and walked on silently. The whisper of the breeze made a sound like music and the sweet smelling grass felt so cool. Then all of a sudden the startling hoot of an owl broke the silence. I went to look for it and found him watching me on the tree that I had been sitting by. It was a big brown bird and it had round shiny eyes. I put my hand up to it, but it rose in the air and fluttered around the branches of the tree. I then looked at my wristwatch and found it time to go home. It was midnight when I got home and I was very tired. So I had a glass of milk and went to bed thinking of the lovely moonlight walk in the woods that night.

IRENE HOLDER,
STANDARD 4, PANTGLAS JUNIOR SCHOOL,
7TH, OCTOBER 1949

30. The Journey

The morning sun shone down upon
This valley oh so green
It seemed to me the finest sight
That I had ever seen.

Although I was but just a lad
And did not appreciate
The beauty of the things I saw
Until it was too late.

The skylark rising from its nest
Among the winberry bushes.
The moorhen swimming with her chicks
In and out the rushes.

Up above a hawk would hover
Seeking out its prey
Some poor little fieldmouse
Would not see the end of day.

The sounds of nature all around
As I walked my lonely path.
The sparrows and blackbirds
Partaking of their daily bath.

I heard the sounds of distant sheep
As they climbed the mountain high
I looked and saw their silhouettes
Against the clear blue sky.

I followed up behind them
As they climbed up to the "Darren".
It seemed to me the grass up there
Was ever much more barren.

A lonely crow stood sentry
While the others nested high
As I got closer to them
I heard his warning cry.

I climbed up to the mountain top
And surveyed the land around me
I seemed to hear the angels sing
"Nearer my God to thee."

I sat and rested for a while
And watched the scene below me
The River Taff meandering
On its lonely journey to the sea.

TOM ABBOTT, 1991

The Darren

31. The Darren's Story

The largest landmark in our locality is the Darren. It is a high cliff gently curving along the mountainside, the scar left by a great landslide. Below it there is a huge mass of broken rock that extends all the way down to the valley floor. This broken mass provided an adventurous playground for children and was popularly called the HAPPY HUNTING GROUND.

There are many such landslides caused by geological faults in the north eastern part of the South Wales coalfield and this one is described in detail in local geology books. The flank of the mountain here is built of sandstone. This hard massive rock appears in our local quarries and it gives us the excellent stone of our earlier buildings and streets. The stone is recognised quite easily because blue, grey and soft rust colours show up all in the same wall.

As I used to come home from work, I always enjoyed a glimpse of the trees on the roadside leaving Edwardsville. Now and again I had the chance to glance at the other mountain. There, often, the afternoon sun would pick out a straight line of shadow marking the fault as it stretched from the Darren past Hughes' or Perthygleision Farm and across to the top of the mountain. This fault caused a spring to rise on the mountainside which fed the farm and its livestock. Besides bringing about the landslide at the Darren, the fault played a more ominous part in our history since it contributed to the cause of the Disaster.

The broken, rocky ground in the Darren was not suitable for farming so it was employed as a 'shoot' by Mr Gray, the Managing Director of Nixon's Navigation. The gamekeeper in charge for some of the time was the grandfather of Mrs Tille Lloyd of Moy Road and she can still remember the thunder of the guns as Mr Gray and his guests enjoyed their sport. The shooting box or lodge on the edge of the Darren disappeared when Nixon's company went bankrupt. Meanwhile the Darren also provided recreation for others - birdnesting boys. The Darren in Welsh is named Tarren Y Gigfran - The Raven's Rock or Knoll. These large birds nest on rocky ledges and so came within the reach of the bold, resourceful and adventurous boys of Bryntaf suitably gloved for the confrontation.

Beyond the cliff, on the top of the mountain there used to be a rifle range. This was the practice ground for the "volunteers". They formed a reserve force for the army and their organisation was left over from earlier times like the Napoleonic Wars when they formed a 'Dad's Army'. The Volunteers met at the Gordon Lennox Club and annually practised their shooting on the mountain top. When Charlie Theyers died, one of the souvenirs of his long life was the scarlet tunic he wore as a Volunteer. The Darren has throughout the years been troublesome. With difficulty the Glamorgan Canal was carved across it. At the end of the last century, the Rhymney railway line was laid across it. Now in the twentieth century a motorway is projected to cross it. As part of the preparation for the new road, bore holes were drilled into the landslide. In one of the bore holes some wood was found. This could only have got into the ground at the time of the landslide and so it was sent for carbon dating. Before this discovery the only clue as to when the landslide occurred lay in the fact that it must have happened after the last glacier had melted. When the wood from the bore was dated it established that the landslide happened about two thousand years ago - almost the last great change in appearance to our valley until coal was mined and our villages built.

W. J. GRIFFITHS
HEADWAY, APRIL 1982

32. Above Aberfan

'Above Aberfan, where I lived, there was a crack on the mountainside 9" wide, as if a slice had been cut out of the mountain. This has always been there, it was a fault in the mountain. Down below Aberfan, towards Bryngoleu, there was a big landslide. There were boulders everywhere, strewn about the valley, hundreds of them, weighing about fifty to a hundred tons.

The new motorway goes over these boulders and along this fault. Looks like a quarry where thousands of tons of rock had slithered down towards the river.'

TED DUGGAN, 1988

33. The Modern Landscape of Aberfan and Merthyr Vale

Like many other valleys' communities the local environment of Merthyr Vale and Aberfan can be described as an interesting juxtaposition of natural beauty and despoilation caused as a result of man's economic activity. Many of the villagers have always been very aware of their surroundings and of the potential for improvement and have worked hard to make changes. When the Merthyr Vale Colliery was eventually closed and subsequently demolished a whole new set of opportunities for change were recognised. The realisation of these opportunities became possible through a Merthyr Tydfil Borough Council Urban Programme Grant and the involvement of the Merthyr and Cynon Groundwork Trust.

The Trust which is part of the national Groundwork network was established in Merthyr Tydfil in 1987 and then expanded operations into the Cynon Valley in 1989. There are currently over 30 Groundwork Trusts spread throughout Britain including four in Wales. Although the various trusts operate in different ways and have to concentrate on different things in response to their specific local conditions and problems they all have three common basis aims. These are the creation of new landscapes and the improvement of existing ones, the promotion of environmental education and awareness and the improvement of facilities for recreation and access to the countryside.

The essence of the Groundwork approach is to tackle environmental problems through a broad partnership approach involving the local community, the local authority and the private sector. The Trust believes that community involvement is extremely important and that community consultation at all stages of an environmental improvement scheme is essential. This type of approach has certainly paid off in Aberfan and Merthyr Vale. From the onset a local committee was formed made up of representatives from the key organisations in the villages. This committee has acted as a steering group for the community environmental improvement programme and has met monthly both to monitor progress and to plan future developments. In addition, before work has gone ahead on any individual project public meetings and open days have been held to canvass as wide a local opinion as possible.

Over the four year period 1991 to 1995 the total amount of Urban Programme allocation for the villages has been £410,000. The projects that this money has been spent on have been tremendously varied and the sites have been distributed through the two villages. The projects fall into four different types: recreation, access, landscape and community.

Recreation projects have included solving the drainage problems that have plagued the Grove playing fields, often making them unusable in the past. Associated landscaping has also helped to improve the general appearance. The other major recreation project has been at Moy Road where incorporating ideas suggested by the local children, an exciting playground has been built opposite the Aberfan Community Centre. This has proved to be so attractive that there have been reports of children queuing to get in.

Work on access has centred on creating the attractive Riverside Walk as an easy footpath to be enjoyed by all and on creating well surfaced links from the villages onto the Taff Trail. Besides a long distance walk, the Trail gets a terrific amount of use as a traffic-free link between the different valley communities. The Groundwork Trust was behind the creation of the Trail.

A variety of landscaping projects have been completed which have transformed previously derelict and neglected pieces of land into attractive roadside gardens; particularly colourful in Summer is the wildflower meadow that has been sown alongside the Grove.

Community projects have been similarly varied. On the small scale school-children have helped to add colour by planting bulbs, whilst at the other end of the scale, a very dramatic impact was achieved by the renovation of the old library. The building which is used by the Merthyr Vale and Aberfan Old Age Pensioners' Association had fallen into an advanced state of disrepair and without the Urban Programme might have eventually crumbled away. The steering committee identified the conservation of the building as a priority and after extensive renovation by the Borough Council it now looks extremely smart. Another community project has been the transformation of an overgrown wilderness into an attractive garden in the grounds of Trinity Chapel. Various members of the community, young and old, together with staff from Barclays Bank in Merthyr Tydfil, who helped to sponsor the project, were seen wielding secateurs, spades, forks and wheelbarrows to help create the garden.

Although there has been a concentration of Groundwork activity in Merthyr Vale and Aberfan because of the Urban Programme, the Trust's association with the villages goes back further than that, for several years during the Easter and Summer holidays, children have "Sprung into the Countryside" with Groundwork. Bugs have been hunted, ponds have been dipped, birdboxes and kites have been built, bicycles have been ridden and a whole host of other environmental activities pursued as the Trust has helped the children to have a better understanding of their local surroundings and hopefully to learn to respect and to care for them.

In conclusion, I would like to say how much Groundwork has enjoyed working with the people of Merthyr Vale and Aberfan. Through the combined efforts of the local community, the Trust, the Borough Council and the Welsh Office, changes have been made, to the environment of two of the Taff Valley's most important villages. Changes which have helped to heal some of the scars of previous heavy industry. The Trust hopes that it will continue to work in partnership with the people from the villages and that future years will see a continued flourishing of environmental projects.

VICKY INSON,
MERTHYR & CYNON GROUNDWORK TRUST,
JANUARY 1994

Above: The playground, Moy Road

Left:Ethel Lloyd in her Groundwork Trust badge at the re-opening of the 'Old Library'

The Old Library

34. Armistice Day

See the poppies with their scarlet heads,
standing as sentries o'er the dead,
Swaying gentle in the breeze
Murmuring music - but not for me.
And see how the grasses are weeping
look at their bended heads -
Silently whispering to the poppy -
Lest they should be heard by the dead.
They in their innocent sphere-forming
with body and soul
A shroud so as to protect them -
They are sacred as God knows.

RALPH HOWARD, WRITTEN ON ARMISTICE DAY 1924,
AT LOCK HOUSE, ABERFAN

35. World Peace Efforts

Many of the residents of Aberfan and Merthyr Vale have already been asked to sign the world-wide petition calling upon the governments of the world to take disarmament very, very seriously and the great majority of those who have been approached have signed. They knew what they were doing and had read the leaflet which was distributed in advance. The deadline for this effort in our community has now been extended to 12th December.

An exhibition will be arranged in the Community Centre in the New Year on nuclear arms and nuclear power.

HEADWAY, DECEMBER 1981

PEACE cannot be kept by force It can only be achieved by understanding

EINSTEIN

36. Sunday School Party

Strolling alone down memory lane when the world lies fast asleep,
I recall a happy occasion, the Sunday School Christmas treat.
This treat was a super party held in St John Ambulance Hall,
All the children were invited, congregation, and Mr Tom Small.
The Chapel ladies would gather on a Saturday afternoon
Busily laying the tables with garlands and coloured balloons.
We looked forward with glee and excitement to that very special date,
Tied thread onto handles of the cutlery, and labelled our names on a plate.
The 'widges were simply delicious, ham and red salmon too
To see us devour those goodies you'd think that we lived in a zoo.
No ice-cream or yoghurt appeared but trifle with lashings of cream
Followed by welsh cakes and pikelets that melted in mouths like a dream.
Then came the nights entertainment led by troupers so rare,
Mrs Gough, Aunty Blod, Mrs Quinlan, their acting beyond compare,
We sang and shouted with laughter, knocked bottles all green off the wall,
We rubbed oil into baby Brown's thorax, and responded to brave Daniel's call.
McNamara's great band earned an encore, Mrs Lewis kept up the beats,
Then a hush, no shouting or laughing as we scampered back to our seats.
The lights in the hall were extinguished as a magical person arrived
In red robe, flowing beard, black wellies, from the chimney Santa Rubery survived.
From the sack on his back to each boy and girl a special present he gave,
We thanked him sincerely and promised that always we'd nicely behave.
So my thanks to the members of Zion for all your great love and your care,
When we meet on that beautiful shoreline, these memories with you I will share.

PAMELA LEWIS (NEE SMALL), 4/5/1991

37. No Goose Grease

I well remember the rag dolls and matchbox furniture my mother made for Christmas and the wooden train for my brother. The cooking of the goose in the bakery at the end of Nixonville and the collecting of the bird on Christmas morning. I'm not forgetting about the jar of goose grease. That was used for sore throats and other ailments.

How fortunate today's children are, no goose grease!

IRENE HOLDER, 1991

38. Oh, what joy!

After receiving your letter I sat down with some nostalgic moments: talk about going down memory lane!

As a girl I remember queuing up outside James' shop at the corner of Perthygleision and Mr James would give every girl and boy an apple and an orange on Christmas Day; as he owned all the houses in Thomas Street, Walters Terrace and a lot more besides, he expected all his tenants to buy from his shop. My mother used to say "Ugh! a sprat to catch a mackerel," but I thought it was wonderful. The doll my gran made for me out of an old black stocking I treasured for years. Then going around the houses singing carols ending up singing:-

A HAPPY CHRISTMAS Bringing toys to little ones, Every Christmastide he comes.

'I wish you a merry Christmas,
Please put a penny in my old box hat.
If you haven't a penny a halfpenny will do,
If you haven't got a halfpenny,
God bless you.'

I remember one Christmas, I belonged to Glyn Humphrey's choir in Merthyr Vale. We had to compete with other choirs in Mountain Ash. What excitement! We all went on a bus to Mountain Ash and sang our hearts out giving a rendering of "The Tempest" and lo and behold we won first prize. Oh, what joy!

Aberfan was considered a distressed area when I was a girl, we were all so poor but, oh! so carefree and happy.

MARY MAGLONA LEWIS,
MELBOURNE, AUSTRALIA,
4TH SEPTEMBER, 1990

39. Winter

The snowflakes are falling
Down to the ground.
The children are calling
From all around.

Toboggans are flying.
Snowmen are found.
Children are laughing
When they fall to the ground.

IRENE M. HOLDER,
STANDARD 4,
PANTGLAS JUNIOR SCHOOL, 1950

40. Christmas Time

Once again it's Christmas time,
And all the World in Blessed
With all the Joys of Christmas time
His love and tenderness.

There's peace for all, and faith for all,
There's love and happiness.
Time to recall the infant small
This day of Holiness.

Once again it's Christmas time,
Let all rejoice anew,
And make His world this Christmas time,
The same the whole year through.

ROBERT LUQUE.
HEADWAY 1968.
(FIRST CARETAKER AT THE YNYSOWEN SCHOOL)

41. Frosting

Happiness, peace and joy
Are remembered in solitude
And spiritual awakening
In tune with God,
With nature, as time suspended,
Cold water through the windows
Is framed by an icicle,
And trickling through my fingers
Is framed by my breath,
Then caught into snowflakes.
The canal bank
crisp and frozen
With Pantglas School
Caught melting
In the Winter sun.
My happy teacher,
Red cheeked is smiling
On friends who are skipping
about with frozen toes.
Watch carefully
Lest the moment be lost
Fading away into noise
And Spring sunshine.

MAUREEN HUGHES, DECEMBER 1988

Memorial Garden in Winter

Chapter Five
Heritage

1.   Introduction

The Merthyr Vale Colliery is an important part of our heritage. But before the colliery there were farms, the Glamorganshire Canal, the Taff Vale Railway and people worshipping together. There are other aspects to our heritage. The people who established the villages around the colliery, the hardships they endured, the work they put in. The girls who went away to service, the evacuees who came here from Deal and Folkestone are all part of our heritage. So too is Timothy Evans, born in Mount Pleasant, Merthyr Vale.

Mattie and Maggie, Glandwr Cottage, circa 1908

2.   Heritage

"December 11th, 1874 - the first tram of coal was raised in Number One Pit, Merthyr Vale," - so recorded Eddie John's grandfather in his diary. Thus was brought into production a pit specially designed with a lattice steel winding tower architecturally described as elaborate and decorative. Coal exploitation up to this time has been controlled by the iron companies so Nixon's Navigation was a new development for the Merthyr Valley. Around the colliery there grew up the compact pit head settlements we know as Aberfan and Merthyr Vale.

In 1874 too, Polly Howe came to live in Aberfan. The house she came to was Glandwr Cottage, Perthygleision. It was one of the buildings in the village that preceded the coal mining development. A canal had been built to carry the iron production of the Cyfarthfa works and others to Cardiff. The stretch of the Glamorganshire Canal from Cardiff to Abercynon was built between 1790 and 1794. The last nine miles from Abercynon to Merthyr were built from 1794 to 1798. Greater difficulty was experienced in the last distance because they had to build locks for the canal to climb from the sea at Cardiff to above five hundred feet at Merthyr. Along the canal sixty feet long boats nine feet wide holding twenty ton loads were horse-drawn at a speed of about two miles an hour. Glandwr Cottage was built to accommodate a boatman and his family; with his animal being kept in the outbuildings.

Three-year-old Polly Howe's father had come from Abercynon. He is described as a "Sawyer, deceased" on his daughter's marriage certificate but, in fact, Thomas Howe was employed as a carpenter by Mr. Griffiths, the owner of the Aberfan Estate which stretches from Bridge Street to Bryngoleu.

At this time, 1874, none of our chapels had been built, but worshippers met in private houses. This is what early Christian worshippers did, so we read in the Acts of the Apostles. In Troedyrhiw, a house in Wyndham Street was such a meeting place and Carmel Chapel was built on the opposite side of the street in the 1840s. In Merthyr Vale, at Danyderi Cottages, Baptists had been meeting in this way. They continued to meet in such places as the Red Cow, a tavern which used to stand where Moy Road and Coronation Place meet.

Thomas Howe's house too became a Baptist meeting place. The family point to a corner of the big kitchen to the left of the door as you enter where the pulpit was for their services. Meetings must have been held in this way for a few years, because it was eventually decided that a Chapel should be built. In 1879, a piece of land was leased from Mr. Griffiths, Aberfan House, for a ground rent of £2.10.0 a year. So, helped by Carmel, Troedyrhiw, Smyrna was built. Polly Howe became Mrs. Thomas and her daughter, Maggie, died in 1981.

One eighty year old daughter still survives to remind us about the house, the family and the history.

BILL GRIFFITHS, HEADWAY MARCH, 1981

3.   A Three Legged Stool

My great grandfather was called William Thomas Angel. He came from Tavistock in Devon. He left there to look for work and at first he settled in Bristol. Then he came to the Merthyr Vale Colliery, where he was the master boiler maker, when the colliery first opened.

When he left Devon, he wanted something to remind him of home and his mother. So he carried with him a three legged stool that his father had hewn out of a tree. As he rested on his journeys, he would sit on the stool. The only other possessions he had were tied up in a knapsack. After he married, his wife, my great grandmother, would sit on the stool to peel vegetables. She would also sit on the stool to bath their babies. I have the stool to this day and the rings of the tree can still be seen quite clearly.

My great grandfather supervised the building of the railway bridge over the Taff Vale railway line. He also had the handling of the building of the Black Bridge in Aberfan, over which the journeys of trucks ran, taking the colliery waste to the tips.

SARAH CHIDGEY **1991**

4. Early Beginnings

In the early 1900s, when work was very hard to find, people either emigrated to America or sought work in the private coal mines that were then to be found in the Welsh Valleys.

So it was that in 1903 my grandfather, Jim Richards, travelled from Cornwall to Wales to seek work in what was then Nixon's coal mine, and having found work, sent for his wife and four young children and settled in Aberfan.

Their first home was in the basement of the old Navigation Hotel which was situated just below the Aberfan Railway Station. Now both places are lost landmarks in our village.

They finally settled in Barrington Street where, in 1911, their fifth child was born, a daughter, who was to be my mother. My grandmother was a tailoress and took in sewing to supplement their meagre wages. Their eldest son was in local government in Merthyr Tydfil before enlisting in the Royal Engineers during the 1914-18 war. He spent much of that time in France where he was honoured with a 'Medaille d'honour'. Upon his demob, he joined an Oil Refinery in Neath, then went on to work with a firm of consulting engineers in 1920 and in October of that year, he joined the Air Ministry.

After two years he was sent to Iraq to supervise the installation of water systems, oil tanks and other equipment at an R.A.F. unit. In 1932-33, working from London, he prepared the complete designs and specifications for the water and drainage installations at the R.A.F.'s fantastic station called Habbaniya, Iraq. 20 years later that unit had become a small desert city in its own right, equipped as no other R.A.F. unit has ever been. It is now in the hands of the Iraqi government. In 1955 my uncle was awarded the M.B.E. for services to his country.

When my grandparent's second son was demobbed from the forces, he couldn't find work so he followed his father down the mines. He was only there a short while when he lost a leg in an accident with a coal dram. He died at the age of 30 as a result of that accident.

Their three daughters, as was the practice in those days, were put into household service until they married.

In 1952 a firm of steeplejacks had a contract to paint all the steel work in the Colliery at Merthyr Vale and also the Black Bridge that spanned the River Taff and carried the colliery waste to the tips above the Grove. My brother joined the firm at that time and when the work was finished, travelled away to other jobs. In 1967, the firm returned to demolish the 225ft square stack that for 95 years had dominated our village. The stack had been built in 1872 and had to be taken down brick by brick because it would have been too dangerous to blow it up because of the nearby houses.

Today, even the colliery has gone, the end of another era!

My brother had travelled away and settled in Cornwall, where he got married. He lived where my grandparents once lived. There he too raised five children. From Cornwall to Wales, and Wales to Cornwall. The wheel as the sheave has turned a full circle.

Irene Holder, 1991

Aberfan Station

5.   The Building of the Village - 2

'Snooks'

The Medical Officer to the Board of Health could report to the Board in 1880 that the standard of housing in Ynysowen and Treharris, and especially in Ynysowen, was such that the inhabitants did not fall victim to the fevers that beset people living in some other parts of the town of Merthyr. In his opinion, the arrangements made for the general health of the population of Ynysowen had been well thought out. The drainage of the area was being completed and the Sewage Farm land, formerly part of the Ynysygored Farm estate, which was to cope with the drainage problems of Merthyr, had been fenced, drained, double dug and handed over to the Farms Committee of the Board of Health. The name of the first farmer there was Snooks and he almost lost his job when a massive hay rick, that was in his charge, spontaneously combusted, and burnt to the ground. Housed on the farm was the donkey that had been purchased to collect refuse in nearby Troedyrhiw. Board members were less than convinced of his efficiency and complained about the number of swedes that the donkey was consuming on the farm. Before very long, the donkey was sold.

Soon after the houses in Taff and Crescent were built by the Nixon Company for their workmen a storm occurred and the houses were flooded by the River Taff. Again in July 1872, there was a terrible storm of rain and thunder and lightning which affected both Aberfan and Merthyr Vale. The storm lasted for twenty four hours and the River Taff overflowed its bank in Troedyrhiw. The bridge near the Ynysowen Colliery was swept away by the flood and the people living in the colliery houses were much alarmed as the flood entered their homes. This is a trend that continued over the years and in 1877 forty yards of river bank was carried away and the debris was spread over two acres of the Sewage Farm land.

Over one hundred years later, after many incidents of flooding in the meantime, on Boxing Day 1979, terrible floods occurred after very heavy rain and many people had to be evacuated from their homes in Pantglas Fawr, Taff Street and Crescent. Most of them, unless they managed to carry their possessions upstairs, lost the entire contents of their ground floors. Carpets were ruined and furniture rendered useless after being deluged by filthy water. Those affected gathered in the Community Centre where the Merthyr Tydfil Borough Council established an emergency centre. Here the homeless were fed and sheltered until they could return home or move in with relatives. The villagers had rallied around to rescue people, with boats and dinghies, from water that was five to six feet deep.

This was the last reported incident of serious flooding. Taff and Crescent Streets and Cottrell Street had been seriously flooded for the last time. Alterations to the flow of the Taff, after such a scare, seems to have solved the problem. But for the first time the river had come straight across the Sewage Farm fields and into the Pantglas Fawr estate, and even today when there is heavy rain those who have been through the ordeal of flooding, watch the river anxiously, afraid that it is going to be turned into a raging torrent, as it has so many times before.

Maureen Hughes, 1992

6.   England Tried to Claim the First Steam Train

I was the eldest of ten children and I started school in 1910 at Merthyr Vale. I was about five or six years of age. They were hard times and no-one could afford to lose work. People didn't want holidays because three days holiday could take six months of work to make up for three days lost. People would rather be in work because they couldn't afford holidays. The river was our entertainment. All of us could swim. We were all like fishes. No-one had anything new. Where would we get it from? Everybody was poor. We were fine workmen but only just scraped home.

The holiday most looked forward to was going down to Quakers Yard Fair. We would have a shilling in our pocket and this would take weeks to pay back. Some people would try to win it back by gambling.

There were three fairs around here. Merthyr, Troedyrhiw and the one that we looked forward to, in Quakers Yard. This would be before the First World War. Everyone would be walking along the Tram Road, where the first steam train ran. This was Richard Trevethick's engine carrying iron from the Penydarren Ironworks to Abercynon. England tries to claim the first steam train but Trevethick's engine ran along there in 1804. Everyone walked because then they would have more money to spend in the fair. Going down by the old Quakers Yard was very pleasant, the weather could be relied on and we could tell the seasons; we would be sweltering. I would be going down with schoolfriends, but whole families made a day of it, going to the fair.

Then in 1914, the war started. I remember the time well. My father's twin brother came to say goodbye to us. He didn't think that "the war was going to last long", he said, but it was four years before we saw him again.

I was fourteen on the 14th September 1918 and I started work on New Year's Day in 1919. The war had finished and we were issued with soldier's trousers which we cut down to use for work in the colliery. Before I actually started work in the colliery, like many other respectable families, we would go down to the Mount Pleasant sidings and unload small coal. Ten or twelve tons would be unloaded and that money would be ours to keep. Going down the line I might be stopped by a policeman. "Where are you going?" he'd ask. "I'm going to collect my pay, Sir, from Mr Dowdesworth and Mr Appleton." "On your way", he'd say. I would come back with my 3/9d. I wouldn't have it for two minutes, it would be given to my mother, but I was proud to have it at the time. I was about twelve or thirteen.

After the war everything started altering in stages. We didn't know what was coming. Cinema tickets were 4d but no-one had 4d to spare. Money for a man underground, 'in the company' as they called it, was £2.2.6d. Stoppages would be 1/11d. Rent 5/10d. The man on the coal-face earned £2.9.0d minimum and was lucky to have it. Everything rose after the war. Coal was 1/2d. My father wouldn't see the light of day - he had to work long hours to get the wages.

In 1912, there was a big strike called the 'Dram of Muck Strike' and then in 1926 came the General Strike. I joined the Labour Party at this time and I have been a member ever since. During the thirties we saw poverty and deprivation, the "bad thirties" we used to call them, but we survived the bad times and the Labour Party got in after the war. If we had stuck to our guns we would have been well away today. People my age don't forget. When strikes came, all against the working class, "we found our friends and we had very few." I remember at the time of the 'Dram of Muck Strike', men were running over to the Aberfan Hall for a meeting and the Manager would be watching from his house "Fernbank" in Merthyr Vale, through binoculars to see who was going to the meeting. A grandfather of mine, Peter Gardner, stood for the Council against the Colliery owner, H. E. Grey, at the beginning of the century; he lost of course, Grey swamped in. My grandfather was a brave man. They counted the votes on the Thursday, he lost his job and his house on the Monday. He was working in the Merthyr Vale Colliery. He had to go to work in the Rhondda. He was a big supporter of the Union.

Union dues were paid in the Coffee Tavern to the Treasurer of the Federation. Young lads paid 3d a fortnight and adults 6d a fortnight. Everyone had to pay their dues. Wouldn't be allowed through the Colliery gates if we hadn't paid our dues to the Union. But we enjoyed ourselves. If only we'd had the 4d to go into the Cinema! But there were dances at the Coffee Tavern, Walter Bell's old Assembly Rooms.

There were good rugby players in Taff and Crescent Streets in those days and we were one big happy family. Most of the disagreements were in the pubs. We did not have much but were contented and survived it all.

After women had the vote, I remember the women of Taff Street would go up the street thirty or forty of them at a time to vote. They would all be voting Labour. I remember my mother going with them - it was her father who had stood against H. E. Grey and lost his job. And people never forget it. Nearly everyone was Labour. But there was a man in Taff Street who was a Conservative. He was the Chairman of the Conservative Club. I have seen him come out of his house with a big blue rosette and his family with blue ribbons, just to show what they were.

WILL JOHN O'BRIEN, 1986
In 1988, Peter Gardner's grandson, Thomas Gardner O'Brien became the Chairman of Mid Glamorgan County Council. He is a younger brother of Will John O'Brien

Will John O'Brien

7.   Mount Pleasant - Memories

I was born in Mount Pleasant, just after my parents came to live there. My mother hailed from London but my father was born in Wenvoe Castle where his father had sought employment. My grandfather came from Worcestershire and had come to work at the Castle as a gardener. Later they moved to Cardiff Castle where my grandfather became gardener for the Marquis of Bute but this time my father, too, was employed as a gardener there. My grandfather told me of the hunts that the Marquis often participated in and, surprisingly, one of his favourite trips was to the Merthyr Vale mountains, to hunt wild boars.

Little did my grandfather realise, at the time, that he too would be making a trip to Merthyr Vale one day, but, as with so many others, he was attracted to the new colliery just built there. So he made another move and settled in the Crescent. He obtained employment as a blacksmith, whilst my father was engaged as gardener to Mr Grey at Ynysowen House, where there were large grounds. My uncle, Ralph Keevill, branched out into his own business and opened a general store at Crescent. The business lasted for many years.

PHYLLIS DAVIES, 1992

8.   A Long Established Family in Merthyr Vale

My Granny Rowlands was born Sarah Edwards in 1858 and lived in Old Danyderi. Her two cousins lived in Danyderi Farm and married the two Jenkins brothers who had come from St David's in Pembrokeshire. She was taken by her father to the fields of Danyderi Farm to see what he called "history in the making", the first clods of turf being turned over for the sinking of the Merthyr Vale Colliery.

My Granny went to the first school in Merthyr Vale, which was held in 1 Cardiff Road. The fees were 1p a week and if she was unable to attend, her mother would send my Gran's sister, Martha, so that she would still have her money's worth! There were only three pupils in the beginning, one of whom was Enoch Morrell who became the Miners' Agent of Merthyr Vale Colliery, the first Mayor of the newly created Borough of Merthyr Tydfil and the guiding light behind the first free secondary school in Britain, at Cyfarthfa Castle.

Granny Rowlands worked as Major Bell's cook in Ynysowen House. She told us that Major Bell used to cross the little bridge by Crescent and go riding on Mr Griffith's Aberfan estate. She also used to sell red flannel in the Market in Merthyr and she cleaned the offices at the colliery. She was the only woman to receive a pay docket from the colliery in the early days. She was given a piece of ground on the tram road, as an allotment, because she had fed the workers in the early days of the colliery. In those early days, the miners paid 4d to the colliery doctor and this covered the whole family should any of them be ill.

My Granny married John Rowlands and they had six children, two boys and four girls. One of these girls was my mother, Mary Hannah, and another was Sarah Rowlands who was to teach generations of children in Pantglas chool.

My father, Bert Michael was a haulier underground. His horse was called 'Yankee' and he was a very big, headstrong animal and only my father could handle him. My father was chosen to take Yankee to London on Exhibition and the horse was brought up from underground. He was put into a field behind our house where he was to stay for a few weeks before the exhibition. My father would often go out to our back yard, which overlooked the field where the horse was kept, and shout "Yankee" so that the horse would raise his head and neigh loudly.

My father loved animals. He kept pigs but he could never bring himself to kill them. He had his favourites among them. I remember once someone was coming to kill one of the pigs so my father told him which one it was to be and left the scene. Dad was most put out when he found out that his favourite pig had been killed instead of the one he had indicated. My mother would salt the slaughtered pig on a stone slab in her pantry, and then the carcase would be hung from a big hook in the kitchen. The carcase would be dripping black brine onto the pantry floor. This is how we, and a lot of people, managed. There were big families in those days and everything was home made. There were small bake houses in all parts of the village and we would take cakes and other things to be baked there, especially at Christmas-time.

There were tram lines running from Merthyr Vale quarry to the colliery. When he was a boy my husband, Stan Jones, used to wait on the corner and as the trams ran past he and his friend would leap on the trams and ride down to the colliery. To stop the tram, for the people to get off at the bottom of Bell's Hill, a man would stick a sprag through the spoke of one of the wheels. In the early 1950s, Jazz Bands were all the rage and Stan was the leader of the Miners' Band. They used to perform in the full miner's gear, supplied by the Merthyr Vale Colliery. The whole village used to participate and a great community spirit was shown. Stan had worked underground at the age of fourteen, and, after twelve years in the army and several as a 'brickie', he became a miner; surprisingly, he hadn't been a miner when he led the Miners' Band. It was Stan who brought the last pit pony up from underground.

I still look back and remember the days when I was younger, and the whole community seemed to revolve around the pit - the pit my grandmother saw sunk and which over a hundred years later, my grandchildren saw close.

EDITH JONES NEÉ MICHAEL, 1991

Cardiff Road, Merthyr Vale. Scene of the first school

9. Great Aunt Jane

My Great Aunt Jane was born in Dowlais in 1880. She lived to be one hundred and five. Her mother, Mary, had also been born in Dowlais nineteen years previously. Mary married David Jones. He had come from a small agricultural village in Cardiganshire called Pennant. At first David Jones had been working on the railway but during the 1880s the family moved to Taff Street in Merthyr Vale and David Jones became a collier in Merthyr Vale Colliery. They had added to their family and eventually they had twelve daughters including my Great Aunt Jane and my own grandmother, gentle, delicate, Emma. There was one son but he was killed on the level crossing when he was a young boy.

When Jane was about five years of age, her grandfather in Pennant died and she went to live with her grandmother in the remote Cardiganshire village. They lived on a smallholding called 'Panteg' and her grandmother kept chickens. Years later Auntie Jane told me that she hated eggs. They had been "two a penny" on the farm. She also revealed that she had resented being sent away to live "even to her own grandmother". Her parents and sisters would have their photographs taken and sent to her but this seems to have been little consolation. Even so, she kept in touch with her Cardiganshire friends and relations right up until her last days. When she was a hundred years old, the Sunday School in Pennant sent her loving greetings. She had been a scholar there in the 1880s.

Mary-Jane was about ten years of age when someone from the village was coming down to South Wales on a visit. They offered to bring Jane down to see her family in Merthyr Vale. She told me that whilst she was here, her father took her out for a walk. They crossed over the little bridge at Crescent and climbed the steep, winding hill towards the Aberfan Farm of the Griffiths', and the Canonbie House of the Bells'. There they saw all the bricks piled up to build more houses in Perthygleision including Thomas Street.

As the village grew around the colliery at such a rapid pace it must have presented a real contrast to the rural communities of Mid and West Wales that so many of the settlers had left behind. The village of Pennant consisted of scattered farms and smallholdings and to get to school, the children, my Aunt Jane amongst them, had to cross fields and climb hills. Their lunch would be wrapped in a large handkerchief and they would all drink from the clear, bubbling mountain streams. When Jane was fourteen years of age, her grandmother apprenticed her to a dressmaker. She had wanted to stay on in school and when she was about one hundred years old, she told me angrily, "Maths I wanted! Maths I wanted! But my grandmother took me out of school." Three years later, her apprenticeship over, she took up dressmaking. She made the wedding dress of the headmaster's bride in Pennant and she and her friends picked wild flowers to throw over her as she came out of the church.

Auntie Jane outside Panteg

In those days girls would work as dressmakers in private houses sewing for all the family. They would work all the week from 9 a.m. to 8 p.m. and would be paid a shilling. When she was seventeen, her grandmother died and Auntie Mary-Jane came back to Merthyr Vale to live. She started to go around houses in Merthyr Vale and Aberfan sewing. This she did for many years. She would spend a week in one house where she would be sewing for the mother, father and perhaps three daughters, taking her own sewing machine. She was a familiar sight in the village, carrying her sewing machine.

She was a skilled milliner and villagers have told me about the hats that she made for the Sunday School Anniversaries. She specialised in bonnets that the little girls wore. They would be trimmed with dainty flowers, forget-me-nots, buttercups and daisies, and crisp ribbons. All the sisters were good milliners and went in a body to buy canvas hat shapes in the haberdashers in Aberfan Road which they trimmed with fruit, flowers and ribbons after covering them in crepe de chine. When she was twenty one Auntie made her own ball gown and wore it to the Rechabite Hall. Her father had her photograph taken and 'went like the wind' to have it framed in Silvergleitz, the picture framers in Aberfan Crescent. Auntie Jane told me that her father had trained as a minister in Lampeter but had lost his certificate in a barn. I thought this very strange at the time because as far as I knew all the family were non-conformists but I later found out that many young men from South Cardiganshire, who were from non-conformist backgrounds trained for the Anglican priesthood. It was a tradition associated with the church before the breakaway of those who embraced Methodism and the certificate awarded was crucial. Apparently, these can be traced in the National Library of Wales.

Auntie Jane married Joseph or Joe 'Baker' as he was known in the village. He was a master baker. He was one of five brothers and several of the brothers were ministers of various denominations. The family came from Llanidloes and there was a large contingent of people from that town who settled in Aberfan. Joe and Mary bought 1 Pantglas Road at the turn of the century, when the houses were newly built. They had been built by a co-operative and Aunt Jane remembered with sorrow the struggle that she and Joe had to pay the mortgage. But the houses were sturdy and well built of local stone. Auntie Jane lived there until the age of ninety five, and then she went to stay with her niece, Eirionwen, in Merthyr Vale. A few years later my cousin, Pauline, bought the house so it is still in the family.

One of the other sisters married Michael O'Brien. He was the twin of the father of Will John O'Brien. He was the uncle who had "gone to war". Her name was Sarah. Will John reckoned that they were the 'smartest couple in the village'. They kept a little shop in Crescent Street and they had two children called Kathleen and Raymond. They were named after friends of the family. There was a large framed photograph of Michael O'Brien on the passage wall and Sarah would hold the two small children in her arms and lift them up to see their father whilst he was away. The glass would be smothered in their fingerprints and a family friend told me many years later that Sarah refused to clean the glass until her husband came home from the war. Sadly, she and her two children died young.

1 Pantglas Road was the scene of the first meetings to establish the now thriving Social and Democratic Labour Club. Joe 'Baker' and four friends met there to be away from the eyes of the "bosses". They gathered in Auntie Jane's front room. She told me that they would take a horse and cart over the mountain to Bedlinog and collect five barrels of beer at a time. She did not tell me how long they took to drink it! When Windsor Cottage was purchased as the new premises for the Club Uncle Joe did not have far to go because Windsor Cottage was just across the road. Auntie Jane was the first woman to pull a pint there and the first woman to sing the 'Red Flag' there.

Aunt Jane survived all her sisters, including my grandmother who died at the age of forty two. Emma and her sister Magdeline had been the youngest of the sisters. Magdeline died at the age of twenty, following childbirth. Aunt Jane was the oldest and lived the longest. By the time that she was a hundred she had become quite a celebrity in the village. I remember her at the village carnival, sitting on the stage, when she spotted my mother and myself. She came smartly towards us. Upright and steady. She was one hundred years old. She refused to have a postal vote and if the car that was taking her to the polling station was not there quick enough for her, she would go on foot. On pension day she would send her niece to get her pension early. This was because of her advanced age. She did not want "Mrs Thatcher" to get her week's pension, in the event of her death. She always seemed surprised that she had lived so long and was very sad when her much younger nieces and nephews died before her.

Auntie Jane, 100 years old, Merthyr Vale

Aunt Jane lived a stone's throw from Pantglas School. My mother and I met her up the Cemetery at the time of the Aberfan tragedy. She was eighty six years of age but had climbed two steep hills. She was as steady as a rock. But she could not understand why the good Lord had spared an old lady of eighty six when so many children had died, including a great niece of her own. She was deeply religious and spoke about the "Good Lord" as if she knew him personally. Although she was very old, nearly one hundred and six, when she died, I was very sorry. She did not have any children of her own but we loved and respected her.

I live in the main road in Aberfan and if I answer my door and am there for a minute or two, I will usually see a cousin passing by. Like me, they are grandchildren or great-grandchildren of Auntie Jane's sisters.

MAUREEN HUGHES, 1992

10. Pennant and Llanon

Placed on your grave
Sweet peas from Aberfan.
Remembered by your graveside
Pennant and Llanon.
Gathered from my garden
Flowers given by Merthyr,
Tinged with coal dust,
Held together by winding gear,
Laid to rest now.

Placed on your grave
Sweet peas from Aberfan.
Covered in coal dust.
Remembered by the grass
Of your graveside,
Shaded by a pine tree,
Shadowed by the little chapel,
The green fields,
Of Pennant and Llanon.

MAUREEN HUGHES, 1989

11. The Building of the Village -3

"A Small Bird" - Late 1870s

The first shop was applied for in Aberfan and the planning application was received by the Board of Health, from a Mr B. T. Davies of Troedyrhiw. The plans were for a shop and dwelling house. From a poem in a 'Merthyr Express' of that period, we learn that this was no ordinary shop-keeper but a crowned bard called 'Ceredwyn' and we also learn from 'Gwilym Gelledeg' writing in the same poem, of the shopkeeper's great humanity and his affection for the people of Aberfan.

Schools were being held in the Bethania Vestry on the Aberfan side of the River Taff and in a 'workman's cottage', later identified as 1 Cardiff Road, on the Merthyr Vale side. But by 1878 agitation and hard work had produced the Merthyr Vale School, the bulk of the population being found on that side of the river.

Then towards the end of 1879 came the news that a two-horse, sprung, covered, van would be running between the 'Perrott Inn', Treharris, and the William Harris shop in Troedyrhiw. The van would be calling at the Windsor Hotel, Merthyr Vale and the fare would be threepence each way. The railway station came in 1883 after great agitation over seven or eight years. Doubts had been expressed that it would ever materialise. At one of the many concerts held in the rapidly expanding community, this one at the Coffee Tavern Assembly Rooms, the visiting artiste was able to sing,

"The Taff Vale Company go ahead,
They never are behind
Except for building stations
For which they are not inclined.
As I was coming down tonight
I heard a small bird cry,
Merthyr Vale will have a station
When pigs begin to fly."

MAUREEN HUGHES, 1992

Merthyr Vale Station

12. Station's 100th Birthday

Merthyr Vale celebrates its one hundredth birthday in June. With due ceremony on 1 June 1883 the double platformed station was opened for public use. Its importance in the history of Aberfan and Merthyr Vale has been immense.

The early years saw hundreds of work hungry men with their wives and families arrive by train to seek work in the colliery. The first glimpse people had of their new home was the station. Their arrival must have been accompanied by a great deal of apprehension and doubt unlike the joy and euphoria felt by those years later to whom the sight of Merthyr Vale station meant that they were safe home from war. Many families have been united in grief and joy on the platforms of Merthyr Vale station.

The opening of the station afforded people the opportunity to travel further afield, it provided a gateway to new places and experiences. People will remember the chapel outings of the 1920s and 1930s which for many was their only trip out of the village in a year. On the morning of the outing, children would be up at the crack of dawn to be at the station in plenty of time, loaded with sandwiches and Welsh cakes specially prepared by mother. On these occasions large queues would form at the booking office and the station would be packed with excited children and equally distraught mams and dads. Barry Island was a favourite place to visit and inevitably, it would rain.

More recently, history was made at Merthyr Vale station when the Queen arrived there to visit Aberfan in 1966. It was the first time Her Majesty had been greeted in such a small village. In fact, the station was too small to accommodate the whole of the Royal Train.

A number of years ago the booking office and original waiting rooms were demolished and later one line and platform were closed down. Today, the station looks rather forlorn, but it has a proud history.

HEADWAY, MAY 1983

13.   The Black Cap

I was in service to the Sankey family in Cardiff. David Sankey was a Barrister and a nephew to Lord Sankey.

Sometimes Lord Sankey would come down to Cardiff to stay with his nephew. He used to come down to have quiet to study his papers. He had a desk upstairs where he used to work. There was a picture of a little girl saying her prayers and an angel hovering above her, hanging over his desk. He liked this picture very much and so did I: it was called "The Consoler".

I said to him one day when he was visiting, "You wear the black cap?" He said "Yes, and I don't sleep for a fortnight afterwards."

A year after he died the death penalty was abolished. When I got married Mrs Sankey gave me the picture that hung over Lord Sankey's desk.

I still have it today.

MEGAN JONES, 1991

14.   10 Rillington Place

Can English justice fail?

"As a realist, I do not believe that the chances of error in a murder case, with these various instruments of the State present, constitute a factor which one must consider …… there is no practical possibility. The honourable, learned member asks me to say that there is no possibility. Of course, a jury might go wrong, the Court of Criminal Appeal might go wrong. But there is no possibility which anyone can consider likely. The honourable and learned member is moving in a realm of fantasy when he makes that suggestion."

These were the words of Sir David Maxwell Fyfe, Home Secretary, speaking in the House of Commons in 1953 - during the debate on the inquiry into whether Timothy Evans had been wrongfully executed on March 9th, 1950.

It was on the 30th November, 1949 that Timothy Evans voluntarily entered the Central Police Station, Graham Street, Merthyr Tydfil, and said to a police officer "I have disposed of my wife down a drain."

Timothy Evans was born in Merthyr Vale on 20th November, 1924. Before his birth, his father left home, never to return. When eight years old, Timothy Evans cut his foot on glass in the River Taff. This resulted in a TB verrucae which never completely healed and led to poor health for the rest of his life. His education suffered and he was never able to read or write other than his own name. Ludovic Kennedy in his book "Truth to Tell" suggests that Timothy Evans was never able to fully comprehend events in which he was involved.

In 1935 the family moved to London, but in 1937 Timothy Evans returned to Merthyr Vale to live with his grandmother. On leaving school he went to work in the mines. His foot continued to trouble him and in 1939 he returned to London. He married Beryl Thornley in 1947, and in the following year they rented a flat at 10 Rillington Place, Notting Hill, London. Their daughter Geraldine was born in 1948.

In 1949, Beryl Evans discovered that she was pregnant again and because of financial worries determined on an abortion.

Also at 10 Rillington Place there resided John Reginald Halliday Christie and his wife Ethel who had leased their flat in 1938.

John Christie, claiming to have medical knowledge, persuaded Beryl and Timothy Evans that he could perform an abortion. On November 8th, 1949 as Timothy Evans left for work, his wife said "On your way down tell Mr Christie everything is all right."

The exact sequence of events on that day is not clear; but on his return from work, Timothy Evans was taken by Christie to see the body of his wife Beryl and was told that she had died during the attempted abortion. (Four years later Christie confessed that he had strangled Beryl Evans.)

Difficulties arose over explaining the disappearance of Beryl and caring for the baby Geraldine. Christie informed Evans he had arranged for a family in East Acton to care for the baby and asked Evans to feed and dress the baby the following morning ready for collection by that family.

In the meantime, Evans had been dismissed from his job as a van driver and seeing no reason to remain at 10 Rillington Place, sold the furniture, informed his mother that his wife and baby were on holiday and returned to Merthyr Vale.

Evans was troubled by his wife's death but was unaware of the fact that Geraldine had been murdered. He was anxious to avoid implicating Christie but nevertheless he decided to report to the police at Merthyr Tydfil. His first statement was a false account of the abortion. In a second statement he told everything that he knew that had happened. The Notting Hill police were informed of the statement and they questioned Christie.

Christie, who had at one time served in the police force used his knowledge to hoodwink them and flatly denied any knowledge of the murders.

Evans' confession at Notting Hill police station was subsequently shown to be false. At no time did he say that he had murdered his wife but that he had "disposed of the body." The 'confession' was written for him by the police: Evans was unable to read it but signed it with his mark. At the trial, Chief Inspector Jennings said that Evans began making his statement at around ten in the evening and it was finished about an hour later. The length of the confession was such that it would have taken the accused a considerable time to martial the facts and to dictate them in the chronological order in which they appear - a feat impossible to accomplish within the hour and half.

The trial took place at the Old Bailey in January 1950. The chief prosecution witness was Christie, who had a previous police record. He was complimented on being an ideal witness. The jury was out for forty minutes and returned a unanimous guilty verdict.

Timothy Evans was hanged in Pentonville on 9th March, 1950, protesting his innocence to the end and frequently saying Christie "did it."

Just before Christmas 1953 Christie strangled his wife Ethel. Early in the New Year he strangled three other women. In a search of the garden at 10 Rillington Place, the police discovered the bodies of two women who he had murdered in 1943 and 1944. Before his execution he admitted a total of seven murders, including Beryl Evans, but not baby Geraldine. However, he said that if the police could find the proof that he murdered Geraldine he would confess to that murder as well. John Christie was hanged at Pentonville in July 1953.

There was considerable public disquiet that there had been an appalling miscarriage of justice in the Timothy Evans case. The Home Secretary, Sir David Maxwell Fyfe, who had declared the impossibility of an innocent man being hanged, appointed Mr John Scott Henderson QC to conduct an inquiry. He concluded in his report that justice had not miscarried: that it was entirely coincidence that the only male occupants of this small house were both strangling women in the same way without either knowing what the other was doing.

In 1961, Ludovic Kennedy published a book '10 Rillington Place' and no critic disagreed with the finding that Timothy Evans had been wrongly executed.

It took a further four years of campaigning before a fresh inquiry was ordered. This inquiry was conducted by a High Court Judge, Sir Daniel Brabin, who concluded that "while Evans had probably not murdered his baby, for which he had been hanged, he probably had murdered his wife on which charge he had never been tried and for which there was virtually no evidence."

This was enough for the Home Secretary Roy Jenkins to recommend to the Queen the granting of a posthumous free pardon; and so, sixteen years after his execution, Evans' name was finally cleared.

Thus Sir David Maxwell Fyfe's claim that a miscarriage of justice was impossible was proved to be wrong and in the years since the sixties a number of other miscarriages of justice have come to light.

It has been said that Ludovic Kennedy's book "10 Rillington Place" centred as it was on the execution of Timothy Evans, was influential in the abolition of capital punishment.

REVEREND KENNETH HAYES, 1993

15. The Sankey Commission

After the First World War a Royal Commission was presided over by Lord Sankey. He was a judge of the High Court and he was appointed to look at the conditions prevailing in the coal industry.

In the final report of the Commission in 1920, the chairman recommended nationalisation. The Government did not act upon any of these recommendations and there continued to be deep dissatisfaction amongst the miners. Another commission under Sir Herbert Samuel failed to recommend nationalisation. Since the Sankey Commission, the miners had been waiting for an end to private ownership. At the end of April the state subsidy which had maintained the level of the miners' wages was withdrawn and this precipitated the General Strike in 1926.

16. For Coal's Sake

From my front door-step, as a 7 year old, I could throw a stone onto our colliery - we lived that near it. Like some giant jungle cat, sprawled on a lounge carpet, it hogged the only flat ground between the hills on either side of the valley. A mass of wood, zinc, brick, stone and steel, combining with man, to wrest from the ground beneath it - coal.

The bitter-sweet relationship between the colliery and man was one of life's early lessons. For into our homes, day and night, came its raucous noises - followed silently, like some master burglar, by the dust which settled in our houses and lungs. Dust, the miner's scourge, had certainly sunk deep into the lungs of the old man who lived in the other part of our house.

His replies to my many youthful questions often came in the form of a cough, a hard cough, a graveyard cough, a premature graveyard cough. He sat in front of his fire for long hard hours - he could go nowhere else. As a change from his chair, he lay on his sofa until the coughing forced him to rise again. He couldn't go to bed, that meant stairs; he couldn't leave the house, that meant hills - the colliery, you remember, had the flat parts. This old man, I realised later, was only thirty five.

The colliery was all powerful; it was a giant, but no gentle one. Many homes it had to warm; industrial wheels to turn, ships to power - and, it was rumoured, even hell's fires to sustain. Our colliery knew of no noise abatement act, paid no heed to public nuisance legislation.

Yet, from the elevated position of my home, the mystery and power of the colliery attracted my young mind. Daily, I watched, like an army of black ghosts, the many men who went to work in it. After passing my house, they were only seconds before stepping onto the colliery. There, to pick up their lamps, and make their way down to the iron cages which dropped them quickly to another world, hundreds of yards below.

I watched them go, frail sons of nature, armed only with a flickering lamp to pit their skills against that which had stood intact for millions of years. Watching my father amongst them, I wondered when he would come up again from 'down there', and if he did, how? For even as children we soon realised the cost of coal - that it sometimes was coloured red.

Before my teens were reached, a tearful sister came to the school playground, "Oliver has been killed," she blurted out, "Oliver has been killed." Poor Oliver, an elder brother, married and now living away, killed two collieries further down the valley. That day he had probably passed some other lad's house on his way to work. Someone else had seen him entering that cage - but no-one had seen the sly heavy stone above him where he worked, until it fell, crushing his very life force. Twenty six years of God's creation snuffed out like some penny candle.

"Death where is thy sting?" toned the minister, "Grave where is thy victory?" A resounding one I thought as they lowered his still body into it, a great victory, a complete victory.

Oliver, a brother of whom the younger were proud. Only a few years previously we thrilled to see him home on leave from the Army. Proudly we touched the buttons of his uniform and tried on his cap. But he swopped the soldiers' khaki for the miners' black; his rifle for a 'pick'; his life for death!

Ironically, as he lay dead, just a few miles away at Merthyr Tydfil and Dowlais, the Prince of Wales, saddened by the dereliction of property and people promised, "something must be done." How I wished Oliver had been one of those who hadn't any work. But as we returned from the graveyard, the wheels of the colliery where he worked, continued to turn. Life was expendable, decreed the colliery- work was not.

In the midst of such sadness and the eventual inevitability of going down the colliery to work, school seemed futile. My school was even nearer than the colliery. Just across the street and I was through the iron gate and safe within the high boundary walls. There, in large classrooms, the staff struggled to give us the means to escape the life which loomed ahead of us - and to their credit they had a measure of success. At least the school offered temporary shelter and safety from the pits.

Yet, we could have no inkling then, that children of some of my classmates thirty years on, were to feel the full and fateful might of our colliery. For years we watched the colliery waste lifted high up the mountainside on the opposite side of our valley - our side was already filled up. Yes, years it took to build up that 'tip', but on a misty October morning, only minutes for it to hurtle back down again towards the colliery. Unfortunately, in its path stood an assembled school and occupied houses, and suddenly one more name was added to the cost of coal.

A climax in suffering, imposed by our colliery, was reached that morning, as a generation of children, together with their older friends and parents, were spirited away from us, as if by some modern Pied Piper.

That earlier teaching as a child delayed my descending a colliery until a year or so ago, but only as a visit of a few hours. When I reached that pit bottom, it was all I had feared, and more.

For miles, it seemed, together with my overman brother, we groped our ways along low narrow dark tunnels; wet, dirty, slippery tunnels. My helmet and lamp were off more than they were on as my head struck the many hidden projections. All this of course, as my brother explained, just to reach the coal-face, work was yet to start!! There were long hours to follow in cramped conditions, cutting at that which could well bring it all down around you, a fate to which more than one widow and orphan could testify.

There could only be one pertinent question for me to ask - 'Why did they strike to keep such places open - why?'

After leaving that Taff Merthyr colliery I walked later that evening to 'my' colliery at Merthyr Vale.

I stood again as a child, looking at that which I had loved and respected, then stooped down and cast a stone onto it - but this time a larger stone - I threw some more. Then I was joined by Oliver, my brother; then the 'old man' with the silicosis' the children and adults of Aberfan disaster and indeed all the people were there. And they all threw stones, large ones, until the colliery was so full that not even a man's finger could pass through it.

"No! No!" they all cried, "No! Not even for coal's sake."

CYRIL JOHNSON

17. CYM-DIFLAS - GLOOMY HOLLOW

Coming home from Quakers Yard School
I climb the hill alone,
My legs aching.
My mother's cousin,
One of many in the village,
Is hanging over the fence
Halfway up the hill
Gasping for breath.
His face grey
His body emaciated
His clothes loose.
He turns faded eyes
Around to meet mine.
I was shaken
By the dust-laden breathing
Of middle aged senility
Caught in the afternoon sun.

MAUREEN HUGHES, 1982

18.   Mount Pleasant Signal Box 1916

My father was the railway signalman for over forty years in Mount Pleasant. He was a very clever historian. He was noted. He had a fantastic memory and he could remember especially Welsh history. He was from a very cultured family and my mother was also a very clever Welsh scholar. She was from Stay-little in Montgomeryshire and her memory was outstanding. As a matter of fact, she was a pillar of Calfaria Chapel and in her younger days was a noted actress who took the lead in the dramas for the Chapel.

My father had the Black Lion box in Mount Pleasant and he was a noted gardener as well. People used to come and see his beautiful vegetable garden and they used to say to my father "Well David, that wonderful garden of yours, there's nothing out of place, everything is in perfect condition; aren't you afraid to leave it in case someone tries to steal something?", and this was my father's answer, "I have been here for over forty years, I love the people of Mount Pleasant, and they love and respect me and I can honestly say to you that I have never lost even one potato", and Dad used to smile over that story, but it is perfectly true.

He came from Pembrokeshire, a lovely village not very far from Crymerch. He came as a porter to start off with, over in Merthyr Vale Station. Everyone knew my father and of course he had to have lodgings and he was most fortunate, he had a lovely home in which to live with Mrs Vale, who lived

The Black Lion Signal Box at Mount Pleasant

in Cardiff Road, Merthyr Vale. He was very, very, happy there, very very happy.

Then he became a signalman and when I was a child I used to love to walk down to the signal box on the Aberfan side and cross over with my mother, and we'd go into the signal box. We would cross over by the Bluebell Field before you came to Pontygwaith. We walked down and crossed the field and then there would be Dad's garden, and then we'd go up the steps to Dad's signal box.

I can remember so well, there was Dad, very, very clever with the 'phone, and he'd be phoning and writing and he was a beautiful one with the handwriting. You couldn't beat him, and I used to think "What a wonderful gentleman my father is to be able to do all that, phoning and then write it down". And then the most exciting thing of all was to see Dad taking the flag, opening the window, the train would be coming and the flag, the right flag, would be put out of the window. All the guards knew Dad and they would signal to him and he would wave the flag and show them the right way. And another wonderful thing, in all those years, Dad, he never had one accident because he always knew the right flag to wave.

MORFYDD HOLDEN, 1987

The signal box at Mount Pleasant also called the Black Lion would have been a very important signal box on the Taff Vale Railway at this time. Not only would passenger traffic be passing this way, but the signalman would have had the responsibility of all the traffic from the Merthyr Vale Colliery during the war time when there was a huge demand for coal. There were numerous sidings and Mr David Evans would have been kept very busy.

19. Aberfan

Decades before the Coal Tip toppled,
the rain and hail of Merthyr Vale
on window panes tapped cryptic warnings
as Dowlais furnace demons danced
against the Brecon Beacons backcloth.
When pyrotechnic dusk descended
the Miners' lamps mimed creeping sparks
on ashes left by burning paper
or glow-worm groups that slowly squirmed
towards the tainted River Taff.
The village crouched below the tall
unslighted wall of spoil, the site
of Doomsday domes as black as night
where undermining muck was massing
in growing might deploying forces
for Operation Thanatopsis,
to form a phalanx and advance
on undefended killing ground.
It made a mindless Kindermord
of Innocents in Pantglas School.
But this is hindsight. Now I write
of Aberfan pre-avalanche
when I was young and green as grass
that grew where now wax flowers fade.
Dull endless Sabbaths I recall
with countless aeons wedged between
the rocks of Early Morning Service,
Sunday School and Evening Sermon
when Zion Chapel sought to grapple
with Higher Thought and low esteem.
The Hong Kong Corner Shop I knew
and Station Hill and Nixonville,
the Crescent libelled Dog-and-Tub Row
and towpath trek to Troedyrhiw
to mix and match with fag-end boyos
who nicknamed noted local voters
'Old Cannonballs' and 'Mochen Pigs'
'Prick Evans Porth' and 'Scratchit Sid',
'Dai Bach' and 'Ianto Spit-a-quid'.
Where have they gone? Where are they now?

Down some wet pit of sweat and grit
or better 'ole more black than coal
that Time has drilled beyond the Blue?
   Still sharp and clear my ear retains
the sound of Nineteen Twenties Sundays,
the dust that widespread underfoot
when Zion Chapel's congregation
behind its Baptist barricade
of crumbling brick and broken glass
defied encroaching gloom with hymns
extolling grief with doleful joy,
- grey faces grave with guilty pleasure.
   From throat of ventilation shaft
of Nixon's Navigation Nine
pulsed groans and rhythmic exhalations
as though pit monsters racked with pain
were stumbling to some mammoth graveyard
while Sunday bells were tolling knells
with choirs that made a shroud of sound
for those unborn but dead too soon
- tone weaving with that silken yell
that threads together song and soul
with grief, belief and exultation
that eases pain and frees the will
yet makes the itching eyelids smart,
confused by joy's obscuring foreboding.
   The vale, too small to stage it all
reveals no Gotterdämmerung,
Apocalyptic Revelation
or Tragic Muse of Sophocles,
but through the arch of absent years
I see the strain of Time and tears
where rows of gravestones line a hill.

SELWYN RUSSELL JONES

20. Service

Before the eighteenth century, men vastly outnumbered women in domestic service but as men became more demanding of better wages and conditions, wages began to rise and women began outnumbering men in the great houses. Also in the eighteenth century came the growth of the middle classes who began demanding servants too, and by the next century every middle class household had at least one servant, usually a woman. One of the reasons that a woman would be employed was that she could be paid less. A household would struggle to keep a servant, even poorly paid clergy would rather economise on other things than do without domestic help. The maid servant was a symbol of social status. Domestic service reached its peak when the numbers of those able to afford resident domestic staff rose sharply. By 1901 domestic service was the major employer of women in the country and with a total workforce of one and a half million people, there were more employees than in mining, engineering or agriculture.

The First World War altered the position of the female domestic servant. Women found that they could become factory workers, bus conductresses, canteen workers, land girls, nurses and shop assistants. Often they replaced men who had been called up. They found that they could pick and choose their employment and if they continued in domestic service, their employer. But after the war was over, the men and women did not return to domestic service. Women began to think that they lost social status by becoming domestic servants whilst the men tended to enter hotels, restaurants and clubs.

The growing economic depression of the 1920s once again saw girls entering into domestic service, albeit reluctantly. Hundreds of girls entered domestic service from the South Wales valleys during the years of the 1930s' depression. The Merthyr Valley, including Aberfan and Merthyr Vale, was no exception. The distinctive dress that they all wore of black stockings, print dress, white apron, cap and collar, evolved from the beginning of the nineteenth century onward and lasted well into the twentieth century. Ex-miner, Will John O'Brien sets the scene from a man's point of view.

21. "She had to go away"

Women in the villages stayed home once they got married and there was little work for girls. They had to go away to service. "They were skivvies." My own sister had to go. The vacancies would be advertised in the "South Wales Echo." All the "nobs" would advertise in there. My sister-in-law went to work in the cloisters of Windsor Castle for the clergy and canon. She was married by the canon in the chapel at Windsor. Poor dabs went away at fourteen. My own wife went away but came home at fifteen when her mother died. Girls thought that it was marvellous to work in a shop like Theophilus in Merthyr and did not have to go away to service. Girls looked after the children in the family but were not paid for that. Boys worked underground but if you had a girl, she had to go away. You can see how things have altered.

WILL JOHN O'BRIEN.

Girls in service, 1930s

22. "Call me Madam"

I went away to service when I was fourteen. That was in 1931. I was fourteen on the 2nd of October and because I had a job to go to, I was able to leave school straight away. I was going into service to a Mrs Phillips of Penylan in Cardiff. There were five children in the house, as well as Mr and Mrs Phillips. I had to wear a brown dress and a white cap and I had them made in the village.

My brother took me down to Cardiff and when we got there I said "Mrs Phillips! This is my brother." "You must call me Madam!" she said. Her husband was a 'bit of a boss' on the docks. I had to call the children 'Miss' or 'Master.'

We didn't arrive until seven o'clock but she told me to go up to my room and get changed into my uniform. When I came down, she had disappeared. After a while my brother said, "Can you find her? I want to go." I knocked at three or four different doors before I found her. She paid him for bringing me from Aberfan to Cardiff, and he left.

I was washing for five children, all by hand, there was no washing machine there. I worked from 6.30 in the morning until half past nine at night. After dinner was over, I had to do silver cleaning or brass cleaning. Then there were the children's shoes to clean and after that I would help the master bath the twins; they were about three years of age when I was there. I was so tired by the time that I finished, that I would go to bed straight away. I was paid 10/- a week.

Every week I would have one afternoon off and I would go into the City with the girls. We would be happy enough until we would see a bus with Merthyr Tydfil on it. We would jump on the bus and I would go as far as Troedyrhiw. From there I would catch a bus down to my mother's house in the Grove, Aberfan. She would make me a meal and I would have just enough time to eat it before I would have to leave to catch the bus back to Cardiff. The fare was 1/6d. which was a lot out of a weekly wage of 10/-.

I remember one evening, I was seeing to the children's beds, as usual and I took one of the hot water bottles out and put it in my own bed. My mistress caught me and when Christmas came she gave me a hot water bottle and half a crown as my present. After Christmas dinner was over, I was allowed to travel home. I met up with some of the other girls on the train. In the compartment they were all showing what they had had for Christmas. One of the other girls had been given a beautiful eiderdown by her mistress. When I showed them my hot water bottle, they all screamed with laughter.

Anyway, I had been there for nearly two years when my mother became ill and I was worried about her. My father wanted me to come home. He wanted me to finish. I said to my mistress, "My mother is ill and I'd like to go home." "I want you to stay. I'll give you a raise of 1/- a week." she said. But when I went home my father wouldn't hear of me staying.

I said to the mistress again, "My mother is ill and I want to go home." "Wait until next week" she said, "and then you can have some time off and stay at home for a few days."

I told my father that I did not like to tell her that I was leaving and in the end I packed my two cases and carried them downstairs and left them in the outside toilet. Then when I had finished work for the day, I wrote a note and left it on my bed, saying that my mother was ill and that I had gone home. When I got to Queen Street Station, I was very nervous but luckily I met up with Mrs Conti, who kept a cafe in Aberfan and I stuck close to her. We went as far as Troedyrhiw and then caught the bus down to Aberfan. I got off the bus and walked the short distance to my mother's house. It was pitch dark by now. I knocked at the door. "Who's there?" called my mother. "Me." I said. "Beryl! Thank God." she said. She opened the door and there she was with a candle in the old fashioned candlestick and my brother's two little boys behind her in their nightshirts.

I soon found another job working for the people who kept the Pontyrhun Stores in Troedyrhiw. I was paid less than I was having in Cardiff, 8/- a week, and I would rather walk than pay 2d a day busfare, but I was glad to be home.

BERYL ROBERTS, 1991

The Grove Bus Stop

THE GROVE BUS STOP

23. Worthy Ambassadors

Invasion appeared imminent and on the last Sunday in May (26th) the announcement was made on the 9 o'clock radio news that children from the East and South East coast towns were to be evacuated, those from Folkestone amongst them. The following week was spent on preparations, the Education Office being in constant touch with the schools and with London: there were medical examinations, and labels to be filled in by parents. Final instructions came on Saturday morning, and these were broadcast overnight by the Ministry of Health and printed in the morning papers. For Harvey Grammar School it was to be - Merthyr Tydfil.

So on Sunday morning, June 2nd, on a peerless day of brilliant sunshine, over 3200 Folkestone school children assembled by 9 a.m. in Radnor Park. People lined the streets, cheering and waving: some parents came to the Park, others watched from the down platform or gathered in gardens along the railway for a last wave. At the Central Station were the Mayor (Alderman G. A. Gurr), the Chairman of the Education Committee (Alderman R. L. T. Saunders) and many other town representatives, gathered to wish them God-speed: also some thirty members of the St. John Ambulance Brigade, whose services were fortunately not needed. The children - carrying gas masks, and food for the day, and with ration cards and identity cards safely packed in their hand luggage - were excited and happy and in good spirits, looking forward to a wonderful adventure: parents realised that their children would be in comparative safety. With the parties went 185 teachers and 100 other helpers: in their luggage were the bare necessities in clothes and equipment - night clothes, toilet articles, change of underclothes, handkerchiefs, stockings or socks, house shoes or plimsolls, and a warm coat or mackintosh - other clothes could be sent later.

It was a hot day and the train was packed - ten to a compartment - rolling stock being scarce on account of the Dunkirk evacuation. Boys brought their own food - sandwiches, packets of crisps, oranges, apples: and though at stops (Tonbridge, Redhill, Reading) kind hearted people handed up lemonade and other drinks, the party suffered a great deal from thirst, except for the wiser ones who had brought drinking water with them. And so continued through the Severn Tunnel to Newport, where water supplies were replenished, and an additional engine attached for the mountain gradient. It was a rush job, extremely well done: journey's end was reached about 5.30 with the party tired, somewhat disheartened, and in some doubt over the sort of reception they would get.

But they need not have worried: there was no mistaking the warmth of the welcome which awaited them. As the train ran into the Merthyr terminus it was met by the Mayor, J. W. Watkin, and prominent townspeople: there was a poster "Folkestone gets a Deal at Merthyr": over the platform was a banner, "Welcome," with lines of flags: there were shouts of "You will get a square deal here, folks" - for there were some Deal children amongst the party.

So the exiles made their way to the Miners' Hall, hauling their luggage up the main street in the evening sun. The streets were lined with people, often five or six deep: foster-parents, sightseers - the whole town seemed to have turned out, and police kept a way for the long line of boys and girls. No doubt there was much scrutiny - and criticism - of appearance and demeanour, but whenever a halt occurred people, and particularly the women, chatted with boys and girls and assured them they would be happy in Merthyr.

Some two hours were spent in the Miners' Hall: checking, a second medical, and then a meal: after which the party left for separate halls, one in each ward of the town, and from there were taken by billeting officers to their new homes. By 10 p.m. everyone was settled in.

Merthyr was in many ways a great contrast to Folkestone: it was an inland, industrial town in a depressed area, predominantly labour in politics and non-conformist in religion. The people were shorter and stockier, had their own ideals and traditions, spoke a different language: the lively Celtic temperament was very different from the reserve natural of Kentish folk. But boys soon came to know and appreciate their Welsh hosts, and entered into Welsh life and customs more easily than might have been expected - and in this the help of Mr R. J. Howells (who was returning, after eighteen years, to within a few miles of his native place) was invaluable. They also began to admire the miners, whose work was much more dangerous (if less spectacular) even than work on the high seas, and who made light of frequent injuries which they regarded as the normal hazards of their work.

Staff from Harvey Grammar School, at Merthyr Tydfil, A B Downing Head Teacher middle of front row

They soon picked up something of the language, and their English speech insensibly acquired a Welsh intonation, and even a Welsh idiom: some of them earned rewards from their hosts for learning by heart (in Welsh) the Lord's Prayer or the xxiii psalm - with, of course, "Land of my Fathers."

Some boys were more fortunate then others in the matter of billets, which might be in larger houses where they could even have a quiet room of their own for study, or with families able to help them in their work. The great majority of billets were, however, in the smaller houses which could not provide these amenities: such foster parents could not give what they had not got, and made up for any lack by kindness and sympathy. They took the greatest interest in the boys' progress, and helped in every way they could, so that a wonderful sense of affection grew between the English boys and their Welsh hosts. There were many cases in which boys were provided with clothing and pocket money if these were needed: some went away for holidays with their hosts: others were helped to secure good posts as they left school.

There was, of course, a billeting allowance, but it was absurdly small: for boys under 10 years, 10s.6. a week: from 10 to 12, 11s.0d: from 12 to 14, 12s.: from 14 to 16, 13s.: from 16 to 17, 15s.6d.: and over 17, 16s.6d. Such sums, even in the early 1940s, would scarcely cover the cost of food. And the headmaster, Mr A. B. Downing, reporting (1942) of 177 boys billeted, classified 63 as "very good", and 63 as "good": 48 were "satisfactory" and only 3 considered "unsatisfactory".

The boys were fortunate in being able to keep together as a unit, and even to draw closer together than at home, for many other schools were scattered amongst a number of South Wales schools, and became integrated with them. The individuality of the Harvey Grammar School was thus strongly maintained, its essential traditions unbroken, and the school spirit undaunted. Nor, strangely enough, does scholarship seem to have deteriorated much during these years.

Schoolboys experienced at first hand a side of life they would never otherwise have known: contact with an industrial community living in a distressed area came at first as a shock, but this was soon replaced by sympathy and admiration. They also came to realise that amongst their fellow citizens were those with a widely different temperament, who had their own traditions and customs, and who even spoke a different language.

Then, away from parental control, boys acquired an increased sense of responsibility, of self-reliance, of self discipline, e.g. in the organisation of their leisure as well as of their work time-table, and in going about a great deal on their own. They learned too, to conquer their shyness and reserve: to get to know people hitherto strangers, and above all to appreciate their hosts. Whether they left any compensating advantages behind them is difficult to tell: it is hoped they proved worthy ambassadors of their home County and of their mode of life.

In September 1944 the return of the evacuated schools from South Wales was seriously mooted, and a formal three months' notice was given by the Education Committee to the Corporation in October: the Governors would require possession of the school premises early in the New Year.

Ultimately, on December 9th, it was decided - with the concurrence of the Kent Education Committee - to open after the New Year, on January 11th: and this in spite of the fact that the Minister of Health had not at that time removed Folkestone from the list of evacuated areas.

Thus it happened that a brief but very pleasant ceremony took place in Georgetown school, when the Mayor (Alderman T. Edmund Rees) and the Mayoress bade the school a formal farewell - not a lasting goodbye, for they hoped to meet again, perhaps in Folkestone. For the school, there was regret at leaving so many friends, and a sense of gratitude to their hosts, which later took a tangible form, when parents combined, with the Girls' County School and the Technical School, to raise a substantial gift (£127) for the Merthyr General Hospital. And so, on December 23rd, 1944, the official evacuation ended after 4 and a half years: a real Christmas home-coming for 550 boys and girls, of whom 140 were Harvey Grammar School boys.

The return journey began at dawn, in a long train of corridor coaches. G. T. Taylor of the Folkestone Education Department acted as their marshal, and the escort of helpers included three nurses, though nothing serious happened to require their services. At Reading, tea and sandwiches were provided: at Tonbridge, more urns of tea and cartons of sandwiches were taken on board: and so, after a stop at Sandling for the Hythe boys to alight, the train arrived at 6 p.m. at Shorncliffe, where it was met by Councillor W. J. Rule. Alderman Stainer was at the Central, and so the train continued to the Junction, Dover and Deal. Everywhere there were cheers, and help with luggage, and loads of good things provided for all.

EXTRACT FROM A 'HISTORY OF THE HARVEY GRAMMAR SCHOOL' BY THE REV. J. HOWARD BROWN, B.Sc.

Inside Cyfarthfa Castle School, Merthyr

24. An Evacuee Remembers

From a holiday resort sandwiched between the English Channel and the North Downs to an industrial town set in lovely Welsh countryside … came the evacuees during WWII.

From a reserved populace with its large proportion of retired folk to be received, with great kindness and sympathy, into a friendly, hard-working, coal-mining community … our Kentish accents mingling unmelodically with the music of Welsh voices.

From schools housed in attractive old residences to a spectacular modern castle … where the girls from the Merthyr Tydfil area uneasily squeezed up to make room for us on the top floor, (while the boys were on the ground floor - and never the twain were supposed to meet!)

From a frontline town which knew fortification and Dunkirk returnees (and later the Battle of Britain, cross-Channel shelling and buzz-bombs passing menacingly overhead) to the peace of a town which knew little of the belligerent manifestations of wartime … we were welcomed.

Among my 'best' friends were Cyfarthfa girls, Sheila Reid and Mair Owen, and there was Fay who played the piano at school lunchtimes so that we could dance. The Jitterbug was the 'in' thing and we gyrated wildly, clattering our heels on the polished floor until the damage to the parquet and the deafening decibels forced an ultimatum from Miss Davenport (Welsh headmistress) - either stockinged feet or NO Jitterbug! (The noise had been half the fun, of course.)

With Sheila and Mair I joined the Woman's Junior Air Corps. We drilled in the Drill Hall and marched behind the boys' Air Training Corps band, and went to summer camp where lollipop bombs, and their like, were demonstrated. We learned to fire rifles and throw hand-grenades. I have the group photo still.

I was fortunate in having my mother and sister with me and, unlike most of the girls, didn't return home for the school holidays. The few who remained behind were taken by our teachers on some wonderful outings. We visited Porthcawl, Penarth and Barry, then explored the Brecon Beacons and had glorious hikes to the Duffryn Valley. The mountains and their sheep were a new experience, and delighted us. We collected sphagnum moss and the tufts of sheeps' wool left on barbed wire fencing; this was sent off to be made into padding for airmen's suits. Wild flower naming competitions were held along the flower-crowded banks of the River Taff, and so the happy days went by.

Back nearer base we gazed in awe at the 'burning tip' at Dowlais, and wondered if the goats tethered there ever got burnt feet. We checked the everchanging torrent which rushed down Abermorlais to see what colour the chemical works had provided that day - the favourite one being a bright turquoise! Close to the Castle Cinema we visited Binah Owen, the blacksmith, who often allowed us to pump the forge bellows. I still have a beautiful copper horseshoe that he made for me.

I have so many memories of my schooldays in Merthyr that they would fill a book. Things like taking 'banana' sandwiches to school (Mam only telling after the war that it was really parsnip mashed with flavouring!); wearing clogs because they were five clothing coupons whereas it was seven for shoes; a wasp diving up my sleeve in a sweet shop and my pulling my jumper right off - to everyone's amazement, (I was only eleven but was still greatly embarrassed;) Mam's war-time elastic giving out whilst on a school outing, and everyone gathering around to shield her whilst she got sorted out! (Quite a feat in those days of the dreadful directoire knickers!) and so it goes on until my last one  ... our family had developed a love of Welsh griddle cakes, so Mam, before taking Frances and going home ahead of my school's departure, had asked our landlady to get a bakestone made for me to take - I shall never forget struggling to the station with my luggage AND that 14lb slab of iron ... our wartime souvenir from South Wales!

Anecdotes from Others ...

Going back to our day of arrival in Wales - Marlene Jones remembers, as a child, sitting on the wall of the old Aberfan station and looking back at the lines of evacuees standing on the platform holding their packages, labels tied to lapels, waiting for the next move.

I doubt that anyone has forgotten the experience of sitting in school-rooms at the end of that long day's travelling waiting to be claimed by the local housewives. They gathered us up, took us home and made us part of their families: bless them.

Many of us were billeted within walking distance of our schools, but those who lived in places like Aberfan went by train to Quakers Yard where the Technical School was housed, or to Merthyr where they walked on to Georgetown School or the splendid Cyfarthfa Castle which had absorbed the County and Grammar Schools.

Aberfan and Merthyr Vale were easy names to cope with but we found many others to be real tongue-twisters.

A few mothers came to stay in Wales; often bringing younger brothers and sisters who then attended Welsh schools. Some children learned to speak a little Welsh especially those who went to chapel; one 'girl' recalls being presented with a bible as a farewell gift from the one that she attended.

Our teachers gave up much of their spare time to dealing with our welfare. They provided entertainment for us and, *in loco parentis*, educated us in table manners, hygiene and the like. They also had the more devastating matters to deal with such as breaking the news of family casualties through enemy action; or offering consolation when members of their Welsh 'families' were killed in the forces.

One small group of girls knitted and sold small items to raise money for Clementine Churchill's Russian Fund, and her handwritten acknowledgement said:

March 1943

10 Downing Street,
Whitehall.

Dear Gladys, Pamela and Dorothy,

Thank -you very much for your gift which I have just received. I am very grateful to you for the trouble you have taken to help the heroic Russians in their terrible but victorious struggle against the wicked invaders of their country.

Your sincere friend,

CLEMENTINE CHURCHILL

Evacuee youngsters joined the cadet forces and the Boys Brigade. We loved to swim in the indoor pool at the back of the Merthyr Hospital and we played in the parks. An abundance of cinemas in the area fed our minds with their colourful nonsense and the chip shops filled our stomachs afterwards. Several lads were so absorbed by the film industry that they found themselves niches in cinema projection rooms (and one later made it his profession) - such was our fascination with Hollywood and its celluloid glamour!

Socials and outings were plentiful, and one favourite trip was to Pontsarn where we gazed in awe down into the ill-famed Blue Pool. We loved picnicking on the mountains; giving wide berth to the many basking snakes we saw, and picking delicious winberries. Another novelty was exploring the tips, and one boy who used to enjoy sliding down the ill-fated Aberfan tip can remember being warned to take care as it was considered unstable - even in those days.

The King, Queen and little princesses came to inspect the so-called sewing-machine factory which, everyone said, was really producing munitions. The first black men most of us had seen, apart from on the movies, were among the lorry-loads of American soldiers which passed through those parts - the men threw chewing-gum and chocolate to children in the streets.

We visited Cardiff to see a pantomime with Victoria Hopper as Cinderella and were very impressed when she later married a Folkestone actor and settled there. Mrs Downing, wife of the then headmaster of the Grammar School, recalls going to the opera in Cardiff and having the opportunity to purchase some fish, (a rather scarce commodity), en route - but, alas, no wrapping paper available, so she and a friend wrapped it in their scarves and stowed it beneath their theatre seats. Despite puzzled complaints from people around about a fishy smell, the two culprits kept very quiet!

Ruth Watkins says that she had 'two lovely boys' staying with her and, as there was a shortage of kettles, one of their mothers sent her one filled with another item in short supply … onions! The boys took pieces of coal home from the tips as momentoes, and she wonders if they have them still?

After the war our Welsh 'families' started visiting the homes of their war-time charges and many of us nostalgically continue to go to our own special parts of Glamorgan - some have married local people and settled there.

Winifred Turner, retired secretary of the Folkestone County School, surely spoke for everyone when she expressed the tremendous sadness we all felt at the time of the tragedy in Aberfan, a place which had been part of our growing up days during World War II.

Acknowledgements for 'memories' to:
I. Downing, D. L. Hewson, Marlene Jones nee Williams, Yvonne Miller, L. G. Petts, W. J. Russell, Margaret Sumner née Horne, Winifred Turner, Ruth Watkin, Frances Wood nee Skeer, T. Wylie.

JOAN SKEER PLANT.

Evacuees and others having
a picnic at Pontsarn .
Mrs Foley, Penydarren in the Centre

25. The Irate Official

During the 1939-45 war, an official came to give a talk to the residents of Aberfan Crescent about air raid precautions. This meeting was held in the Navigation Hotel.

The official said that in the event of fires breaking out after a bombing raid, they would have to be tackled in order of importance. "If there is a fire in this hotel and one in the end house opposite, you would have to tackle this one first."

"No, I wouldn't", said one of the audience, Bomper Jackson. "Yes, you would", said the irate official. "Well, I wouldn't", came the reply once again, "because I live in the end house."

NORMAN JONES, 1991

26. My mother lived in an end house

On a warm Summer's day, about the 5th or 6th of July 1941, I was in work at the munitions factory at Bridgend. I was working the 2 p.m. to 10 p.m. shift. Sometime during the afternoon, someone came into our department and enquired who lived in Merthyr Vale. On being asked why he was enquiring, he replied that an aeroplane had crashed into an end house there and that someone had been killed. My mother lived in an end house so I made tracks for home without delay.

You can imagine my horror and shock when I eventually saw the end house of South View, demolished and the wreckage of two aeroplanes nearby. Then I was told that Mrs Cox, the occupier of the house, together with her two children, had been killed. Also dead were the two pilots. What a sudden tragedy to befall a small close community.

Phyllis Davies, 1992

27. The whole field shook

At the age of seven, my father was playing down in Munkley's Field, Mount Pleasant, when he heard the sound of aeroplanes, very loud. He looked up and there were two aeroplanes flying one above each other. They were flying very close when their wings must have clipped because the next moment one plane crashed into the field that he was playing in. The whole field shook and the other plane carried on to crash into Mrs Cox's house in South View. The house went on fire and he was very frightened. He scrambled up the bank of the field to the main road and ran home. He told me that he will always remember hearing his mother calling his name as he was running home. She had heard the noise of the planes crashing and she knew that he was playing in the field.

Later he ran up the street because the fire engines were there. He was not sure if the hose pipes were taking water from the Mount Pleasant pub or out of the river. He seems to remember talk of the train cutting the hose pipe.

One pilot was found on the fence of the playing field.

JULIE JEFFERSON NÉE EVANS, 1992

28. A Fateful End

The Sgt. Pilots were Canadians serving in the Royal Canadian Airforce. Their names were Louis Goldberg, known as 'Curly' to his mates, who was twenty seven years of age at the time of the incident, and Jerald Fenwick Manuel who was twenty five years old at the time of the incident. They are both buried in the cemetery in Cefn Coed, Merthyr Tydfil. Louis Goldberg is buried in the Jewish Cemetery about a quarter of a mile from his comrade.

Eye witnesses are known to have said that three aeroplanes had been flying over the village in close formation when the wingtips of the two came into contact, hurtling them groundwards to their fateful end.

Enquiries revealed that relatives had been known to visit the graves but no-one had visited in the last twenty years, as far as is known.

CYRIL JOHNSON, 1992

29. Nixon House

When the day's surgery was over on Friday, 28th February, 1986 that, presumably, ended Nixon House as a doctor's premises.

It had started, certainly by early this century and, possibly late in the 1890s. (We are sure that one of Headway's readers knows the exact date. We'd like to know.)

Nowadays we are familiar with the description 'purpose-built'. Nixon House was purpose-built then.

Nixon's Navigation, the colliery owners, had it built for the company doctor. It was designed to be home, surgery, consulting room, treatment centre and pharmacy. An interesting feature is the side door allowing colliery accident victims direct access to the treatment room.

A half-century before the National Health Service was launched, when all local males over fourteen worked as miners, money was stopped from each man's wages to pay for his family's medical attention at GP level. Nixon House's first resident doctor was a practitioner named Draffin. We know that he lodged with Miss Eileen Goldsworthy's family at no. 3 Nixonville.

For readers of a certain age, though, the figure always to be identified with the house is Dr Charles Richardson White. He was memorable for reasons other than his professional qualities. He was a character. The be-spatted, ex-army doctor was chauffeur-driven on all his rounds. His uniformed driver, Adams, lived further down Nixonville.

The well-tended garden was, we believe, sometimes used for parties, ceremonies and presentations. Its flagpole flew the appropriate flag on the home countries' patron saints' day.

Dr White, an obvious Scot, had married a Miss Livesey whose family had the Glantaf Hotel, Troedyrhiw. There will be many with memories of Mrs White dressing their wounds.

In days, not so distant, quite major treatment, now only undertaken in hospitals, was performed in the village surgery. Medicines, too, were made-up there. It is, therefore understandable that for the people of Merthyr Vale and Aberfan, Nixon House, no matter to what future use it is put, will always be the surgery.

HEADWAY, APRIL 1986

30. As if they stopped breathing only yesterday

Merthyr Vale, Aberfan, to me these names are synonomously linked with my childhood, with a past that is daily growing less tangible, with a heritage that I can never own because I don't live in Merthyr Vale to reap the benefits of the community spirit that my ancestors took for granted and the people of Merthyr Vale still enjoy. That feeling of togetherness, if it even exists in some other part of Merthyr, certainly doesn't thrive the way that it does in Merthyr Vale and Aberfan, the way that I appreciated even though I only lived in Aberfan a few years when I was very young.

It saddened me to learn of the pit closing because it played such a huge part in our family history. My great-great-grandmother saw it sunk, my grandfather brought out the last pit pony and so many other members of my family were associated with it in so many different ways. And now it has closed, its life ended, just like the lives of my ancestors whose life it fulfilled.

Although I no longer live in the Merthyr Vale community I still visit my Nan often, and as she speaks of people who died decades ago, as if they stopped breathing only yesterday, I am reminded how proud I am to be part of a "long established family in Merthyr Vale".

LISA JONES, AGE 16, GRAND-DAUGHTER OF EDITH JONES

Colliery visit, Merthyr Vale, 1970s

162

Chapter Six
Memories

1. Introduction

Living in this close knit mining community we have so many memories. In an age before the supermarkets and supertores our shops were all-important and many of the memories recorded here concern our shops. Mary Rees née Emanuelli remembers her father " A Welshman with, an Italian accent" who kept a local cafe for 26 years. Also remembered are children's games, significant buildings, the soup kitchens and the war years.

The Soup Kitchen Helpers 1911

2. Memories

It is commonplace today to hear of the closing down of old buildings, so we are apt to accept the news with a matter of fact attitude, but when it happens in our own village, we immediately become alert and start to recall what part that particular building may have played in our own lives.

The Rechabite Hall, better known as the Coffee Tavern, is such a building. It evokes many happy memories especially for the older generation of our community.

Around fifty years ago one could have called it our community centre, but having less amenities than our present day centre. None-the-less, many happy hours were spent there by the people of the area. One could spend a whole afternoon or evening in a happy, friendly environment for very little cost. We can hear the older folk saying 'those were the good old days'.

The Rechabite Hall was built in the 1880s after the Taff and Crescent Street houses were built for the workers of the, then, privately owned, Nixon Navigation Colliery. The 'Assembly Rooms' as the Coffee Tavern was known in its very earliest days, was provided by John Nixon for 'the workmen of that area'. The quarry workers employed at the nearby Oaklands quarry could buy soft drinks, cigarettes and snacks there. Indeed the building itself is built of solid stone hewed from the same quarry. The same quarry supplied the stone for the archways that were made underground in the Merthyr Vale Colliery. It is said to be the most solid building in the vicinity, never having been flooded by the notorious River Taff, but allegedly very cold, due to the flagstone floor. In its heyday it had two billiard tables and one bagatelle table. There were many good players and a billiard team which participated in competitive games. There was also a soccer team of high repute, winning many top trophies, even in its first year of competition. The top floor of the building was a dance hall, said by some to have the best sprung floor in Wales. Regular weekly Whist Drives and dances were held with special long dances in aid of various charities also helping many local residents in paying for medical appliances, on one occasion, a wooden leg.

The Hall was also used for Vaudeville shows and plays. There were the regulars, such as the Fox Family and their troupe who came and put on a different play each night. They played for a couple of weeks staying at various houses in the village and becoming 'part of the family'.

The Hall was used by both Anglican and Roman Catholic churches whilst their permanent places of worship were being built.

One memory for the residents of Taff and Crescent Streets is of when the River Taff flooded through their houses. When the water reached a certain level, a shout went out to carry furniture, lino, rugs, to the top floor of the Coffee Tavern for safety. Initials and house numbers were hastily marked on belongings in white chalk for later sorting. The Hall had a connecting door to No.1 Crescent Street, where the caretaker usually lived. In later years the hall has been used by the DSS and local doctors, and the top floor by St. Mary's Church for the youth of the area.

HEADWAY, APRIL 1985

The building was subsequently demolished. A block of flats has been built on the site. The name of the Rechabite Hall has been kept for the flats

Rechabite Hall conversion to flats

3.   I love Aberfan

I have loved Aberfan from the time that I was born in January 1906. On a Saturday night Aberfan would be like Piccadilly. The shops were open until gone 10.30 p.m. and you would see all the people going to these shops. The butcher boys would be out on their bicycles, a lovely arrangement of meat in front of them, and a clean tea-towel. They would be going in all directions, even to Merthyr Vale.

Kent's Shop. A noted shop for many reasons.
There was Mrs Kent, a very buxom lady from the country, up Hereford way. She was in charge of the sweet department and had a bad chest. I often laughed when I went there. She had oil in the other department. She was a lovely person and she had two children, Albert and Sarah.

Now they had living accommodation behind the shop and down below. There was a side entrance to go around the back. Every Sunday there was a great performance and my mother and I would never miss it for anything. My mother would say, "Morfydd. Dewch i weld nhyw yn mynd i ddechra., i'r Eglwys yn Troedyrhiw?" Great commotion. A horse and trap in those days. They were great people for Troedyrhiw Church, and father in his topper, very aristocratic, and a gold chain. Mother, very buxom in black satin and a huge hat. She would come up the side of the house and Albert would also come up the side of the house, to help get mother into the trap. And that was a performance because she was rather buxom. Eventually father and Albert would get mother into the trap, then once she was safely installed would call, "Sarah! Sarah! Come along Sarah!" Now Sarah was rather slow. She would come with button up shoes. "I'm coming mother. I'm coming mother." "Come along Sarah." Sarah would be taken into the trap, father at the reins. "Are we all ready, mother?" "Yes dear." Quick trot, trot, trot, trot, trot and off they would all go to Troedyrhiw Church.

And then next door to Kent's shop there was a lovely shop, J. B. Evan's shop. It was a fruiterers shop. J. B. was a clever gentleman and he had a delightful wife and lovely children. And on a Saturday night if you looked outside J. B. Evans', there would be two queues, one each side, by the two windows and if you wanted anything, you took your turn and there would be at least half a dozen assistants serving as quickly as possible at that time of night.

Then there was Davies' the Outfitters. He had a shop and it was something like Pontypridd Market. He was an outfitter and he would put some of his goods to hang outside. He did well, very, very well there indeed. And then they moved from Aberfan and went to Cardiff.

Martin's Shop.
Further along Aberfan Crescent, there was Martin's shop. I remember the old gentleman, George Martin, a delightful character and his delightful wife. It was lovely to go into that shop. And as soon as the old lady would see me, she usually sat behind the left hand side counter, she would say, "Oh come in my dear. It is always lovely to talk about the olden days." Then there was Mr Mytton. He was a lovely boy, Alby Mytton. He was in charge of the wireless, not the television in those days, the wireless. And I bought a wireless and Lionel, George's son brought it up and said "now if anything goes wrong, I'll send Alby up," and Alby was only too pleased to come to our house to see to the wireless. We all loved our wireless. We were all musical, the four of us. Mam, Dad, myself and also Eluned, my late sister.

Then further on there was a lovely, lovely Jewish family, the Silvergleitz. They had a lovely shop and Mr Silvergleitz was a watchmaker. There were watches and picture frames in that shop. They were a real aristocratic family.

Navigation Hotel.
The Navigation was a very famous hotel and it was there that our brass band practised and had rehearsals. The conductor was Mr George Thomas. His sister was Miss Evelyn Thomas, the music teacher; she was outstanding. She had pupils from all parts of Merthyr Vale and Aberfan. I would stand there and listen to the wonderful band rehearsals - and they were wonderful.

The Police Station.
On the end of Noel Terrace there was the Police Station. It was a lovely house with a lovely green in front of it and I can remember Sgt Howells. He was a real sergeant, very smart and he was living in

that police station, and he had a lovely wife and children. And over in Merthyr Vale in the police station there, was Inspector Roberts. And Inspector Robert's wife was a sister to Sgt Howells and when I was young, it was such a joy to see Sgt Howells and Inspector Roberts walking together the whole length of Aberfan Road and you sort of looked up to them as if you felt safe. They were on the beat. And another little point of interest; I can remember them using a torch and going late at night to every shop door to see that it was locked properly. Those were the police we had in those days.

India-China Shop.

This shop was the first shop, on the other side of Aberfan Road, opposite Smyrna Chapel, and was called India-China Shop. And I have very happy memories of India-China Shop and I'll tell you why. In those days they sold little, tiny biscuits and they were iced all over with the alphabet. A, B, C, etc., on each biscuit and you had a big bag full for 1d.

The Milliners.

We had a great milliner's shop. Mrs Hughes was the Milliner and she was a real court milliner. She had a mirror that reached from the floor up to the ceiling where you could view yourself in your new hat. She made all her hats and they were beautifully made out of crepe de chine. She was my mother's milliner and my late sister's milliner and my milliner; we were only young in those days. And when my mother wanted a new hat, Dad was always delighted; she'd take us down to Mrs Hughes the Milliner and she would order a certain hat for herself and one for me and one for Eluned and they were made and lined in crepe de chine. There was either a bunch of cherries or plums at the side. Well, we thought that we were little princesses. Mrs Hughes would wrap them up carefully in tissue paper and there'd be a big box with string at the top for carrying. And there would be my mother's hat, my hat and dear Eluned's hat, all in this box.

Then, where Jean Gough's shop is now, there was Price the Drapers. He had come from Brecon originally. He was charming and his wife was charming too. They had many assistants in the shop who had been trained there, so many of them. They had the lower department and then you went upstairs to the upper department if you wanted bed-linen or anything like that. Mrs Price had a nanny for her children and her nanny was lovely - she was from Troedyrhiw. I was very, very fond of Mr and Mrs Price. They were real characters, they were aristocrats.

Richards' the Jeweller.

Richards' the Jeweller was the noted jeweller from the top of Dowlais to the bottom of Trelewis. There was no other jeweller like Richards the Jeweller. His shop was outstanding. He happened to be friendly with my father. They were both brought up in Preselli. In those days they had the most outstanding grandfather clocks in Richards the Jewellers. They were a sight. He had a lovely wife. She was very clever. She was Catherine Dyer from Troedyrhiw. She was a noted organist and a talented painter as well. Mr Richards was a deacon in Smyrna Chapel. He more or less adopted his nephew, Luther. He brought him up and Luther was the mainstay of that shop. He saw to everything and everything was in apple pie order. Everything was shining like glass.

MORFYDD HOLDEN, 1987

Aberfan Crescent, the Coronation, 1911, showing some of the shops and the Police Station

4. Carlo

Carlo was a big black Labrador, he had big brown eyes, and a shiny black coat. His nature was as beautiful as his looks; to think that he was an ordinary dog would be quite wrong. In fact he was extra-ordinary.

He belonged to George Martin, the Paper Shop in Aberfan Crescent. Everybody knew him, friends and customers, but most of all the children of Aberfan Crescent, who invaded the shop regularly.

Carlo also had a job to do. In those days the railway ran through Aberfan, the Rhymney Line, and every morning at eleven o'clock, Martin's "Mid-day Echo's" would arrive on the train; there were only a few sheets of information for the racing fans, only nine copies, a small bundle. Carlo would sit on the shop step and listen, he could hear the train long before anyone else could. A few minutes before eleven George would say, "Go fetch", and up the Navi steps he would go straight on to the platform.

All the station staff knew him, one of the Porters would put the bundle in his mouth and off he'd go, down the Navi steps and back to the shop. He had done what he loved to do.

The First World War was raging in France, the Prince of Wales started a Fund to collect money to buy comforts for the troops. George put a collection box in the shop, outside the shop, Carlo also paraded up and down with a placard in his mouth. It seemed to do the trick, no one could refuse Carlo. Although Aberfan wasn't a wealthy village they soon filled the collection box, in record time.

The War went on, and it was decided that because of the increased traffic between England and France, there was an increased risk of Rabies, and all dogs outside their own homes should be muzzled. That was the beginning of the end for Carlo, he couldn't fetch the papers anymore, he couldn't sit on the step and be fussed by the children and the customers - nothing was the same for him.

In four months he was dead, he wasted away. George always said that he died of a broken heart, he just couldn't live his new way of life.

People would ask for months afterwards "Where's Carlo then?", when the train came; the Porters would look for him, but he never came.

TINA MARTIN, 1991

5.   Aberfan in the 1920s

I started work in Mrs Owen's shop at number 5 Aberfan Road when I was 15 and a half years of age. I had just left school and I started in the shop soon after Christmas 1920.

I earned five shillings a week, but one shilling was stopped out of my pay for the laundering of the smocks which were to be worn in the shop. I also went around on my bike on a Saturday afternoon to collect debts as most of the people bought on the 'slate' or on credit. I was paid a shilling in the pound for every debt collected. Mrs Owens was from Cemmaes in Mid Wales where her father had a farm and she went back there to live. I visited her there several times and I think that she eventually bought a public house there but I cannot be absolutely certain about this.

In 1923 I went to work in the local cinema in Aberfan. They needed a pianist and I could play the piano. The manager of the cinema, Mr Ferguson, lived next door to us in Wingfield Street and he had probably heard me playing the piano through the wall. I was very pleased to be offered the job, in fact I jumped at it. I started as an assistant to a lady who came down from Merthyr. She used to take snuff and this made the piano keys brown which used to annoy me very much.

Owen's Shop, 1920s

I was supplied with sheet music for the film but I was also very quick at picking up music by ear and as I was able to see the screen from where I was sitting. I often played what I had heard before to fit in with whatever was on the screen, for example a cowboy film.

Another thing that used to cause me annoyance was that young lads would flick peanut shells and empty cigarette packets into the piano, during the performance, thereby jamming the notes. I would ask the projectionist, Mr George Clees, to stop the film and then Mr Ferguson would harangue the audience from the front stage. These disturbances happened at the matinees. Because I was the Junior I was expected to play at the matinees. These same boys, when they came in, would try and pay me for their tickets with live mice and frogs and such like, but I gave as good as I got.

Underneath the cinema there was a billiard hall which was run by a girl friend of mine. The billiard hall was heated by a large fire, the cinema was cold and I used to get frozen stiff, so in between times I would go down to the billiard hall to keep warm. Sometimes I would have a game of billiards with the village lads. This doesn't sound much today but if my father had found out I would have been in for it. In those days, it was a cardinal sin for a girl to enter a billiard hall.

ANNIE MAY COLES, NÉE GEORGE,
BRISTOL 1991

6.   Pegler's Shop, Aberfan

I went to work in Pegler's shop when I was fifteen, straight from school. This was in 1931. I was working there for fifteen years and then I became the manager of the Pegler's shop in Abercynon.

Peglers was the last shop to be built in Aberfan.

Eira Hardy was the first cashier there. There was another girl working there with her and when Eira was leaving, Kitty told me about the job so I became the new cashier. The manager was a man from over the valley and he lodged with Mrs Rees in the Grove. There were two boys working there as well as the manager and myself. There was also a boy 'carrying out'.

We were kept busy because people were coming from over Merthyr Vale to do their shopping. We used to run a Christmas Club every year and people would save all the year round for Christmas. The people would buy mats, ironmongery, buckets and that sort of thing; they wouldn't buy luxuries. The grocery business was hard work in those days. Cheese, butter, all had to be weighed and wrapped separately. We had to weigh flour, sugar and dried fruit and the fruit had to be flat wrapped. Before the flaps were all tucked in the package would look like a rabbit. We were open until eight o'clock on a Saturday. We had ten days annual holiday and we always started back to work on a Friday.

The most popular sweets were liquorice all sorts and jubes. Sweets and cream biscuits were only sixpence a pound. A big bar of chocolate was two pence halfpenny. A two pound pot of jam was six pence halfpenny, plum jam. Hartley's was eleven pence halfpenny for a pound pot and was the best. Edam cheese was four pence halfpenny a pound. A small packet of Persil was three pence halfpenny and the best tea was eleven pence halfpenny a quarter. Loose tea was eight pence a quarter. A tin of pineapple chunks was three pence halfpenny and butter was ten pence a pound. A large tin of pears was eleven pence halfpenny. A large picnic ham was three shillings and eleven pence. This was a very large ham weighing about four pounds. The price of a mat was twenty five shillings for a very big mat and twelve shillings and sixpence for a sizeable mat. Club biscuits were two pence each and the area manager for Jacob's would come to the shop and give us samples of the biscuits.

There was sawdust on the floor of the shop and when it got dusty, it was swept up and fresh sawdust put down. The sawdust was there so that people wouldn't slip.

I was still there during the war. People had their ration books and their coupons. They were allowed only two ounces of butter and eight ounces of sugar. One old lady couldn't understand why she was allowed so little butter. She used to think it was my fault and tell me off.

I used to go around for orders. I remember going to one customer. Diptheria was raging and she had lost two of her daughters. I was there for a long time with her. She just could not stop crying.

MAIR PRICE NÉE PHILLIPS, 1991

7.   Merthyr Vale in the Past

There was an orchard where the Action Garage is now situated, also allotments on the Tramroad where there are now garages. At Easter time we would have the pleasure of two fairs, namely Scarrats and Freeman's.

There was also a social centre on the field alongside the Tramroad which was built by the workmen. The men would go there for a game of snooker or cards or draughts. Also there were whist drives held there. Often there would be concerts in the centre where you could go as a family for the cost of a few coppers and have a good night's entertainment. This has all long gone and we are left with just a playing field.

There was a billiard hall between Brynteg Terrace and a few houses known as Beehive Cottages but now known as Windsor Place. Men passed many happy hours there either playing billiards or having a chat. It was eventually put to use as a Salvation Army Chapel. Now it is just a seating area.

The local school was situated in the upper part of the village but was demolished in the late 1960s. The school yard still exists as a playground. The school house was occupied by the headmaster but was later used as a police house. Now it is used as flats.

There was a time when the people of Merthyr Vale could say "You needn't go from the village for anything you require." We had quite a variety of shops. In Cardiff Road there were Pierces and Michael's, two small shops selling a variety of goods. There was also Thornes shop and bakehouse where the villagers would take their Christmas cakes to be baked. Oh, the delightful smell when they came from the ovens, which were heated by coal, not gas or electricity.

There was also a dentist in Cardiff Road. Also in Cardiff Road we had Calfaria Chapel, which has been demolished in latter years. The Trinity Chapel was in Wesley Place but this has also been demolished and only the vestry remains which is still used for worship. There was also the Wesleyan Chapel and the Post Office which was kept by Miss Powell. Later this became "Cotters the Newsagents." On the corner was Thomas's the Fish and Chip shop. Also sold there was confectionary.

Nearby was the Merthyr Vale Station. Having obtained a ticket from the booking office the passenger would then go onto the platform and on a cold day there was a spacious waiting room with a cheery coal fire to warm you for the start of your journey.

The Station Square boasted the Royal Stores, always well stocked with mouthwatering groceries, and Dai the Barber. Then there was Arnotts which later became Hales the Chemist and then Mrs Gittens who later transferred her Milliner's business to Grey's Place on the opposite side of the square. Next we had Disgwylfa Chapel which also no longer exists as a place of worship. In Grey's Place, Mrs Ida Rees had a newsagent's shop.

Prospect Place was on the main Merthyr to Cardiff Road. There were a few houses and then the Hibernian Working Men's Club, Maggie Davies' sweet shop and William Harris's the Grocers. Next came Clive Place, nicknamed 'the Barracks', which is now demolished. Then there was another Fish and Chip shop, Rob the Cobblers and then Edwards Shoe shop later to become a doctor's surgery. Then came Windsor Place where there was Ham the butcher, the Co-operative Grocery store. Powell the butcher, George the barber and of course "The Windsor".

There were other shops in Merthyr Vale. We had Price the Bakers, the baking was done in the basement of the shop, where groceries were sold. Continuing on the main road we came to Jones Lozenge shop which is now a fish and chip shop. We had a faggots and peas shop but now it is a dwelling house. Crossing Victoria Street brings us to Rees' shop selling groceries and sweets and next Bill Beddis, the cobbler. Cross the road and retrace our steps and there we had Jim Harding's shop where we could get fruit, veg., fresh fish, rabbits and groceries. Lower down we had Paynes the drapers where you could buy anything from a pin to a bedspread.

In Belle Vue Terrace we had Prossers' sweet shop and Colston's sweet shop which was in Lena House. In nearby Alberta Street, we had Prosser the butcher.

Money was short in those days but the men worked hard in their allotments, both on the tramroad and behind Brynteg Terrace where they also kept poultry. They enjoyed the fruits of their labour when it came to eating the veg. they had grown and the eggs that the chickens had laid. The chicken eventually finished up on the dinner table.

The children also made their own fun, going up the mountain to play and maybe taking a picnic with them. Perhaps they would paddle in the pools by the tanks.

I must not forget to mention Maggie Williams and "Lil the Milk", who used to bring the milk in jacks and measure it into a jug at the door.

So many memories of Merthyr Vale. There is very little left now. Just Lewis the Newsagent and Doreen the Post Office at Station Square and Eirwen's, previously Tommy Clements, Windsor Stores at the top of Alberta Street and of course, "The Windsor".

BEATRICE CHAMBERS, 1991

The Windsor Hotel", Merthyr Vale

8.   A Walk in the Mind

A walk in the mind. Sounds a daft title doesn't it but it's true in as much as that's all that's left for me to do now. As I sit and ponder, my memory goes on a journey through time, and fifty odd years pass as quickly as an express train, and there I am walking down Bryntaf Street with the sun shining down on my bare head. Isn't it funny, whenever you think of your childhood, it seems that the sun was always shining.

As I stroll along I hear the sound of children playing. I look around me and see girls skipping with an orange rope that had been given to them by England the costamonger. Now that's a name to conjure up memories. Mr England and his beautiful high stepping pony that pulled his cart around the streets of the Borough. It seems I can still hear the clip clop of his horse, or is it Hughes "the Farm", selling milk from the churn, still warm from the morning's milking. As I wander down the street and come to Hughes "the Shop", I stop and look at all the goodies in the window. Monster bags, lucky dips, liquorice novelties and sweet potatoes that you sucked until you reached a little gilt toy in the middle. Duw! Like Aladdin's cave it was. Before I got to the corner, I had to pass another three shops in quick succession, Will Richards', Harris the Grocer's and Swift Jones. It was hard to be poor and not have any money.

I remember the school holidays quite clearly. Wasn't it good to get a few weeks from "Slogger" Williams, Gertie Lewis and Archie Powell? Little did we realise how important these people were until it was too late. But that is always the way. Is my memory playing me tricks or can I still smell the potatoes roasting on the bucket fires that the kids had scattered around? I can see them now with the black around their mouths after eating those potatoes. A real delicacy they were. The thought of them makes my tummy rumble even now. Memories are coming back of Sunday School trips to Barry Island or Porthcawl which was the nearest thing I ever had to a holiday. Another treat was a cornet from Jack Llewellyn. Now Jack Llewellyn sold cockles and wet fish on some days and ice cream on others, and it was said that he used the same ice cubes for them both. But whatever that truth of that, I can only say that ice cream has never tasted the same since.

In my mind's eye, I can see the men winding their way from the colliery after a long hard day. And for those who lived in Bryntaf it was more wearying because whichever way they went they had to climb a hill to get home. The first hurdle they came to was the long flight of steps at Nixonville;

if they turned left at the top, they would have to negotiate the Subway Hill, and if they went right they would have to go up the Navigation steps and the top half of the Station Hill. Mind you, if they fancied a quick pint, then the latter direction was the best to take. The Navigation Hotel was en route. When they reached the top of either hill, some of them would be spitting black; it was either the coal dust hanging heavy in their lungs or twist tobacco, or a combination of both.

When the men got home their dinners would be waiting for them, and while they ate the mams would be preparing the baths in front of the fire. And do you know, when I was a kid, I used to wonder how they washed themselves clean and preserved their modesty at the same time.

As I continue on my walk I can see the Bryntaf Men's Band marching up the street with the Leader Dai Thomas at the front and Ron Cartwright the base drummer at the back keeping the right beat. As they pass you can see the pride in them. they were world champions. They won the title at the Crystal Palace. As they march up the street to reach the Bryntaf Quarry, kids fall in behind and try to keep in line. They feel even prouder than the men.

Now as my memories begin to fade, a lump comes to my throat and although I wasn't born in Aberfan, I arrived there when I was 4 years old, the village and the people helped to fashion me for adulthood and even if I say so myself, it didn't do a bad job. One thing you can be sure of, no matter how long I live, I will always remember and feel proud of the time I spent in Aberfan.

TOM ABBOT **1991.**

Bryntaf

9.   The Hot Tears I Shed

Born on 16th January 1928 in Aberfan, I have spent most of my life here. Though for brief intervals moving away, I have always returned.

Pondering memories that stand out from my childhood in this small coalmining village, my thoughts turn to my own childhood, five daughters born between 1950 and 1963. I feel that, although my early days were much poorer, materially speaking, than theirs, I was lucky to be without the pressures and dangers imposed upon them by the culture of today.

Though my family were poor, no television or radio, no holidays, few new clothes, almost everyone else in the village was in the same position. A sense of camaraderie prevailed, and we produced our own entertainment. There was always some activity in Aberfan, "Penny Reading" (a form of talent contest), concerts in the hall and much involvement with our churches and chapels.

I also loved school. What joy in learning to cook! During those war years sugar and fat were scarce but schools were allocated special rations to enable the children to carry on these lessons. "Cleanliness in next to Godliness" Miss Davies Cookery (as we fondly called her) drummed into the minds of all.

Art was also a favourite subject of mine. Pantglas School had submitted several entries to an art competition open to the whole Borough. I had painted a "May-Day Scene"; children dancing and laughing around a colourful maypole accompanied by a man playing a fiddle.

One morning at assembly, Miss Gordon, our Headmistress, announced with pleasure that our school had taken a first and a third prize. It was with great pride and happiness that I learned that my picture had won the first prize. I was awarded a beautiful book of fairy tales from the school and the sum of 2/6d from the officials of the competition. The money seemed an awful lot then, (as indeed it was!) and I was thrilled when my mother told me that I was allowed to keep it all and spend it how I chose. So thrilled in fact, that even now, after all these years, I can still remember how it was spent. A brand new green swimming costume and bathing cap from the "posh" Llewellyn Jones Emporium, with enough left for a sketch pad and pencils from Martin's, a small village store. Try getting all that for 12.5 pence today!

As I have already mentioned, we created our own entertainment, therefore there were always rehearsals for concerts and such. For one concert at Bethania Chapel, I was chosen for an item in which I had to recite a story to a doll. My own (and only) doll was far too small to be used, so for the performance someone was kind enough to lend my teacher one.

I shall never forget being handed that doll. I can still see the wonderful clothes she wore made from shining, smooth yellow satin and her beautiful face made so special by her "sleeping eyes" that opened and closed like a real baby.

By today's standards, perhaps she wouldn't seem much - to me she was the most marvellous doll I had ever seen. The heartache I felt when I had to return her at the end of the concert, the hot tears I shed that she was not mine....

I still recall the feel and smell of her. I have only to touch satin and close my eyes and I am transported once again to Bethania Chapel.

EMILY GRIFFITHS (NÉE LLOYD), 1991

10. Soup Kitchens

I remember going to the Soup Kitchen in the 1926 Strike. My friend was Maud Davies. She was longing to go to the soup kitchen, she used to try and sneak in with me, but her father was Mr J. L. Davies the shopkeeper, so she wasn't allowed.

She would wait until I had finished my meal and then she would carry my empty plate. She seemed so proud carrying that plate.

Mr Harvard was in charge of the Soup Kitchen; he was a big Labour man, he was a very good man.

When you went for your soup - depending on what you liked - you would ask for 'a bit of thick or a bit of thin' depending on the thickness of the soup.

MEGAN JONES, 1991

11. Soup Kitchens, 1920s

Referring to the soup kitchen days, in the 1920s I had two sessions, one in 1921 when I was eight years old and the other in 1926 when I was thirteen years old. We had breakfast and dinner there. We started taking china cups and plates but they did not last long so we started taking condensed milk tins for cups until we got enamel cups and plates. We carried them in a 7lb cloth flour bag. We queued from Aberfan Road to the hall at the end of Coronation Place, and everybody would be singing. Also I went to 1, Moy Road, for second hand clothes which were distributed to people who were on strike. My mother was a good dressmaker and would alter them for trousers. I will always remember them issuing new suits to the very poor; they were of a reddish colour and everybody knew where they came from. It was very embarrasing for them that had them.'

TED DUGGAN, 1991

12.   Experience

In 1931 I left school and obtained employment at the Deep Navigation Colliery in Treharris as a Blacksmith's striker. The pay was 13 shillings and 8 pence for a six day week. I was laid off during the Depression; I had been one of the last in, but later I found a job in Castle Pit, Troedyrhiw in the lamp room on the night shift and the pay then was sixteen shillings and ten pence. I worked as a navvi for a while after that pit closed but when Hills Plymouth pit opened up again I went there and was paid £2.17.9 per week. I worked there until I got married.

Donald S. Young

13.   Keel Slugs and Caterpillars

8th August, 1939 I got married. September or October I had to go for a Medical, the Second World War having started. On the 4th April, 1940 I reported for duty at No. 10 Driver Training Centre (R.A.S.C.) Luton.

We were stationed there for about 8 weeks; during this time our main training consisted of drilling and only about two weeks tuition on driving. I had some difficulty in being kitted out because of my size, all my uniform was too small, and I still wore the boots that I worked in at the Colliery, because they could not fit me with a size 13. It was almost two years later that I was eventually fitted out with a uniform by the Indian Division while we were up in the Lebanon and Syria. I looked smart in my new uniform and boots; many an Indian Officer, because I was so tanned, and in the right colour battledresses, used to speak to me in Hindustani when delivering despatches; this caused some laughter and smiles from the Indian Clerks. We were posted to Cromer while Dunkirk was being evacuated.

Two things happened here which still make me smile when I think about them. The first was that I was detailed for duty on a road block, on the Runton Road; the password was 'Lifebuoy'. After dark, at approximately 10.30 p.m., a man approached my side of the road block. To my question 'Who goes there?' came the reply 'Friend'. I requested him to advance and be recognised. On approaching me I asked him for the password, he replied 'Sunlight'. That of course was the wrong password. The outcome was that this Officer had to spend one and a half hours in the Guard Room until we were relieved of our posts, whereupon the Guard Commander recognised him and took him through the road block, muttering under his breath, as he went.

Secondly, during one dinner hour I was head of the table and as such had to relay to the Orderly Officer any complaints about the meal before us. There were caterpillars in the cabbage and keel slugs in the potatoes; the boys at the table were moaning so I asked them if they would back me up if I complained. They said, 'Yes! Of course.' The said Officer arrived at our table and asked the usual question. "Any complaints?" I said, 'Yes Sir.' and went on to explain about the caterpillars and slugs saying, "this is meat extra to what is on the menu." He turned to the rest of the men and asked them if they too were complaining, to which the reply came, "No Sir! It is alright." I then showed him the slugs on the edge of my plate. He told me to take my plate to the cook house and tell them to give me another dinner, this I did, and was given a perfect dinner.

Later we were told that we were going up to Scotland and from there we would receive leave, but they pulled a 'flanker'; we boarded a train and landed in a place called Goo-Roc and there awaiting us were three liners; the Queen Mary, the Mauretania and the Aquatania and between these three, one Division of troops were boarded; our liner was the Queen Mary. Ports of call were Sierra Leone; Symonds Town; Trincamalee; Colombo; Bombay and Suez, the last four were aboard the S.S. Egra.

After disembarking at Suez we were taken to Genifa where we erected bell tents for all the R.A.S.C. drivers. For the next few weeks our job was to travel to Suez, Port Said and Alexandria to collect Bedford 3 tonners, Chevs and Matador trucks. A short time later we moved to Abbassia Barracks near Heliopolis and Cairo, where we had to camouflage our Bedford trucks with paint; and we then moved to El-Daba. Here there were scorpions, snakes and poisonous spiders (shivers), to contend with. A request came from Western District Headquarters for two Despatch Riders to contact all units in the Western Desert. A boy named Jimmy Jones from West Wales and myself volunteered and we were issued with Matchless G.3 350 cc ohv motor cycles, no air filters on the carburettors; I used to put half a pint of engine oil in with every three gallons of petrol to help save the cylinder wear. Jimmy Jones worked from H.Q. to Mersa Matruh and down to El-Daba. I worked from the Advance Supply Depot at El-Daba to Mersa Matruh over 1,000 miles per day. Whenever we saw feathering, sand coloured clouds we knew that the following day there would be a sand storm, some of which were so violent that you could hardly see three feet in front of you; it spoiled your food and drink.

When the rains started the thunder and lightening were very frightening. We have never seen such weather in this lovely land of ours. Dug-outs were flooded to their tops, and lakes of water were standing on the surface ground.

Came the Christmas of 1940, Jimmy and I were to have our Christmas dinner in a place called Bugush; the Camp Commandant carved the meat, the Sergeants served the vegetables, likewise the Christmas pudding, and our C.S.M. Bone of the Coldstream Guards, came around with the tea bucket out of which he served a brown liquid; after the second mug of this I realised it was the good old Stingo! After listening to the C.S.M.'s speech both Jimmy and I ended up under the table. When we eventually got back to our beds, Jimmy was calling to stop the bed from moving; sad to say, it took us nearly a week to recover.

Our next station was a place called Barce. Here there was a big change in the terrain, the further we went the greener the grass. It reminded us of home. As we were passing through Cyrenacia we had great difficulty in getting down the hill into Barce. I was now driving a 3 ton Bedford. The enemy had blown up the bridge that crossed the gully. We were the first British troops to arrive in the town closely followed by the members of an Australian Division. It was night time and the sound of rifle fire went on all night long. My bed that night was a double thickness of blankets under the back of my truck accompanied by a stray black and white smooth haired terrier which was really terrified. I calmed him down and he soon snuggled under the blankets with me. The following morning I had to go in search of petrol so that I could return to Derna. I eventually found a petrol dump being guarded by the Aussies. I explained my mission and was given a supply and returned to Derna. We then moved camp to Cyrenacia.

I came to be friendly with some farming people, and although they couldn't speak our language, between our signs and drawings we managed to understand one another. I gave them a tin of corned beef and a tin of pilchards which I had managed to acquire; they were so grateful - Gratis! Gratis! The following day I returned and they had made a lovely dinner of curly greens, corned beef and potatoes which they asked me to share. It was my turn to be grateful, what a pleasant feeling there was in that house, for a while I could forget the horrors of war. The following day I managed to obtain a few luxuries, carnation milk and some jaffas, which I took to the farmer and his family; imagine, a Police Inspector's son turned renegade! However, for this they washed and ironed my uniform, for which I was most grateful. Happy days, but on with the war.

Our next job was to take equipment up to the M.T.S.D. in Ben Ghazi. Nearing this place I saw big oil fires and heard the sound of exploding shells; it brought back to mind the horrible sights I had seen in and near Siddi Barrani. On arriving at Ben Ghazi, I found the troop had already moved out, on their way to Alexandria, so I had to return 75 miles back to where I had come from, and report to my Senior Officers. Three hours later we had orders to make our way to Tobruk the best way we could, Gerry was on our tails.

The Retreat and Siege of Tobruk.

Two hundred and fifty miles back down the line we were on the outskirts of the harbour and town of Tobruk. Drivers were checked by Military Police and told where our site was to be. A few days later we were surrounded; dive-bombers attacked all ships in the harbour and sank them. There was only one ship left in the harbour and that was a Red Cross Hospital ship. We watched one day as a dive-bomber tried to hit this ship and fortunately missed. As it levelled out over our site one of our gunners, a boy named Dai Salter, who was from the Rhondda, scored a direct hit, then one of our hurricanes came into view and finished the job, doing a victory roll over our site as he went on his way. The German pilot had bailed out and was taken prisoner. It was Easter Sunday and the Germans attacked. It was Hell let loose on us, but they were beaten back with heavy losses. Our rations were meagre and when we found out that the Officers were having potatoes on their menu, while we had only rice, my friend and I decided to do something about it, so on our next trip to pick up our supplies we also lifted a sack of potatoes, so we had our share too.

A week or so later I was in hospital with injuries sustained when my lorry had a near-miss. We had several air-raids while I was there, and some of the men cracked from the strain and their injuries; it was a sad sight; a few days later I was taken down to the harbour to board a Red Cross Hospital ship named the Kara Para. What a feeling that was, we were like sitting ducks waiting for the enemy to strike. Panic stations were reached when we thought we had hit a mine, instead the ship had grazed the booms across the harbour mouth.

We docked at Alexandria where I was taken to the 27th General Hospital which is near Moasscar and Tel-el-Kabir. I was in Ward 5, and was able to help out a little, thanks to my civvy experience in the St. John Ambulance. I soon recovered and was then posted to 364 Company R.A.S.C. and saw duty in Palestine, Iraq and Lebanon. We crossed the Jordan valley through Rutbah and on to Habaniyah where there was an R.A.F. Aerodrome. After doing some guard duty there we were moved yet again to Kirkuk and the Oil-fields. It was a stinking place, bitterly cold with snow on the mountain range and heavy frost on the ground; I will never forget the discontent we felt. Later we moved on again back to Palestine, and were sited in an olive grove not too far from Haifa. We had our Christmas dinner there but it was nowhere near as good as the one we had in Bugash.

The Officer commanding the section I was in was a Lieutenant P. Emmet; he had heard that I had been a Despatch Rider with A.D.S.T. in the Western Desert, and had been on the advance as far as El Agelia 100 miles west of Ben Ghazi. He asked me if I would like to be a Despatch Rider again, I said, of course, and a few days later I was given the post. From there we were detailed to carry carcasses of meat, beef and mutton, from the docks at Haifa to cold storage at Tel-aviv, needless to say we did not go without our share of the meat. We were later moved up to the Lebanon, but not before we had a carcass of mutton dropped off at our camp.

Baal-bek in North Lebanon was a small town; African troops, Basutos and Bechuanas, were stationed there. These soldiers were very tall, between 5ft. 8 ins. and 6ft. I was told that they were a labour battalion and were constructing a railway line up to Aleppo. Snow carpeted the surrounding hills. I was detailed to take despatches to Haifa via Beirut, which was a distance of one hundred and forty nine miles, a round trip of 298 miles. The weather was bitterly cold, and some days I had to wait for the snow ploughs to clear a passage down the hill into Beirut. Then something happened which leaves my mind a blank even to this day. I only know that I woke up in a New Zealand Casualty Unit in Beirut, many soldiers were in the beds in the ward and many were lying between the beds also. I caught sight of my face in a mirror in the toilet; what a sight, bulging eyes, face black and blue, I also had a facial paralysis down the left side. I was led back to my bed from the bathroom, tucked in and given orders to stay there. The next time I awoke, I was in a hospital bed in Beirut, in and out of comas for five months, eventually recovering and finding out that I had five fractures to my skull, followed by cerebro-Spinal-meningitis.

I was boarded home on the S.S. Laconia leaving Suez for Durban; on arrival there I was taken to the Springfield Hospital. (The S. S. Laconia later sank in the South Atlantic.) Later, when I was better able to travel, I boarded the S. S. Largs Bay, once more on my way home; we stopped at Port Elizabeth and every available space including the holds was filled with cases of Navel Oranges. When we docked at Stranraer, I was examined by doctors and given my discharge on 60% Disability Pension.

The result of this illness was that I ended up on Health Insurance for a while before getting new employment as a Shipwright's Labourer at Junction Dry Dock in Cardiff. The wages in this employment were £4.16 shillings per week.

My next employment was with the Parks and Cemeteries Department of Merthyr Borough Council. I worked where required at Aberfan, Treharris and Cefn Cemeteries, and at the following parks, Thomastown, Troedyrhiw, Aberfan and Cyfarthfa. While working at Cyfarthfa, we grew fruit and vegetables for sale to the public. I applied for the post of Groundsman at Treharris Park; what a pleasure working on the gardens and bowling green. The flowers were my joy, cactus, dahlias, pansies, pelargoniums, even the Superintendent commented on the profusion of blooms.

The winter of 1962 again saw me in hospital very ill; however I recovered and went back to my job in Treharris Park. One day I was approached and asked if I would like to take charge of a Parks Police Force that was to be formed of six men and myself. I remained in this employment until I was 65 years of age, having served thirty three years in the Parks and Cemeteries Department.

My grateful thanks to my dear wife for all the worry and sickness she has put up with all these years.

DONALD S. YOUNG, 1991

14. Megan the Ironmonger

Megan Jones, "Megan the Ironmonger", looked up from cutting wallpaper. "So-long, Meg" her husband called to her. He was off to fight in the Second World War. Mrs Humphreys from Crescent Street, and her friend, were in the shop. Megan was surprised to see their tears falling onto the wallpaper. She was twenty three, had been married to 'Trefor the Ironmonger' only one year and now she had been left in charge of the business.

The shopkeeper's wife from next door came in and asked her how she was going to manage. She offered her husband to do the books. "But I thought to myself - how can he make money for me? How can he make the business pay?" So I told her that I would manage fine.

At that time it was very hard to get goods. If you hadn't anything to sell you could go down to the Chamber of Trade in Cardiff. I took the two evacuees who were staying with me down to Cardiff and we went to the Chamber of Trade offices.

This big chap came along. He said in an officious manner, "What are you doing here?" "Rather, what are you doing here!" I said "My husband's gone to fight. He may lose an arm or a leg, so I've got to keep the business going and I haven't anything to sell."

He looked on a map of all the shops in the South Wales area. He let me have a load of saucepans. You couldn't get saucepans at the time. The two girls and I carried them bit by bit to the station. Word got around about the saucepans and a queue formed and they were soon sold out. The same thing happened with a crate of cups and saucers. Dai Robbins was working in the goods yard of Aberfan Station before being called up. He came with the cups and saucers and a great long queue formed. He always reminds me of that when he sees me. People used to say to me 'Keep me a kettle', or 'keep me a coconut mat' and those who were living the nearest were, very often, the luckiest.

One day I had quite a few kettles in. They looked a bit drab, I thought, so I painted them with black paint to smarten them up, and I put them on a high shelf so everyone would see them. Mrs Keogh from Noel Terrace came along - she was a well known character in the village, and bought one of the kettles. She came back the next week, "What the hell was wrong with that kettle', she said. "I put it on the fire and it went up in flames." My father used to help me in the shop sometimes. "What have you been up to again." he asked me. He was with me in the shop one day when a German who was working in the colliery came in and asked me if I had some things in stock. "Yes Mr Otto, no Mr Otto, " I was saying. My father was waving his arms at me behind the man's back. After he had gone, my father told me that the man's real name was Helmut. He had been given the nick name of Otto by the men on the colliery because he kept telling them they "ought to do this" and "ought to do that."

Another time my father was in the shop helping me; he was a lovely man, everyone liked him, when the local vicar came in. He was living in Aberfan House; the church had taken it over as the vicarage. He was looking for some distemper to colour the walls. He 'hum's and ha's'. "I only want a little bit see," he kept saying "only a little bit." When he had settled on the smallest amount possible for his purposes, he asked my father how much water was needed to mix it. My father had a dry wit. "Spit on it", he told him.

The two evacuees that I had staying with me were from Deal in Kent. They had stayed in Merthyr with another family for a while, but then they came down to me. I was only twenty three and I think that I was the youngest around here to take evacuees. So I was a little bit reluctant. The elder girl was called Margaret and was thirteen years old. "If you let us stay" she said, "I'll wash your dishes, clean that big grate in your kitchen and bring you a cup of tea in bed every morning." They were with me for four years. I was very lucky because I would have been alone in the house, and as it was, Margaret looked after things whilst I was in the shop. She was a lovely girl. She reminds me so much of my own daughter Marina. Quiet and dependable.

I remember Margaret wanted to do the spring-cleaning. She was home for a week, spring-cleaning. A letter came from the school asking where she had been for a week. My uncle came to see us. He spotted the letter. "I know you, Meg" he said, "I bet that girl was doing the spring-cleaning."

The youngest girl, Doreen, had made friends with another little girl in the village. She would come home and tell me about extras the family was having. I went to the grocer who had our ration books and I said to him "I have three books here, and I never have any extras. I don't care for myself, but I would like something for the children. I want a Swiss roll." I knew that he had them in. "People are having to queue in Merthyr for Swiss rolls," he told me. I answered him back. "I haven't got time to queue in Merthyr for Swiss rolls", I told him. "I am running a business." I had the Swiss roll. His wife told me later that he'd said to her, "Megan was quite right, I had overlooked her and the children."

But life wasn't all work and rationing. Thursday afternoon the shop was shut and we'd go for a walk along the canal bank up to Merthyr or so, and then on the way home we'd call to all the farms, Ynysygored, Nant Maen and then up to Hafodtanglwys. We had a wonderful welcome and many happy hours. Thursday was also our day for the cinema in the Miners' Welfare Hall and I remember that one Sunday we went picking winberries instead of going to chapel. I couldn't go picking winberries on a Saturday because I was in the shop. As we were coming back along the canal bank the chapel people were coming towards us, all out for a walk after the evening service, so I tried to keep out of their way but the youngest girl gave the show away.

I loved those girls, but I realised more how much they meant to me when I had my own children. When the time came for them to go back to Kent, I took them to the Aberfan Station and said goodbye. This was a very sad occasion. I had even knitted their socks for them. I came home and the house was strangely quiet. For weeks and weeks I could hear them calling "Mrs Jones, Mrs Jones." I missed them terribly. I still keep in touch with Margaret. I tell her that she is still one of my daughters.

My husband Trefor came home in 1945 to a thriving business. I was over fifty years in the ironmongery business. I was a good business woman. Everyone in the village came to the shop. From Mount Pleasant and Merthyr Vale as well as Aberfan. They were good people. When I finished I was owed less than one hundred pounds. A very small sum for an ironmongery and within a few weeks, they had all called to the house to pay me, they were good people.

MEGAN JONES, 1991

15. Merthyr Vale – Merthyr Express, June 8th 1940

Children evacuated from Deal arrived at the Gordon Lennox Hall, Merthyr Vale, close on 9 p.m. Outside the Hall hundreds of local residents gave them a rousing welcome. About 210 children, with their teachers and a few adults, were handed over to a competent staff of workers, drawn chiefly from the teaching profession, and the difficult task of placing the children in their new homes began. All the clergy and ministers of the village, together with local members of the St. John Ambulance Brigade and the local Police (with Inspector Young in charge) worked as one, and many of the children brought letters of introduction from their clergy to those of their new home. Praise must be accorded the women helpers who served the children with a warm meal. All worked together, and tribute must be paid to Mr W. J. Williams, headmaster of Pantglas Boys' School, and Mr A. James, headmaster at Merthyr Vale Boys' School, through whose energy the children were all placed in good homes.

16. There for me to find

Grandpa was Chauffeur-Gardener to Dr White. Before Nixon House was ready for Dr White and his wife, Edith, to move in they stayed with Nan and Grandpa. From what I can gather, they were very good friends, as well as being employer and employee. In the 1914-18 war, Dr White was in the army so a Dr Draffin was the GP. I remember that Dr White had two Scottie dogs, one white and one black.

I thought that I was a princess when I used to be taken to see Mrs White and go around the garden, as well as play with the dogs. I also used to be allowed to sit in the back of their car whilst Grandpa was seeing to it and I remember skipping down the street to tell Mam all about it. I was not very old at the time. Grandpa used to exhibit fruit, flowers and vegetables in shows and always won prizes. As well as growing produce in the grounds of Nixon House for Dr White, he had his own allotment opposite his home. In the allotment, he grew everything, name it and he grew it, from tall sticks with beautiful kidney beans on, to broad beans, peas, potatoes and rhubarb, to name just a few things. At the back of his home, I'll always remember the apple trees grown along a low wooden fence, and always expecting one to fall, just for me. There were sweet peas too and when I used to visit, he used to disappear for a second, come inside and tell me to see if an apple or pear was waiting for me to pick up from underneath the trees. Because I was small at the time, I didn't know that they were put there for me to find, on a bed of straw so they wouldn't be marked.

What a riot of colour Grandpa had in his own and the Doctor's gardens. I wonder how he found the time to look after his children, his allotment, his driving and the both gardens, yet when his grandchildren were born, he found a lot of time for us as well. I remember when Mam, Dad, my sister and myself used to get ready to go home, he used to sit on a chair in the front window to watch for the bus coming up the road; he didn't want us to get cold. We always kissed him and Nan on the cheek and put our arms around them because we loved them and of course we had to leave for Merthyr. I remember his moustache on my cheek as we said "Bye.Bye."

As you went out of the back door into the garden, the gorgeous smell of flowers was a delight. There was a rose arch which you went under to get to the bigger gardens. Sweet peas of every colour that you could name with their curling tendrils and I would be given a scissors to cut some off, to help him in the garden. He had orange and yellow lilies by his back window, these were brought from Cardiff, from Grandpa's Mum's house, and still there in the year he passed away. He grew marrows and cucumbers in the cold frame and his garden shed was as tidy as his gardens and I loved to go and round up his tools for whatever job he was doing and almost underneath grew his Christmas roses and different coloured hyacinths. On the right hand grew his prizewinning dahlias, from the button type to the large feathery king, as I called them, again the colours were wonderful. The crysanthamums were very large and bright yellow, like small suns and pink, white, all different types as well as colours. The button dahlias were from pure white to nearly black and very perfect. On sticks Grandpa used to put upturned plant pots with straw inside which was regularly inspected for earwigs. Grampa used to exhibit his fruit, vegatables and beautiful flowers in all the shows and showed me his many first prizes.

There were large gypsophilla bushes that looked like white clouds, nodding snowdrops, love in the mist, pretty different coloured cheeky faced pansies of which my late dad used to like to have a buttonhole. Roses, every different kind in reds, pinks, yellows, too many to mention, like climbers, standards and bushes, my favourite being the tiny roses on the the rose arch. I still have his bluebells today and I loved to walk in the rain to smell all the lovely perfumes of pinks, carnations and all the lovely flowers he grew, so numerous and beautiful. Grandpa used flowers in St Mary's Church just up the road from his home where Nan and the family went to worship. Every time we went to visit, there would be a bunch of flowers and Nan used to put them in a bucket of water until we were ready to leave. Our house always had flowers in it.

LYN ROBERTS **1992**

James and Mary Adams in the garden at Nixonville

17. Italians in South Wales

Towards the end of the last century and the beginning of this one, Italians from the area of Bardi began settling in South Wales. At first when they came, they lived and worked in Cardiff. But as the valley towns and villages grew they began to open businesses in these areas. By 1938 there were over three hundred cafes in the valley communities. The Italian businessmen who were already established would recruit young men from Bardi to come to South Wales to work. Many of them came to escape rural poverty in Italy. Because the newcomers were scattered around South Wales and most of their days were taken up by hard work, they became well integrated into the host communities. Their cafes became the equivalent of Temperance Bars and were described as a Godsend for the young people of the valleys, who had somewhere warm, comfortable and friendly to meet. The Italian cafe was a popular alternative to the pub for all ages, who mixed together in an amicable fashion.

As the young Italian settled into work and the community, he would be encouraged by his employer, to set up in business for himself, so that by this means, the influence of the Italian cafe and fish-shop spread. By 1921 there were 1500 Italians in South Wales*. Such a young man was Giovanna Emanuelli who came to Wales in 1919. He was in business in Gowerton, Swansea, before he came to Aberfan in 1944 to open a cafe in the centre of the village. Commonly and affectionately known as 'John's' cafe, the coffee was superb, as was the raspberry and ice. Mr Emmanuelli retired in 1970 after keeping the cafe for over 26 years. His widow still lives in Aberfan Road, not too far from where she spent so many happy years. She remembers especially the children who came to the cafe, many of them just taking their first steps and how 'John' would hold them by the hand and take them to help themselves to the Dolly Mixtures.

Her daughter Mary, shares some of the memories of her father, 'An Italian Welshman.'

* Colin Hughes, 'Lime, Lemon and Sarsaparilla, The Italians in South Wales 1881 - 1945', Seven Book, 1991, ISBN 1 85411 055 1.

18. A Welshman with an Italian Accent

My memories of Aberfan - my dad

When I look back, I see Dad in his short, grey, shop coat sitting by the open fire with his best pals, Matt George, Howell Roberts and Bernard Morgan. They sat and chatted about soccer. It had to be Merthyr Town. If they won, that was O.K. but if they lost, gracious me! They obviously would have done everything differently if only they had the chance to play. If only!!

Thursday afternoon was such an important time for them, half day closing, filling out the coupon. Everything was filled out statistically, not just a simple cross here and there: this usually took them an hour or two, but oh the enjoyment that they had.

Memories of Dad behind the counter giving chocolate drops for new born babies, giving sweets to children, teasing the youngsters. He was also 'Father Confessor' to the courting couples, often trying to get them back together again after a tiff.

The café was his love where he met all the villagers. He loved Tuesdays and Fridays. Shopping days for the women. Not just from Aberfan but the gang from Merthyr Vale, too. They would come in for coffee, tea, toast and also plenty of teasing and back-chat.

Memories are also of the regulars, who had their own corners, chairs and tables. Nan Mobley and Mrs Manuel, who spent their time together with Dad. Tom Lloyd, whose favourites were hot pies and Chelsea buns. Dad loved them all.

Memories of Dad when he joined the Ynysowen Choir and had to learn to sing in Welsh. I had lots of laughs when he was telling me about it, but I think he managed.

I could go on and on but I really mustn't get carried away. I just want to finish with one more thing. My last memory of Dad was when he died and the village was so wonderful. I can still hear the singing of the choir and some in Welsh too, and I know that Dad could hear it as well. He must have been as proud as I was to know that he was loved and accepted as a Welshman with an Italian accent, known simply as 'John'.

MARY REES (NÉE EMANUELLI)

19. Heaven on Earth

Aberfan was heaven on earth to me. I had come here from Essex during the Second World War, where we had been surrounded by American air bases. My Mam-Gu, Ann Hughes, lived in Pleasant View, beneath the hills and amongst the green fields of Perthygleision, Aberfan. My mother, father, brother and I lived close by, first in Bryngoleu and then in Canonbie Crescent.

My Mam-Gu's was open house for all her friends and neighbours. Her son's friends were made welcome as well. My Uncle Tom cut hair and he was a lovely, jolly, man. He was in the fire service in Hayes, Middlesex during the war. When I was a little older, he was going up to London to the theatre and I remember that he would bring back the programmes of Ivor Novello's musicals for me to see. My father and his two brothers were very musical. They could all sing well and sang in Ashton's Choir. My Uncle John could play many musical instruments by ear. We all spent happy evenings in my Mam-gu's listening to my Uncle playing the banjo, which was the favourite of the children in the family. He would play so fast that it made us out of breath just listening to him.

I would spend hours watching my Mam-Gu baking and on a Sunday morning I would usually take an apple pie to her friend, Mrs Williams, who lived further along Pleasant View, for her to cook in her gas oven. I liked to help my Mam-Gu but I was also fascinated by the Gas Cooker. I had never seen one before. Also on a Sunday morning, I would take her chapel envelope to another friend of hers in the next street, Kingsley Terrace.

On a Saturday morning, when I was about nine or ten, I would scrub Mam-Gu's steps. For this I needed clean water, sand, which was always kept in the same old rusty tin, a good piece of cloth, a scrubbing brush and a special stone. The stone I would find in the Nant Aberfan, the stream which ran alongside Pleasant View. The perfect stone would be fairly large and blue-grey in colour. Having found a good stone, hopefully, I would return to the steps, five in all, and set to work. I would wet the top step liberally, sprinkle sand on it, scrub the sand off and wash the step down. Then came the hardest part, the special stone would be rubbed into the wet step. This done, the step would be left to dry. I would repeat this for the four other steps. When they dried, the steps would be a sparkling blue-grey clean. I would be tremendously proud of my handiwork. I loved those steps. There was a low wall where we would sit and look down the Canal Bank or over to Merthyr Vale, our feet on the tiles between the steps, my Mam-Gu's privet hedge alongside with its crisp leaves perfect for squashing and crackling between our fingers. I remember sitting on those steps before I could read, I must have been about three years of age, with a very large book, the sort of old fashioned book with a moral tale or rhymes, for children. There were big pictures and not many pages. I can see that book in my mind's eye. There was a cherubic child with a lovely bonnet, on the front cover, in pastel colours. And the sun was always shining.

My grannie gave me two pennies every day for my busfare to school. I would save the pennies because if the weather was fine I preferred walking along the Canal Bank to school. I had a red post box money box made of tin and I kept it in my grannie's. Every so often I would sit on the steps and count it. Sometimes I had as much as 44d. in there. I cannot remember how exactly I spent it but I think that it probably went for exercise books in Martin's shop.

My Mam-Gu loved pictures. There was a picture of her friend from Bethania Chapel on the wall. She was Mrs B. M. Thomas and was on the Council. There was a framed illuminated address of my grandfather's that he was given in the colliery when the engineering and boilermaker's unions amalgamated. There was a photograph of the four colleges of the University of Wales framed together. I knew the history of how Aberystwyth University had come into being from a very early age. "The pennies of the poor" was printed underneath the picture of that college. Above the rocking chair, in the corner where I always sat, was a photograph of my father's sister, Ellen Ann. She had died at the age of seven. She was a beautiful child, lovely hair and huge dark eyes. I used to look at her little bath chair, brown and shiny, on the top shelf of the 'cwtch' and wonder at how she was taken about, unable to walk, having to be carried or pushed everywhere. One Summer's day, I remember coming along the Canal Bank, past Glyndwr Cottage, with my Grannie, I was about six or seven years of age, and Mrs Thomas, who lived there, coming out and calling after us "Ellen Ann. Back again." My Mam-Gu and I just looked at each other. Not another word was said. We had that sort of relationship. No need for a lot of talking. I don't know what she thought but the incident had a timeless quality about it and has always stuck in my mind.

All the children loved my Mam-Gu. She would sit on the steps and the children from Bryntaf would call on her for bread and jam and water to go down to the 'pipes' to play. The 'pipes' were a special feature of our childhood. They were near the 'Lock House' and had been left by the men who had piped water from the reservoirs, up above Merthyr, to Cardiff, during the 1920s. We spent many hours playing in and on them. In Spring and Summer they were surrounded by beds of pink and blue forget-me-nots. My father and his brothers were never allowed to throw away a lemonade bottle, they were for the children of Bryntaf, for water for the 'pipes', not small children, they weren't allowed down the 'pipes'.

Also near the Lock House was a spring of beautiful crystal water coming straight off the mountain and falling conveniently down a ledge. Whenever the tap water went off in the Perthygleision area, which seemed quite often in those days, everyone would trek to the spring. A queue would form. Water has never tasted better. Wonderfully cold, even in Summer, and with a zing to it.

Other children, all friends, came for the loshen (sweets) that Mam-Gu brought home in her round basket. One little girl loved the sweet fish that Mam-Gu brought. She would run along the street to meet her. Her sister would call through the letter box for bread and butter. Bread and marg would not do! "We've plenty of that in our house." Other children would come for bread and butter and sugar, especially if they were feeling 'down in the dumps'. All the children called her Gu. She loved them. She would be down on her hands and knees telling them stories.

Mam-Gu died in May when the lilacs were in bloom. I was chosen that year, with two other girls from Pantglas School, to dance on the bandstand of Cyfarthfa Park, dressed in mauve taffetta dress, as a lilac domino. I went to dance to please my mother but my heart wasn't in it. After the dancing was over my friend and I met Mr Beynon our teacher, and his wife, as we walked down from Cyfarthfa Castle. His wife lifted up the hem of my coat to see, as she thought, my lovely dress but I had already changed back into my serviceable checked cotton. I missed my Mam-Gu.

A few weeks later the results of the scholarship came out. Most of us in Mr Beynon's class had 'passed' for Quakers Yard Grammar School. We were allowed to go home to tell our family. In my excitement I ran all the way along the Canal Bank and was nearly home when I realised that I had no-one to tell. My mother and father were in work and Mam-Gu was no longer in 4 Pleasant View. I stood in my mother's garden looking down at my shoes and thought about the lovely furry caterpillar I had found in the garden the Summer before and that I had taken up to show my Mam-Gu. A dark brown, pussy like caterpillar, huge and soft.

Yes. Aberfan was heaven on earth for me.

MAUREEN HUGHES, 1991

20. Mam-Gu

You were often in your garden
Picking long branches
Of blackcurrants,
Sticks of rhubarb,
Next door's sweet peas
That were hanging
Over the fence,
And all for we children.
But now I see you
In your long clothes
And black hat
Planting blue flowers.
Do you remember
Me picking your hydrangea
With Rosalie's sister Marjorie?
"I'll tell your father",
You called from the door,
Your eyesight was poor
At a distance.
I looked in dismay at my
Beloved Mam-Gu,
You were always giving me
Things from your garden.
Now I know that you were good
And if you could,
You would have given
Dear Marjorie, your life.

Blue hydrangeas then
Now blue flowers
Tall, bell shaped
Clumping together.
Blue flowers, green leaves.
"I am nearly ready Aelfryn."
I saw the blue flowers
Through a wonderful vibrant
Living haze.

Mam-Gu was in the garden
Building low walls in warm stone
Conjuring vitality from her fingertips,
Preparing him a place.
I felt the hum of life
Not death.
My father began to rest.

MAUREEN HUGHES, 1989

21. Memories

After the first year the pain should be less,
After the round of Birthdays, Anniversaries.
October 23rd will be that magical day.
Will it really hurt less to remember?

Most memories you relate without choking
then unwares it catches you, the physical touch,
Of one whom you owe your existence.

Precious, precious, Memories.
Precious, precious, Father.

JUNE VAUGHAN 20TH OCTOBER 1981

Chapter Seven
Pastimes

1. Introduction

Some of the first activities recorded in the village centred around music and drama. This was to be the pattern for nearly a century with every chapel having a drama group and several successful choirs. Almost every place of worship had a youth group and there was a wealth of children's games and activities. Despite the harshness of the working day, there was contentment and happiness to be found amongst friends and neighbours. The men had their 'clubs' and sporting activities and the women their bosom pals. Today the community is still lively and receptive to new ideas and pastimes.

Merthyr Vale Choir

2.   The Building of the Village - 4

Social Activities - 1870s

The number of concerts being held contributed to the social life of the village. Often they would include Eisteddfod winners with such names as 'Gwilym Bryncerddin', 'Gwalch Alaw' and 'Gwilym Baullt'. There was a strong link between Merthyr Vale and Mountain Ash because of Nixon's ownership of their respective collieries, and choirs came regularly to the developing community from the small town. Many of the concerts were benefit concerts held for the ailing of the village, some of whom had been injured in the colliery. One of these unfortunates was James Rule. He was a representative of the workmen and was a keen advocate of compensation especially after the explosion at Abercarn in 1878. The workmen in Merthyr Vale had contributed nearly forty pounds to the Abercarn Disaster Fund by taking a collection and a further twenty pounds from their Sick and Accident Fund. Mr Rule had himself proposed that the Merthyr Vale men support the moves that were afoot to establish a permanent relief fund to meet every case of accident in the Monmouthshire and South Wales collieries. Shortly afterwards, Mr Rule had fallen victim to an accident himself. The concert in his benefit was held at the Coffee Tavern Assembly Rooms and he must have been very popular for "everyone was eager and willing to forward the object in view, which was to aid James Rule".

There were a few hiccups. Some of the concerts held attracted a rowdy element and boys, also termed 'a colony of scamps', were castigated for shooting peas at the rest of the audience. At another concert some of the audience were represented by the press as being "uncultivated". They had been talking loudly and waving their programmes in the air, annoying respectable people who had an ear for music.

In 1880 the Ynysowen Volunteer Band played on the green outside the National Schools in Troedyrhiw. This was in support of a fair and bazaar being held to pay for the improvements to the school buildings in Pentrebach. The lady of Cyfarthfa Castle, Mrs W. T. Crawshay, visited the bazaar with her mother Mrs Woods. The refreshments were supplied by Mr Howfield of Merthyr.

Lord Aberdare, whose mother's family had originated on one of the farms in Merthyr Vale, and who owned the Danyderi Colliery, had agreed to open the Coffee Tavern with its spacious Assembly Rooms.

The Mount Pleasant Hotel had its licence restored after a period as a dwelling house and the Windsor Hotel played host to a sheep shearing match revealing the partly rural economy that was still in existence in the area in 1880.

Meanwhile, workers from the Merthyr Vale Colliery were taking part in the Troedyrhiw Flower and Vegetable Show and were regularly winning prizes. Other prizewinners from the village were Rhys Rhys, the landlord of the Aberfan Hotel, who won prizes for his leeks and rhubarb, and the occupant of Lock House who had prize winning currants. Mr James Ball, who became a well known marksman, won a prize for the best garden of a workman.

There were still otters to be found along the River Taff and fox hunting was taking place.

A cricket club had been formed and the cricket team from Mountain Ash were regular visitors. A rifle club was started and a branch of the Volunteers.

By 1880 the social activities in the village were being well established.

3.   Mount Pleasant - 'The Mount'

One important loss at "The Mount" was the absence of a large enough public hall or something similar, where events could be held, so the community turned to the hospitality provided by the Mount Pleasant Hotel and to the Long Room, in particular. Most, if not all of the functions normally held in a village were held there and Mrs Williams' family played an important role in the people's lives, whilst outside was the quoits pitch. There strength, or lack of it, was displayed on many Saturday afternoons.

The Mount Pleasant Hotel, with just a few others, was one of the early residences in the area and date back almost 150 years or more. Also to be found in these early days was "The Old Tavern - Yr

Hen Dafarn." Here lived Rachel and Joseph Hughes who hailed from Carmarthern. Joseph was working as a railway labourer. There were two Mount Pleasant Cottages. One was occupied by John and Anne Evans and a baby, of three months, called William. The other by a coal miner from Amroth, Pembrokeshire called Thomas John and his wife Phoebe. The house called Mount Pleasant was home to Morgan Joseph, a retired mineral agent who now had 15 acres of land. His son was living with him, and he was still a mineral agent, who was twenty four years of age. His name was Morgan Joseph as well. There was another house called "Tyr Mount 'or' Tyr Rhyd' and this was occupied by a blocklayer John Elias, his wife Ann and seven children.

Nowadays there is one main street left of the Old Mount Pleasant. There was at one time the street called South View, the same street involved in the accident with the two planes in 1941. South View was destined for further trouble in the 1950s when, after some unusually high winds and storms, the roofs of two houses were completely lifted off. The exposed situation of this row invited the strong winds from every direction. The Local Authority decided later to demolish the remaining houses and move the occupants to other accommodation in Merthyr Tydfil. So ended the story of one of our streets.

The area was chosen after the war as a site for twenty four prefabs. These were later demolished for more substantial buildings. An estate of council housing was erected on the allotment site which had been the pride of the local gardeners. My father had been included in their number; he had continued as leisure something he had worked at for most of his life.

As with many villages the coming of modern transport and the ownership of cars has altered the interests and pastimes of old and young. But the essence of the community hasn't been lost and there is still an affinity between those who can lay claim to having lived in "The Mount".

PHYLLIS DAVIES, 1991

4.   An Awful Calamity

There is a memorial in Aberfan Cemetery to seven young Volunteers drowned at Lavernock on the 1st August 1888. The Volunteers were the forerunners of the Territorial Army of today and there were many battalions throughout the South Wales area.

Exactly eight years before the tragic occurrence at Lavernock, the Volunteers were camping on the Merthyr Vale mountain beneath Heol Cymro. "From here was commanded a view of the whole Merthyr Valley." There were 195 tents and a thousand men in the camp and water was pumped from Ynysowen. Among the tents was a tee-total tent which was fairly well used and a tent for entertainment where the men sang comic songs and did some "jigging". Reveille was at 4.30 a.m. and everyone was expected to be washed and dressed by six 'o' clock. There was plenty for the men to do around the camp and everyone was expected to do their share. Rations were collected and the men were eating beef, bread, cheese and vegetables. There was a twenty four hour guard duty, whatever the weather, and plenty of steady drill. Divine worship was held on the Sunday and the Vicar was present. Some men went to Mass in Dowlais.

But eight years later when the Volunteers went to camp at Lavernock an "awful calamity" took place. The "Merthyr Express" described it as one of the saddest tragedies that had ever agitated the public mind of South Wales. Seven young Volunteers, the youngest, J. Webber, a fitter, of Cardiff Road, Merthyr Vale, was only 17 years old. The oldest, W. Coulston, a plasterer from the same street was only twenty. Both of them, with five companions, were drowned when an over-loaded boat ran into difficulties on a journey from Lavernock to Penarth. Two of the young men were from Treharris, the others from Aberfan and Merthyr Vale.

The story is as follows. Ten Volunteers had asked a boatman, called Joseph Hall, to take them to Penarth at 3d per head. The name of the boat was "The Maggie". The boat sailed into rough waters and water started coming into the boat which frightened the boatman. Suddenly, a wave lifted the bow of the boat and it overturned. The accident occurred 500 yards from the shore and in about eight feet of water. The boat turned over about a dozen times and everyone who perished seemed to have lost their presence of mind. When "The Maggie" turned for the last time only three men and the boatman were to be seen. "We were all getting weaker and weaker", said one of the survivors. One of the soldiers clung to the mast of the boat which kept him up in the water and saved his life.

A courageous young fellow called Daniel Maloney, who was only seventeen years of age, rescued three of the survivors, including the boatman. Despite the very real danger of his own boat capsizing, he went to the rescue of the drowning men. He saw that they were in great danger. A fourth man was almost saved by him but at the last moment, "he sank like a stone, we saw him no more".

The boatman went to the police to give a statement. "The policeman told me to go home and rest and when daylight came to go and search for the bodies of those who had perished. I went home but could not sleep and lay awake until daybreak and then proceeded to the beach. I walked to Lavernock and remained searching until nine or ten 'o' clock". The first bodies were found the following Monday, the accident having occurred on the previous Wednesday. There were thousands of excursionists there to see the bodies of J. Webber and E. Brown, both of Merthyr Vale, being brought in. Then the body of J. Potter, a collier of Perthygleision was found. He was just nineteen years of age. The bodies had been found at the edge of the whirlpool by a boatman by the name of David King.

The Sergeant to whose company most of the men belonged sobbed convulsively when the grief stricken relatives arrived. He was unable to speak and could only grasp their hands. The three young men who had survived had been allowed to leave hospital.

At the inquest the boatman was censured. He was found to be grossly negligent but not criminally liable. The coroner told him that it would be a long time "before you will forget the circumstances under which this sad affair occurred."

On the Sunday a service was held at the camp. Three sides of the square were formed by up to a thousand Volunteers belonging to the third battalion of the Welsh Regiment. The fourth side was made up by the band and a large number of people from Cardiff, Penarth and the neighbourhood. The Chaplain, Rev. Mr Leigh concluded his sermon by saying, "Their dust has returned to the earth as it was and their spirit unto the God who gave it". Among the hymns sung was "Onward Christian Soldiers". On the same day in Aberfan, Merthyr Vale and Treharris, "most affecting pulpit references were made to the mournful disaster off Lavernock at the various places of worship".

On the 11th August at 4.30 p.m., the bodies of the young soldiers were brought to the Taff Vale Station at Merthyr Vale for burial in the cemetery at Aberfan. The "Merthyr Express" reported that this funeral cortege and subsequent burial was one of the saddest sights that ever presented itself to the inhabitants of the Taff Valley". An overcrowded boat, a sudden lurch, formed a description of the calamitous event which spread "Horror and grief" everywhere throughout the Eastern portion of the country.

There were some 750 Volunteers present in the funeral procession. Sergeant Ball headed the firing party, composed of men from the Merthyr Vale detachment. They were followed by the three survivors, Moss, Williams and Dowdeswell. The Dowlais and Mountain Ash band played the "Dead March" in Saul and their drums were draped in black. Then came the compliment of buglers and the three officiating clergymen. The respective mourners followed each of the coffins carried by six of the Volunteers. Then came the privates of the Merthyr Vale detachments and the privates and officers of the Battalion.

"The progress of the procession along the winding road to the ceremony was witnessed by an immense crowd, spectators having taken up their positions even on distant hillsides. A more imposing demonstration of sorrow and grief in a rural district could scarcely be conceived." The blinds to every house 'en route' were drawn, and there was a solemn, affecting, stillness in the air disturbed only by the moving strains of the muffled drums and the grief stricken lamentations of the relatives which pierced every heart

When the procession arrived at the cemetery at Aberfan the Rector began his address. He referred to the river running through the beautiful valley and exhorted the comrades of the stricken men to lead better lives from that day forward. The anguish of the mourners as the coffins were lowered was something terrible and there was scarcely a dry eye amongst those who witnessed the sorrowful scene.

"Over the graves it is intended that a monument shall be erected at the expense of the regiment in honour of the deceased. Upon it will be set their names and a description of the awful disaster to which they fell untimely victims".

Reading and writing about this "awful calamity" brought back the vivid memories of October 1966 and the funeral of the victims of the tragedy in Pantglas School and Moy Road. The crowds that gathered on the hillsides, the sorrow and the terrible lamentations were the same. The difference lay in the overwhelming numbed grief of a whole community. My mother and I stood together in the cemetery. We joined in the service, sang "Jesu Lover of my Soul", with trembling hearts and voices but apart from this we spoke very little. There was nothing to say in the face of such an awesome, dreadful happening to such a small, close knit community. Thoughts lay too deep, numbed by disbelief and shock.

MAUREEN HUGHES, 1991

St Marys Well Bay, Lavernock

A. Lloyd

5.   Lavernock Point

I came here with two teachers
And form four girls
from Quakers Yard School.
I cannot remember what year it was
But no doubt
I could work it out
If I put my mind to it.

The Summer was cold
And we all shivered
On the beach.
Today, the January
Winter day seems warmer
Than that Summer afternoon
So long ago.

I also came here
With a friend and her family
When her father was on holiday
from Merthyr Vale Colliery.
Many years later
He had a 'Stroke'
And I used to visit him in hospital.
When he died
I went to his funeral,
And sat
At the back of the Church.

Now I listen to the rush
Of the waves
The sea here is whirlpool
Treacherous.
In the cemetery at Aberfan
There is a memorial to
Local Soldiers
Who drowned here long ago.
Weatherworn rifles,
But not the soldiers
Stand together
In a green ring.

MAUREEN HUGHES, 1990

6.   Colour Sergeant Ball

The sergeant in charge of the firing party at the funeral of the seven Volunteers drowned in Lavernock, was James Ball.

One of the first organisations to be formed in the growing community of Merthyr Vale was a rifle club and Sgt Ball was a prominent member.

In July 1894, some six years after the "awful calamity" at Lavernock, Sgt. Ball won the Prince of Wales Cup at Bisley. This prize was second only in importance to the Queen's Cup. And the feeling throughout the Merthyr Valley was that Sgt. Ball should be given a hearty welcome on his return home. He would be arriving at the Aberfan Station, and near the bridge there was a banner proclaiming the "Merthyr Vale Detachment Forever." A banner displayed in Aberfan Road said, "Welcome to the shot of the 3rd V.B.". The villages were gaily decorated, flags and banners being displayed from nearly every window and vantage point.

The Merthyr Vale Volunteers assembled at the Drill Hall in Nixonville and marched to the Rhymney Railway Station in Aberfan. There was a detachment of Volunteers from Merthyr already in position on the platform and they lined up together to await the hero's train. Signals had been placed along the metals of the track and the booming of these as the train approached drew hundreds more people to join the hundreds of villagers who were already on the station. The train drew in at a quarter past seven and "loud cheers rent the air". "A feu de joie" was fired and the band played the salute. Colour Sergeant Ball was greeted by loud cheers from his comrades and was carried shoulder high, by members of the shooting club, to the Drill Hall. The villagers had turned out in hundreds and cheered the marksman lustily, as he passed. Merthyr was

Train along the Rhymney Railway

intensely proud of Colour Sergeant Ball and Merthyr Vale was even prouder. Even torrential rain did not "dampen the ardour of the inhabitants nor affect the heartiness of the welcome".

At the Drill Hall the hero was enthusiastically received and was cheered loudly when he said that he could hardly express his feelings of gratitude for the great kindness shown to him. In his speech of thanks he assured them that he always tried to do what was right and to do his duty and that he would never forget this welcome home as long as he lived.

The next day the townspeople gave vent to their feelings about the brilliant achievement of Colour

Sergeant Ball when the principal streets of Merthyr lost their "everyday dullness" by numerous banners and bannerettes which flew gaily from windows and chimney pots. They indicated "good feeling and respect for an event of extraordinary importance."

Colour Sergeant Ball arrived by train from Merthyr Vale. He was carried in style to the Merthyr Drill Hall, the band playing, "See the conquering hero comes".

He paid tribute to Major Bell, "to whom he owed his success. He had always found him willing to assist. When he thought of these kindnesses, he was convinced of the fact that if a man would do his best, others would help him."

Compiled from the Merthyr Express and South Wales Daily News, 1991

Colour Sergeant James Ball

7.   The Building of the Village - 5

Fun and Games - 1870s

For many years at the Annual Sunday School treats, 'Bobby Bingo' and 'Kiss in the Ring' would be played.

Bobby Bingo was a game played with a ring of children. By tradition, the children would represent sheep, chickens or pigs. Inside the ring would be the child who represented the farmer and outside the ring, the child who represented 'Bobby Bingo'.

The game would start with the farmer saying "Who is that walking around my stoney wall?" And the thief, Bobby Bingo, answering "only Little Bobby Bingo". He would then try and steal one of the sheep, chickens or pigs. The game was popular all over Britain and was known by many different names in various localities. In Scotland, for example, it was known as 'Johnnie Lingo'. Perhaps the game was brought to the new mining community from the West Country. Here the game was known as 'Bobby Bingo'. Certainly there were numerous settlers in Merthyr Vale from Somerset and Cornwall.

'Kiss in the Ring' was another popular game which would be played by an equal number of girls and boys. A girl would touch a boy and a boy would touch a girl. The other players would then chase them. If either of the two were caught, they would go into the ring and kiss. Then it was their turn to try and catch the people who had taken their place. These would be the persons who had successfully caught them plus that person's partner. Such was the popularity of this game throughout the Merthyr district, especially at Midsummer, that there was a lively correspondence in the "Merthyr Express", as to whether it was proper for chapel deacons to participate.

8. Cymdeithasu Yn Aberfan Ar Ddechrau'r Ganrif

Sut oedd pobol yn cymdeithasu yn y pentref as dechrau'r ganrif yma? Rhaid siarad âg hen bobol i gael gwybod. Roedd e'n amlwg bod bywyd cymdeithasu yn ganol bwyntio o gwympas y capeli. Roedd bobol yn sôn am côr meibion Merthyr Vale ag Aberfan, yr arweiydd oedd Septimus Ashton, fy hen dad-cu, bandiau jas, capel tairgwaith as dydd Sul, band of hope, penny readings, côr ieuenctid y capel, cyfarfodydd bron pob nos ag yr adfwyiad.

Soniodd yr hen bobol am weinidogion enwog yn ymweld â'r capeli. As ôl capel yn yr hâf bydda'r bobol ifanc yn mynd am dro, as hyd y camlas. Weithiau roedd cymaint o bobol yn mynd i'r capel, roedd rhaid iddynt sefyll tu fas ar y stryd. Mae hi'n anodd credu y fath peth yn digwydd heddiw.

Ond gan siarad â fy nhad-cu, ces i stori wahanol. Daeth ei deulu o Iwerddon a dim gair o Gymraeg yn gael ei siarad yn y gartref. Roedd crefydd ei deulu yn Catholig a ffordd o fyw yn wahonol iawn i'r un a chafodd fy Mam-gu. Ymweld â tafarnau gwnaeth ei dad nid y capel. Pan siardais i â'm tad-cu gwnaeth e son am gemau pêl droed, ban Jas Aberfan, yn cystadlu gyda chefnogaeth pawb. Roedd menywod hyd yn oed yn aros lan trwyr nos i wynio gwisgoedd ag ati.

Mor wahanol oedd bywyd fy mam-gu. Roedd ei thad yn arweinydd y côr meibion. Hefyd roedd ei theulu yn mwynhau cyswyllt cryf â Chapel Bethania. Ei chofion hi yn cynnwys, eisteddfodau, gwersi piano, ysgol sul a phopeth trwyr iaith Cymraeg.

Ond ar y pwll glo roedd y ddau deulu yn dibynnu am eu harian ag i'r 'Soup Kitchen' aeth y ddau deulu yn ystod y streic 1926-27. Felly er bod na wahanol math o gymdeithas. Roedden nhw'n yn dda iawn. Yn y dyfodol fydd ddim pwll glo i ddod â phawb gyda gilydd. Felly sut bydd pawb yn cymdeithasu yn y dyfodol?

GAN NIA HELYDD LYNCH,
11 BLWYDDOED,
FEL RHAN O WAITH AM BENTREF ABERFAN

Bryntaf Girls Band

194

9. Social Life in Aberfan at the Beginning of the Century

How did people socialise in the village at the beginning of the century? One must talk to the old people in order to know. It was obvious that social life concentrated around the chapels. People spoke about the Merthyr Vale and Aberfan Male Voice Choir, which was conducted by my great grandfather, Septimus Ashton, Jazz Bands, chapel three times a day on Sunday, Band of Hope, penny readings, the youth choir, meetings almost every night and 'the Revival'.

The old people spoke of famous ministers visiting the chapels. After chapel in the Summer, the young people would walk along the canal. At times there were so many people attending chapel, they would have to stand outside on the street. It is difficult to believe that this kind of thing could happen today.

However talking to my grandfather, I had a different story. His family came from Ireland and not a word of Welsh was spoken in their household. His family were Catholic and the way of life was so different to that of my grandmother. My grandfather spoke of football games, the Aberfan Jazz Band, which competed with the support of all around them. Women even stayed up all night to sew costumes etc.

The life of my grandmother was so different. Her father was the conductor of the Male Voice Choir. Her family also enjoyed a strong connection to Bethania Chapel. Her memories included eisteddfods, piano lessons, Sunday School and all activities in Welsh.

But it was on the coal mine that the two families both depended for their earnings and it was to the soup kitchens that they had to go in the strike of 1926-27. Therefore, although there were differences in the way people socialised, it was obvious that the two societies co-operated very well. In the future there will not be a mine to bring everyone together. The question thus is how will people socialise in the future?

NIA HELEDD LYNCH,
11 YEARS OLD,
TAKEN FROM PART OF A PROJECT ON ABERFAN

Bryntaf Men's Band

10. Our Photographer

My mother came from Corwen, in North Wales. She was one of 10 children and she had seven brothers. Most of them came to South Wales and did well. My mother's favourite brother was a well known photographer at the beginning of the century here in Aberfan and later in Oakdale, where he was in charge of the Lamp-room in Oakdale Colliery.

At first his mother used to develop his photographs in Corwen, she was a photographer herself. She used to go around taking photographs of the farms in North Wales. Amongst photographs Uncle Alun took were some of the Soup Kitchen helpers in Aberfan School in 1914, and of George Martin's dog Carlo.

MEGAN JONES 1991

11. Life in Aberfan in the Twenties

I was born on May 21st 1921 at 46 Bryntaf and lived there until I was twelve, when we moved to the Grove.

Looking back, they were happy times with long hot Summer days and bitterly cold Winters. I can remember snow piled high above window-sills and roads piled high with snow-drifts.

My mother came from Llanidloes and although settled in Aberfan, she always hankered about 'Llani'. She was of small stature, with black hair and dark eyes; she was always 'on the go', full of energy - she made and sold faggots and peas every Friday, she also made brandy balls and peppermints; they were sold to a wide variety of people. Times were hard and it brought in a little money. There was a miners' strike in 1921 and in 1926, I often went to the Free Soup Kitchens in the Summer holidays.

My father came to Aberfan in 1912, and had to learn English. He hailed from Blaenau Ffestiniog and was studying for Mining Management. He passed all his exams, but in 1914 war broke out and he went to Wrexham and joined the Welsh Fusiliers. Her served four years in the Army and when he returned, like a good many more, had to take any job in the pit. My grandfather never forgave him for wasting his education, and my father was cut out of his will.

The only thing my father never lost was his voice; he had been trained to sing and had a framed certificate from the Trinity College of Music. In his time he was a member of a few choirs, but the last and main one was Mr Devonalds, who was the conductor and Mrs Goldsworthy was the pianist. I went with them a few times when they went to Llandrindod Wells to compete. My mother's sister Mary was the head waitress at the Manor Hotel; I stayed for the day with her and was petted and made a fuss of and usually had a purseful of money to return home.

I remember coming home over the Beacons with the choir singing, "All in the April Evening." They had won the competition with this song, and as we came over the mountains, the lambs were bleating and the beautiful countryside, the memory of all that is still with me, and when I recall that night, I get a lump in my throat. I love music and it must have been instilled in me from an early age.

I used to be so proud of Dad. He was so handsome in his tails and bow tie. I can remember one special occasion when he sang in the City Hall, Cardiff at a Doctors' Conference.

He sang at any concert and the money went in the kitty; he was a semi-National winner, but never won the National Eisteddfod which was a great disappointment to him.

MAIR WILLIAMS (NEE LLOYD), APRIL 1991

12. The Golden Age of Soccer by "Old Timer"

"The Golden Age of British Soccer." These words were used in reference to the years immediately following the First World War, that is the 1920s. Large gates, now enjoyed by the elite of the First Division, were then the lot of teams in the minor leagues. The standard of football then played was high, and the number of young men who preferred playing themselves to watching others do so, was colossal. Sharing in this prosperity were the towns and villages of South Wales.

So keen was the competition between these towns and villages that inevitably many capable players emerged, so many in fact, that Wales became a happy hunting ground for the professional clubs. It was said that if any manager was in urgent need of a man he had only to phone down the pit and up would come a ready made player. Many small clubs were adopted as nurseries by the bigger ones.

Among these villages were those of Merthyr Vale, Mount Pleasant and Aberfan. So great was the supply of capable players that one club was insufficient to accommodate them. This led to the formation of new clubs and it is interesting to note that in recalling the names of these teams, one always associates them with certain areas in the district, thus … 'The Crescents' and 'Rechabites' with Crescent and Taff Streets; 'The Crusaders' with Bryntaf; 'The Albions' with Perthygleision; 'The Stars' with the Cinema. Others like 'Mount Pleasant' and the 'Windsors' and the 'Church' need no guesswork.

Mount Pleasant, in those days consisted of two streets, if South View is included. It seemed impossible that such a small area could form a team but form one they did and more surprisingly a successful one as well.

Financially, the old days were far from being good old days, but from a sporting standpoint, they were happy days.

HEADWAY, SEPTEMBER 1970

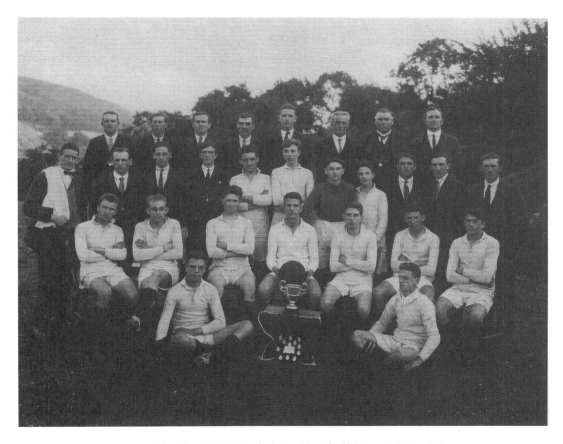

Merthyr Vale Rechabites Football Team 1925 - 26

13. "Strides" by Old Timer

Sport has certainly made great strides from that day some fifty eight years ago when as a boy I took part in my first football match, one street against another.

Our field was the street itself; the football - some newspapers wrapped up in stocking and tied with string; the goal posts consisted of two piles of coats placed at either end of the street; the captain was usually the boy who supplied the stocking. Normal football kit was of little importance; stops to re-tie a loose string were frequent, finesse may have been absent but enthusiasm there was in plenty.

In those days, before the advent of the bus and motor car, we kids were imitating our idols, "The Crescents". The greatest difficulty of these ardent supporters was the entrance fee, even though it was less than today's packet of chewing gum. Many were the ruses adopted to gain a free entry. Some of the more venturesome gained access, but the more patient, realising that the gatekeepers left their posts at half time, waited until then to get a close up of the game.

HEADWAY, OCTOBER 1970

14. Sport

Headway takes the liberty of quoting from the "Football Echo" of 22nd April, 1989. It's from a report of Cardiff City's home game against Southend in the Football League's Division Three. It relates to "defender Gareth Abraham."

"City - could do little right until Abraham surprised everyone by threading in a 31st minute goal shot. The ball fell invitingly to Abraham whose apparently harmless twenty yard low drive crept inside an upright for his second league goal of the season. In fact 20 year old Abraham had done his best to pep-up City's front line.

Abraham warmed up for his eventual success with a fierce 17th minute volley ... with an obvious taste for goal, Gareth also headed wide at a corner. The score certainly lifted City."

All this from, you will notice, a 'defender' sets one wondering what Gareth would do if he were in the team as a 'striker'.

It's good to see a Pleasant View boy, Gareth, doing so well in his chosen profession. Congratulations to a 'defender' doing his best to lift the "Blue Birds" up in the League Table.

HEADWAY, MAY 1989

15. My First Driving Lesson

My Instructor arrived and we travelled as far as the Old Library, here he stopped and gave me instructions on what I should know about the car.

We exchanged seats. I then started the car, driving towards Merthyr Vale. On manoeuvring the bend by St Mary's Church, I did so with only one hand on the wheel and that, I now know, was a dreadful mistake. We travelled along Nixonville without any hitches. On approaching the level-crossing gates of Merthyr Vale Colliery there were a number of cars waiting for the gates to open; my Instructor directed me to use my clutch and make sure that I kept my engine running. I had my moments of doubt whether I would be able to start without stalling the engine but fortunately everything went well. What a relief!

I managed somehow to get up Bell's Hill, but I can't recall how I got on the main road to Merthyr, but I must have followed the instructions correctly.

We were travelling along and I was enjoying my new skill when suddenly there was a piercing noise from behind. I thought that it must be the siren of an ambulance. The noise persisted and I couldn't understand why the ambulance was unable to pass our car because the road was clear and besides, they should have been able to see my L plates. Suddenly, the Instructor dived for the steering wheel of our car and stopped the dreadful noise.

We continued until we reached the furthest end of Merthyr Vale, then quite out of the blue I looked at the wheel and to my horror it appeared to be on fire. There were sparks coming from it. I just couldn't believe that this could happen to me! I carried on driving because I could not stop, the other cars were too close behind me; I again had to draw the Instructor's attention to my predicament and he again pounced on the steering wheel and extinguished the flames, much to my relief.

I thought how very peculiar it was that all this should happen to me on my first driving lesson; it seemed more like a test of nerves or how to manage difficult situations. However, we continued and all seemed to be going well when my Instructor suddenly said, "If I were you perhaps it would be better to slow down, it would be rather embarrassing to be stopped by a police car because you are exceeding the speed limit." I rectified the situation and we arrived at journey's end without any further mis-haps.

The next incident was when I asked my husband to take me for a driving lesson. He wasn't too keen, thinking his car was too powerful for a learner. However, I was persuasive, and when we arrived at the Slip Road, near Leo's Supermarket, he said "You are not going up that hill are you?" I assured him that I always did with my Instructor, so we proceeded without mis-hap but returning down the hill, my foot slipped off the brake and I free-wheeled all the way down. I found my footing just as we reached the bottom, but not before my husband realised what happened. I just explained that I was afraid that he might have panicked.

I expect that many learner drivers experience anxious moments, but they are hilarious on recollection.

VIOLET CHILCOTT, 1990

St. Mary's Church

16. Swinging on the Old Iron Gas Lamps

I recall swinging on the old iron gas lamps. There was one outside my granny's house in Pleasant View. We used to get the orange ropes from Tommy Breeze's vegetable shop in Aberfan. The oranges used to be delivered to his shop in wooden boxes with rope tied around them. If you bought vegetables from his shop he would give you a rope and an empty box free if you asked, hence the rope for our swing on the gas pole.

Then the old top and whip. I used to start at Pleasant View and whip my top right past Kingsley Terrace and all through Bryntaf and back again. No cars in those days so we had a free run.

MARY MAGLONA (LEWIS), MELBOURNE, AUSTRALIA, 1990

17. Childhood

When I sit and think of days gone by,
And the things we used to do.
Like walking up the river bank,
To get to Troedyrhiw. We'd go swimming in the Lido,
On a lovely summer's day.
Then walk back home to Aberfan,
At the finish of the day.
We'd have sandwiches and sherbet pop,
And maybe sweets as well.
When we got home in the evening,
We had many a tale to tell.
The games we played as children,
Had seasons like the weather.
When I was young I often wished,
Those days would last forever.
We would play L.O.N.D.O.N.
It was always lots of fun.
Then we'd get our homemade cricket bat,
And have a game of Nip and Run.
We played Buttons on the pavement,
And Rounders in the street.
Or a game of Marbles down the "backs"
With whoever we did meet.
With Hook and Wheel we'd bowl along,
Then puffed we had to stop.
While other kids around us played,
With their Leather Whip and Top.
We went walking down the "Old Road"
To go swimming in the Taff.
The water wasn't very clean,
But we always had a laugh.
On winter nights when it got dark,
We would gather around the lamppost.
Put lighted paper up the drainpipe,
To see which one whistled most.
We never had much money,
Because our dads were on the "Dole"
But they earned an extra couple of bob,
Up the mountain picking coal.
So now I sit and think about,
What the kids are doing now.
Did they ever learn the games we played,
Or have they forgotten how.
Our lives are very similar ,
And the circle is complete.
Their dads are on the "Dole" you see,
And they are hanging around the street.
It seems society hasn't learned,
From their mistakes of yesterday.
So I sit and think and wait for,
My chance on Judgement Day.

Tom Abbot, 1989

18.   The Queen and her Throne

Golden hair with silver ribbons.
Muslin dress as white as snow.
Pretty shoes made of silk
And socks of pretty pink too.

Golden throne with silver lanterns,
Pretty carpets made of cobwebs
Pretty too and oh! so old,
And pretty curtains made of Gold.

MARY EMANUELLI,
STANDARD 4, PANTGLAS SCHOOL, 1950

Estlyn Williams, Fete and Gala Pageboy, Whitsun 1966

19.   The Red Waters

If reading these words has no special meaning for you, it can be said that you haven't lived, at least, you haven't lived at the top end of Merthyr Vale, that small but integral part of the story we tell. Almost one street, it could be said: certainly one people, a sentiment expressed by no less than Mr Idwal Evans, a teacher of excellence at Merthyr Vale School. Too young to integrate into the wider community, we were content, no doubt, in such a compact area, to develop quite naturally in a cocoon of adult stability based on religion, diligence and high moral standards.

Discovering, as a child, the Red Waters, which stood on the doorstep, as it were, of the Danyderi colliery and coke-ovens, was to gain, unawares, one's first geographical, historical and political experience, as we would have pondered over the implications for our forefathers in that industrial venture. There was just a hint that we may have been standing on "Holy Ground".

Pushing on from the Red Waters we hadn't far to go before reaching 'the Sidings', yet another site which spoke to us of history, but we hadn't come here for that, no, there were far more important things for youngsters to do. Yes, you've guessed correctly, FOOTBALL. Ignoring its lack of size, 'the Sidings' became, in winter, our Wembley, and it took little conversion, stone wickets instead of stone goal posts, to make it the Oval in summer, with certainly Vitae Lampadae's 'bumping pitch and blinding light'. Here, our characters were being formed playing cricket, no less than those formed on the playing fields of Eton; two contrasting worlds, of course, but inevitably destined in later days to clash like noisy cymbals with each side having to concede that there was a place for each in the commercial, industrial and political life.

But enough of that for the moment and so to return to our sweaty sessions of soccer and cricket, which lasted for hours on end and the yearning for a cooling off. Oh and weren't we lucky in having a choice of super venue for that. Yes, firstly it was down to 'The Hazel' and a dip in the freezing fast flowing Taff itself: But with compensation in mind in being able to swim at no cost and no limitation on time spent in that 'ice-box', how privileged we were!!! But on returning to the bank how thankful we were to some of the older lads who had lit a fire with wood and we stretched out gratefully, cold, blue hands and feet to meet the smoky flames; ah, life was good after all, as circulation was felt again. Towels were a luxury. Secondly, our choice was the Donkey Field and the Blue Pool where, on the 9th August 1932, one of our friends, Leslie Sims, was to tragically lose his young life when he accidentally drowned, a traumatic experience indeed and a scar on immature minds, but we still think of you, Les!

Not easily suppressed however, is the vitality of youth and we continued throughout the long days of summer and the short ones of winter, to explore and enjoy the back lanes and streets around us, for our playing areas were certainly limited. We were hemmed in by the close proximity of the mountain running at the rear of Brynteg Terrace and the ominous mound of colliery waste sitting precariously on that. We fared little better on the other lower side, where we were hemmed in by the colliery and the railway. So we were left with the longish, narrow Tramroad as an alternative playground, shades of Trevethick, more history, and was it any wonder that we often wandered onto the danger sites of the colliery to play around and get grease from the axle-boxes of the trucks for our hair; Brylcreme was still a long way off.

But, through it all, we just carried on happily kicking our footballs, when we had one, climbing trees on our hillside below Danyderi Farm; picking our blackberries and winberies; playing 'guessing' in front of shop windows; shoeing the 'white horse; weak horses, strong donkeys; catty and doggy; hooking our wheels and dozens of other games, sometimes under the hot sun of long summer days, and just as enjoyable, sometimes under the friendly gas-lights before going 'in' for a wash, bit of supper, and then up the wooden stairs to 'Bedfordshire', but not before, 'Lord keep us safe this night'.

There were the occasions when we climbed onto the window ledges of the Windsor Hotel hoping to find out why our elders wanted to spend so much time there. We would creep quietly into the Billiard Hall pretending we weren't there until some small indiscretion provoked the thunderous voice of Jack Pendducae and it was the door, before we were helped through it. We washed up and slipped down to Calfaria Chapel and the Penny Readings, in a vain attempt to win a few coppers for singing or reciting; we usually drew a blank there, no budding Eisteddfod winners amongst us I'm afraid. And the Aberfan Cinema too, made its call, so it was not easy finding 2d and over the colliery we ran to find out how Tom Mix and Rin-tin-tin were getting on every Saturday morning. What a life we lived. Who could ask for more?

We didn't, but we got it every summer when amidst whoops of delight we ran down the road to see clanging steam traction engines drawing, onto the Tramroad, long colourful, trailers full of impending delights, yes! Freeman's Fun Fair was rolling in and soon from Jack Taylor's house at the bottom of Alberta Street down to Disgwylfa Chapel, would be set up an Aladdin's arcade of fun and laughter. Take your choice from the Horses, the chair-o-planes, swinging boats, dodgems, and the many stalls, coconut shies, skittles, roll-a-penny, ice-cream, toffee apples, and when the mighty Wurlitzer organ set it all off, the village turned out. Days of depression? Not on your life, it was an occasion for joy and laughter, to turn the dark clouds inside out.

Yes, the top end of Merthyr Vale enjoyed itself despite adversity, indeed adversity was the spur to make life all the more successful; we learned the meaning behind the adage, 'the best things in life are free!'

Today, the Red Waters has lost its vivid colour, and other things, too, have become lost. But life is like that. It changes despite our desire to retain what was. A new generation takes the stage as we move gently to the wings and we sincerely hope happiness and enjoyment will be their experience no less than it was ours within those few pulsating acres.

CYRIL JOHNSON, 1992

DAN Y DERI FARM, MERTHYR VALE

20. The Fellowship of Youth

The large black and white photograph shows a group of teenagers sitting around a long trestle table covered with a white cloth. Most of those featured are now grandparents; even the boy making a face at the camera. Three of the girls no longer live in the locality having moved away more than twenty years ago.

The photograph was taken sometime in the 1950s. The occasion was a 'tramp's supper', hence the rather scruffy clothes. The setting was the vestry of Hope Chapel which used to stand between the old library and the garage. The 'tramp's supper' was just one of the unusual events provided by the Fellowship of Youth; a youth movement sponsored by the Churches of Christ.

There is evidence to suggest that the Fellowship of Youth existed as far back as the inter-war period. Some local people remember attending youth meetings at Hope Chapel near the end of the second world war. But it was the 1950s and the obsession with keeping youngsters 'off the streets' that marked the start of the FOY's golden age. At the beginning of the decade it was led by Percy Adams, a telephone engineer living in Glyndwr Street, Merthyr Vale. He provided a varied programme, with a strong bias toward traditional chapel activities. There were anglicized versions of the penny readings, dramas were produced with a strong temperance theme, quizes mainly on the Bible. Adults came along to talk about their jobs, whilst once a month there was a 'devotional meeting', which usually brought a sudden fall in the attendance figures, though others relished the chance to perform in front of an audience. The Fellowship of Youth succeeded in attracting youngsters from a wide range of backgrounds and areas. They came not just from the churches and chapels of Aberfan and Merthyr Vale, but also from neighbouring villages.

The mid-1950s saw a change in leadership and with it a change in approach to youth work. Philip Morgan, a young minister just out of college, came to Hope Chapel with a wide experience of the type of youth activities being provided by the Churches of Christ in England. One obvious difference was in noise levels; much of it due to Philip Morgan himself. It marked the end of the time when young people were expected to be a passive and attentive audience. Under this new regime they were expected to help run the show. Furthermore, there were none of the old restraints on the content of the programme. Events did not have to be overtly religious or educational. The 'tramp's supper' was a good example of these radical ideas. At one level it was entirely frivolous and silly, with funny speeches and the throwing of bread rolls. Yet those involved found that they were practising social and other skills.

The same was true of other events such as the mock trial and the mock parliament. Some of those who in earlier times baulked at the idea of reading a passage of scripture in public, found it relatively easy to give evidence in a crowded noisy 'courtroom'. And the sheer silliness of some activities and the free periods of table-tennis and general running around gave greater emphasis, and meaning perhaps, to the serious moments. The once a month service of worship had gone. In its place was 'the epilogue' at the end of each Monday evening. It began with campfire songs - this old man and the like - sang around the open coal fire in the vestry or under the stars in the chapel garden. Then hands would be joined to form a circle for prayers, a short talk and more religious songs like "Kumbya" or a negro spiritual.

At the end of the 1950s Philip Morgan moved on and was replaced by another young minister, a Scotsman named Henry Bell. In some ways he was even more liberal than Philip Morgan and the new generation of FOYers enjoyed a great deal of freedom, especially to express their opinions and wishes. Yet the FOY was a carefully organised movement. Only members could attend meetings, and their attendance and subscriptions were recorded on the register. When the new session was due to begin in January 1960, Henry Bell outlined the conditions for membership in the Sunday School magazine. All members had to be between 11 and 16 years old. [There was a Junior Fellowship of Youth for under-11s for a short time.] All new members would be initiated at a special membership epilogue, and official FOY badges were available for 1/3 [6p approx.]. Forthcoming attractions included a new quiz league with a cup for the winning team; the FOY festival; and in March, Mr Adams and his filmstrips.

Not much there to excite the more sophisticated modern teenager. But for most of the fifties and early sixties, Hope Chapel was bulging at the seams every Monday evening. Part of the attraction lay outside the chapel building; there is at least one old-married couple that started 'going-out' together at FOY. And there was always the possibility of a game of postman's knock to look forward to. Whatever the reason in the response, the fact remains that on several occasions the books had to be closed and prospective members placed on a waiting list. True, for most of that time there were few counter-attractions, but the opportunity to meet a wide range of people of your own age, and to have a lot of fun in a free and friendly atmosphere was enough to ensure that the Fellowship of Youth would have a special place in the memories of a lot of local people.

KEN ROBERTS, 1991

21. With Great Gusto

I also recall the Dramatic Societies, amateur of course. They performed at the Rechabite Hall in Crescent Street. I remember especially their performance of 'Maria and the Red Barn' and the 'Ghost Train'. We used to cheer the hero and heroine and boo the villain with great gusto.

MARY MAGLONA (LEWIS), MELBOURNE, AUSTRALIA, 1990

22. Drama

There were a lot of drama societies and choirs during the war years. Our chapel, Capel Aberfan, had a drama society. The producer was a North Walian who had much more Welsh than English.

Anyway, in this play there was a scene where the couple had to kiss. The man said that he would kiss the woman in the actual play but he thought that it wasn't necessary in rehearsal. "After all, I am a married man." He explained that this was war-time and a lot of men were away, everyone had to be careful, people could talk. Anyway the night of the play came, the producer was more than determined that things were going to be done properly. As the big moment drew near he stood up in his place in front of the audience and shouted in broad Welsh "Kisher, kisher." The players collapsed with laughter and couldn't go on.

I remember one night the film broke down in the cinema and the audience came up in a body and piled in to see one of our dramas. I liked the plays and choirs very much but if we went to Merthyr to perform I would always be worrying about my evacuees, Margaret and Doreen, in case there was an air-raid warning.

MEGAN JONES, 1991

Smyrna Chapel Drama Society

23.   It was a Joy

Every chapel and church had a drama society. They performed in the old Aberfan Hall, now regrettably demolished. It was a beautiful place with a lovely stage and gallery. The Aberfan Hall was the focus for all these happenings. One chapel would bring their play and then in a month's time there would be a play by another drama society.

And then once a year there would be a drama week that was outstanding. The week would begin on the Saturday and run through the Monday, Tuesday, Wednesday, Thursday and Friday, and then Saturday again. Every evening a different play would be performed and on the final night a grand finale and the adjudication. And believe me, the charabancs came from all over Wales supporting the competition. I wouldn't like to tell you what time the proceedings finished on the Saturday night but it was a joy.

MORFYDD HOLDEN, 1987

24.   Penny Readings

We had something in Aberfan that was rather unusual. We had what was called "Penny Readings." This was when I was very, very young. We paid a penny and went in. The Aberfan Hall would be absolutely packed. There would be prizes for the best stories, the best singers and for elocution.

There was also a prize for something that our present generation would know nothing about. In Welsh it was called "Donath at a nodau". The person would be given a reading with no punctuation mark whatsoever and had to read it straight through, it would all be bundled up hopelessly. Occasionally someone rather clever would go so far and stop, go so far and they would win the prize.

Then there was a noted singer from the Grove, Mr Tommy Lloyd. He won every singing adjudication in that hall. He had one of the most beautiful voices, a lovely voice. His daughter is living in Pantglas Fawr, Mrs Emily Griffiths, and is a noted artist and her father was a noted singer.

I can remember that in the adjudication in the hall a little bag was given, as a rule, with a sixpenny piece inside and this was the prize. The bag would be in crochet work, in pale lavender. There was a string to go around the neck. Now a sixpence nearly seventy years ago was a fortune.

MORFYDD HOLDEN, 1987

25. Englynion Ceredwyn - B. T. Davies

B. T. Davies, "Ceredwyn", degreed.
This gentleman was a Bard,
A pure, satisfied, refined shopkeeper,
Upright, an extremely good man.

He was a natural, literary genius,
He was generous with what he witnessed
with his own eyes.
His pure belief in the talents of Aberfan.
Were in abundance, worth money.

His musical contented days were faultless,
Only he was lonely,
Really we will have to find a kind woman
for this widower,
Whilst keeping her there in reverence.

He had a pure original talent, in his work.
It was not superficial.
He was a teacher, he wouldn't turn back,
Or muse, on his gifts.

Great was the success of his many endeavours
To live good.
He was pleased with his success.
His benefit was to inherit a clean virtuous mind
And a good heart, making a perfect pair.

He was a good, virtuous, protector.
The destitute benefited by the gifts
of his hands.
The old people were never forgotten.

On he went, untiring, and soon became
a Chaired Bard,
He lived in great respect, and anon,
He had a long gifted life,
Above his crowning.

TAKEN FROM THE
MERTHYR EXPRESS, 20 APRIL 1878
TRANSLATED FROM THE
WELSH BY ETHEL LLOYD 1991
*B. T. Davies was a composer
of Welsh alliterative stanza.
He was probably Aberfan's first real shop-keeper.*

26. A Noted Welsh Bard

Amongst the mourners at the funeral of Walter Bell was Michael Thomas. He was to become a very well known and popular inhabitant of Merthyr Vale. He was a very talented man and his name was among the noted Welsh Bards.

Born in Cwmllynfyll in 1861, Michael Thomas was one of ten children. His beloved mother died in 1886 and after looking around various colliery towns in South Wales he decided that Merthyr Vale appealed to him the most and he settled here in 1887. Some of his Bardic chairs were won at Pontypridd, Dowlais, Pwllheli, Blaenclydach and Pontneddfechan. He won twenty pounds for an essay at the National Eisteddfod in Pontypridd and altogether won fifteen Bardic chairs.

The minister of Bethania Chapel Rev J. T. Rogers, where Michael Thomas worshipped, visited his home on several occasions when there was illness in the house. He noted that two of the Bardic chairs were upstairs, unused. He decided that this was because they were too uncomfortable so he wrote to the Eisteddfod Committee saying that Bardic chairs should be improved. He thought that gifted Bards like Michael Thomas, deserved more comfort to sit and enjoy their worthy proclamation.

Michael Thomas died in 1928. He never married but has several great nephews and nieces in Aberfan.

Drawing of one of Michael Thomas Bardic Chairs

BEDD FY MAM!

SEF

MRS. SUSANNAH THOMAS,

PENYGRAIG, CWMLLYNFELL,

Yr hon a fu farw Chwefror 19th, 1886,

YN 53 MLWYDD OED.

Hwnt yn ngorwel ddu marwolaeth
  Heulwen bywyd mam aeth lawr,
A daeth nos dymhestlog alaeth
  I amdoi ei theulu 'nawr.
Ryfedd nos! heb wên un seren
  Yn ei nen yn gwasgar hedd,
Dim ond caddug drwy'r ffurfafen,—
  Pruddaidd gaddug glyn y bedd.

O! fy mam! fy mam anwylaf!
  Nythle gofid yw fy mron,
O! na chawn ei gwên hawddgaraf
  Eto ar y ddaear hon.
Heddyw gwn beth ydyw galar,
  A'i bicellau'n myn'd i'r byw,—
Galar nad oes ar y ddaear
  Ond y profiad ddwed beth yw.

Y mae'r gwyneb siriol hwnw
  Wisgai wenau ar bob pryd,
Wedi newid heddyw'n welw,—
  Cilio wnaeth ei dlysni'i gyd:
Y mae'r hon a fedrai leddfu
  Holl drallodau'i theulu cu,
Arnom heddyw wedi cefnu,—
  Wedi myn'd i'r beddrod du.

Caled meddwl fod y tafod
  A'n cynghorai ni bob pryd,
A'i gynghorion wedi darfod,—
  Obry'n ngwaelod bedd yn fud.
Y mae'r galon gynhes hono
  Gurai drosom yn mhob clwy',
Yn y beddrod, wedi peidio
  Curo drosom bythol mwy.

Mae'r nefolaidd hyfforddiadau
  Roddodd ini lawer gwaith,
Fel angylion ar ein llwybrau
  Yn ein gwylio ar ein taith;
O! mor werthfawr ei "dymuniad"
  I'w hanwyliaid hoff o hyd;
Fel yn eigion môr ei chariad
  Boddai hi ein beiau'i gyd.

Mae fy meddwl megys gwallgof,
  A'i grwydriadau oll yn ffol;
Mae'n tramwyo llwybrau adgof,
  Gyda brys yn mlaen ac ol.
Mynych gwel'd fy mam yr ydwyf,
  Gwrando'i llais, ac amheu'r bedd,
Er fod trwch y gweryd rhyngwyf
  A chael gwel'd ei hanwyl wedd.

Agor bedd fy mam oedd agor
  Bedd o fewn fy mynwes i,
Aeth fy nghysur ar ei helor
  Tua'r gladdfa gyda hi.
Huan gwyn holl hedd fy nyddiau
  I'w orllewin roddodd lam,
Claddwyd fy ngobeithion goreu
  Yn y bedd lle claddwyd mam.

O! mor gyfyng oedd ffarwelio
  Am yr olaf waith â hi,
Pan wnai'r olaf awr ei gwthio
  I afaelion angau du.
Y mae'i "hanadl byr" yn treiddio
  Drwy fy nghlyw yr adeg hon,
A phob adeg fel yn suddo—
  Suddo'n ddyfnach glwyfau'm bron.

O! 'rwy'n cofio'r noson hono—
  'Rwy'n ei gwel'd drwy ddagrau'n lli'—
Pan ddechreuodd mam a pheidio
  Ateb ein galwadau ni!
O! gyfyngder diymwared,
  Methu'n clywed wnai'r pryd hyn,—
Yn rhy bell oedd wedi myned
  Obry i ddyfndderau'r glyn.

Fel ar bruddaidd len fy hiraeth
  Eglur ganfod wyf o hyd
Ymyl gwely ei marwolaeth,
  Ninau'n yr ystorm i gyd;
Ac yn ngrym y 'storom ddigllon,
  Gododd fel o'r dyfnder du,
At ein gilydd gwasgem weithion,
  Gan mor enbyd oedd ei rhu.

" O, na b'ai fy mhen yn ddagrau,"
  Fel y gwnai ngofidiau cudd—
Nofio llif fy nagrau'n lluoedd
  Allan o fy nghalon brudd.
O lan bedd fy mam, dywylled
  Yw dyfodol ffordd fy oes,
Nid oes belydr gwyn i'w weled,
  Dim ond nos o gorwynt croes.

Gydag eraill o'm hanwyliaid,
  Hedd fo hun fy anwyl fam;
Ar ei hol i'r bedd yn ddibaid,
  Dyfod 'ym o gam i gam.
Cystudd, ing ga'dd yn yr anial,
  'Nawr o'i hol maent hwy i gyd;
Crefydd Iesu fedr gynal
  Ei holl ddeiliaid i well byd.

Cwmllynfell.   MICHAEL THOMAS.

The funeral hymnsheet of Michael Thomas's mother,
on which appears his poem about her, on the next page

27. A Poem by Michael Thomas

at his beloved mother's graveside, who died in 1886, 53 years of age.

On the horizon of her life, dark death took away her sun and there came a
tempestuous night that enshrouded our family now.
Strange night; without the twinkling of one star in the heavens, dispersing
peace, only the dark misty firmament, only the dark earth of the grave.

O, my beloved mother, my dearest mother, my breast is the nest of my sorrow,
we shall not see your beautiful smile again on the earth.
Today I know what is sorrow, with its' sharp stabs going into the living.
Sorrow, there is not on earth, only the experience says what it is.

The pleasant face that wore a smile at all times, by today has changed
tearfully, hidden is all its' beauty, this one who could disperse the whole
family's troubles, has left us to enter into the dark grave.

Hard to realise that the tongue that advised, and encouraged us at all times
is finished, and now lies below this grave, dumb.
The warm heart that beat over us in every trouble, has stopped beating in the
grave, having failed to beat over us ever again.

O! I remember that night, I can see her through a storm of tears, when Mam
began to fail to answer our calls, she could not hear at that time, she had
gone too far into the black grave.

With others of my dear ones, peace was the sleep of my beloved mother, behind
her we are coming step by step. Illness overtakes you in the wilderness.
All that has left her now. Her faith in Jesus will sustain her on her journey.

MICHAEL THOMAS, CWMLLYNFYLL, 1886
TRANSLATED FROM THE WELSH BY ETHEL LLOYD

28. Rivalry

"Rivalry and comparison between North and South will always be part of the Welsh pattern of
life, however closely the two peoples may be united in future by trunk road or helicopter."
A South Wales man who glimpsed a recent reference here to the once renowned home spun
erudition of the famous bootmakers and cobblers of Llanerchymedd, Anglesey, challenges its former
fame with the achievements of the small mining village of Cymllynfyll at the head of the Swansea
Valley. Its famous school of poets of the late nineteenth and early present century, used to meet in the
little engine house of "Gwaithy Mynydd" high up in the picturesque Twrch Valley. Is it small wonder
that Watcyn Wyn, Dyfnallt, Ben Davies, Mafonwy Gwilym Wyn and Michael Thomas developed
their muse so tunefully to the murmer of the river or the breezes of the Black Mountains?" he asks.

CRWYDRYN. WESTERN MAIL, 6TH OCTOBER, 1956

29. A Noted Singer

Aberfan has always been a village of great culture especially music and drama.

Every chapel and the church had a drama society and a choir. There was a noted brass band, under the direction of Mr George Thomas. They used to practice in the old Navigation Hotel.

There were a number of choirs apart from the chapel choirs. There was Septimus Ashton's Choir, and John Devenold's Madrigal Choir and Bob Roger's Mixed Choir. We also had a wonderful singer in Aberfan, Mr Johnnie Thomas, who won the National Eisteddfod. He had the newsagent's shop in Aberfan Road. News came that he had won the tenor solo. He was a noted singer. The news spread quickly and we all got together and hired the band from Troedyrhiw. We found out the exact time of the train and when Johnnie Thomas would be returning. The band and the people went down Bridge Street, along Nixonville and up Bell's Hill. We stood there and waited in silence for the train to arrive, watched one or two doors opening and then one of us spotted him. "There he is. There he is." Two men ran down and they had him on their shoulders, before he knew where he was. Then the band started playing "See the conquering hero comes". Well, we came back down Bell's Hill, along Nixonville and up Bridge Street; we turned left by the Aberfan Hotel and we lined the roads. Johnnie was taken into his shop which was opposite Smyrna Chapel. We all stood there shouting "We want Johnnie. We want Johnnie". He opened his bedroom window and expressed his thanks to us all.

MORFYDD HOLDEN, 1987

30. Ashton's Choir

"Bethania Chapel was always full. Septimus Ashton was the Precentor. On special occasions there would be benches in the aisles. Septimus Ashton was outstanding, a noted gentleman."

MORFYDD HOLDEN, 1984

Hovering around the fringes of the practice hall, Selwyn Russell Jones would listen to Ashton's Choir and see his neighbour Mr Richards, the Jeweller, balding, plump and bespectacled, singing along with his fellows under the conductor's watchful eye. They would be singing such rousing choruses as "The Spartan Heroes", "The Crusader" and "Crossing the Plains".

Septimus Ashton conducted with everything that he had. Not for him the flick of the finger, the nod of the head or the pursing of the lips. On occasions, he would let out shattering ear splitting yells and if the baton had flown out of his hand, it would have brained someone. When he would be conducting a sacred song his eyes would grow moist and tears would run silently down his cheeks.

Septimus Ashton came to Aberfan in 1907 in answer to an advertisement in 'Y Tyst' the newspaper of the Welsh Independents. Bethania Chapel had advertised for a Precentor to lead the singing and teach music in the Chapel. Septimus Ashton was short listed along with two others and they came on three consecutive Sundays to take the singing in Bethania. This was their audition and from this Septimus Ashton emerged as first choice. Thus he moved from Treorchy with his family, when he was about thirty years of age. The new conductor soon established himself in Aberfan and became highly respected in the community because of his love and knowledge of music. Meanwhile the Chapel became noted for the quality of music to be found there. He taught 'tonic sol fa' to the congregation and everyone who joined the choir had to read music. For his services he was paid the 'Silver Collection' taken in the Chapel every month. By day, when there was work there, he worked in Merthyr Vale Colliery.

Glyn Roberts of Aberfan Road, formed an early ambition to join the choir. His father was Choir

Secretary and his grandfather was also a member, when, at eighteen Glyn told his father, "I want to join the Choir." Glyn went for an audition to Mr Ashton's house in Coronation. "He told me that I was a bottom bass and that I could join." This was a very proud moment for Glyn, he would be joining his father and grandfather in Mr Ashton's Choir. Glyn also sang in Bethania Chapel.

"We would practise on a Sunday. The doors would be closed at five past four. No one could come in afterwards. Mr Ashton wasn't strict but he was firm. A lovely man and a wonderful musician. He had a wonderful voice himself; the full range from top tenor to bottom bass. We would go to the chapel for the first service, then come out and cross the road to have a smoke, then go back into the chapel for the second service and then stay for the singing school until nine o clock at night. The choir would compete in all the Eisteddfods and won the National in Cardiff."

Ada James, nee Carpenter, sang in Ashton's Mixed Choir. The very way that she came to join the choir was unusual. She was auditioned by Mr Ahston without her even knowing. "I was working for Miss Florie Davies, Cookery, as she was known, in Aberfan Road. I was lucky, I did not have to go away to service. I came here to work for Miss Davies straight from school and I have been here ever since, for over seventy years. Mr Ashton and his family lived next door. One day I was singing in the pantry and he heard me. He told me to join the choir. So I did and my friend Grace came with me for company. I was about twenty at the time."

"There were about one hundred and fifty of us in the choir. People came down from Troedyrhiw and Abercanaid. Petula Clark's grandmother, Mrs Phillips, came down from Abercanaid to sing in the choir. She sat down the front. She was a small round lady with rosy cheeks. Two cousins of Petula Clark also sang in the choir. I met my husband when he came down from Troedyrhiw to sing in Ashton's Choir. There was a good choir in Troedyrhiw and they were conducted by Herbert Llewellyn. They were the Royal Male Choir. They had sung on the Royal Yacht and my husband had sung with them. Herbert Llewellyn's wife sang in Ashton's Choir. Also singing in Ashton's Choir was Septimus Ashton's wife and sister. Singing in her father's choir was Nesta. She still lives in Aberfan and is the sole survivor of his five children. She has retained her love of singing.

In 1939 Johnnie Watkins became the Mayor of Merthyr Tydfil. His Civic Service was held in Bethania Chapel, Aberfan. The choir sang "Worthy is the lamb". "We sang as if we were possessed" remembers Ada James. "The Chief Constable of Merthyr was there and he said that he had never heard such singing. Our singing, he said had sent shivers down his spine".

"We had a marvellous accompanist. He could make the piano talk. He would tell us that he had never had a music lesson. My father and two brothers also sang in the Choir and we would travel away to sing, usually travelling by train from Aberfan Station. I remember going to Machynlleth and Liverpool, amongst other places, to sing and we went to Llwydcoed, Aberdare, to sing in the open air. We often sang in open air Eisteddfods. On that particular occasion we sang "We will never bow down."

Idloes Owen had a choir in Merthyr Vale and when Ashton's Choir finished some went to sing in that choir. But we had a lot of sacred music with Mr Ashton, "Elijah" and the "Messiah" for example. And we were all one".

This sentiment was echoed by Beryl Roberts. "We are all treated the same. He had no favourites. He had something to say to us all as individuals. He was a very friendly man. I remember that four of us had entered a competition, singing together. We went to a musician in Moy Road but it was Mr Ashton who sorted us out. He had us around the piano and soon put us right".

Her friend, Mair Price, recalls that he was a good man, jovial and humorous. "We had great times and didn't realise until afterwards what good times they were. We paid 2d a week, in contributions and as long as we had that 2d then we knew that we were alright. We had a lot of fun in the choir".

During the 1930s, in the "bad times", Septimus Ashton and some of his choir went singing on the "Hunger Marches". They would sing around the streets of London. They found this hard, not least the choir master himself. They were proud men and worth listening to. Often they would be given a singing engagement on the strength of what someone had heard in the street. They would probably sing in a local church or chapel. Then they were able to send extra money home to their families.

In 1944, when Septimus Ashton died, the choir fell apart. Glyn Roberts and some of his fellow choristers formed the "Gleemen" and they would go around the clubs singing. Glyn went on to sing in the Ynysowen Choir. Glyn recalls the first conductor of this choir, John Haydn Phillips. "Like Mr Ashton, he was a fine musician". I travel a lot to Mid Wales and am surprised to know how popular John Haydn's hymn tunes are there. "Bro Aber" especially is sung regularly.

Many friendships were made in Ashton's Choir which held a special place in the hearts of the singers. In the 1960s two middle-aged men met for the first time in over thirty years. Broad grins spread over their faces as they realised that they had sung in Ashton's Choir. The excitement in their voices revealed that their membership of the choir had been a precious and special time in their lives, an experience that they had treasured over the years.

There have been many noted choirs in Aberfan and Merthyr Vale. But, whenever people start talking about choirs of the past, Ashton's Choir is sure to be mentioned.

There are four generations of Septimus Ashton's family still worshipping in Bethania Chapel, his daughter, two grand-daughters and a grand-son; four great- grandchildren and two great-great-grandchildren.

MAUREEN HUGHES, 1992

31. 25 Years of Music

'Born out of tragedy like the precious pearl out of the shell of pain'.
Sir Alun Talfan Davies, Q.C., President of the Choir.

The first discussions on the formation of a Male Voice Choir took place at one of the meetings of the Tip Removal Committee when it was realized that its work would soon diminish after the agreement to remove the tips. Posters were placed in the local shops in the Winter of 1967 and the first practice was held in Tommy Small's Chapel. Rev Erastus Jones was the conductor and John Haydn Phillips became the Musical Director soon afterwards. Gwyneth Evans was the accompanist. Three of the founder members are still with the choir and they are Cled Davies, Victor Jones and David Pryce.

By their twenty fifth year, the choir had travelled 75,000 miles and raised £75,000 for charities all over Britain and on the Continent. They have sung at many Cathedrals including Canterbury.

"We sing to help others
We sing because we like to
We like helping others
as they once helped Aberfan."

Born out of tragedy, not only has the Choir helped many other people and causes but has played a vital role in rebuilding the heart and soul of our community. The story of the removal of the tips under the leadership of Mr Tom Price is an epic one and from the Tip Removal Committee grew the Ynysowen Male Choir.

"We give thanks for all that Ynysowen Male Choir has done." - Reverend Kenneth Hayes, Aberfan and Merthyr Vale Churches Council.

COMPILED FROM YNYSOWEN CHOIR 25 ANNIVERSARY PROGRAMME 1968-1993

Ynysowen Male Choir 1968 - 1998

*Mayoress Linda Matthews receives Leicester's Coat of Arms
from Mal Jones, oldest member, Arnold Davies, Treasurer, and
Ray Jones, Secretary, of Ynysown Choir*

Chapter Eight
Schooldays

1. Introduction

Our schools and schoolteachers have played a crucial part in the life of the community. Because so many of our teachers lived in the village we were able to see them in their off duty times as well as in the classroom. Many of these teachers are remembered with gratitude and affection. With hindsight they are appreciated more then they were in our youth but they seem to have been respected and in many cases, loved. Susie Olwen Thomas is an example. Fourteen of her first cousins also became teachers, many of them remaining in the village schools. There are happy memories of schooldays but our fortunes were tied to the colliery and bad times there showed up in the school log-books with descriptions of children struggling to school in unsuitable clothing and bad footwear. The log-books also revealed much infectious disease. Creative writing was encouraged in our schools and still is today.

Ynysowen Nursery School

2. Pantglas Infants School 1911-1913

I was a little girl of five years of age going to school, Pantglas Infants School. I had a lovely dress with frills on each shoulder and a bow in my hair. My first teacher was Miss Jinnie Morgan, Iltyd Villa, Aberfan Road. My mother took me to school. My mother was allowed to stay with me until I stopped crying. Well, of course it was a new experience for me. I had always spoken the Welsh language and now I would be going into a room where I would be hearing the English language. I did not know whether I would understand it or not, but my teacher was lovely.

Miss Lydia Davies was the headmistress in those days. She was a very lovable, good natured lady and I loved that school and there was no need for my mother to take me the next day because I was quite alright and quite happy.

MORFYDD HOLDEN, 1987

Pantglas School, Aberfan

3.   Pantglas Junior School 1913-1917

After the Infants school, I went to the Juniors. My headmistress was a Miss Davies from Penydarren. She took the scholarship class. Miss Fanny Barley was in Class 1. I loved her. I loved her very much. And then in Standard 2 I had Miss Sal Rowlands whom I also loved.

In Standard 2 we always had our Scripture. This would come to start the day and then sums and writing.

Then we had a Welsh class and I can remember Miss Rowlands, she always depended on me to give her the meanings of some Welsh words. She said that I taught her 'the Welsh' language.

In Standard 3 and Standard 4, I had two lovely teachers again, Miss Minnie Lewis and Miss Beattie Lewis, and they lived in 'Y Wern', Aberfan Road. That was a lovely home to go to. I knew their mother well and I was often invited later on to go for a special evening to 'Y Wern', and that would be packed with all teachers whom I knew very well and we would have a lovely evening talking over old times.

I remember Miss Davies the headmistress used to take the scholarship class, up the stairs in her own private room.

The scholarship was our 11+ and she would take us every day for about an hour in arithmetic and essay writing, a bit of geography and a bit of history, and my word, she was an excellent teacher, and the great day came for the scholarship examination. In those days we had to go to Cyfarthfa Secondary School to try the examination. We had to have a little case ready with our pen, pencil and all that we needed, then we sat the examination and came home on the train. In those days there weren't so many buses running. The train was more popular. Then we had to wait for the result of the examination. Well it seemed a long time waiting for that result, but the result came. I had passed, much to the joy of Mam and Dad; they were absolutely thrilled.

And I remember Dad, he was so pleased that I had passed and he said "Morfydd, I am going up to see Miss Davies the Headmistress today." "Are you Dad?" "Yes I am going up. I want to say thank you to her for what she has done." And I thought how lovely of Dad to do such a kind thing.

MORFYDD HOLDEN, 1987

4.   Mount Pleasant School

At five years of age I went to the comparatively new school at Mount Pleasant and many happy years I spent there until the age of fourteen. My headteachers during this time were Mr Jenkins and Mr Lewis. The school and community were so closely intertwined that even when I left school I did not forget the happy years I spent there. This was borne out just a year or so ago when an exciting invitation was received from the headteacher, Mr Bond, to attend a pageant magnificently presented by children and staff to commemorate the school's 80th year. There followed a nostalgic look at photographs of 'old' boys and girls and the event was brought to a successful and happy conclusion with refreshments.

PHYLLIS DAVIES, 1992

5. Cyfarthfa Secondary School

Passing the scholarship meant that I was to go to Cyfarthfa Secondary School. Quakers Yard School hadn't been built so I went to Cyfarthfa in September. We were quite a number of valley pupils. We went by train and then walked up to Cyfarthfa Park. We caught the train at Aberfan. There was an Aberfan station and an Aberfan railway.

The headmistress in those days was Miss Davenport. She was very, very regimental. The main doors would be open and when we had assembly every morning we could hear Miss Davenport's strong footsteps walking down the corridor.

"Good morning girls."

"Good morning Miss Davenport." We'd have assembly and prayers and then we'd go to our classrooms for our lessons. Miss Davenport, I must say this, was very, very fond of the Merthyr pupils. She tried to get the valley girls to pronounce words the same way she did. She didn't always succeed. "Theatre" was an example. We Welsh girls would say it in our own way. She had a very soft spot for the Merthyr pupils but not for the valley pupils.

I had an excellent lady teaching me Welsh. I was fluent in Welsh and Miss Hettie Morris was from Pembrokeshire, not very far from Dad's home and of course mutations came to me naturally and I never had to swot mutations because they came automatically. But I felt very sorry for those pupils who had to swot and swot. I remember Miss Morris coming up to me and saying "Morfydd. Read this book, you know all this. It's wasting your time. You'll love this book. Read this book while I go around the other pupils." We happened to talk about my name. And she said to me 'Do you know the meaning of your name?"

"No I'm afraid I don't Miss Morris." "I'll tell you the meaning of your lovely name Morfydd - of great value." And that was the first time that I knew the true meaning of my lovely name.

We were there for a year. I can't say that I enjoyed it there because I felt that Miss Davenport was not on our side; and then the great news came that Quakers Yard School was going to be built and the valley pupils who had to go to Cyfarthfa would be installed in Quakers Yard.

MORFYDD HOLDEN, 1987

Miss Davenport's Study

6.   Quakers Yard School

The great day came and I shall never forget it. As a matter of fact, the headmaster was my next door neighbour. He lived in "Llewelfa" on Aberfan Road. He was a noted poet. "Sarnicol" was his Bardic name. He was a great friend of my father's. They were both pillars of Bethania Chapel.

I remember going down with great enthusiasm for my new school and I was one of the first two prefects to walk in through that door. It was a wonderful feeling. We were put into our different classes and I was going to excel in my Welsh language. Eventually I sat a very difficult Welsh exam paper, about which there were letters in the 'Western Mail'. I passed with a merit and decided to go in for teaching and had to apply for college.

In those days, before you went to college, you had to do one year as a pupil teacher and I was chosen for Merthyr Vale School.

MORFYDD HOLDEN, 1987

Girls outside Quakers Yard School, dressed up for performance of a Form Play

7.   Melbourne Australia, 1 December 1990

Dear Maureen,

Thank you for your letter. It would be remiss of me if I did not recall on paper the fond memories I have of Miss Lowe and the characteristics that endeared her to me, and I am sure to most of her pupils.

Miss Lowe introduced me to good literature and read to her class all the classics, such as 'Jane Ayre'; 'Anne of Green Gables' and of course, Shakespeare. She would read with feeling and if anyone would fidget, she would stop reading and gaze straight at the culprit with those deep grey eyes of hers, as much as to say, "How dare you!" The culprit would immediately sit up straight and give full attention, whilst Miss Lowe resumed her reading. Miss Lowe's rendering of Wordsworth's "Daffodils" was memorable.

She was very keen on deportment, always saying, "Shoulders back and sit up straight", and when walking, "walk tall!" She certainly set a good example herself. Her back was as straight as a rod. I remember the year 1933, my last year in school, Miss Lowe instilled in us the importance of good manners, her favourite phrase being "manners maketh the man and woman." On my last day, Miss Lowe called me aside in the corridor and said, "Maglona, you will be going for domestic training to Gwaelodygarth House, Merthyr Tydfil. You will be going out into the world, try to remember all that I have taught you; walk tall, mind your manners and if you ever need any advice I shall always be here for you."

Gwaelodygarth House was an old mansion set up as a domestic training centre for school leavers. I am not sure if it was the council or the government that was responsible for setting it up. During the 1930s most of the valleys of Wales were in a poverty trap; from Dowlais to Treharris girls were sent to Gwaelodygarth House where they were trained for service to the aristocracy, the middle classes or work in hotels. The members of staff were Miss Grant, who was the Head Housekeeper, Miss Farmer who ran the cookery department and Miss Devrill, who was laundry and sewing. After our training, a post was found for us. I was sent to a hotel in Bournemouth. I was just fourteen and a half years old.

I shall never forget that journey from Aberfan to Bournemouth on the train. I cried all the way and felt homesick for a long time before I eventually settled in. Although Bournemouth is a lovely seaside place, everything seemed so foreign to me. I often remembered Miss Lowe's advice when sometimes in England I was treated as a second class citizen. I would retaliate by walking tall and putting on my best manners - that usually deflated them. I hasten to add, I also formed a very good friendship with some English people. Miss Lowe was a compassionate and dedicated teacher but, alas, with the intolerance of youth, I did not appreciate her worth at the time. But as the years have passed by, I have. Despite all my travels, it is no wonder that I miss the mountains, the singing and comradeship of my native Wales.

Maglona

Mary Maglona Lewis and great grand-daughter Charlotte at Wayundah, Melbourne

8.   Sheer Bliss

Of course it is with sadness that I remember Pantglas Girls' School. My favourite teachers were Miss Rowlands, Miss Lowe; she lived in the Grove and Miss Gertie Lewis; she lived in Troedyrhiw. They could teach every subject and were all disciplinarians but also kind when needed. On reflection, I don't think we will ever see the like of those dedicated teachers again. During the school holidays we used to worry our parents for a penny or a halfpenny and wait for the street vendor, Rabbiotti the ice-cream man, to buy an ice cream cornet. Nectar from the gods and sheer bliss!

MARY MAGLONA LEWIS,
MELBOURNE, AUSTRALIA, 1990

9.   Portrait of a Teacher

Dorothy Gwendoline Lowe BEM

Miss Dorothy Gwendoline Lowe was the third child of William Henry Lowe and Alice Emily Lowe. Her father, William, was one of the engineers who sunk the Merthyr Vale Colliery. He had come to the village from Rhyl, in Flintshire. He and Emily were married in St Tydfil's Church, Merthyr Tydfil. She was the daughter of Mr Benjamin Thomas Phillips who was a Merthyr tradesman. He owned a 'Fancy Repository' in the High Street, next door to the Red Cow public house. Today the shop is a hairdressers. Before William was married, he lodged in the Rechabite Hall, Merthyr Vale.

After the birth of their first child in Merthyr Vale, the family moved to Ogmore and it was there on the 3rd February 1894, that Miss Lowe was born. When William's work was completed in Ogmore, the family moved back to the Merthyr area and eventually to Aberfan where they settled in 'Ashcroft', the Grove. The house had been newly built.

Miss Lowe was about sixteen years of age at this time and she started pupil teaching in Pantglas Girls' School, Aberfan, before going at the age of eighteen to Fishponds College, Bristol. Here she specialised in Needlework and Religious Studies.

In 1914, fully qualified, she returned to Pantglas Girls' School, teaching the subjects of Needlework and Religious Instruction throughout the school. In 1924 she took over the 'scholarship' class. All of the girls passed except one poor child - this was twenty four out of twenty five children.

Miss Lowe was still teaching there when the school became a mixed school, now to be called Pantglas Senior School. The headmaster was W. J. Williams, 'WJ' as he was affectionately known. Under his headship she became Senior Mistress. She retired in 1954, after teaching in the same building for forty years.

She knew many people in the village and many still remember her fondly today. She moved to 'Fronheulog' Aberfan Road, in 1966 to live with her sister. She died on 7th July 1980 aged 86. There are three nieces and one nephew of Miss Lowe still living in Aberfan. I am one of the nieces.

DOROTHY SMALL, 1993

10.   Deeply Peaceful

I remember Miss Lowe taking sewing classes in the Youth Centre of the Pantglas Senior School. She must have been on the point of retirement, in the last few years of her teaching career.

The Autumn nights would be drawing in and my friend Rosalie and I would walk from Perthygleision through Aberfan Road and enter the quiet corridors of the school in Pantglas.

Miss Lowe second right front row.
W. J. Williams, headteacher,centre front row.
'Old Timer' J. Evans centre back row.

I did not know Miss Lowe as a school teacher, because I went to a school outside the village. But we all knew her to be a very lovely lady of quiet strength. She sewed beautifully, a skill I came to appreciate when I developed a love of sewing myself.

Her whole demeanour was one of patience and gentleness. She had a steady gaze and a deeply peaceful face.

Many years later, twenty or more, I would call each year at Fronheulog for her Christian Aid envelope. She hadn't changed at all to me. She had the same beautiful, serene face and kindly steady gaze. She must have been over 80 years of age by this time.

Everyone liked Miss Lowe. She is firmly woven into the many faceted tapestry of our village life.

MAUREEN HUGHES

Aberfan Infants School 1919

Susie Owen Thomas and Her Class 1919

NOTES OF THE CHIEF ORAL LESSONS.

Birds & their nests

W.R. End. Mar: 13th 1923

Appat: Picture of birds, model of nest & B.B. sketches.

Observ & Exper.	Inferences
1. Why nests are made.	They are built for cradles for the baby birds.
2. Where they are built	Some birds build nests in trees e.g. Crow blackbird thrush while swallow builds its nest under the roofs of houses.
3. Can describe how nests are made.	Birds carry straw wool grass, moss, twigs & even mud to make their nests. Each bird makes a different kind of nest.
4. The Mother Birds care	Not only does the mother bird keep her young ones warm & feed & attend & teach them to fly but she keeps the nest clean & in good repair.

SYLLABUS
FOR THE

WEEK ENDING.................

Reading (a) Story Readers "Cinderella".
(b) Sentences on B.B.

Story Lessons
(a) The Birds of Killingworth
(b) Fairy Tale

Word-building to correlate with reading lesson.

Writing Simple sentences & Names

Dates

Number Analysis of No. 16.

Observations or Nature Lessons Birds & their nests.

Occupations
(a) Brush Work Birds nest.
(b) Clay Modelling of Birds
(c) Freearm Return of the birds
(d) Chalk Drawing free - first 3
(e) Paper Cutting Bird
(f) Playwork Mosaic Bricks

Drill or Games Simple Table N. S. E. W.

Singing

Needlework

Conversation Spring
Welsh Common Objects
Recitations "Birds' Nests" "To the Cuckoo".
Geography Children of Norway.

11. Susie Olwen Thomas Syllabus Book

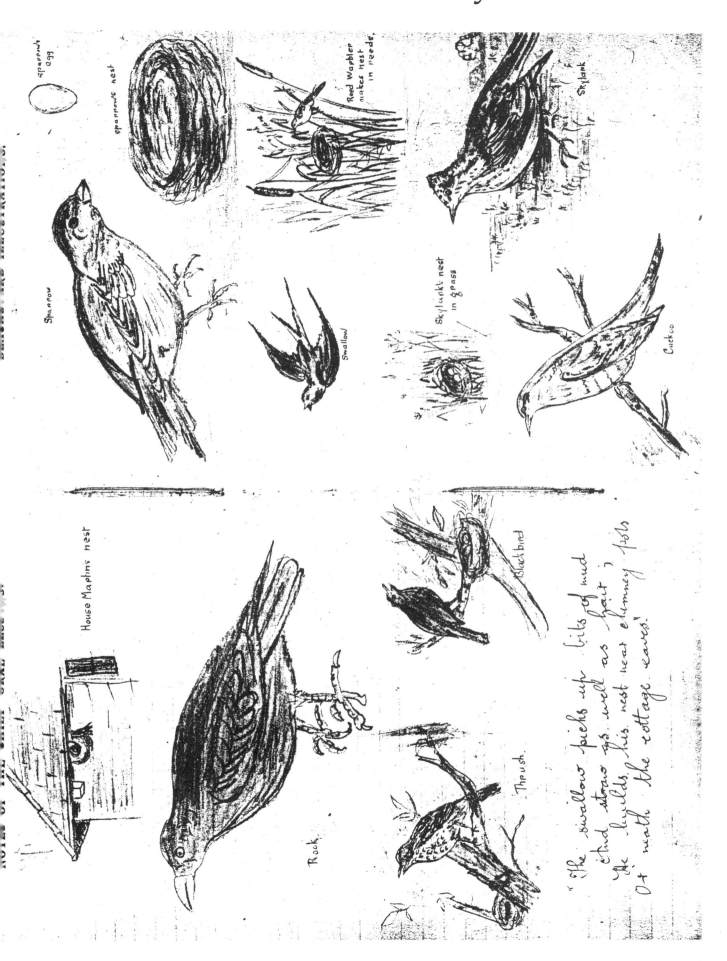

Sparrow's egg

Sparrow's nest

Reed Warbler makes nest in reeds.

Skylark

Sparrow

Swallow

Skylark's nest in grass

Cuckoo

House Martin's nest

Rook.

Blackbird

Thrush.

" The swallow picks up bits of mud
and straw as well as hair ;
He builds his nest near chimney tops
Or neath the cottage eaves."

12. Pantglas School Log-book 1918-1940

11 Nov 1918 … A half holiday was given this afternoon as a celebration of the signing of the Armistice terms and the end of the war.

21 March 1919 … The school was closed for the afternoon because several fires had gone out and there is no coke or coal in the school. The temperature is too low for the purpose of holding school with the influenza spreading and the children living on rations.

23 May 1921 … Eighteen pairs of boots were bought this week and given to boys who are in need because of the stoppage in the coalmines. His Worship the Mayor sent me £5 from his "Children's Distress Fund".
The staff made two collections. In addition to the purchase of new boots, several pairs have been repaired and old boots sent to the school by some kind persons have been repaired and given to needy cases.

27 March 1923 … This afternoon, in accordance with the wish of the L.E.A. we celebrated the centenary of the late Henry Richard once a M. of P. for Merthyr Tydfil and the "Apostle of Peace" of modern times.
I delivered an address to Standards 4 - 6 dealing with his work for Wales and Peace. The boys sang suitable Welsh airs.

30 Nov 1923 … I spoke to every class this morning with reference to the General Election. I told them that no party colours are to be exhibited on school premises during school hours. In addition they were told that they are free to wear any colour they choose after school hours and that I expect them to be respectful to all parties and that their behaviour will reflect upon the school.

13 July 1925 … School closed for whole day owing to the large number of children away with the English Baptist Sunday School Treat.

10 March 1928 … The boys were all assembled in the Central Hall at 3.15 to witness the opening of our new piano. Every class sang their favourite song and the whole school sang "Jerusalem".

9 Nov 1928 … The attendance has been very low this week owing to illness. The dire poverty of the people is having a marked though gradual effect upon the disease resisting powers of the children. Clothing and boots are getting worse and worse. This week representatives of the S. W. Miners Federation of Great Britain brought some clothing here for distribution.

18 Dec 1931 … The boys sang carols etc. in their classrooms during the first lesson of the afternoon. St. 1a had tea and presents with the Infants. The rest had a long play from 3.30 to 3.50.

11 Nov 1932 … By the kindness of Mr Way, who lent us a portable wireless set, we were able to assemble the whole school in the hall today to listen to the Cenotaph Service. A dry, cold but sunny week. There is a very high percentage of children attending with very bad boots. A higher percentage than we have ever seen here.

8 May 1935 … His Worship the Mayor, Coun D. Davies J.P. and Canon J. Richards Pugh Rector of Merthyr, visited the school this morning in connection with the Silver Jubilee Celebrations. Tea was given to all the boys this afternoon and each received a Presentation Mug.

1 March 1938 … Gwyl Dewi Sant.
St. David's Day was celebrated this morning. The whole school was assembled at 11 am in the Central Hall. Welsh folk songs were sung and an address on the 350th Anniversary of the Translation

of the Bible into Welsh was given by the Rev. Islwyn Evans, Congregational Minister. School was closed in the afternoon for the customary half day.

3 Sept 1939 … At 11.15am today Britain declared war on Germany. School was closed for a further week's holiday.

11 Sept 1939 … Time table will be considerably disrupted this week because of Gas Mask, Fire and Dispersal Practice.

9 Nov 1939 … Head teacher accompanied 5 boys and 5 girls (Girls Dept.) to Town Hall, Merthyr, to witness installation of Coun J. W. Watkins, Merthyr Vale, as Mayor.

2 June 1940 … Over 1600 evacuees from Folkestone and Deal arrived in Merthyr. 211 children with 8 teachers and 7 helpers were allocated to Aberfan and Merthyr Vale.

3, 4, 5 June 1940 … School closed by order of the D. of E. for teachers to engage in billeting work.

10 June 1940 … School recommenced. 22 evacuees from Deal admitted to Standards 1 - 5.

11 July 1940 … No swimming instruction today - very wet. In view of daylight air raids by the Germans, it is doubtful whether the journey to the baths should be undertaken.

23 August 1940 … Pantglas Boys' School as such, comes to an end today. Re-organisation takes effect from 2 September, this school becoming a Junior and Infants School with Mr A. J. James in charge and the Girls and Infants School becoming a Senior Mixed School in my, Mr W. J. Williams, charge.

Mr A. Pearson completed 25 years service in this school on his appointment as Headmaster of Abercanaid Mixed and Infants School. He has rendered signal service to this school and community over a long period of years and he carries with him to his new sphere, our best wishes.

Other members of staff will also be transferred as a result of re-organisation. To all for their splendid co-operation during the past three years, I record my sincere appreciation and thanks. We have been a very happy team.

13. Pantglas Boys' School Log-book 1918 -1940

My father was a pupil at the school for some of the earliest years that are covered in this log-book. The only thing he ever told me about the school was that if any boy was late the headmaster would stand on a box, he was a very short man, and bring the cane down as hard as he could on the offender's outstretched palm. My father was a boy of nine and a pupil at the school when his father, an engine driver at the Merthyr Vale Colliery, died during the Christmas holidays. The entry in the school log-book for the day of his funeral recorded that one of the teachers was away suffering from a cold.

The entries in the log-book began just as the First World War was ending and finish as the Second World War reaches its first anniversary. The Boys' School was amalgamated with the Girls' School in August 1940. The Boys' School building then became the Pantglas Junior Mixed School and thus it remained until October 1966, when it was engulfed by one of the coal tips that had loomed over the school and the children taught there, for generations.

In the very early days teachers were returning from War Service and the married women teachers, who had filled the breach, had their contracts as war supply teachers ended. Women teachers had to give up their posts when they married so their employment had been a concession to the times. For some years afterwards the anniversary of the Armistice was celebrated by the whole school. On one of these occasions, a young woman teacher fainted during the two minutes silence and had to be sent home.

The first entry in the log-book, which was for 31 October 1918, reveals that an epidemic of influenza was affecting school attendance. And a few days after the Armistice terms had been signed, the school was closed. The closure lasted from 14 November until 2 December and was due entirely to the epidemic. When the school eventually re-opened, attendance was below 50%. This became a recurring theme in the log-book revealing how much illness, especially epidemics, was affecting attendance. By the beginning of March 1919, the spread of influenza was "seriously affecting attendance." Also in that month, the school was closed because several fires had gone out. The temperature was low and there was no coal or coke in the school. The influenza was still spreading and this was made worse because the children were "living on rations." By the end of the same month the 'flu' was "still raging." Incongruously, the coal that was being used to drive the ships of the Royal Navy, was not sent a quarter of a mile up the road to feed the school fires. The epidemic did not start receding until the middle of April.

In succeeding years, scarlet fever became an additional hazard and on the 10 September 1920, the headmaster noted, "scarlet fever has broken out here and attendance is affected." The disease was still spreading six weeks later and a continuing problem throughout November. When the new term began in January, scarlet fever was still in the area and new cases were being notified well into February. But finally, on the 18th February, improved attendance was noted in the log book and was maintained the following week. The disease had been in the area for nearly six months and throughout this period had seriously affected the children's school attendance. The following year influenza became a problem as well and the school had to close intermittently between the 27 January and the 13 February with up to seven school teachers, nearly the whole staff, being absent on any one day. When the school did re-assemble, 30% of the children were still absent. At the end of the same year came an epidemic of measles. The first cases noted in the log-book were on the 1 December. The school did not start getting back to normal until the middle of January, some six weeks later. In April came diptheria and scarlet fever, with the "dip", as it was known locally, re-curring later on in the year. This was September 1923.

The next widespread outbreak of influenza was in February 1927 and the headmaster noted on the 15th that there was an epidemic. By the 25th, attendance was down to 65.6%. There was no improvement noted until the middle of March and even then, fresh cases were still being reported. A similar situation existed the following year with influenza "raging" in the early months of 1928. In March of that year the headmaster noted that the children were badly shod and that there was a considerable amount of illness prevelant. When heavy snowdrifts were recorded in March of the following year, many children were ill. Some of the children had struggled through snowdrifts but there were only 33% of them present in the Junior Department. Some children were too badly clad to come through the snow. Also noted by the head was the continual lack of coal for the school fires and on occasions the children had to be taken out into the school yard for physical exercises, in order to keep warm. Because of the lack of fuel, the school was often closed early.

In the Autumn of the following year, diptheria struck again, was soon 'raging' and affecting attendance. The Winter of that same year brought no respite and the headteacher could only continue to record poor attendance. Tonsillitis, too was being noted in the log-book, with scarlet fever as an added hazard. Not until the third week of December did the headmaster note an improvement in the number attending school. Even so, when school re-assembled in January 1930, the head teacher reported once again "diptheria is still here" and this fact was being noted until the third week of the month. When the school re-opened after the Easter holiday, diptheria, small-pox and scarlet fever contacts were affecting attendance. The Winter again brought the usual seasonal bouts of illness with influenza and diptheria being the main culprits. These two illnesses, in particular, hung around throughout the months until the school re-opened after the Easter holidays.

Early in 1934, chorea, diptheria and scarlet fever were affecting school attendance with diptheria re-appearing in the Autumn. New cases of diptheria and scarlet fever were reported in February 1935 and measles in March. Attendance was down to less than 74%.

Every year boys from the school were taken to Summer camp. The Summer of 1936 was no exception and twenty eight boys were taken to the camp at Ogmore. They were in the care of two teachers. The trip was tragically marred by the death of one of the pupils from diptheria. He died at the isolation hospital in Bridgend. Over the next few months all the school pupils received three immunisation injections against diptheria. The beginning of the year only brought influenza and scarlet fever.

In 1938 school resumed after the Summer holidays and in the Winter came the usual crop of illness. There were several weeks of measles among the younger children and this was closely followed by German measles.

The Winter before the school was re-organised, was just the same and the head noted in the log-book that illness was prevalent in the Winter months, something which had been noted by all five of the headteachers who had served the school from October 1918 to August 1940.

MAUREEN HUGHES, 1992

14. School Log-book 1918 - 1940 Pantglas School, 'Piteable Condition'

Something that received a lot of comment in the log-book was the vagaries of the weather. A wet and boisterous period would affect attendance. Many of the children did not have proper clothing to cope with bad weather. Sometimes they struggled through the elements only to be sent home because of their piteable condition and the school would be closed. Footwear especially was a constant problem and the stoppage in the Merthyr Vale Colliery in 1921 "brought distress with it". Constant efforts were being made to provide children with footwear. In May 1922 the school staff organised a jumble sale in aid of the Children's Boot Fund and the following month a concert was given at the school by the "Demobs" in aid of the same cause. But in September of that year wet weather and a lack of boots was given as the reason for poor attendance and eighteen pairs of boots were distributed. The General Strike of 1926 saw carnivals being held to raise money for the Soup Kitchens and again attendance at school was being affected because of bad or no footwear. "Some boys badly in need of footwear" and "large numbers of boys with footwear in a very bad state" were some of the entries in the log-book of this time. Children were badly clad and shod because the Nixon Company had gone into liquidation and the Merthyr Vale Colliery was awaiting a new buyer. Some children were suffering from malnutrition and were examined by the school doctor. Thirty two children were given a pint of milk a day. Meanwhile forty eight pairs of boots were distributed from the Miners' Distress Fund and boot repairing was going on at the school. This resulted in improved attendance. The Miners' Distress Fund also paid for boys to take part in the school holiday camp at Pendine. In November 1931, 100 pairs of boots were distributed to "necessitous children" and in 1938 a boot inspection at the school revealed that there were ninety four good pairs of boots, forty pairs of boots in a mediocre condition and seventy two pairs of boots in a bad condition. In December of that year boots were distributed from the Mayor's Permanent Boot Fund. Footwear was still a problem in bad weather when heavy snow affected attendance. And because of the lack of suitable footwear, on one particular day in January 1940 there were only 30% of the boys present.

MAUREEN HUGHES

15. School Log-book 1918-1940 Pantglas School, 'Lighter Moments'

In July 1919 a Peace Celebration Sports and Open Air Concert was held in the school yard. The headmaster recorded that the programme "raised the enthusiasm of a large gathering of parents".

An excellent tea was served after the concert. The function had been "a most enjoyable entertainment which greatly helped in establishing the school in the good esteem of the people". A few months later, in October, a Whist Drive and Dance was held to raise a fund to purchase "requisites for organised games for the three school departments". A parcel of footballs was purchased soon afterwards for the Boys' Department and a system of organised games was declared "workable".

March of the following year saw St. David's Day being celebrated with a talk by the head teacher on "St David as a Patriot". Suitable songs were sung by the whole school and the customary holiday given. This was a day celebrated assiduously throughout the years with songs and Welsh lessons and sometimes visits from the local ministers of religion. Also celebrated in 1920 was the centenary of Henry Richard, the Apostle of Peace.

The whole school was gathered in March 1928 to see the opening of the new school piano. And in the Summer term there was a concert and a visit by parents to see their children's craft handwork. The Christmas festivities of 1937 were made special by the contribution of a Baptist Chapel in Leeds. And in February 1938 there is a mention of the first school assembly. Also mentioned for the first time was a school trip to London, to see the Tower of London and the Houses of Parliament. The boys were taken regularly to the baths at Gwaenfarren and Edwardsville and some became very good swimmers, winning the Borough Cup at the Swimming Galas regularly. A regular visitor to the school was a Miss Thornly B.A. from the Temperance Union who gave lectures under the heading of such things as "alcohol, its affects and dangers".

Music features in school life and the school joined with others in Festivals and Concerts. In October 1935 a school trip was organised to see the film of "David Copperfield". This seems to have been another first in the life of the school. The school premises were used as a polling booth in the local municipal elections and in the General Election. The first Monday in May, Labour Day, was a holiday and to generations of children, the day for visiting the Troedyrhiw Fair. During July the school would be closed on half a dozen days or half days for Sunday School Treats. In 1936 there was a holiday for the visit to the Borough of the Prince of Wales. This was when he uttered the famous words that something must be done about the poverty and unemployment that were to be found in the valley communities. In 1939 came the declaration of war and the Sunday School trips to Barry Island and Porthcawl, thereafter reverted to the old style celebrations of Sunday School teas.

In 1940 the school was re-organised into Pantglas Junior Mixed School with a separate Infants Department. The new head was Arthur James and he stayed until his retirement in 1953. Thus the school served a few more generations of children who celebrated successive St David's Day, with plays and pageants, songs and stories. They went on Sunday School trips to Barry Island and Porthcawl as their parents had done before them, on school trips to Bristol Zoo and Windsor Castle, had a day off for St David's Day and the Troedyrhiw Fair, and thus it was until October 1966.

MAUREEN HUGHES

Above: E. J. Price, third from left front row (son of Price the Draper)

Right: A Report of Progress from 1924

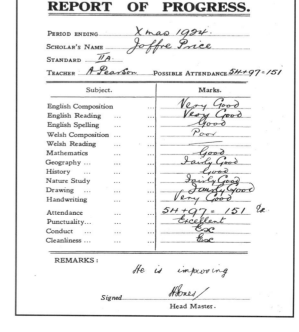

230

16. Letter Mount Pleasant School

Mount Pleasant School
Merthyr Vale
17 December, 1935

Rhys Elias, Esq. MA
Director of Education
Merthyr Tydfil

Dear Sir,

The school clock is quite beyond repair, so I am told by Mr Richards, Watch and Clock Maker, Aberfan, who repaired it, or tried to repair it, last. He told me that it was he who supplied it, and that the then School Board would not go beyond fifteen shillings.

I really do not think any more money should be thrown away on this one, as it never goes for six hours immediately after being repaired. Therefore I beg to apply for a new clock.

Yours faithfully,

E. W. Jenkins
Headmaster

17. Merthyr Vale School

I had a wonderful year in Merthyr Vale School. A wonderful year, and Mr E. L. Jones of Aberfan was the headmaster.

He put me into Standard 1 to start off with Miss Powell, 'the Post Office'. Miss Powell in her fancy boots and her stick up collar and her gold chain going around her waist. She walked from the Old Post Office in Merthyr Vale and she was the organist in the assembly and the things that I remember from all those years ago. This is one of them.

Miss Powell was at the organ. Mr Jones, the headmaster said "Now then Miss Powell. What would you like our first hymn to be in assembly?" And this was nine o' clock in the morning. This was dear Miss Powell's reply. "Now the day is over" and it hadn't started. We just held our heads down not making a sound. We couldn't look at Mr E. L. Jones, the headmaster. Then the next day it would be "Fight the good fight" and while we had gone on to fighting the good fight in the second verse, she would still be fighting the first verse!

My salary for the month was £1.11.8 as a pupil teacher.

At the end of the year I applied for college and the Minister of Calfaria, Rev. D. P. Evans was my referee. I was a staunch member of Calfaria Chapel.

MORFYDD HOLDEN, 1987

Happy, smiling faces. Merthyr Vale School yard

18. Milk Bottles

They appeared mysteriously in our classrooms. As children we gave no thought to their transport or disposal, so different from the urge to bottle-bank nowadays or follow the "Return to your Milkman", message on the present milkbottle.

Eager anticipation of the play time to come and quenching of thirst encouraged us to get our heads down and work. The 1/3 of pints of milk were counted carefully, one of our earliest maths lessons. If you'd been 'good', the giving out of straws or the sticking of them into the lids of the bottles was your reward. How different were the tops, no shiny foil which we now collect for dogs for the blind, but discs of cardboard, scored in the centre to pop open easily or stick and scatter the contents all over you - this always happened when your clothes were clean and mingled with the fine particles of coal dust which soon made you a little grubby.

Those tops were precious - carefully washed and dried, the odd one which slipped through soon made its presence known by smell and sight, they were then stored for future use. The school mice must have enjoyed them.

An exciting day came when with coloured wool begged from knitting relations or even found in classrooms (the small box of handi-craft equipment would not satisfy the creative experience today's children enjoy) was used to make pom-poms, carefully the wool was wound around two tops - too tightly and lopsided would be your result, and oh! the agony of pushing through those last strands.

Next the frightening part, taking up the scissors, their sharpness a great deal to be desired, and cutting so carefully each strand until they separated. The two tops were then prised apart, a tricky operation this, too much, everything fell apart, too little and the winding centre wool was difficult to tie. Nimble fingers which poked the wool around resulted in a knot so secure it could have held the Black Bridge over which trundled the drams.

The atmosphere was tense every eye was on you for the final stage. The discs once yielding when used for their original purpose were hard and stubborn to tear or pull apart, but oh! the joy when the threads bounced their miraculous way into a ball - a many splendid sphere, if like the old gob stoppers, different colours were used. A little trimming and the finished result was taken home with pride. Where are they now? Aberfan at one time must have been awash with them.

Contents of the bottles were enjoyed with glee. The Seasons of the year bringing each different flavour.

Spring - a sweet taste reminiscent of local meadows, buttercups and daisies, do you like butter? played with many a bright glowing flower.

A summer too hot and the taste was "off" and bitter. Small amounts left in the bottom of the bottles soon resulted in a rather strong smell.

Autumn had no special taste just the enjoyment of rich milk.

Oh! but Winter - this depended on the positioning of the bottles. Black, deep black fires, which blazed on one side of the classroom, our only heat, a source of pleasure if on chilly days your desk was near, of envy if you were farther away, was the deposit for the bottles.

Like tall white snowmen with hats aloft, some lopsided, they waited in the hearth. Carefully carried by your teacher or by big strong boys and placed around the glowing red tiles to sit surrounded by the iron black of the fire guard, they waited and were warmed. Slowly the frozen top receded and the milk took on a different texture, cream thickened and the taste altered. Memories of clotted cream from Devon brought back from holidays, mingled in your taste buds.

Slurp, gurgle, bubble blowing, wonderful the sounds which echoed around the classroom at playtimes, the wicked ones amongst us vieing for the most outrageous noise and most bubbles.

Clutching our precious three pence piece be it silver or many sided bronze, we rushed on Friday to school knowing the joy of the half-penny change from the payment for the milk which was 2 $^{1/2}$ d per week.

The great half-penny was spent in the shops near the school. Lucious red-lips in wax, chews, liquorice sticks, sticky multicolours and glorious hews, smells that sent the nostrils tingling greeted the opening of the front door which rang the message to the back of the house - many a front room was used as a small shop to keep the wolf from the door.

The joy of choosing was immense, you pondered longingly until the decision was made. And sticky or many coloured homewards you returned.

Did you ever get a spare afternoon bottle of milk?
Weren't you good!

Hazel Knight neé Small

19.   A World Away

A world has gone as
Bright eyed with laughter
Down the path
The children ran.
A canal with boats on!
A dream to them.
The school gate and the wall
So toffee smooth and
Round topped,
they slide, fall
Down it's surface.
Inside the teacher
And the children
Make a roundabout
Of pipecleaners,
Cheesebox wheels and
Powder paints.
Outside the crisp air and
A bouncing ball,
Sunlight and the teacher's call,
And overall
A green and black looming.

Maureen Hughes, 1987

Mr Stanley Beynon and his class

20. Our Mag

A young man alighted from the bus at the Mackintosh Hotel. He and his companion climbed the hill towards the Pantglas School. As they walked together to the Secondary School, his companion turned to him and said "Stan! I think that you are down for the Junior School." "I can't be." he protested. But his friend was right and thus it was that Stanley Beynon, newly demobbed from the Army Education Corps, came to be teaching in Pantglas Junior School. Many years later he told me that he couldn't believe it when he had to report to the Junior School. He had been teaching soldiers and now he found himself with a class of seven year olds. To crown it all, Miss Havard, also on the staff, would not speak to him because she maintained that he had pinched her class.

I was not in Mr Beynon's class for the first two years. Children from Perthygleision stayed together for standards one and two. My only contact with him came when he visited our classroom and admired some marsh marigolds that I had picked for Miss Wanklin, who was our teacher. During the lunch hour I went to the little wood behind Bryngoleu, where we lived and picked some for him. He seemed pleased and our friendship spanned the years and lasted until his death a few years ago. The next year I found myself in his class and there I remained until I left Pantglas for Quakers Yard School.

There are many highlights of the years spent in Mr Beynon's class. One is when his wife was having her second baby and he brought his son Alan to school with him. He was a dear curly headed toddler in a blue suit and was a great favourite in the classroom, and so good. That same year we made a carousel of cardboard. What pleasure to be released from reading, writing and arithmetic for the afternoon, the sun streaming into the classroom and onto the children. We were all happily working together making horses out of pipe cleaners and cotton reels, splashing brightly coloured powder paint onto cardboard and paper. The following year we all worked together to produce 'Our Mag'. Every child in the class contributed something and one of the boys had a picture in it of a painting that Mr Beynon had sent to the 'Daily Mirror's Children's Art Exhibition, where it had been put on view. Mr Beynon had the magazine duplicated so that we all had a copy and it was quite substantial, the size of a large exercise book with as many pages. There were many different coloured covers and 'Our Mag' was printed in large letters on the front. Then there was the time that we visited Bristol Zoo and ate stale sandwiches, supplied on site, out of paper bags, in a huge room with hard seats. I can see Mr James, our headmaster, waving his hands around directing us. I wondered at the time what he thought of us being given stale sandwiches to eat. After the lunch I sat on a bench outside, my feet too short to touch the ground, and a kindly lady asked me where I was from. "Merthyr Tydfil" I said solidly. The County Borough of Merthyr Tydfil was printed on the front of our school books and I was proud to come from there. "I have heard of that place" she said thoughtfully.

I remember visiting the children's department of the Merthyr Central Library where Mr Beynon borrowed the "Odyssey" to read to us. He also read to us from the 'Daily Herald' on a Monday morning. This was to improve our general knowledge. Then he would ask us about Marshall Aid and the Schumann Plan, and who was Foreign Minister of what country and about their capital cities. But we loved all sorts of learning and twenty-two of us passed the scholarship examination to Quakers Yard School.

I never remember Mr Beynon being absent from school. The only time that I can remember any one else teaching us ordinary subjects was when Cyril Vaughan came to the school as a student teacher. This caused some excitement because he was courting June Small and her sister Pamela was in our class. I can see him now, leaning on the classroom windowsill whilst he talked to us, the morning light streaming into the room, catching the rising dust in its rays. Many years later I was to see a photograph of him in the 'Guardian', his head in his hands in utter despair, standing alone, surrounded by the enormity of the Aberfan Disaster, as he had made his way to school.

Before we went to Quakers Yard School, Mr James came to explain to us some of the intricacies of geometry and algebra. I was chosen to present a copy of 'Our Mag' to him. This had been a very happy period in my life, my years in Pantglas School.

Some years later, Mr Beynon told me that he had an exercise book that we had written in when we were in Pantglas. I had bought Mr James' house and one day Mr Beynon turned up on my doorstep with the book. When I saw its rust cover, I travelled back years to a time of wooden pens with scratchy nibs made worse by blobs of soggy blotting paper, picked up from the ink-well. How I struggled to copy up those stories. Some of the children, now adults, have written in this commemorative book.

Their stories and poems as children have also been included along with some examples of children's creative writing today.

Stanley Beynon had come to teach in Pantglas School, a rather surprised young man but he turned out to be a dedicated and enlightened teacher of Junior children.

MAUREEN HUGHES, 1993

21. A Winter's Day

Nov 29 1949

It was snowing and John and Janet were very bored. It was the Winter holidays from school and it was snowing hard but the children longed to go out but their Aunt Caroline persisted that it was far too cold. Were the children glad when their mother returned from her Christmas shopping, now they could go out!

They ran into the hall shouting merrily and nearly knocked their mother over. "Goodness" said their mother when she got her breath back. "What's this?" "Oh please can we go to call for our friends", said Janet. "Yes you may", said their mother. Aunt Caroline came down the stairs. She was a thin crusty faced old woman and was very old-fashioned and strict. "You are looking for trouble" she said to their mother, letting them go out in this." "Don't be so old fashioned, Caroline", said Mam. Aunt Caorline's face went livid with fury. She turned quickly and made her way to her room. "Put on your mufflers, coats, hats and gloves children" said mother. They did as they were told and soon on their way to their friend's house. By this time the snow had stopped. The children played snow-balls on the way. "Lets build a snowman," said John. "That will be lovely" said Janet, "But lets go and call for Jack and Jill first." "Allright" said John. By the time they'd reached their friend's house their noses were like cherries. Their luck was out for their friends had very severe colds. They turned away from the house and slowly made their way home. The wind bit into their skin making their blood run cold. After they had left their friend's house a blinding blizzard of snow started and the children didn't know which way to go. What a joyful sight it was to see their house in the distance. They managed to stumble up the path and soon they were in their own room looking at the snowflakes whirling and twirling to the ground. Aunt Caroline was still pouting away upstairs in her room.

MAUREEN HUGHES,
STANDARD FOUR, PANTGLAS JUNIOR SCHOOL

22. The Smugglers

One dark and dreary night
Some smugglers came in sight
And on their backs were sacks of gold
To take to the secret cave so old.

They wore old and tattered clothes
And out of their shoes peeped their toes
For although they were rich
They were mean and wouldn't sew a stitch.

MARGARET ABRAHAM, 1950
STANDARD 4, PANTGLAS JUNIOR SCHOOL

Pantglas Junior School

23. A Race Against Time

David was hurrying, running as fast as he could to try and get to school on time. It was his own fault that he was having to rush like this now, he had wasted so much time daydreaming after his Mam had called him to get up. He had slept so well, and had such pleasant dreams that after she had gone back downstairs, he had just lain there, hands behind his head, just thinking. He spent a lot of time just thinking, that was why he was now having to run so fast to catch up with himself, as Grandad would say.

He was still thinking now, at first he ran a while, then walked a while to try to get there on time. He wished they lived a bit closer to the school but Mam said they must think themselves lucky they had somewhere to live at all. He had thought at the time that was an odd thing to say, why should having a house be considered lucky? Didn't EVERYONE have one? He had only been round the country a little bit in his short life, but he had seen some great big houses, surely LOTS of people could live in those? When he said this to Grandded, he'd laughed and said David would be a Member of Parliament yet, but David didn't know what he meant.

Oh, bother, he'd got a 'stitch' in his side, he'd have to slow down to walking pace, he wished he had a bicycle, some children did, not anyone HE knew of course, but he had seen them. Mam said that was because they had Fathers that could pay for them. His Father had been killed last year in the colliery, so they'd had to leave their house and come to live with Grandad. Pity he lived such a long way from everywhere.

Funny about some people not being able to have bicycles, though, he had an Aunty and Uncle who had a car! They lived in England, and last Easter they had come and fetched him, and taken him on a holiday, the first he'd ever had. Mam would have liked it, he knew, but she'd had to stay and look after Grandad. He had a bad cough and couldn't do much for himself. When David had asked him how he'd got such a cough, he'd laughed and said, "Hard work might not kill a man, but it doesn't always do him a lot of good."

He'd better start running again, he had no idea of the time, but he must get there before the bell stopped or he'd be in the 'late' book and have to stop in after school.

As he ran he looked up at the sky, funny, there was a bit of moon still up there, why was there sometimes the sun and moon in the sky at the same time? If he asked his Mam, she'd say "Go to school and find out." All the same, it was strange to think that earlier this year there had been a spaceship up there, and the men were going to visit that moon. He knew the name of the spaceship, too, because his birthday was in June so teacher had said that he was a Gemini, and that was also the name of the spaceship! He felt somehow that that made it his, he felt quite possessive about it, as if it belonged to him, somehow.

Oooh - whoof - he'd got another 'stitch'. He bent down and touched his toes and then stretched up again, that was easier. Better walk for a while now, but as fast as he could, he didn't want to be kept in after school, he wanted to be able to go back to Tom's house with him.

Tom's Dad was very clever, he could make little figures and animals out of bits of wood. He couldn't go to work any more, he had lost a leg in a pit accident years ago but he kept very busy carving these lovely things. People used to buy them from him, there was a shop in the town that bought them.

Better start running again now, time must be getting on.

David was hoping to be able to buy one of the little wooden figures for his Mam for Christmas, there were still two months to go, yet, and he was saving every penny he could. He did any jobs around the village, a bit of delivery for the butcher, washing dishes at the local club, anything that anyone would pay him for. His store of pennies was mounting.

He hoped Tom's Dad would be able to make a lady carrying a basket of flowers, Mam loved flowers. For her birthday in April he'd bought her a packet of seeds and she'd sown them in the bit of ground behind the house. Real pretty they'd looked in the Summer.

When he'd been on holiday with his Aunty, there had been loads of flowers in a huge garden, the lady had let him take a big bunch of them home for Mam. She'd taken them from him, and buried her face in them, when she'd looked up again David thought she'd been crying, but she'd said how happy they'd made her, and you didn't cry if you were happy, did you? Mind you, he didn't think his Mam was very happy sometimes, she was always telling him not to dream but he often caught her looking sad, as if she were dreaming about something she couldn't have.

Surely there wasn't much further to go, was there? He'd never realised how long it took to get to school, but then he'd never had to run like this before, he usually set off much earlier. He mustn't let himself drift into that habit of dreaming or he'd never get anywhere in life. Mind you, it had been pleasant, just lying there, drifting. He'd been pretending that he'd won lots of money, and he was planning all the things he'd do for Mam and Grandad, first, new clothes for everyone, then a holiday such as the one he'd had.

Suddenly, he tripped and fell flat on his face. He sat up and looked at the damage, his knee was a bit grazed, but never mind, that would grow again. What WAS a problem was the toe of his shoe. There was a loose bit of leather, that's probably what tripped him. Mam would have to do a bit of 'cobbling' as she called it. She always mended their shoes.

Up he got, and started running again, his knee was a bit sore but he daren't slow down. He was getting close to the village now, he could just hear the school bell ringing. Hurry, hurry, he should be able to reach there in time, he kept going.

He turned the corner into the school lane, yes, he was going to be in time after all. He slowed down to a walk, he was beginning to limp a bit now. Everyone knew him and spoke to him as he passed. Then he was within sight of the playground, he could see his friends, Tom and Edward, Megan and Mair, they all waved and called out a greeting to him as he entered the gates. He felt a sense of belonging.

Mam was always saying she would like to go right away from the district, away from the pit and the grime, but he was happy here among all these friendly people, they were good and kind. The sense of belonging touched him again as he joined his friends.

Yes, he would be quite happy to spend the rest of his life here, in Aberfan.

CAROL WHELAN,
LOWER EARLEY, READING

Aberfan Road, Aberfan

24. Merthyr Vale School Log-book 1968

1 March … St David's Day. A concert was held in the school this morning to celebrate our Saint's day. All classes contributed items and thanks are due to the staff for their hard work.

15 November… The headmaster left school this a.m. to meet Mr Beale, Director of Education, to be informed that he was to be recommended to take over the new school at Aberfan.

16 November … I had to visit the Education Department again to confirm my appointment to Aberfan and to discuss with Mr Beale various topics ensuing.

14 December … The school Christmas party was held today. Thanks are due to the staff, both teaching and ancillary, for the great effort they put in to make the party a resounding success. We presented the children with their gift, purchased from the Aberfan Disaster Fund Grant.

6 June … School re-opened. From this day onward, preparations are being made to close the school at the end of term, ready for the transfer to the new school at Aberfan Park. We will certainly experience many interruptions of the normal running of the school and it will be difficult for staff and pupils alike.

16 July … A concert was held this evening to mark the closing of Merthyr Vale School. The attendance was exceptional and an excellent concert was given by the children of the school aided by Miss Merryman of Mount Pleasant and Miss Jennifer Colston, an old pupil of Merthyr Vale, as soloist. It was quite a nostalgic evening and many of the older residents of the village who attended, were quite obviously deeply moved. The Deputy Mayor and Mayoress, honoured us with their presence, also the Chairman of Primary School Managers and the Ward Councillors. The Deputy Director and the Senior Organiser, plus Infant Organiser, were also present. The staff are to be complimented on the fine work done at a time when many problems beset them.

18 July … It is with very mixed feelings that I make this, the last entry in the annals of Merthyr Vale School. The school has always maintained a high standard of work in all spheres of Education and has served its purpose well, over the last century. Consequently, there is great regret that this is now to cease; but the exciting future that lies ahead in our new school, with all its extra amenities is a challenge that we are now anxious to face. Reality must be faced. The building at Merthyr Vale has served its purpose well but the changing face of education has alas, forced the realisation upon us that it is no longer suitable. The opportunity has come to enter a new environment more in keeping with the needs of today. The opportunity arose from the starkest tragedy but let us hope that we can make the new school as great an influence on the community of Merthyr Vale and Aberfan as this old establishment has been before it. Let us hope that we can take the spirit of the two schools, whose time has now ended and weld together a great and powerful influence for the good of the community.

TUDOR J. EVANS

25. Ynysowen Junior Mixed School 1968 - 1969

3 September … This new school, built in less than twelve months, to replace the Pantglas Junior School and also to accommodate the merger of Merthyr Vale Junior and Infants School opened this

morning. A new infant school has opened in the same campus. There are eight members of staff and two hundred and seven children were admitted on the opening day. A very fine site indeed has been prepared and the impression made upon the children has been quite startling. All the construction work has not yet been completed and this fact has added a little to the confusion. I would like, here, to compliment the staff, teaching and ancillary, for all the work put in during the weeks prior to the opening of the school. Without this co-operation, we would never have been able to open.

5 September … Mr G. Jeffreys, Headmaster of Kelvedon Hatch County Primary School, Brentwood, Essex, with members of his staff and family, visited the school this afternoon to present a lectern which had been donated to the new school.

13 September … School seems to be settling down well. The children are extremely happy in their new surroundings

30 September … Mr Ellis of Manchester visited the school. He has been responsible for organising a collection amongst Sunday Schools in his area with which they had purchased a Bible. It is thought that the Bible must still be in the Education Office.

4 October … This afternoon a short Harvest Festival was held at the school. Produce was sent to the local old age pensioners.

21 October … Mr Williams and Mrs Williams, the two members of staff who had served at Pantglas School during the disaster of two years ago, attended a dedication ceremony at the Cemetery this morning. The Memorial Arches were being dedicated. At the same time a short service was held in school.

21 October … Mr Beale, Director of Education, Mr Selwyn Jones, Town Clerk, and Mrs Jones visited us this morning. Mr Beale wished to show the Town Clerk the new features incorporated in the school.

24 October … The Round Table (Merthyr), presented over a thousand books to the school this evening. The books had been donated by the Publisher's Association. An informal presentation took place in the evening. Mr Beale, the Mayor and Mayoress, Mrs Lambert, Coun. M'Ginty, Mr Roberts and a representative of the Publisher's Association, also of the Round Table, met members of staff and were entertained to refreshments.

6 November …Rev. Erastus Jones visited the school to discuss arrangements for a conference to be held at the school on 23 November.

22 November … Rev. Erastus Jones and a member of the committee visited the school to finalise arrangements for tomorrow's conference.

23 November … School was taken over for a conference on the future of Aberfan. Conference held between 2 and 8 p.m.

16 December … Professor Charles Gittens called at the school to view the lay-out. He was accompanied by Mr Beale and Mr Roberts.

17 December … School party held this afternoon - very successful.

18 December … The Infant children were invited to the school today to hear the school carol service.

8 January … Mr Luque, caretaker, called at the school and reported that there were several small jobs needing attention in his bungalow which he hopes to move into at the weekend. The architect has been informed and has promised to try to get them seen to.

15 January … Miss Davies and Mr Richards attended a Welsh Language course at the Teachers' Centre this afternoon.

16 January … The Alberta Paintings were delivered to the school today. These will be selected from, to hang in the Junior School and Infant School, the remaining paintings to go to Afon Taf High School.

17 October … A party of Russian musicians, who have been touring the country, came to the school this morning. They were extremely interested in the organisation and their questions, through an interpreter, were extremely searching. They were quite astonished at the degree of autonomy allowed the schools. They enjoyed the singing of the children and one of their number - a magnificent lass with the true gift of the clown - responded with two songs which the children enjoyed hugely.

17 October … In the afternoon, a Harvest Festival service was held in school. The display of fruit and vegetables had been set up in the morning, arousing the curiosity of the Russian visitors.

21 October … On the third anniversary of the tragic disaster at Pantglas School, a short service was held in school.

TUDOR EVANS

Ynysowen Junior School, 1996

26. Pwll a Rhiannon

Far, far away in the far distant past, Pwll, ruler of Dyfed lived. The wise men in his court decided that Pwll would have to marry and have a child to carry on ruling when Pwll was deceased. He married a beautiful young woman called Rhiannon. Very soon Rhiannon gave birth to a beautiful baby. There was something about this baby that was very rare; he was extremely large for a baby and had beautiful blonde curly hair. Pwll selected six nurse maids for Rhiannon to help her look after the baby.

One day, when Pwll was out hunting, Rhiannon decided to have a nap, and told her maids to look after the baby, the maids, who were rather lazy went to have something to eat and drink, then they got dozy and went to sleep. When they awoke the child had disappeared. The maids were very frightened, they looked in every nook and cranny for the baby. Then one perked up and said "I have the most terrific plan". She told the other maids to look for a dead animal; unfortunately, there was a dead fawn in the bushes, they took the dead fawn indoors and pulled a few bones out of it, and ripped some flesh of it, then they squeezed some blood out of the unfortunate animal and rubbed it on Rhiannon's arms and hands. The maids then scurried behind the door to wait for their mistress to awaken. When Rhiannon awoke she gave the most horrific scream and the sly maids ran in and said "Mistress! We trusted you and you killed your only child." Poor Rhiannon said "But I couldn't have killed it! He was in the next room!" The maids said "We put the baby in your bed, we thought it would be nice for the baby to sleep with its mother." Rhiannon was devastated, she was helpless.

Later when Pwll returned, he couldn't believe what he thought Rhainnon had done. The wise men and Pwll had a meeting, the wise men wanted Rhiannon to be put to the death sentence but Pwll had other ideas. "I do not want my wife to die, why can't we put her outside the city gates and tell people what she has done, and she must carry them on her back." So that was her punishment.

A few miles away a horseman and his wife were having a discussion, "I am going to stay out in the stable all night, because every mystical and magical eve of May one of my beautiful young colts gets stolen." Teyron was an extremely brave man, but he couldn't have children. He was sitting in the stable when a hideous hand shot through the window and grabbed the colt. Teyron drew his sword and cut off the creature's arm; there was an unearthly scream, neither animal nor human, then there was silence. Then Teyron heard a chuckling, gurgling sound of a young baby, he dashed outside and picked up the infant; the baby was wrapped in silken sheets and had blonde, curly hair. He took the infant to his wife. His wife was very, very happy.

As the baby grew older he began to look more like Pwll, when he was two years old he looked more like a four year old, when he was four he looked more like an eight year old, and at eight looked more like a teenager.

One day Teyron's friend came by and said, "Do you remember Rhiannon?" "Oh yes" said Teyron, "Beautiful sweet Rhiannon." "Well," said Teyron's friend, "she's not like that any longer, haven't you heard?" "No" said Teyron, "will you tell me." "They say that Rhiannon killed her child." Later that day Teyron had a word with his wife, he told her the story, and they realised that the child they had found on the eve of May was Pwll, Rhiannon's child.

Teyron's wife wanted to keep the child but Teyron persuaded her to give the child back. They went to the City gates and Rhiannon spoke to them, "I have been very evil, I killed my son, would you let me carry you on my back?" "No," said Teyron "I wouldn't." When Rhiannon looked up she knew that the boy with Teyron and his wife was her son. Teyron took his wife and Rhiannon's son to see Pwll. Pwll ran out to Rhiannon and picked her up, swung her around and said to her, "I knew you didn't kill our son." He imprisioned the six maids, then he turned to his child and called him Pryderi, because in Welsh, pryderi means worry.

And they all lived happily ever after.

AMY ROBERTS, AGE 9,
MOUNT PLEASANT PRIMARY, 1991

Rhiannon and the six nursemaids

27. Math Fab Mathonwy

A long time ago there was a cunning woman called Arianrhad, she had two sons. The oldest son Dylan, was tall and handsome, but Arainrhad didn't have enough time to look after the youngest son, so after a couple of days Arianrhad gave the youngest son to a friend of hers, his name was Gwydion.

Gwydion took care of this child, the next day Gwydion gave this child a name, he named this boy Lleu Llaw Gyffes. Years went by and Lleu grew up to be a tall handsome boy.

Gwydion decided it was now time for Lleu to visit his horrid mother, when they arrived there Arainrhad was jealous because he was so handsome. So she said "I will not allow you to be happy, you shall never marry anyone off this earth." So Gwydion thought and thought until he came up with an idea.

He went to his friend Math and asked him to join him in the forest, when they arrived there Math cast a spell and made a lady of flowers and called her Blodeuwedd. Soon as Lleu saw her he fell in love with her. Llew and Blodeuwedd went to live in a castle. A few months later Lleu went to visit Math, while he was away Blodeuwedd fell in love with a man called Gronyw. They plotted how to get rid of Lleu, until Blodeuwedd remembered that there had to be a special way to kill Lleu.

So when Lleu returned home Gronyw hid in the woods, Blodeuwedd said to Lleu, "Could you show me what you have to do to die?", so Lleu said, "Someone has to make a spear every Sunday for a year. Then I must take a tub of water down to the river-side and place it under a canopy, then I must put one foot in the tub and another one on a goat and only then will I die." Blodeuwedd grinned, and that night she crept into the woods and told Gronyw what he had to do.

Gronyw went away for one year, when the year passed he came back with a spear, Blodeuwedd and Gronyw had a problem, they had to get Lleu down to the river-side, Blodeuwedd came up with a cunning idea, she said to Lleu, "Lleu, it's a lovely day, will you please show me what you have to do again, I know that no-one will want to kill you, but I would still like to see you." Because Lleu loved her so much, he showed her and while he showed her Gronyw threw the spear and drove right through his heart. But Lleu didn't die he just changed into a huge eagle and flew away.

Blodeuwedd and Gronyw were jumping for joy. After a few days Gwydion went to visit, Blodeuwedd said that Lleu had died, but Gwydion knew that he had to die in a special way.

So Gwydion went out looking for him and he went to a farm and asked a farmer "Have you seen anything suspicious going on?" The farmer said, "Well there are a lot of dead pigs around that tree." Gwydion went to the tree and began to sing and Lleu flew down from the tree and sat on Gwydion's knee. So Gwydion used one of his last spells and turned Lleu back to his normal self, Lleu was very frail he could hardly move. Gwydion fed him until he regained his strength.

Then Lleu and Gwydion went after Gronyw. Lleu said to Gronyw, "I shall kill you the same way as you killed me." Gronyw said that wasn't fair, so Lleu said "Go down to the river and get a big rock, Gronyw went to the river-side and found the biggest stone he could, he then placed the stone over his body, Lleu threw the spear so hard it shattered the rock and killed Gronyw. They then chased Blodeuwedd but they did not kill her, they turned her into an owl so that she could only show her face by night.

Lleu and Gwydion lived happily for the rest of their lives.

Emma Tovey, age 10,
Mount Pleasant Primary School, 1991

Lleu resurrected as an eagle

Chapter Nine
Sunday Schools

1.   Introduction

We all attended Sunday School. For many of the earlier generation, attending Sunday School was the only way that they had a trip to the seaside. But the teachers were lovely and dedicated and there was an opportunity to make friends other than those made at school. There was a wonderful excitement about the Sunday School Anniversary, so accurately described by Harvey Small. I thought about my dress for weeks beforehand and can remember them all to this day. The special smell that there was on that day of extra lashings of furniture polish combined with copious flowers on pulpit and table has stayed with me over the years. Relatives and friends all dressed in their very best clothes would be arrayed in the pews and after weeks of rehearsal we sang and recited our way through some very noble and inspiring sentiments. This would last from morn until night with a break for Sunday dinner and tea. Certainly religious worship played a very important part in the lives of the people of Aberfan and Merthyr Vale and still forms an important backdrop to village life today. The pattern is varied and includes a Quaker and a Greek Orthodox priest.

Aberfan and Merthyr Vale combined Sunday Schools, July 1994

2.   The Gallery

The 'gallery' occupies an honoured place in the story of the churches; the rise and fall of the faith can be echoed in the gallery, when there was not enough room in the congregation then the gallery was added. In Zion, the gallery's main support were two huge oak beams which ran the length of the chapel, in themselves wonderful pieces of craftsmanship. In Zion in 1905 the gallery seats were free. The downstairs seats were rented at 6d. a quarter payable a quarter in advance. George Evans was appointed secretary, and William Jones as treasurer, of the Pew Funds. In was arranged that nine sat in each centre seats, there were partitions in the seats - and they were to seat 5 and 4. Five were accommodated on each side pew, the lower floor looked towards the pulpit, which had the Baptistery under it, and usually closed. In the front of the pulpit, the Big Seat, here sat the deacons, they faced the congregation while hymns were being sung, they took the collection. In many churches the collection was taken on a plate, or a collection bag with one deacon passing the plate and another deacon recording. The one recording was often asked, "How much has she given" and the loud reply would echo, she gave nothing. What a marvellous place the gallery was, to watch these carryings on!

It was at the beginning of the century, that gallery life got a bit lively, as the deacons lift their eyes, it was usually to see trouble up above, the boys were on the one side, and the girls were on the other side of the gallery, a fact in itself to cause trouble during a 50 minute sermon. A letter in the Merthyr Express waxes eloquently and hotly over these disturbances, and a number of churches have reference to it in their records. In Zion's case a number of remedies were adopted. Gallery stewards appointed, extra deacons drafted in to keep order, in one case the whole disconate was sent up. The minister spoke to them, all remedies it seems were of no avail. Those in the gallery had a good vantage point, a feature of many services, was to see programmes floating down from the gallery. One tells of the Baptismal Service, when he lost his cap, and as the Baptism began his cap was sailing on the waters!

The gallery was used for Sunday Schools concerts, the choir used it for concerts, and all testify to a real sense of enjoying the fellowship of the church.

A sad comment on many churches, is the empty gallery, in 1919 Zion was able to use the vestry for morning worship when the heating broke down. In 1926 the gallery was closed for morning worship, a sure sign of the declining congregations. In Zion when the chapel closed, the gallery was still used by a handful.

ZION, MERTHYR VALE BAPTISTS.
REFERENCE - "HAVE FAITH WILL BUILD" 1876-1976

The Gallery, Smyrna Chapel

3.   The Building of the Village - 6

In Fine Spirit

The years of striving to sink the Merthyr Vale Colliery were over by 1875 and the community began to grow. By 1880 there were 374 houses and a population of 1,790 people. With this growth came increased social activities. The chapels were crucial in this. The Baptists and the Independents had been very active in the winter months of 1877, and in the Spring of 1878 they "borrowed the Capel Aberfan for an Eisteddfod to which all the chapels in the vicinity came in 'fine spirit'". The Merthyr Express was able to report that 'the vocal powers of this vicinity are rapidly spreading, notwithstanding it is but a new mining district."

The Sunday Schools of the various chapels were also in fine spirit. These were the days before the annual chapel outing to Barry Island and Porthcawl. The Sunday School treat in the 1870s was a walk around all the main streets of the village. The Baptists and Independents would usually walk together and later returned to their places of worship. Here they would be regaled with tea and cakes. The girls would be dressed in their ginghams and everyone would have fun and games in a field adjoining the chapels. After the playing of games was over, there would be more tea and cakes and concerts with 'interesting programmes'.

Perthygleision Farm, Aberfan

Perthygleision Farm - Aberfan
Cradle of Quakerism

4. Verses on the Union of the Sunday Schools in Ynysowen

In the vigour of gladness my museing
    has pleasure,
Not over in the dismal noise of the gun
To look in grief on the dead with their
    pale grey faces,
Only here, above the fascinating foundations
    of Ynysowen and its charms -
I will outfall my talents, still praising
    the united chains brought to bear,
On the Breast of the Sunday Schools.

Some beautiful threepenny chain they
    plaited from the twigs of the three
    pious branches.
It was good in its intentions, according
    to the Bard -
In order to shake the sleepiness of the
    School,
It is a rather slow swelling Ocean,
The sect quite hidden, an overflowing Love
    from it ran.
Heaven's smile on its face is swimming.

This is not an Union to destroy the plan
To kill every kind of joy,
Only the means to attract every age
And grade to smile at one another.
The Calvin and others become dissolved in one,
In the knot in the ring of unity
And from it will flourish the essence of
    Brotherhood,
They will have millions there to
Praise them.

Let not the immoral breezes of the times
Blow, until it kills the influences of the
    three Schools, only cling to the subject,
Under the banner of the Cross to beautify
The white fields of the future.
The success of the Instruction, will be
    Crowned with Divinity,
Is the last wish of the Poet,
To bring sinners to run free with their
    talents,
Under their Wings.

WILLIAM JONES (GWILYM IAGO)
DANYDERI.
MERTHYR EXPRESS, 27 JULY, 1878
TRANSLATED BY ETHEL LLOYD, 1991

Y Golofn Gymreig.

At ddarllenwyr lluosog y *Merthyr Express* : Wrth weled y cynnydd parhaus sydd ynghylchrediad ein newyddiadur, a'r boddhad mawr y mae ein darllenwyr yn eu gael yn yr adran Gymreig, ac ar ddymuniad taer lluaws o'r beirdd, yr ydym yn ostyngedig yn cydsynio a'u cais, i ruoddi un golofn o'n papur at eu gwasanaeth : i gyhoeddi barddoniaeth, llofion, difyrion, ffraetnebion, &c. ; ac yr ydym yn addaw, os bydd y cyfryw i fyny a'n safon, y cânt ymddangos yn brydlawn yn eu tro.

PENILLION AR UNDEB YSGOLION SABBATHOL YNYSOWEN.

Yn nwyfre llawenydd fy awen gaiff wledd,
    Nid draw yn eron drwst yn magnelau—
I syllu mewn gofid ar glwyfau y cledd,
    A'r meirw a'u gwelwon wynebau ;
Ond yma uwch sail Ynysowen a'i swyn,
    Arllwysaf fy noniau er cammol
Y Gadwen Undebol, osodir i'w dwyn
    Ar ddwyfron yr Ysgol Sabbothol.

Rhyw gadwen deirceiniog a blethwyd yn
    hardd,
    O frigau tair cangen grefyddol ;
Yn dda yn ei bwriad 'nol meddwl y bardd,
    Er ysgwyd cysgadrwydd yr ysgol.
Mae'n undeb mal cefnfor ymchwyddol ei led,
    Enwadaeth yn hollol orchuddia ;
A chornant o gariad o hono a rêd,
    Gwên nef ar ei gwyneb a notia.

Nid undeb yw hwn o gynlluniau er lladd,
    A difa pob math o lawenydd,
Ond moddion i ddenu pob oedran a gradd,
    I wenu y'ngwyneb eu gilydd.
Y Calfin, a'r Armin ymdoddant yn un
    Yn nghwlwm y ddolen undebol,
Blagura o honi frawdgarwch a rhûn ;
    A chanmil a geir yn ei chanmol.

Na chwythed awelon anfoesol yr oes,
    Nes lladd dylanwadau'r tair ysgol,
Ond glyned eu deiliaid dan faner y groes,
    Er harddu gwyn faes y dyfodol :
Coroner dwytoldeb eu haddysg a llwydd,
    Yw olaf ddymuniad y prydydd,
I ddwyn pechaduriaid i redeg yn rhwydd,
    A'u doniau o dan eu hadenydd.
          WILLIAM JAMES (Gwilym Iago).
Danyderi.

DYDD GWYL SANT SWITHIN.

Yn gymmaint a bod hen draddodiad yn mhlith y Cymry er's oesoedd mewn cyssylltiad a'r sant uchod a'r tywydd, yr ydym yn credi mae nid annherbyniol gan ddarlleuwyr lluosog y *Merthyr Express* fydd cael ychydig o'i hanes yn y

5.   Sunday Schools, The Welsh Baptists

"On the evening of Thursday week the scholars of the Baptist Sunday School attended a tea party in Carmel Chapel, and were joined by the scholars from Danyderi and Perthygleision. The proceedings commenced with the perambulations of the children and friends of the school, who, sang several choice selections as they passed through the village of Troedyrhiw, on their way to chapel, which having reached, a liberal supply of tea and cake was provided, to which they did ample justice, after which an address was delivered by the Rev. J. Lewis, minister of the above chapel and the arrangements were ably conducted by Messrs. Price and other friends of the school, so that the whole affair gave great satisfaction."

This report appeared in the "Merthyr Express" for 8 October 1870, under the heading of "Tea Party".

The Welsh Baptists who were meeting in Danyderi, Merthyr Vale, eventually had their own Chapel building which they called Calfaria. The building had an interesting history. Originally it had been constructed, at the instigation of the colliery owner, John Nixon, as a Presbyterian Chapel. The chapel was the scene of many concerts but for some reason the Church in Wales began meeting there. This must have been in Nixon's lifetime for the story goes that he would not let them hang a bell in the actual building. They had to hang their bell in a tree.

The Welsh Baptists of Aberfan, who were meeting in Glandwr Cottage, Perthygleision, became the Smyrna Welsh Baptists.

Calfaria Chapel

6.   Swede Hunting

Then the times we climbed the fences into old Price's fields to pinch his cow swedes. We'd take them home and mam would cook them and add butter and pepper. Delicious, especially as they were free! Old Price would see us sometimes and start galloping on his horse to chase us away but he never caught us, being young, we could run like the hare.

One Saturday, a gang of us went swede hunting and got away with quite a few, Price's presence being absent. The next day being Sunday, I went as usual to the Methodist Chapel. The preacher started his sermon on the evils of stealing. He seemed to be preaching his sermon for me alone. I sat there petrified. He was a great orator as only the Welsh preachers of that era could be. Well, I can assure you, that put a stop to my swede hunting, for a while anyway.

MARY MAGLONA, MELBOURNE AUSTRALIA, 1990

7.   The End of the World

The end of the world has been predicted several times this century. It does seem that an actual date and time were given on one occasion and that it was taken seriously by a small group in Aberfan in the first decade of this century. My grandmother, Mrs Agnes Piggott, who would then have been living in 'Marshfield' Aberfan Road near the Mackintosh Hotel had heard of this prediction and she looked on as a group prepared themselves to climb the mountain in the hope of preserving themselves. And possibly in an attempt to follow the Biblical direction of 'ascending to high places' in the event.

There was singing and there were prayers and upward moved the group. My grandmother was not convinced however, and went about her day as uaual, only to emerge from her home in the evening to see the group disband and return to their homes, crushed and deflated but also very glad that the ordeal was over.

I don't know who the group were or if they were members of any particular sect, or even if it had anything to do with the Revival, the dates certainly seem to fit together. The story was told always with a smile about the fact that they were rather shy on the way home following the explosive nature of the start of the day, a contrast which was too full of comedy to miss repeating. What she did not do was to call the people silly and as a child I always thought her most brave to stay down in the village.

HILARY CLARKE, 1991

Pulpit, Capel Aberfan

8.   The Valleys are Set Alight

Just before Christmas 1904, Evan Roberts, leader of the 'Revival', visited first Merthyr Vale and then Aberfan as part of his religious crusade. He had been studying for the ministry at Newcastle Emlyn when a conviction that he had to return to his home town of Loughor, near Swansea overwhelmed him. There he began his work in his own local chapel of Moriah.

The original Revival had begun in a muted form the year before in Newquay, Cardiganshire, under the influence of a Calvanistic Methodist minister. Evan Roberts had been waiting for the opportunity now afforded him and he became joyful and courageous in his crusade, willing to spend his life-savings on taking his mission around Wales.

In the weeks before he came to Aberfan and Merthyr Vale, the 'Valleys had been set alight' with his preaching and with the singing of Welsh and English hymns. These hymns could be heard resounding through the valley streets sometimes until two thirty in the morning.

A crowd gathered at Merthyr Vale Station on the evening of 14 December anxious to know where Evan Roberts was going to speak. When it became known that he was going to preach in Calfaria, Merthyr Vale, the chapel soon became crowded. Many of the people could not get in and crossing the Taff, crowded into the three chapels in Aberfan Road, hoping that Evan Roberts would decide to preach in one of these places of worship.

But it was to Calfaria Chapel that he came first, a tall young man of twenty six with brown eyes, dark auburn hair and a gentle face. He was greeted by a huge throng of people. Outside the crowd were singing hymns. Inside the chapel was too full for comfort and the preacher spoke under difficult circumstances. The people were full of religious fervour and began praying and then they too began singing hymns incessantly. This formed the main part of the service, the singing being magnificent. Many mothers had brought their babes in arms with them.

The next day Evan Roberts was to be found in Aberfan. The people gathered together in hundreds and sang and prayed in the streets. News had spread of Evan Robert's triumph in Merthyr Vale and the enthusiasm of the crowd had gathered momentum in Aberfan.

Crowds gathered outside Capel Aberfan from nine o' clock in the morning and by ten o' clock the chapel itself and the surrounding area was so full that Evan Roberts had difficulty in getting through the crowd to address the congregation. He had tired from his exertions of the day before but the congregation were delighted by his presence. They sang over and over again "Mai cariad ydw Duw" to the tune of 'diadem", their voices rising to a crescendo. When at last they had finished, Evan Roberts was obviously overwhelmed and he was unable to preach in his usual manner. Someone in the 'Set Fawr' offered up a prayer and the singing was taken up again. Another prayer was given by a young man in the chapel gallery and yet again the congregation began singing. Evan Roberts preached in three Aberfan Chapels that day to huge crowds, many of whom had travelled long distances. Some people were unable to see him, the crowds being too great. But everyone was prayed for and no-one condemned by the preacher or his followers for they preached "God is love. - Duw cariad yw."

Later, it was announced that over six hundred converts had been made during the visit of Evan Roberts to Aberfan and Merthyr Vale.

All denominations joined in the crusade. Even the Church in Wales was influenced and there were clerics assigned to work in parishes that had been affected by the Revival. There was a general increase in church and chapel attendance which now became more regular. The Bible became more widely read with the demand for Bibles increasing three or four fold. The Revival brought benefits for the whole community, for no longer could local ministers content themselves with ministering to respectable and well-to-do congregations. Now they were impelled by the spirit of the times to work out of doors amongst the less fortunate.

Effective preaching had always been an essential feature of the non-conformist hold over the Welsh people. Henry Richard noted that "wave after wave of emotion would pass over and thrill through the vast congregation at open air assemblies". There were numerous religious revivals and they kept the chapel congregations firm. These revivals were usually of a temperate nature but the Revival led by Evan Roberts was extraordinary and scenes never witnessed before or since, took place in the valleys of South Wales.

Evan Roberts had come from mining stock. His father had been a collier. At the age of twelve Evan Roberts became a door boy in the Colliery and by the age of sixteen he was working cutting coal, probably earning five shillings a day. Because he had worked in the mines for twelve years before entering college at Newcastle Emlyn, he understood the way of life in the valley communities. He was able to use this knowledge and his background to communicate to the people. He was able to speak to them naturally and with sincerity. A London newspaper of the time was able to report that because of the Revival there was less idleness, less drunkenness and less gambling. Hauliers had even stopped swearing at their pit ponies.

The Revival came at a time when the political climate of the late nineteenth century was bringing about profound changes in the life of the South Wales mining communities. The chapels were beginning to lose their potential leaders to the new creed of Socialism. The revival of 1904-05 masked the impact of these changes but by the 1918 General Election, liberal politics and religious non-conformity had been superseded by the Labour Party and the new gospel of Socialism.

MAUREEN HUGHES, 1992

Mr Evan Roberts

9. John Haydn Phillips

John Haydn Phillips died after a long illness, borne with faith, on September 4th aged 68.

He brought honour to our community by winning the hymn tune competition in the National Eisteddfod at Llangefni and Lampeter, two years running. The Llangefni tune, 'Bro Aber' immediately took wing, is regularly heard on radio record programmes and sung in services and is regularly becoming a 'must' in Cymanfaoedd Canu', Welsh and English. His many other tunes have been sung and some of them will quietly take their place in future hymn books. John as a boy was for years unable to walk. His characteristic determination took him from his chair to work as an office boy at Adler's Button Factory and he ended his career there as Managing Director of the Welsh Products. With the same determination and devotion to duty he taught generations to sing and gave them a foundation in life in the Sunday School at Capel Aberfan. In later years he was the secretary and the leader of the Church there.

He played his part in our community recovery after 1966, attending the Community Conferences, freely giving of his accountant experience to the Community Association, conducting in turn, the Ynysowen Male Choir and the Aberfan Youth Choir.

Music was his delight. He conducted a number of "Cymanfaoedd Canu" in Wales and London. His enthusiasm and organising ability will be sadly missed in the Merthyr 'Gymanfa Ganu' of the Presbyterian Church of Wales and in the wider field of the annual selection of hymns for such events, for which he also composed. He took his place in the inter-church life of Aberfan and Merthyr Vale and served for many years on the Churches' Council.

Our sympathy surrounds his family.

REV. ERASTUS JONES,
HEADWAY 1985

715 BRO ABER 10.10.10.10.10.10

J. HAYDN PHILLIPS, 1917-85

A - men.

867

O! tyred i'n gwaredu, Iesu da,
　Fel cynt y daethost ar dy newydd wedd,
A'r drysau 'nghau, at rai dan ofnus blâ,
　A'u cadarnhau â nerthol air dy hedd:
Llefara dy dangnefedd yma'n awr,
A dangos inni greithiau d'aberth mawr.

Yn d'aberth di mae'n gobaith ni o hyd,
　Ni ddaw o'r ddaear ond llonyddwch brau;
O hen gaethiwed barn rhyfeloedd byd,
　Hiraethwn am y cymod sy'n rhyddhau:
Tydi, Gyfryngwr byw rhwng Duw a dyn,
Rho yn ein calon ras i fyw'n gytûn.

Cyd-fyw'n gytûn fel brodyr fyddo'n rhan,
　A'th gariad yn ein cynnal drwy ein hoes;
Na foed i'r arfog cry' orthrymu'r gwan,
　Ac na bo grym i ni ond grym y groes:
Rhag gwae y dilyw tân, O! trugarha,
A thyred i'n gwaredu, Iesu da.

JOHN ROBERTS, 1910-84

10. The Building of the Village - 7
Social Activities, 1870s

In the Autumn and Winter 'Penny Readings' were held. These were an early feature of village life and were to continue for the next sixty years. In Aberfan and Merthyr Vale the readings were taking place in both Welsh and English. There were debating, reading and singing competitions, with small prizes for the winners. The chapels all co-operated with each other. Those denominations who already had chapel buildings lent them to those denominations who were still raising funds for buildings of their own. A ventriloquist from North Wales gave a show in the vestry of Bethania, Welsh Independents, towards the chapel building fund. And to Bethesda, English Baptist, Merthyr Vale, came a black preacher from Birmingham, to tell of his own experiences as a fugitive slave in the Southern States of America. A celebrated woman preacher, Martha Griffiths, probably a Welsh Independent, was preaching to capacity congregations on account of her eloquence. The Smyrna Welsh Baptist Choir, conducted by John Davies, formerly of Cwmdare, participated in a concert for a young man called William Sage who had had to have a leg amputated following an accident in the colliery.

MAUREEN HUGHES, 1992

11. Smyrna Sunday School

Merry notes, happy notes,
Red and blue and green.
Joyful notes of children
Singing in anniversary.
All dressed
In double Sunday best,
With caring teachers,
Tendering preachers,
Psalms and songs
And Bible verses,
"Duw cariad yw."

MAUREEN HUGHES, JANUARY 1988

Ysgol Sul Smyrna

Nodau llawen, nodau hapus,
Coch, a glas, a gwyrdd.
Nodau llawen y plant
Canu yn yr cylchwyl.
Pawb wedi gwisgo
Yn ei dyblig Sabath goreu,
Gyda athrawion,
Gofalus Pregethwyr tirion.
Salmau, a canu,
A pennillion o'r Bibel
"God is Love."

TRANSLATED BY ETHEL LLOYD, JULY 1992

Merthyr Vale mountain, the River, the Grove field and Smyrna Chapel

Smyrna

The Sunday School drew the children of Bryngoleu, Perthygleision, Thomas Street, Aberfan Crescent and Bryntaf in good numbers. There must be a number of people who feel fond when they see Mrs Ethel Lloyd remembering her efforts as the Sunday Schools Infants teacher and perhaps their happier and more innocent days. Throughout the villages, chapels had their dramatic societies which usually put on their shows in the Aberfan Hall. These were not only lively, they were quite popular. Quite a number of boys belonging to the chapel were called up to the forces during the war and John Jones (Pontygwaith) never failed to pray for them by name in the weekly prayer meeting. When the war was over, the church became very active in raising funds under the guidance of Mrs Gwyneth Williams, wife of W J Williams the school master. I remember a house full of people patiently unpicking parachutes for the women to convert the cloth into pinafores and the like at the weekly sewing class . This was the prelude for the annual jumble sale. Then the Disaster occurred, and where would the village have been without our chapels. While Bethania became the mortuary with its mortally wounded queues, Smyrna became a *" casualty and refreshment centre". The reference continues that 'the chapel's communion table was covered, not with bread and wine, but with bandages and antiseptic'. The building and the members were heavily and indelibly scarred by that experience and it is most painful to recall the horrors of the time. Although our losses then was the beginning of the end of our Sunday School, the most important fact that emerged was that denominations never mattered afterwards. Now we are eight members on the book, but we remain hopeful.

BILL GRIFFITHS

*Christianity in Action Today, Topic 8 "Aberfan" Book 8 the Story of the Scriptures Page 35

Athena Hill - St Marys Sunday School

12. One of the Happiest Days of my Life

I remember Haydn, my son, was just six and he had only recently come out of Llandough Hospital after an operation on his spleen. He couldn't read or write because he suffered from cerebral palsy. He started going to the English Baptist Chapel, to the Sunday School. Reg Wakely was his teacher; Mr Wakely taught him to sing "Jesus Loves Me", he was marvellous, he also taught him a verse.

The Chapel Anniversary came and Melba Taylor's mother, me and my Aunt went to hear him. I was more nervous than he was, I was quaking. Haydn didn't bat an eyelid. He was word perfect and had a lovely singing voice. His father's family were very Welsh and known for their singing.

A neighbour of ours used to take Haydn to sing to some of the people in the street. She used to tell me that his voice should be trained. I was so proud of Haydn that day. Of course, the Sunday School Anniversary was very special. We used to dress up in our very best clothes, hats and all. Haydn kept going to Sunday School until Mr Wakely retired as his Sunday School teacher. He thought the world of Mr Wakely.

That Anniversary day was one of the happiest days of my life.

ADDIE WATKINS, 1991

13. Zion English Methodist Chapel

Zion Chapel was built a little over a hundred years ago. Over this period it has had various names. At first the members were known as the "Prims" which was short for Primitive Methodists, who were a breakaway group from the Church of England. Secondly, the chapel itself was known as Noah's Ark, attributable to the Nant stream that ran alongside and Mr Noah Morgan, one of its earliest members. Thirdly, it was known as 'Small's Chapel', its seating capacity is less than a hundred and Mr Tom Small was a Steward and Sunday School Superintendent for over fifty years.

The founders are not known as records were not kept in those early days. Two commemorative stones on the front of the building bear the names of Mr Snape, the manager of Merthyr Vale Colliery and a Dr. G. M. Jones. A debt of £100 remained after the chapel was built.

There were several High Days in the year of the Chapel. Harvest Festival, when the little Chapel looked even lovelier adorned with flowers, fruit and vegetables. On the following evening a Thanksgiving service would be held, when the produce would be sold and the money went into the Trust Fund. Like other chapels in the village, the Sunday School Anniversary Service was 'standng room only', children were even put to sit on the window sills. Another important day was the Annual Tea and Concert when everyone took part. The water for the tea was boiled on an open fire on the lawn and the tea brewed in the pulpit. Table tops were placed over the seats and non-members helped to make this a festive occasion. The young boys and girls would continue the 'Fellowship' by taking a walk up and down Troedyrhiw Road. In later years the Christmas morning service at 8.30 a.m. became an important date. The preacher for that date was a great local Preacher, Mr Bill Rubbery, who lived on the side of the mountain in Troedyrhiw and was collected by Mr Tom Small in his Raleigh Green 3 wheeler. When after 20 years it failed to make the hills, Mr Rubbery became a pillion passenger on Cyril Vaughan's Vespa Scooter. To this day Mr Vaughan still conveys the Church and Chapel members to their places of worship, alas, not on his Vespa.

The Chapel had unknowingly been built on a geological fault causing severe cracking in the walls and front porch; this was remedied by expert and voluntary help. The women organised the fund raising; sewing classes were held and there were faggot and peas suppers in the chapel. There were many stalwart supporters.

The Chapel was first licensed for marriage in 1953 when June Small and Cyril Vaughan were married there and the Rev. Morgan Slade officated.

In 1966, 144 children and adults died in the Aberfan Disaster. Among those were 17 children from

Zion Methodist Sunday School and Sunshine Corner. To the villagers of Aberfan, the Chapel will always be referred to as 'Tommy Small's Chapel'.

REFERENCE - ZION ENGLISH METHODIST CHAPEL - A HUNDRED YEARS

14. The Little Tin Chapel

Acts 2 v 41 and 42

Some eighty years ago a few people dedicated themselves to gather together to follow their Christian conviction. They resolved to meet in a house in Barrington Street, Aberfan but eventually purchased the chapel premises in Aberfan Crescent known as Mount Hermon. Latterly the chapel became known as the Gospel Hall, Aberfan, but locals soon affectionately re-named it "the little tin Chapel". The Chapel was indeed constructed of corrugated sheets of tin but painted a lovely shade of green it did not look out of place and peacefully and gracefully blended in with the green grass and trees that surrounded it. The building itself was indeed small, as Aberfan and Merthyr Vale Chapels went, but that made it all the more endearing.

Many activities were held there during the weekdays and on Sunday there would be the Rememberance Service, Gospel Addresses and Sunday School Prayers.

During the Disaster of 1966 the Hall was open for all who wished for help and relief, and many names of Brethren were mentioned in the relief work. Five Sunday School scholars were lost in the Disaster.

The venture has been worthwhile but age has had its' effect. The repairs and upkeep of the Gospel Hall was mainly done by our Brethren. Now I am the only person left to tell the tale and I am 85 years old.

Eternity will reveal ALL.

GEORGE WILLIAMS, TROEDYRHIW, 1991

Gospel Hall, Aberfan

15. Sunday Schools - The Little Tin Chapel

When my children were small I taught them all to go to Sunday School. They went to the little tin chapel because the teachers were so good to them, Mr and Mrs Williams and Mr Jones.

They always had an outing to Barry Island every year and also packed lunches. There was a party three times a year. My children loved to go up until 1966. I had Mr Jones to the house when my two kiddies died in the disaster, to pray for them. I had my brother's little boy Royston in my room with my little Pat and Tommy because they were always together. I was sorry to hear that they had pulled the chapel down.

The children looked forward to going on the outings and to the tea-parties. They used to have ten shillings in a little envelope. I wouldn't give it to them until it was time for the fair. We would all be sitting in a circle on the sands and then they would give us our packed lunch. The teachers would be there with us.

The children used to have little prayer books given to them by the chapel and they would take them to Sunday School every Sunday. It was a fine little chapel.

GWYNETH PROBERT NEE HODKINSON, 1991

16. My Children

You are the rock I build my dreams upon.
You are the strength I need when things go wrong.
In life you play a most important part
And regulate the beating of my heart.
You are the children I carried with much bliss,
All my life I will remember this.
You gave me hope
When things seemed all in vain,
Made me smile and the sun came out again.
There is a purpose to life they say,
And you are mine.
For this I bless each day.

CHRISTINA LLEWELLYN, 1991

17. Our Little Girl - in memory of

I think of her eyes when open
So bright serene and so trusting,
Asleep in the night.
I think of her face, so rosy and warm,
With lips red and 'kissful' ee'n after the storm.
I think of her hair, so gleaming and brown,
Just like a bird's wing, just fresh from the down.
I think of her spirit, so loving and giving
Aglow, and so strong with the joy of her living.
I think of her love, her sure faithful love,
Pray God, that she sends it from heaven above.

Dear God, our Creator in heaven above,
Look after our Sharon, and give her our love.

SHEILA LEWIS, 1967

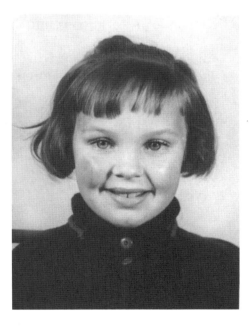

Sharon Lewis Age 7 1/2 Years
School Photo October 1964

18. Virginia Iles Moseley

Virginia wrote to me from her home in Texas, shortly after the Aberfan Disaster. I replied to her letter and we began a long friendship which exists to this day. In 1975 Virginia visited me for the week of Christmas. She was a joy to have as a visitor and fell in love with the country of Wales, the people and Aberfan in particular.

We filled up our spare time in a very busy week with non-stop talking, often into the early hours. It didn't matter how late we went to our beds, she was always up before me, and was busy outdoors, wandering through the village streets and up to the cemetery. She is an ardent Southern Baptist, and, amongst others I introduced her to , was the Rev. Kenneth Hayes.

That week we attended Christmas Eve Midnight Mass at St. Benedict's Roman Catholic Church and on Christmas morning we attended the Baptist Chapel Service at Nixonville. Christmas afternoon we joined the congregation in the Communion Christmas Service at Smyrna Chapel.

SHEILA LEWIS, 1991

19. Your House Blessing

December 22, 1975.

A sacred Mass, your home to bless, to think I shared this happiness, to be asked by the Father to have a part, in something so near and dear to my heart.

We are told * to be kind to the stranger outside, for angels may seek the right place to abide.
And angels visit to minister our needs, their mission to go wherever God leads, the home is the true test - the trials are sore, and we take a chance when we open the door, lest we cause someone's faith to suffer despair, by some idle word or deed, unaware.

But to have a home where Jesus can rest, as the Silent Listener, the Unseen Guest, your home is one, stripped of pretence, it's God's dwelling place in every sense.

I pray for your home, its' walls and doors, the sheltering roof, the halls and floors, the windows, each room, and the hearts inside, to be kept unspotted from worldly pride.

And Oh! that your home will ever be, a refuge, a haven for others to see, God's fullness and glory, transcended, supreme, and maybe again fulfil someone's dream.

It did this for me and you'll never know love, as I lay there in bed how I prayed God above to shower abundance of manna and grace, on your household, and keep you in His embrace.

* 1st Peter 4 v. 9
Hebrews 13 v. 2

VIRGINIA, 1975

258

20. A Reverie

The mountains, majestic, await to give birth to treasures in deep pits half mile in
the earth; our first visit down there, to share with you seems fantastically,
unbelievably true!

The eve of my parting was Oh! such fun! You helped me pack, tied up every one
of my beautiful gifts with loving care; we joked and laughed, had so much
to share!

On parting, I wondered how I could hold tight; but no need for break - you made things
right; God used you to plan every move in it's place, how easy if I'd trust more in
His grace. (How needlessly heavy my heart can yearn; so many lessons I fail to learn;
for my God is sufficient, true Grace He avails, if only I'd let him; He never fails!)

I've stood on the mountain, transfigured, renewed, by God in Wales, new courage ensued;
so I must go now to the Valley's depth, for there's work to be done by those of us left.

And one day in Heaven, no deadlines to meet; no time, no distance, but at Jesus' feet,
we'll spend Love, eternity, soul's joy, delight, in reunion, all of us and never more night.

VIRGINIA, 1975

21. Father Barnabas

Father Barnabas came to live in Aberfan on the 6th November 1989.
He is a Greek Orthodox priest and for thirty years has been a monk.
He has had a very interesting life and for some years worked in Paris amongst the Russian emigres;
as he says "with the down and outs".
In 1965 he joined a Monastery in Devon, and in 1973 he founded a Monastery in Mid Wales which
is dedicated to the Prophet Elias. The Monastery is in a beautiful old farmhouse in the village of New
Mills, near Llanfair-caereinion; there is a truly beautiful garden and in the garden "a lovely chapel".
The Monastery is devoted to prayer and to giving a welcome to visitors.
Father Barnabas came to Aberfan because of the relatively cheap housing, but also to be a presence
in the Valleys. He is in semi-retirement but feels now that
he is an "Orthodox presence in the Village". He is devoted
to a life of prayer and finds the People of Aberfan, 'so kind
and so friendly'.

He is a Welsh speaking Welshman who went to school
in Pennal, near Machynlleth, he was born in 1915 and
trained in St. David's, Lampeter, as an Anglican Priest. He
became disaffected with the Church when they began
departing from tradition and found his spiritual niche in
the Greek Orthodox faith.

Now he has become a familiar sight in the village with
his long flowing white beard and his black robes almost
trailing the ground. He has made a lovely "Monastery
Garden" at his house in Bridge Street where all is peace
and tranquillity. He too, welcomes visitors and is kind and
courteous to all. A gentleman of firm convictions, he has
made a very welcome addition to our community.

MAUREEN HUGHES

22. A Voice from the East

In Aberfan and Merthyr Vale there are, and have been many Christian places of worship. Anglican, Roman Catholic, Non-Conformist, Pentecostal and Evangelical. Although not as well attended as in previous years, they still witness to God and proclaim his presence through their services of praise, prayer and instruction.

All churches have their roots in the teachings of Christ given 2,000 years ago in Palestine. The Ancient Church of the East, called the Orthodox Church, claims to have remained closer to the Jewish Church, to which Christ, in his human form, belonged. He would go to the synagogue, in Nazareth or Capernaum, regularly to hear the word of God. This was contained in the Old Testament. He would go to the Temple at Jerusalem, from time to time, to take part in the sacrifices offered there every day. After His ascension to heaven and the descent of the Holy Spirit at Pentecost, there emerged the Christian Church. This was no longer confined to Jews but open to all believers. The worshipping church which emerged thus combined in its worshipping, elements from the synagogue, that is bible reading and prayer. There was also an element from the Temple, that is sacrifice, but no longer of birds and beasts but of the body and blood of Christ, as celebrated by Him on the eve of His death. The Orthodox Church is faithful in the command of Christ to "do this in remembrance of me" and has its altar of sacrifice and Icon Screen, like the Temple and its pulpit for God's word, as in the synagogue.

Because God became man in Christ, an image of God, he can be depicted in pictures, which we call Icons. In every Orthodox Church there are Icons of Christ, His mother, the Virgin Mary, and the Saints. They are painted to rules that are in force to this day.

We need divine help to get through life and this we obtain through prayer and sacrement. The Church is at hand at our birth to give us baptism, confirmation and communion. In adult life it is at hand to bless our marriage, ordain men as deacons, priests and bishops, to forgive our sins and to ease our pain through anointment with holy oil. And underlying it all is the life of prayer whether it be in church or in private, perhaps at home, in silence. This is our life link with God when he speaks to us and we to him. Thus the eternal is never forgotten if we pray and are guided through the various crisis that arise in life.

An Orthodox Christian is one who believes in the faith as taught by the Apostles. They heard it from the lips of Christ. They did not add to it nor subtract from it as it developed down the ages. Christ is acknowledged as the head of the Church, uniting those who have died with those who are still on earth. Patriachs and Bishops are only under him, not absolute rulers. They are guides to eternity and when they speak on serious matters in a General Council, they speak with Christ's authority and cannot lead us astray. The Church, the Bible and Tradition speak with one voice. We pay heed to their teaching.

FATHER BARNABAS, 1991

Father Barnabas' Monastery, Mid Wales

23. Conclusion

Our story has been told in these pages. But nothing remains the same and Merthyr Vale and Aberfan are no exception. The biggest change that we have had to accept is the closure of our colliery. Now the site is the scene of a local reclamation scheme and the empty space is tinged with sadness. Walter Bell envisaged new industries and technology bringing employment to the area when coalmining came to an end but insufficient jobs have come to replace those lost.

We have made new friends through the book - people who have sent contributions into the village which are included in this manuscript such as Tom Bellion, Carol Whelan and Audrey Wilson. We have rediscovered old ones such as Irene Downing of Folkestone and the evacuees.

We have lost friends in the villages. Beatrice Chambers, Morfydd Holden, Megan the Ironmonger, Gwyneth Probert, Donald Young and latterly Rev Kenneth Hayes have died and our community is diminished by their loss. But there are positive things in our community. A survey* conducted in the villages in 1994 revealed a widespread interest in caring and concern for our environment. The shooting of wildlife was wholeheartedly condemned and nature reserves called for. People knew their villages well enough to know where these should be and were prepared to look after them. Broadleafed woods, roadside trees, dry stone walls and hedges were the best loved features. The young people identified farm buildings as being important to them. The Taff Trail along the Canal Bank has brought a resurgence in cycling and walking amongst all ages. Cycling is now the most popular sporting activity in the villages. When asked what they liked about their village for the purpose of the community map, the people of Mount Pleasant identified favourite walks, friends and the schools, the Post Office and Newsagents. These meant a lot to everyone. There is a quiet but keen interest in the Welsh Language and culture. In the Jigso survey 72% of those questioned who were eligible favoured a bi-lingual village school.

Meanwhile life goes on. New life has been breathed into "Headway". As a sub-committee of the former Community Association, "Headway" has been vital to the well being of the villages and it is good to know that it is still capable of making an impact in these post-Disaster days. Another sub-committee of the Association, continually looking for improvements in the community has been the catalyst for establishing a Community Co-operative. Through these shops we have come to know some of the newcomers to the villages and some of them have joined our co-op and they are welcome. There are other activities taking place in Trinity Chapel through the Ynysowen Project and they have established a community Cafe where once Mr and Mrs Emanuelli reigned. The return of the £150,000 to the Aberfan Memorial Charity has given our gardens and Memorials security for the foreseeable future and peace of mind for all of us who lost loved ones in October 1966 and for those who share our concern.

The Chairman of the former Community Association, Cyril Vaughan, looks forward to the days ahead with the colliery site improved. His hope is that we can go on making progress, being capable of accepting change and embracing new ideas whilst cherishing those things that gave us our strength in the past and our foundation for the future. All of us in the Writers and History Group join him in his hopes and thank all those people who have thought of us and helped us in any way in the preparation of this book "Aberfan - Our Hiraeth".

Maureen Hughes 1998
Co-ordinator
Aberfan and Merthyr Vale
Writers and History
Group

*Local Jigso Committee Survey - published October 1994.
Assisted by Dr. Liz Hughes
The Jigso Co-ordinator
Rural Surveys Research Unit
University of Wales
Aberystwyth.

Photographs supplied by

Viv Evans
John Yates
Mary Jones
Adrienne Murphy
Robert O'Keefe Video Services
Bryn Carpenter
W. A. Humphreys
Bernard Donoghue
Bryan Davies
Edward Perry
Winnie Williams
Victoria Winkler
Stephanie Davies
Ken Jones
The Guardian Newspaper
Cyril Vaughan
Maureen Hughes
Eirionwen Williams
Sara Mclean
Sheila Lewis
Joe Probert
Mary Maglona Lewis
Julie Jefferson
Stuart Phillips
Marlene Jones
Emily Griffiths
Denver Coles
Ray Jones
Megan Jones
E. J. Edwards Folkestone
Mrs. F. Kilby Folkestone
Pat Davey
Dorothy Small
Wendy Howard
E. J. Price
Lance Jenkins
Neil Sumner
Father Barnabas
Dorothy Parker
Lyn Roberts
Pontypridd Town Council
Menna Lloyd Davies
Ann Price - retired nurse

This book has been brought into being by the Writers and History Group of Aberfan and Merthyr Vale. All proceeds will be used for the benefit of the two villages.

Dedications

To our wonderful parents - John & Eileen Davies (nee Adams) - God bless you. Lyn & Lorna

Wonderful memories of Nan & Grampa - James & Mary Adams. Love Lyn Lorna.

In rememberance of a loving Mum - Madge Fielder (nee Adams). From Graham.

To my four children, their partners and their children - Mary Gaynor Williams, Crescent Street, Merthyr Vale.

To honour our beautiful valley and also my beloved family - All in Christ's care. Sheila Lewis, Nixonville, Merthyr Vale.

Audrey Wilson MBE - October Memories, Dr Kiedon & the children - Roby Huyton, Merseyside.

To Grampa - Tommy Breeze. All our love - Lisa & Erin.

Loving memories of Mary & Crad Hibberd from all their children & grandchildren.

Loving memories, Idris Jones & Michael Jones, Bryntaf, Aberfan.

Loving memories of John & Elizabeth Morgan (nee Hopkins) Great-Grandparents of Beci & Joss Jones and Polly & Lottie Mossman.

To our children - David & Pauline Vaughan, Stephen, Angela, Alan & Andrew Phillip Vaughan. Our grandchildren - Rebecca Angela, Gareth David & Katie Ann Vaughan. All our love from Joan & Trevor Hopkins, Coronation Place, Aberfan.

Anthony David Hill, Born April 25th, 1958 died October 21st, 1966.

Sidney John Hollett 1908-1965 last miner killed in the Merthyr Vale Colliery.

John Crawford East 26.8.32 - 21.9.59

Barry Civil Defence Rescue Team and all those who came to help.

The Bryn School, Basildon, Essex - Happy memories.

Silver End School, Braintree, Essex - Happy memories.

Pantglas Infants & Junior School - Precious memories.

Pantglas Secondary School - Precious memories.

"The children sing like blackbirds at the dawning; No shades of memory lie on their faces, lifted to greet the morning." - Lady Wilson of Rievaulx.

Jennifer Claire Sutton, Aberfan
Anne Hallam, Llwydcoed, Aberdare
Eira E. Gough, Ty Bryngoleu, Aberfan
Adrienne Murphy, Aberfan Fawr, Aberfan
Valerie E. Rees, Troedyrhiw, Merthyr Tydfil
Rachel M. Hosgood, Christchurch, Dorset
Robert O'Keefe, Heolgerring, Merthyr Tydfil
Carolyn Jacob, Brecon, Powys
Arnold & Elvis James, Barry, South Glamorgan
Arthur & Mary Elizabeth James, Aberfan
'Ted' Beedle, 'The Garage', Aberfan
Selwyn and Grethe' Russell Jones, Macclesfield, Chesire
Joan Wilson, Folkestone, Kent
Sara McLean, Newtownards, County Down
E. J. Price, Barry, South Glamorgan
Stan Jones, Morgannwg, Merthyr Vale
Carol Whelan, Lower Earley, Reading
Lyn & Ron Elston, Lower Earley, Reading
Chris Whelan, Lower Earley, Reading
Alan Mytton, Pantglas Road, Aberfan
Cyril Davies, Moy Road, Aberfan
Elizabeth Ann Drage, Bryntaf, Aberfan
William Drage, Bryntaf, Aberfan
David Thomas Jones, Bryntaf, Aberfan
Roy Jones, Bryntaf, Aberfan
E. J. Edwards, The Harvey Grammar School, Folkestone, Kent
Ted Duggan, Knighton, Powys

Cynthia Langdon-Davies, Abergavenny, Gwent
Vivian Wall, Pontefract, West Yorkshire
Dr. F. Holley, Heolgerrig, Merthyr Tydfil
Stuart R. Jones, Pantyscallog, Merthyr Tydfil
W. Russell, (Harvey Grammar School Evacuee, 1943), Folkestone, Kent
Mansel Richards, West Grove, Merthyr Tydfil
Nesta Lewis, Denbigh, Clwyd
Margaret Sumner, Colne, Lancashire
Matthew Payne, Bryntaf, Aberfan
Cyril & June Vaughan, Kingsley Terrace, Aberfan
Olive Lloyd, Llanbradach, Caerphilly
Carol Small, St Fagans, Cardiff
Iris Knight, Caterham, Surrey
Harvey & Joyce Small, Hereford
Judith & Ralph Jackson, Rayleigh, Essex
Peter & Suzanne Vaughan, Cwmdare, Aberdare
Michael & Vannessa Vaughan, Quakers Yard, Treharris
Freda & Cecil Edwards, Woldingham, Surrey
Hazel & Jim Knight, Woking, Surrey
Dr. Gerald Lewis & Mrs Pamela Lewis, Sketty, Swansea
Hugh Watkins, Merthyr Tydfil Historical Society
Michael Gibbon, Islington, London
Erastus & Eiluned Jones, Ty Toronto, Porthmadoc, Gwynedd
Cyril Jones, Pleasant View, Aberfan
Gemma, Ben & Jordan Mabbitt, Canal Locke Close, Aberfan
Morgan Chambers, Trefechan, Merthyr Tydfil
Satwant Kaur Singh, Aberfan Road, Aberfan
Fred & Jeanette Evans, Gurnos, Merthyr Tydfil
Catrin & Bethan Rees, Pontsarn, Merthyr Tydfil
Sir Alun Talfan Davies, Penarth, South Glamorgan

Barbara & Michael Maybank, Aberfan Fawr, Aberfan
Gilbert & Beryl Minett, Lyme, Cheshire
George Williams, Troedyrhiw, Merthyr Tydfil
Kenneth William Owen, Ely, Cardiff
Reg Jones, Vale of Glamorgan
Neil, Gerda & Gareth Hammond, Gelli Pentre, Rhondda
Rhondda Community Development Association
Dr. R. W. J. Smith, Mid Glamorgan Health Authority
Effie & Graham Hughes, Treharne Street, Merthyr Vale
David Edward Evans, Bedlinog
Graham John Evans, Barrington Street, Aberfan
Lord Hooson Q.C., Llanidloes, Powys
E. R. Beynon, Muriel Terrace, Bedlinog
Mrs M. Steel, Howell's School, Denbigh, Clwyd
M. Turner, Abergavenny, Gwent
Dafydd Cwyfan Hughes, Anglesey, Gwynedd
Connie Sara, Stroud, Gloucestershire
Joan Johnson, Fish Hoek, South Africa
Glyn & Madge Phillips, Alberta Street, Merthyr Vale
M. J. Watkins, Oaklands, Merthyr Vale
Malcolm & Sadie Aylward, Mervyn Street, Aberfan
Sarah Chidgey, Aberfan Road, Aberfan
E. Pole, Bridgewater, Somerset
Mrs Irene Buttrey (nee Thomas)
Long Ridings Tutorial Centre, Brentwood, Essex
Keith Miller, Heston, Middlesex
Mr W. Wills, Headmaster, Maiden Erlegh School, Earley, Reading
Bill Thomas, Dowlais, Merthyr Tydfil

Janet Kirwan, Perthygleision, Aberfan
John Andrew Kirwan, Perthygleision, Aberfan
Nancy Woodward, Perthygleision, Aberfan
South Glamorgan County Libraries, Frederick Street, Cardiff
Rhiannon Pearson, Barrington Street, Aberfan
Joyce Sawday, Angus Street, Aberfan
W. Lavagna, Cemetery Road, Porth, Rhondda
Ynysowen Primary School, Aberfan
Dan Griffiths, Ynysowen Primary School, Aberfan
Shelagh Barnard, Crescent Street, Merthyr Vale
I. B. Hofayz, Abergavenny, Gwent
Ronald Marshall, Canonbie Crescent, Aberfan
G. Tidmas, Cwmpennar, Mountain Ash
Brenda Morgan, Ynysowen Nursery, Aberfan
Harold Lewis James & Mrs Mair Eirwen James, Aberfan
Lewis Morris James & Mrs Evelyn May James, Aberfan
The Local "Jigsaw" Committee
William Robert Evans & Mrs Tydfil Ann Evans, Merthyr Vale
Kate Evans, Oakfield Street, Aberfan
Michelle Channon, Barclays Bank, Aberfan
Dewi & Gerwyn Morris, Mervyn Street, Aberfan
June, Maldwyn & Tyrone Foulkes, Bryntaf, Aberfan
Mark Maldwyn Morgan Foulkes, Bryntaf, Aberfan
Maglona Dimmer (nee Lewis), Melbourne, Australia
Margaret Harries, Perthygleision, Aberfan
Dr & Mrs K. Edwards, Denbigh. Clwyd
Yvonne Miller, Folkestone, Kent
William Pye, Pontsticill, Merthyr Tydfil
Reg & Lily Davies, Pentrebach, Merthyr Tydfil
Evelyn Davies J.P., Alnwick, Northumberland

Kathryn & Christopher Davies, Pontypridd
Maldwyn James Colin & Megan Lavinia Colin, Cottrell Street, Aberfan
Shane Maldwyn Evans & Jessica Evans, Barrington Street, Aberfan
Elsie, Harold & Colin Davies, Nixonville, Merthyr Vale
David Robert Tovey, Cardiff Road, Merthyr Vale - Mayor of Merthyr Tydfil 1990-1991
Paul Davies, Chapel House, Aberfan
William James Williams, Edith Annie Williams, Taff Street, Merthyr Vale
Rev Stephen & Jenny Barnes & Elizabeth, The Vicarage, Merthyr Vale
Iris Roderick Thomas, Courtland Terrace, Merthyr Tydfil
Austin Griffiths, Hardingstone, Northants
Hilda Harris, Bridge Street, Aberfan
Betty Davies, Mackintosh Street, Aberfan
Dai Hollett, Ontario, Canada
Vera Prosser, Ynysygored Road, Aberfan
Jean, Tim, Alan & Jane Wickens, Nixonville, Merthyr Vale
Anne-Marie & Ronald Carpenter, Walters Terrace, Aberfan
Bryn, Betty & Phillip Carpenter, Griffiths Terrace, Aberfan
Paul, Carole, Michael, Gareth & Gerwyn Carpenter, Kingsley Terrace, Aberfan
Diane & Geraint Price, Cottrell Street, Aberfan
Bess Burford, Cilfrew, Neath
Ian & Danielle Green, Lock House Drive, Aberfan
Richard & Susannah James, Aberfan
Gerald & Thurza James, Aberfan/Rossiter, Pennsylvania, U.S.A.
Sara Ellen James, Lancaster, Ohio, U.S.A.
Andrew Richard James, Lancaster, Ohio, U.S.A.
Natalie Roubina Yoel, Madison, Alabama, U.S.A.
William James Yoel, Madison, Alabama, U.S.A.
William Henry James III, Bethesda, Maryland, U.S.A.
Shannon Marie Davies, Moy Road, Aberfan

Laura Ellen Evans, Bryngoleu, Aberfan
Improvements Committee - Community Association
Reverend Neil Davies, Vicar of St Luke's and St Bartholomew's, Reading
Len & Joan Rees, Hillside Close, Aberfan
Jackie Morgan, Brecon, Powys
Ynysowen Male Choir, Aberfan
Councillor Ray Thomas, Mayor of Merthyr Tydfil 1995-1996
Robert Rogers, Choirmaster, Merthyr Vale
Derek Evans, Thomas Street, Aberfan
Idwal & Eileen Jones, Moy Road, Aberfan
W. J. T. Jones, Swansea Road, Merthyr Tydfil
Olive & Tom Lucas, Bryntaf, Aberfan
Robert Price, Ynysygored Road, Aberfan
Soar Maes Yr Haf Independent Chapel, Neath, West Glamorgan
Kylie & Nicholas Lambourne, Bryngoleu, Aberfan
Debra Leyshon, Mervyn Street, Aberfan
Sian Mamwell, Rochdale, Lancs
Janett, Kerry & Eleanor Smart, Enoch Morrell Close, Troedyrhiw
Sheila & Roger Lewis, Ynysowen Fach, Aberfan
Rebecca Ann Louise Williams, Aberfan Road, Aberfan
Charlotte Joanne Davies, Treharris
Samuel Murphy, Canonbie Crescent, Aberfan
Stephanie Louise Murphy, Mackintosh Street, Aberfan
Thomas Edward Freeman, Cottrell Street, Aberfan
Jenna Lloyd Williams, Bryngoleu, Aberfan
Christopher Royston Davies, Cottrell Street, Aberfan
Aberfan & Merthyr Vale Community Co-operative
County Library HQ, West Glam House, Swansea
Emma & Arthur Marshall, Taff Street, Merthyr Vale

Arthur Large, Cannon Hill, London
John & Janet O'Regan. Ynysygored Road, Aberfan
Arfon John Williams, Northwich, Cheshire
Sal Rowlands, Cardiff Road, Merthyr Vale
F A Whelan, Eltham, London
Dr G J Davies, Weymouth, Dorset
Beryl Painting, Llangranog, Dyfed
Arthur John Yorath & Evelyn Martha Williams, Pleasant View, Aberfan
Reg Chandler, Moy Road, Aberfan
Hughie & Greta Evans, Pantglas Fawr, Aberfan
Suzanne & Emma Williams, Aberfan Road, Aberfan
Bill Donoghue, Ynysygored Road, Aberfan
Maxine Woolgar, Abergavenny, Gwent
J Jones, Clwyd Trawscae Farm, Bedlinog
D. Thomas, Newport, Gwent
The Thrift Shop, Aberfan
Thomas J Corkrey, Llantwit Major, South Glamorgan
J H Jones, Moy Road, Aberfan
Aberfan & Merthyr Vale Community Association
Vicky Inson, Abercraf, Swansea
Catherine Williams, Cardiff
Wyndham Hughes, Crescent Street, Merthyr Vale
Margaret Rees, Ynystaf, Cardiff Road, Merthyr Vale
John Rees, Northwood Hills, Middlesex
Fred & Ethel Kernan, Hythe, Kent

Canon Michael Short, The Rectory, Caerphilly
Jean Donoghue, Ynysowen Fach, Aberfan
Alf Iverson, Ynysowen Fach, Aberfan
Groundwork Merthyr & Cynon, Llwydcoed, Aberdare
Sofie & Mark Bates, Hillside Close, Aberfan
Kitty Davies, Ynysowen Fach, Aberfan
Walter Davies, Maureen Stack, Ynysowen Fach, Aberfan
Clive Thomas, St Mary's Close, Merthyr Tydfil
Beryl Roberts, Cottrell Street, Aberfan
Tom & Pam Swinhoe, Bristol
Elizabeth & Laura Iken, Aberfan Road, Aberfan
Derek Vaughan, Neath, West Glamorgan
Hannah Bates, Ynysowen Fach, Aberfan
Hugh Devine, Carmarthen, Dyfed
Michael & Auriol Lynch, Ty Toronto, Aberfan
Janice & Ted Rowlands M.P., Park Crescent, Merthyr Tydfil
Owain, Alun & Bethan Rowlands, Park Crescent, Merthyr Tydfil
Mair George, Cottrell Street, Aberfan
Betty Evans, The Grove, Aberfan
Marion Mossman, Llandysul, Dyfed
Virginia Moseley, Dallas, Texas
Merlin Lloyd, Ashlea, Merthyr Tydfil
Brett, Tammy, Michael & David Barton, Bryngoleu, Aberfan
Gwyneth Jane Probert & Joseph Thomas Probert, Pantglas Fawr, Aberfan
Catherine, Graham, Christopher, Robert & Carly, New South Wales, Australia
Robert, Pauline, Gareth & Beverley, Benidorm, Spain
Harold & Patricia Davey, Aberfan Road, Aberfan
Dewi Jones, Dinas Powys, South Glamorgan
Paul Thomas & Lauren Jade Thomas, Beaufort, Ebbw Vale
Elizabeth James, Bishops Road, Whitchurch, Cardiff
Margaret Fawcett, Radyr, Cardiff
Peggy Scott, Hartlepool

Tom O'Brien, Perthygleision, - Chairman, Mid Glam County Council 1988-1989
Christine Marie Crocker, Crickhowell, Powys
Richard Morton & Dilys Moore (nee Morton), Perthygleision, Aberfan
Jean Boyland, Ystrad Mynach, Mid Glamorgan
David Chilcott, Post Office, Troedyrhiw, Merthyr Tydfil
Terry & Molly Matheison, Hounslow, Middlesex
Les & Eileen Wilcox, Telford, Shropshire
Simone Wilcox, Bristol, Avon
Terry & Falmai O'Brien, Bryntaf, Aberfan
Clive Lewis, Graigwen, Pontypridd
Marianne G Jones, Aberfan Road, Aberfan
Ken Murphy, Walters Terrace, Aberfan
Malcolm Aylward, Angus Street, Aberfan
Ann MacDonald, Poulton-Le-Fylde, Lancashire
Sylvia & Denver Coles, Henleaze, Bristol
Captain N Lloyd-Edwards, Llandaff, Cardiff
Olwen & Bill Oliver, Llandudno, Gwynedd
Malcolm & William Oliver, Llandudno, Gwynedd
Derek & Joan Arthur, Moy Road, Aberfan
Emanuel, Jacqueline, Alisha & Azaria Azzopardi, Aberfan Road, Aberfan
F Heaton, Folkestone, Kent
M T Breeze, Aberfan Road, Aberfan
Lowri & Thomas Breeze, Pant, Dowlais
Councillor Ellen Jones, Bryntaf, Aberfan
Councillor & Mrs D L Jarrett, Mayor & Mayoress of Merthyr Tydfil 1992-1993
Eunice Williams, Ynysowen Fach, Aberfan
Cyril Edward Williams, Ynysowen Fach, Aberfan

Peter & Mair, Ian & Kevin Bowden, Pleasant View, Aberfan
Edna & Ken Bowden, Aberfan Road, Aberfan
Trevor & Eleanor Abraham, Pleasant View, Aberfan
Beryl Rowe, Moy Road, Aberfan
Wendy Howard, Denbigh, Clwyd
Mr & Mrs Arthur Jones, Cwmbran, Gwent
F J Abbott, Cwmbran, Gwent
Janet Passey, Cwmbran, Gwent
Paul Abbott, Cwmbran, Gwent
Carl Abbott, Cwmbran, Gwent
Charlotte & Melissa Thompson, Aberfan Road, Aberfan
Ashley Curnow, Moy Road, Aberfan
Mary V Davies, Wingfield Street, Aberfan
Lil & Lionel Martin, Aberfan Crescent, Aberfan
Norman & Marlene Jones, Belle Vue Villas, Aberfan
Ffion Elen Wilding, Aberfan Road, Aberfan
Jack McGinty, Nixonville, Merthyr Vale
David Jenkins, Barrington Street, Aberfan
Mair E Jones, Pentrebach, Merthyr Tydfil
Herbert B Lowe, F.B.C.O. Optometrist, High Street, Merthyr Tydfil
Gwen Owen, Oakfield Street, Aberfan
Valmai Mary Owen, Oakfield Street, Aberfan
Jean & Patrick Thomas, Wingfield Street, Aberfan
Helen & Neil, Elaine & Brian, Ontario, Canada
Bill & Roy Gibbon, Pantglas Road, Aberfan
Dan (Harry) & Betty Gibbon, Pantglas Road, Aberfan
Jack & M'Liz Humphreys, Rita & Lawrence Humphreys, Crescent St, Merthyr Vale
Mel & Joyce Jenkins, Perthygleision, Aberfan
Hannah & Alfred Pearson, Kingsley Terrace, Aberfan
Nancy & Douglas Pearson JP, Kingsley Terrace, Aberfan
Peter & Thelma Hughes, Kingsley Terrace, Aberfan

Anthony Wayne England, The Grove, Aberfan
Joe Richards & Jane Ellen Richards, Bryntaf, Aberfan
Mr & Mrs Roberts, Mount Pleasant, Merthyr Vale
Clwyd County Council Library & Information Service
Mr & Mrs Trefor Jones, Ironmongers
Bernard & Barbara Payne, Trehafod, Rhondda
S E Medd, Afon Taf High School, Troedyrhiw
Phillip Atkinson, Afon Taf High School, Troedyrhiw
David M Owen, Haverfordwest, Pembrokeshire
David & Olwen Mason, Cardiff Road, Merthyr Vale
Sir Ronald Mason, Weedon, Bucks
Glenys Kinnock MEP, Newport, Gwent
Ken & Megan Davies (nee Arscott), Moy Road, Aberfan
Terry & Jean Gerlach (nee Evans), Moy Road, Aberfan
John Huw Thomas, Gerrards Cross, Bucks
Laurie Thomas, Sudbury, Suffolk
Margaret Jane Jones & Betty Jones, Troedyrhiw, Merthyr Tydfil
Raymond Price, Church Village, Pontypridd
Margaret Nuttall, Clifton Rise, Berkshire
Edward O'Donnell, Westmeath, Ireland
Nesta Flynn (nee Ashton), Bryngoleu, Aberfan
Haydn Howell Richards, Pantglas Road, Aberfan
'Headway' Production Team
Caitlin Victoria O'Brien, Penydarren, Merthyr Tydfil
Bette Richards, Pantglas Road, Aberfan
Michael John Donovan, Aberfan
Kathleen & Stuart Phillips, The Grove, Aberfan

Ioan Berwyn Jones, Quakers Yard, Treharris
Mick Boaden, Civic Centre, Merthyr Tydfil
Gaynor Boaden (nee McGovern), Heolgerrig, Merthyr Tydfil
Eileen McGovern, Aberdare
Geoffrey McGovern, Aberdare
Jennifer Edwards, Aberdare
Melissa Louise & Jordan Lee Thomas, Pentrebach, Merthyr Tydfil
Tarian Cai Jenkins, Troedyrhiw, Merthyr Tydfil
Steele Lewis Harvey, Troedyrhiw, Merthyr Tydfil
The Rt. Hon. Lord Wilson of Rievaulx, Prime Minister 1964 - 1970 and 1974 - 1976
Michael K Burke, Cwmbach, Aberdare
Gavin Peter, Donna & Jemma Sawday, Aberfan Fawr, Aberfan
Kath & Geoffrey Marshall, Bryngerwyn Avenue, Quakers Yard
Stella & Lou Ramsey, Basildon, Essex
Helen & Eric Batchelor, Basildon, Essex
Rae Vic & Clive Bolt, Basildon, Essex
Amy Edwards, Ynysowen Fach, Aberfan
Sarah & Steven Walker, Troedyrhiw, Merthyr Tydfil
Richard, Victoria & Catrin, Whitchurch, Cardiff
Bryan & Suzanne, Harriet Town, Troedyrhiw, Merthyr Tydfil
Stephanie Wynne Davies, Aberfan Road, Aberfan
Anthony Topham, Newcastle
Bryan & Esme Hughes, Troedyrhiw, Merthyr Tydfil
Kieran Morgan, Oakfield Street, Aberfan
Kayleigh Morgan, Nixonville, Merthyr Vale
George & Mary Ellen Morgan, Pantglas Fawr, Aberfan
Matthew & Carly O'Brien, Pantglas Road, Aberfan
Frank & Berenice O'Brien, Pantglas Fawr, Aberfan
Darren & Kimberley Minett, Ynysygored Road, Aberfan
Lee & Jodie Minett, Quakers Yard, Treharris
Steven & Tracey Minett, Bryntaf, Aberfan

Ann & Richard Hughes, Perthygleision, Aberfan
Winnie & Aelfryn Hughes, Canonbie Crescent, Aberfan
Sidney & Elizabeth Ellen Berry, Bryngoleu, Aberfan
Violet Harvey, Troedyrhiw, Merthyr Tydfil
Fred & Anne Read, Cardiff Road, Merthyr Vale
Peter & Jean Rees, Troedyrhiw, Merthyr Tydfil
Karen O'Brien, Pantglas Road, Aberfan
Tonia Richards, Pantglas Road, Aberfan
Krystal Richards, Abercynon, Mid Glamorgan
Tammy Leigh Richards, Abercynon, Mid Glamorgan
Emma Louise Gerlach, Joanne Gerlach & Johnathan Michael Gerlach, Barrington Street, Aberfan
Emily Francis Morgan, Twynyrodyn, Merthyr Tydfil
Menna Joanne Needs, Quakers Yard, Treharris
Bryan & Jean Tilling, Richmond, Surrey
Thomas David Hancock, Pentrebach, Merthyr Tydfil
Des & Lorna Eames, Peterborough, Northants
William & Miriam Olive Eames, Angus Street, Aberfan
Christina Lorna Macdonald, Stockport, Cheshire
Sally & Alwyn Jenkins, Pentrebach, Merthyr Tydfil
Iris & Thomas Bernard Marshall, Earls Colne, Essex
The Mayor of Merthyr Tydfil 1996-1997, Councillor Bill Smith
Myfannwy Morgan, Mackintosh Street, Aberfan
Allison & Lance Hardiman, Ruislip, Middlesex
Robert & Gillian Hardiman, Ruislip, Middlesex
Smyrna Chapel, Aberfan